*Winner of the Jules and Frances Landry Award for 2022*

# CONFEDERATE CONSCRIPTION AND THE STRUGGLE FOR SOUTHERN SOLDIERS

JOHN M. SACHER

LOUISIANA STATE UNIVERSITY PRESS
BATON ROUGE

Published by Louisiana State University Press
lsupress.org



Manufactured in the United States of America
First printing

DESIGNER: Mandy McDonald Scallan
TYPEFACE: Arno Pro
PRINTER AND BINDER: Sheridan Books, Inc.

Some of the arguments in this work first appeared in the following journal articles: "The Loyal Draft Dodger? A Reexamination of Confederate Substitution." *Civil War History* (June 2011): 153–178; and "Reconsidering the 'Twenty-Negro' Law as the Overseer Exemption." *Journal of the Civil War Era* (June 2017): 269–292.

Library of Congress Cataloging-in-Publication Data
Names: Sacher, John M., 1970– author.
Title: Confederate conscription and the struggle for southern soldiers / John M. Sacher.
Description: Baton Rouge : Louisiana State University Press, [2021] |
Includes bibliographical references and index.
Identifiers: LCCN 2021017961 (print) | LCCN 2021017962 (ebook) | ISBN 978-0-8071-7621-4 (cloth) | ISBN 978-0-8071-7654-2 (pdf) | ISBN 978-0-8071-7655-9 (epub)
Subjects: LCSH: Draft—Confederate States of America. | Draft—Confederate States of America—Public opinion.
Classification: LCC UB343.5 .S23 2021 (print) | LCC UB343.5 (ebook) | DDC 973.7/42—dc23
LC record available at https://lccn.loc.gov/2021017961
LC ebook record available at https://lccn.loc.gov/2021017962

*To Ana, Michael, and Emily*

# Contents

# Acknowledgments

Like many books, this one had seemingly random origins. Almost twenty-five years ago, my dissertation advisor, Bill Cooper, offered me a copy of the reissue of Albert Burton Moore's 1924 *Conscription and Conflict in the Confederacy.* While I had no interest in the topic, I followed the unwritten graduate student rule of never turning down a free book. The book's red spine stared at me for several years before I read it (by that time it had faded into a pinkish color). As I did, I began to wonder how any Civil War topic could go so long without a new study. Also, I noticed that conscription was not the dry bureaucratic topic that I assumed. Instead, as one of the main points where the military intersected with civilians, it touched upon many of the key historiographical debates about the Confederacy. So began my much too long process of researching and writing this book. While many times over the years I have cursed Bill for unwittingly starting me on this project, I am much more in his debt, not only for the inspiration for this topic but also for the high standards and examples he sets with his own work.

Taking almost twenty years to write a book means that I have far too many people to thank. The book's research officially started when I received a summer research grant as assistant professor at Emporia State University and was aided by the receipt of a fellowship at the Virginia Historical Society. Staff at that institution, the Virginia Library, the Southern Historical Collection, the Louisiana and Lower Mississippi Valley Collections, and the Rubenstein Rare Book and Manuscript Library were very helpful.

After I moved to the University of Central Florida, the book's progress slowed while I pursued a variety of time-consuming administrative positions. I owe special thanks to Jose Fernandez, dean of the College of Arts and Humanities, who not-so-gently pushed me to block out time to get back to writing. An informal writing group in the History Department also nudged me along and provided excellent feedback on many of the chapters. In particular, Barbara Gannon was always available to share her Civil War military expertise with me. The university also provided me with a timely sabbatical in the fall of 2020 to help get the book across the finish line. Two graduate students, Matt Patsis and Elizabeth

Klements, did an incredible amount of fact checking, undoubtedly saving me from many errors. Rand Dotson, Todd Manza, and the rest of the staff at Louisiana State University Press have also contributed to helping my manuscript finally see the light of day.

If writing is a generally solitary quest, the rest of life is not. There are many friends who deserve thanks for making life such an enjoyable ride. They might not have helped speed this project up. In fact, they probably made it take even longer. Nevertheless, their company has made the process more pleasurable, and I will be happy to finally have the right answer to their "How's the book coming along?" question. Thanks to the Sheehans, Marko, John, Lee, Tom, Sudhir, Jesse, Dick, and many others. Thanks to my parents for their support in this project and everything else in my life. One of my last conversations with my mom involved her comments on my first chapter. I am sure that the rest of book would have equally benefited from her keen editorial eye.

It is hard to believe that I have been working on this project since before I married Ana and before Michael and Emily were born. While it might be difficult to imagine waking up and not having this book somewhere on my to-do list, it is impossible to imagine life without the three of them in it. For making my life such a joy, I dedicate this book to them—even if this might be the only part of the book they read!

# CONFEDERATE CONSCRIPTION *and the* STRUGGLE *for* SOUTHERN SOLDIERS

# Introduction

In 1881, Confederate veteran Sam Watkins penned *Company Aytch,* which has become one of the most popular Civil War memoirs. It colorfully describes his four years in the Army of Tennessee. Writing from the perspective of an ordinary private, Watkins does not hesitate to criticize Confederate leaders and policies, and he reserves some of his sharpest attacks for the nation's enactment of conscription. In April 1862, the Confederate Congress passed the first national conscription law in American history. Watkins condemns the measure, which "was mighty rough on the rebels . . . All our pride and valor had gone." Having enthusiastically volunteered in 1861, the private now considered himself "simply a machine." His reflections on the law continue by denouncing one of its most controversial aspects: the exemption for men owning twenty or more slaves. The private believed this provision defined the Civil War as a "rich man's war, poor man's fight," with the common soldier now just wanting to leave the army, for "the glory of the South, the glory and the pride of our volunteers had no charms for the conscript." Watkins sadly concludes that "the war might as well have ended then and there."[1]

Many historians have echoed Watkins's hostile attitude toward conscription and his harsh assessment of its impact on the South. In 1916, in one of the first scholarly treatments of conscription, Robert Brooks termed it a "failure" and branded the men drafted as "almost worthless as fighting material." Eight years later, Albert Burton Moore wrote *Conscription and Conflict in the Confederacy,* which has remained the standard scholarly work on the topic. Moore finds conscription to be anathema to Confederates, arguing that it "did not harmonize with the individualistic instincts of Southerners and with their conception of genuine manhood." Alluding to states' rights, he adds that it was "contrary . . . to the genius of the Confederate political system." The only other book-length treatment of the topic, Walter C. Hilderman's *They Went into the Fight Cheering!,* comes to a more extreme conclusion. Focusing on conscription in North Carolina, Hilderman depicts the "absurd contradiction" in passing a national draft in a country based on states' rights, and he succinctly condemns it as "the most hated law in the Confederacy."[2]

Unsurprisingly, scholars who believe the South collapsed from internal stresses agree with Watkins. Along with policies such as the suspension of habeas corpus, impressment of military supplies, and the tax-in-kind, conscription represented an unprecedented national governmental intrusion into southerners' lives. Highlighting conscription policy, Paul Escott makes one of the strongest cases that the centralizing tendencies of the Confederate government did not create nationalism but destroyed it. Conscription measures neatly correspond to Escott's thesis that the Confederacy disintegrated from within as Davis failed in his attempt to build a Confederate nation because he failed to respond to the common people. For Escott's yeomen, conscription policy proved that all men did not share the burdens of the war equally, as the wealthy could purchase substitutes, avoid service in the army through their ownership of twenty slaves, or take advantage of exemption laws. Stephen Ambrose sounds the same chord in an article on yeoman discontent, concisely concluding that conscription "grossly favored the planters." David Williams stands as one of the most unequivocal advocates of the "rich man's war, poor man's fight" thesis. In several books, Williams pulls no punches in his analysis of Confederate defeat, arguing that conscription's class biases unfairly benefited the rich. In his view, for ordinary southerners, the Twenty Negro Law was "the most widely hated act ever imposed," and it led them to abandon the nation. Even James McPherson, who does not subscribe to these internal explanations of defeat, portrays conscription as "the most unpopular act of the Confederate government."[3]

At one level, such negative evaluations appear irrefutable. After all, national conscription both infringed on states' rights and forced nonslaveholders to fight a slaveholders' war. Yet, these assessments do not fully explain the measure and its effects. Watkins unintentionally reveals some of the weaknesses in a simple dismissal of conscription as detested and divisive. First, while he contends that the war might as well have ended with the law's passage, it did not. Confederates, significantly including Watkins himself, fought hard for three more years, with conscription providing the army with much-needed reinforcements. Consequently, southerners, rather than blaming the measure for their defeat, often credited it with staving off that defeat for three years. Also, while Watson condemned the measure, he notably neither advocated reunion nor turned against the Confederacy. Instead, like soldiers in almost every military conflict, he complained but served loyally. He questioned the policy, but he did so out of his southern pride, not out of disloyalty. As a Confederate, he was frustrated by what he considered to be an anti-Confederate measure, but this did not lead him to abandon his cause.

Second, Watkins and some of these scholars see conscription as a single policy that forced yeomen into the army and stripped them of their liberty, while allowing rich men to stay home. Conscription, however, is a moving rather than an easy target. It evolved over the course of the war. Watkins inadvertently makes this point as he misses the target in his description of the measure. He inaccurately implies that Congress passed the twenty-slave law as part of the original April 1862 act. Actually, the overseer provision was part of an October 1862 amendment, and it stemmed from concerns about slave unrest and crop production. From the act's initial passage until the end of the war, Confederate congressmen continually modified the law, trying to balance the needs of the army with those of the home front. Striving for a perfect conscription involved a three-year debate among Congress, President Jefferson Davis, state politicians, the army, the Bureau of Conscription, soldiers, and men and women at home. At times, members of all these groups disagreed on how to balance the Confederates' various needs, but generally they accepted the measure, only wanting to make sure it was fairly enforced.

Overall, Confederates deemed conscription the best way to mobilize southern manpower to win the war and achieve independence. While some southerners decried the measure, it received some praise from a surprising source: Union president Abraham Lincoln. In 1863, writing to New York governor Horatio Seymour in the wake of the New York City Draft Riots, the president contrasted the Union draft with Confederate conscription. Perhaps jealous of the lack of draft riots in the South, Lincoln contended that the Confederate system puts all men into the army: "no time is wasted, no argument is used . . . It produces an army with a rapidity not to be matched on our side." While lauding the streamlined nature of Confederate conscription compared to the Union draft, the president criticized its methods, as its compulsion sent men into the army "very much as a butcher drives bullocks into a slaughter-pen." In contrasting the ends versus the means, Lincoln, as he often did, quickly and colorfully got to the heart of the matter.[4]

For the Confederacy, the end was putting enough men in the field to defend itself against the numerically superior Union army. As an officer put it in 1864, "The Confederacy wants more men. Lee wants men. Bragg wants men. They are wanted everywhere; but where are they to come from?" In a February 1865 speech, the secretary of state reiterated this view, reminding his audience that "War is a game that cannot be played without men." The goal of conscription was to provide these men. Thus, dividing the number of conscripts by the total number of soldiers in the southern armies theoretically offers an easy way to evaluate the measure's success.

Unfortunately, the absence of comprehensive Confederate military records makes such an assessment impossible. The only official figure for total conscripts is 81,993, but this figure admittedly is an undercount. Compounding this problem, the total number of soldiers who served in the army is also unknown. In his 1950 study of the Confederacy, E. Merton Coulter expressed the frustration of all who have sought these elusive figures, bemoaning that "It is an exercise in utter futility to attempt to arrive at the exact number of Confederate soldiers, either throughout the whole war or at any specific time." Time has not resolved this issue. The *Historical Statistics of the United States,* based on information from the Department of Defense, declares that "authoritative statistics for the Confederate forces are not available," with estimates ranging from 600,000 to 1.5 million.[5]

Furthermore, conscription ideally did not just put men in the army but, through exemptions and details, allocated men to where the Confederate government felt they best contributed to victory. Thus, the straightforward conclusion that the army always needed more men ran up against the reality that the home front needed men, too. Civilians and the army required farmers and other producers, and conscripts expected that someone would help their families survive their absence. A Virginia soldier described this predicament to his sister in 1864: "Every man seems willing . . . to continue in the service until our independence is achieved provided they are fed and their families taken care of." The *Charleston Mercury* likewise articulated the dilemma: "Taking of all men under 45 will bring all work in the country to a stand still, and not taking them will leave the armies depleted and incompetent for the work in hand. This is a quandary, indeed."[6]

My work analyzes how Confederate political and military leaders tried to resolve this quandary over the course of the war. While Watkins and some scholars might consider conscription the most hated measure in the Confederacy, a careful study reveals that conscription is more accurately dubbed the most *debated* measure in the South. Fortuitously, studying this debate does not require knowledge of precise statistics but instead relies on how southerners understood and responded to the measure. From April 1862 until the war's end, the government repeatedly modified the measure, trying to find an ideal equilibrium, striving to have both guns and butter, and attempting to avoid accusations of violating states' rights or creating a military despotism. Lawmakers added and subtracted exemptions and expanded the age range.

One of their biggest adjustments was first allowing prospective conscripts to provide substitutes, and later ending this practice. They also considered whether the process should be controlled by the army or a civilian bureau, and they debated the efficacy of details versus exemptions. In sum, the outnumbered Confederacy tried to use conscription to put its entire white male population on war footing while still respecting the rights of Confederates and honoring obligations to take care of its citizens. As an 1865 order stipulated, "there ought not to be one man in the Confederacy whose relation to the service remains undefined."[7]

The Confederate Congress created the Bureau of Conscription to enforce this mandate, and a circular issued by the bureau describes its daunting duties. Enrolling officers had to balance "the recognized demands of armies in the field, the necessities of manufacture, transportation, production, and supply, and the claims of law equity and humanity." In short, the bureau had to decide "how every man shall be required to pay . . . his tribute to his country's cause." In an 1864 letter, the bureau's head, General John Preston, explained the breadth of its responsibilities, which "embrac[ed] the entire sphere of the civil, social, and military economy of the citizen and the Government." His officers were charged with "ascertaining, developing, and maintaining the military capabilities of the country for the defense of the public liberty and preservation of the social order, investigating and deciding personal and civil rights."[8]

While Lincoln had envied Confederate conscription's efficiency, the reality of trying to enforce these myriad and potentially conflicting responsibilities belied his assumption. Enrolling officers strove for an unachievable goal. They were on the front lines of determining how to satisfy the competing demands of the army and the home front. In August 1863, John Coke, an enrolling officer in Virginia, received a petition for the exemption of Joseph Schappers, which epitomized this conundrum. The petition explained how Schappers was "an honest worthy man" whose thirty-acre farm would be a "total loss" if the army conscripted him. Remaining at home, he "is infinitely more serviceable to our cause . . . [than] as a soldier." His skill and industry enabled him to produce more than two or three ordinary farmers could. Recognizing that Schappers did not qualify for any of the enumerated exemptions, the petitioners pleaded for "a wise *discretion*" rather than "a blind control of arbitrary rule." They concluded by reminding the officers that "defenders and defended must eat." While the case appears compelling, Coke frequently heard seemingly deserved appeals like this one. He merely scribbled on the back, "No comments I think are necessary," with another officer tersely adding, "No grounds for exemption."[9]

In *A Shattered Nation,* Anne Sarah Rubin explains that "Confederates lived in a world where the battlefield and homefront . . . were . . . intimately linked together." As Schappers's case demonstrates, conscription served as one of those links. Sending men into the army concomitantly produced ripple effects across communities. As the government acted, civilians reacted. Men had to decide whether to accept conscription or try to avoid the army, and their masculine sense of duty could push them in contradictory directions. Defending their country meant accepting conscription; providing for their family could mean staying at home. Further complicating things, deciding to try to remain home presented a spectrum of alternatives demonstrating various degrees of loyalty. These choices included legal options such as requesting a detail, finding a position that carried an exemption, or purchasing a substitute, and illegal options such as faking an illness, lying to enrolling officers about one's age or occupation, or hiding from officials.

Women also responded to the challenges of conscription. While President Jefferson Davis urged them to "use [their] influence to send all to the front [and] make the skulker a marked man," they might have preferred that their husbands, brothers, friends, or fathers stay home. Women's responsibilities could also push them in oppositive directions. Confederate loyalty meant serving as a conscript guard, but family needs might lead them to help a male relative find a substitute, to petition the government for his exemption, or to aid him in evading the draft.[10]

The army, politicians, and ordinary men and women all had vital interests in the operation of conscription. The Confederacy had to pursue a delicate, maybe impossible, balancing act. Men such as Schappers were needed both at home and in the army. Should a rigid adherence to the rules or wise discretion dictate policy? Thinking in these terms, the editor of the Augusta *Daily Constitutionalist* gave two opposing perspectives on the law: "Was the law enacted for the purpose of testing the loyalty of the Southern people and ascertaining how much they could or would suffer for the great cause?" Or "was it simply for the purpose of filling up the dwindling ranks of the army and reinforcing our troops in the field?" While the editor maintained it was the latter, for many Confederates, especially when officials inflexibly adhered to the law, it unfortunately seemed to be the former.[11]

Given these predicaments, asserting that conscription was not universally hated is not the equivalent of asserting that Confederates consistently celebrated the measure. Conscription policy is best considered as a lens to analyze competing loyalties in the Confederacy. Southerners believed in states' rights and feared military despotism, but the national government needed expanded power in wartime. Southerners believed in liberty for white men but had to consider the need for temporary mandatory service to ensure permanent liberty. Southerners recognized that the Civil War required sacrifices but wanted these sacrifices to be shared equally. Southerners admired the efficiency of an army-run conscription but realized a civilian bureau provided a greater protection for civil liberties. Southerners believed in defending both their families and their nation.

Conscription revealed the unfeasibility of satisfying all these beliefs simultaneously. As the governor of Arkansas informed President Davis, "Soldiers do not enter the service to maintain the Southern Confederacy alone but also to protect their property and defend their homes and families." What was the best way to defend both home and country? For some southerners, sending men to General Robert E. Lee's army in Virginia protected both spheres. For others, fighting hundreds of miles from home neither protected their family from Union invaders nor prevented their relatives from suffering from lack of provisions.[12]

My goal is to examine the evolution of conscription policy over the course of the Civil War as Confederates struggled with these dilemmas. Conscription does not prove that southerners either possessed or lacked Confederate loyalty. Instead, it demonstrates how they debated how much they were willing to sacrifice—both materially and ideologically—to satisfy the nation's insatiable demand for soldiers. In *Virginia's Private War,* William Blair articulates a similar theme. He examines several counties in Virginia, considering a wide array of policies, whereas my work looks at a single issue across the Confederacy. However, we come to an analogous conclusion: complaints did not signal defeatism but rather served as a catalyst for change in the Confederacy. Civilians protested and Confederate leaders listened. Southerners remained Confederates even when their nation's policies infuriated them. Thus, while the main focus of this work is not what caused Confederate defeat, it supports those scholars who contend that external forces—specifically the Union's willingness to apply its numerical superiority—rather than internal divisions led to this loss.[13]

In order to explain these evolving debates, this book is divided into seven roughly chronological chapters. The first chapter looks at the background of the measure, explaining why Confederates turned to conscription in April 1862. The second chapter examines how state leaders, soldiers, and ordinary people reacted to the operation of conscription in the summer of 1862. The third chapter addresses the revisions in the law in the fall of 1862 as Confederates, after hearing concerns from across the Confederacy, sought to improve the measure. The fourth chapter steps away from the chronological organization and instead views conscription from the perspective of enrolling officers. It underscores the difficulties they faced as they interacted with prospective conscripts, family members, and their superiors in Richmond. The fifth chapter explores the policy in 1863, when the civilian bureau faced a challenge from a strictly military conscription, and when voters had the chance to elect candidates to the second Confederate Congress. The sixth chapter considers 1864, when Confederate leaders ended substitution and greatly reduced the number of exemptions as the nation's need for soldiers and the home front's suffering both increased. The final chapter focuses on conscription in the final six months of the war as legislators debated drafting African American slaves, and as the war ended. It concludes by trying to make sense of the contradictory and incomplete extant figures for conscription.

Every chapter considers the interactions among politicians, soldiers, and civilians. Throughout the three years of conscription, three problems occurred repeatedly: reconciling national power with states' rights and individual liberty, achieving an equilibrium between the battlefront and the home front, and spreading sacrifices equally across families and communities. Confederate leaders struggled with all of these unattainable goals. They put policies in place, listened to the reactions from civilians and soldiers, considered the policies' effects, adjusted the policies, and listened once again. While President Davis, with a hint of gallows humor, declared that "the Conscript Act has not been popular anywhere out of the Army," conscription did not destroy the Confederacy from within. Instead, it revealed the potentially insurmountable challenges the nation faced. Confederates had competing loyalties to home, state, and nation. For certain southerners at certain times, conscription worked in tandem with all of these fidelities. For others, however, the measure's preference of nation over state and home forced them consider what sacrifices they were willing to make—and what sacrifices others refused to make—in an to attempt to achieve victory.[14]

CHAPTER 1

# The Confederacy Adopts Conscription, April 1862

On March 28, 1862, Confederate president Jefferson Davis sent a brief but urgent message to Congress proposing a solution to the vexing problem of raising troops for the Confederacy. Approaching the anniversary of the first shots fired at Fort Sumter, and eight months after the Battle of Bull Run, the reality of war had dispelled any hopes that it would be short. A year earlier, Davis had expressed the seemingly simple wish that the Confederacy just wanted to be "let alone." Abraham Lincoln and the Union army, however, had not cooperated with that plan.

As Davis penned his letter to Congress, southerners, pressed from all sides, recognized the military's imperative need for more soldiers. Union General George McClellan's Army of the Potomac, soon to grow to more than 100,000 men, camped on the Virginia Peninsula, less than seventy miles away from Davis's office in Richmond. In the western theater, the Union posed a similar threat, with as many as 75,000 men marching south toward the key railroad junction of Corinth, Mississippi. In the Gulf of Mexico, Admiral David Farragut's navy sat poised at the mouth of the Mississippi River menacing a lightly defended New Orleans—the South's largest city.[1]

The size and status of its own army compounded the Confederacy's military problems. From the outset of the conflict, the Confederacy faced an uphill struggle, with the Union having a much larger pool of potential soldiers. According to the 1860 census, the Confederate states possessed 1,064,193 white men between the ages of eighteen and forty-five, while the Union states contained 4,559,872. Adjustments for border state men who fought for the Confederacy reduced the Union advantage, but it still most likely exceeded 3.5 to 1. Therefore, President Davis needed to ensure that as many of the South's military-age men as possible entered the army.

In March 1862, he sought both to add to the 300,000 men currently in uniform and to address the fact that many of the Confederate soldiers who had enlisted in the spring and summer of 1861 had signed up for only a single year of service. Within a few months, the outnumbered Confederacy stood to lose the majority of its soldiers. These soldiers had enlisted under a confusing, and sometimes contradictory, hodgepodge of national and state laws, which further complicated administering the army. The most recent policy had called for the states to furnish quotas of soldiers but left the method of satisfying these quotas up to each state government, with some using volunteering, some employing bounties, some using a draft, and some combining these methods.[2]

Irritated by these frequent alterations in Confederate policy, the conflicts between state and federal laws, and the lack of uniformity in recruiting policies, President Davis's short message proposed a straightforward solution: the passage of an act declaring that all white southern men between the ages of eighteen and thirty-five should be enrolled in the army. Davis contended that conscription would be equitable in that it would ensure "that the burdens should not fall exclusively on the most ardent and patriotic" men who had volunteered and willingly left their communities and families during the conflict's first year. It now would force men who had remained at home to do their share and join their countrymen in the army. In his proposal, the president matter-of-factly brushed aside any potential objections, asserting that "the right of the State to demand, and the duty of each citizen to render, military service, need only to be stated to be admitted."[3]

Less than three weeks after receiving Davis's request, the Confederate Congress passed the first national conscription law in United States history. The April 16 law heeded Davis's suggestion, conscripting all white men from the ages of eighteen to thirty-five, though it allowed for an eligible man to provide a substitute in his place. In order to enforce this policy and to maintain civilian control over the process, Congress assigned this task to the War Department rather than to the army. As a concession to the rights of the states, it specified that men could only be conscripted in their state of residence and that they would serve in state units. The act not only compelled men to join the army but also required those already serving to remain there, extending the service of soldiers of conscription age from twelve months to three years or the duration of the war, whichever came first. In other words, Confederate volunteers, who believed that they would be discharged and allowed to return to their homes in May, June, or July, now found themselves forced to remain in the army, generally denied even a furlough to visit their families.[4]

The Wilmington *Daily Journal* immediately proclaimed the conscription bill "beyond question, the most important measure that has ever passed the Confederate Congress." Indeed, conscription raised a series of hard and fundamental questions about what the Confederacy stood for and what it meant to be a loyal Confederate. These questions included: Why had volunteering failed to provide a sufficient army? Could national conscription be reconciled with the Confederate doctrine of states' rights? Would southerners see the measure as a challenge to their notions of individual liberty? How would the Confederacy balance the needs of home and the battlefronts? What did loyalty to one's nation mean? Did the need for more troops trump all these concerns?[5]

In the short run, most Confederates believed that they needed a stronger army to win the war, and they were willing to accept conscription's temporary intrusion on their liberty if it led to victory. A year of conflict had demonstrated that Confederate leaders felt that other recruiting methods—particularly twelve-month enlistments—had not worked. While recognizing conscription's necessity, southerners remained wary of an act that threatened their liberty and that caused suffering on the home front. They would spend the next three years wrestling with these questions, and their answers reveal the complexity in assessing Confederate loyalty. Southerners possessed multiple loyalties, including to family, community, state, and nation, and their attitudes toward conscription depended on their calculation of the relative importance of these competing fealties—a view that could change over time.

A year earlier, when the Confederacy initially called for soldiers, no one had seriously considered conscription, as the number of southern volunteers exceeded the army's demand for troops. Young southern men rushed to the standard, fearful that delay could mean that they might miss the war entirely. They hoped to enlist, fight in one great battle, and return home as heroes. When President Davis spoke at the Spotswood Hotel upon his arrival in Richmond on June 1, 1861, great cheers met his claim "There is not one true son of the South who is not ready to shoulder his musket to bleed, to die or to conquer in the cause of liberty here." A Louisianan described her brother as "wild to be off to Virginia" as he "fear[ed] that the fighting will be over before he can get there." An Alabaman predicted "we are going to kill the last yankey [*sic*]" within a year, and he would "whip 25 myself." In 1861, many others shared their *rage militaire*. The new nation lacked supplies not fighters. A few weeks after Davis's speech, a war department official worried that the Confederate army could not equip all of these volunteers, and a month later a report from the secretary of war admitted that the army had turned away men because it lacked the means to arm them. With more weapons, the secretary optimistically predicted, he could add as many as 200,000 soldiers in two months.[6]

When the Confederate victory at Bull Run in July 1861 did not end the war as swiftly as had been hoped, volunteering slowed. With soldiers having "seen the elephant"—their phrase for experiencing combat—and having witnessed friends wounded or killed, army life lost some of its appeal. The Union had not conceded, and the idea of a quick triumph followed by a return home to accolades proved to be a mirage. Most soldiers spent the rest of 1861 in military camps, often bored, sometimes cold, and frequently ill. They also resented military discipline, which challenged their ideas of liberty. Having enlisted for excitement and glory, they had not dreamed of a life characterized by monotonous drilling in a muddy Virginia camp, shivering through the night, and suffering from dysentery. Letters from these soldiers, rather than calling on their fellow southerners to enlist, now often advised the opposite: "Don't never volunteer." A Louisianan complained to his mother that army life was "not what it is cracked up to be," and a Mississippi soldier concurred. He cautioned his father, "Please stay at home" as a "soldiers' life is the dirtiest meanest life in the world."[7]

Three soldiers in Stonewall Jackson's Shenandoah Valley army articulated these same concerns. In January 1862, one carped to his mother, "The romance of the thing is entirely worn off, not only with myself but with the whole army." Complaining to his fiancée of the hardships that he had suffered, which included marching, fighting, and watching soldiers suffer from disease, a second soldier avowed that he would not reenlist but would come home until he was drafted. A third declared, "If I live this twelve months out, I intend to try mighty hard to keep out of [the army]. . . . I don't think I could stand it for another year."[8]

As they pointed out, fortunately for disgruntled soldiers but not for the army, their departure was in sight. This initial group of volunteers did not intend to be long-term professional soldiers and had enlisted only for twelve months. Many of them were farmers who had families at home that depended on their labor both for financial support and for food. Their parents, wives, and children could survive a short enlistment, but a long-term absence would be devastating. Even early in the war, the army preferred men to enlist for more than a year, but a shortage of resources led them to compromise on this matter. If units equipped themselves, they could enlist for just a single year. If they relied on the Confederacy to supply them, they had to enlist for three years.

By the conclusion of 1861, Confederate leaders attended to the twin problems of declining volunteerism and the probability of losing much of the army in the late spring and early summer of 1862. In a November report to Congress, recently appointed Secretary of War Judah P. Benjamin listed fourteen problems with the army. In this list, he singled out "the radical vices of a system of short enlistments" as the most important subject that Congress needed to address. In doing so, he reminded Congress that these twelve-month men did not really even serve as fighting soldiers for a whole year. According to his calculations, after deducting time for instruction, transportation, recovery from camp diseases, and winter encampment, their actual effectiveness as combat soldiers rarely exceeded three months. In order to overcome this challenge, Benjamin recommended that Congress offer bounties and furloughs to current troops to entice them to reenlist for the duration of the war.[9]

In December 1861, General Robert E. Lee, serving as commander of the Department of South Carolina, Georgia, and Florida, assessed the Confederate army's prospects there. He shared Benjamin's fears and came to the identical conclusion: "the troops should be organized for the war." In suggesting this method, Lee, who three months later helped author Davis's conscription plan, pointed out that transitioning men in and out of the army during peacetime was wasteful enough but that in wartime it could "prove highly disastrous." Looking toward the new year, he "tremble[d] to think of the consequences that may befall us next spring when all of our twelve-months' men may claim their discharge." Other Confederates also recognized the impending problem. An officer serving in Virginia "fear[ed] the consequences of the looming departure of the twelve-month men." He termed it "a very serious matter," since "no feasible plan as yet has been proposed to induce them to re-enlist." Another soldier agreed that the current system caused "great injury," for it sent troops home "just as they are getting well drilled." In sum, these men concurred that an army based on an ever-rotating merry-go-round of twelve-month volunteers would never produce enough seasoned soldiers to defeat the Union army.[10]

In a prominent November 1861 editorial, described as having "the odor of official inspiration," John Daniel, the editor of the influential *Richmond Examiner,* proposed a drastic yet simple plan for solving this conundrum: a military draft. Daniel pointed out that the enemy would put 500,000 men in the field for the summer 1862 campaign. He maintained that the time for "half measures" had passed, as a force of volunteers, especially volunteers whose enlistments would expire by the middle of the summer, would lose a conflict against "an army under the iron rule of enforced enlistment and regular discipline." He called for a draft, albeit one done by the states rather than the federal government. In his plan, the government would demand a quota of men from each state, which in turn would demand a number from each county. Men would be selected by drawing lots, with those drawn entering the army, providing a substitute, or paying a fee to avoid service. In the editor's opinion, not only would this method supply an army capable of defeating the enemy but also it was the "only system that is really just to all classes of the population," as everyone stood an equal chance of being drafted.[11]

Despite this call for a draft, in December 1861, the Confederate Congress still preferred to rely on incentives rather than compulsion. To encourage twelve-month men to reenlist for the war, it passed legislation providing each reenlistee with $50 and a sixty-day furlough. In the short run, this "bounty and furlough act" weakened rather than strengthened the army. Units immediately lost men who eagerly departed the army on their two-month furloughs, and when these soldiers returned, they did not necessarily return to the same companies. The act also stipulated that men who reenlisted could form new units and elect their own officers, thereby further depleting the units in the field.

Reflecting on this policy a year later, the secretary of war stressed the harmful impact that it had on the efficiency of the army, with men joining units that only existed on paper or that could not quickly be made fighting ready. Citing these problems, a leading scholar on the draft posited that the measure should have been called "an act to disorganize and dissolve the provisional army." Lee biographer Douglas Southall Freeman went even further in his criticism, claiming, "A worse law could hardly have been imposed on the South by the enemy."[12]

The numbers bear out these negative appraisals. Despite pleadings and inducements, the plan neither increased the army's size nor resulted in an army of men enrolled for the duration of the war. In February 1862, according to Secretary of War Benjamin's figures, the army only had 92,275 troops enlisted for the war, with an additional 240,475 enrolled for twelve months. Thus, if nothing changed, the Union army's projected 5 or 6 to 1 manpower advantage might end the war by the middle of the summer. Moreover, in that same month, President Davis's message to the newly seated first Congress blamed recent Confederate reverses, including those at Fort Henry and Fort Donelson in Tennessee, on the "evil" of short-term enlistments. Congress had already decided that the failure of carrots demanded the use of sticks. It passed a bill allowing the president to require that each state provide up to 6 percent of its white population to serve for the lesser of three years or the duration of the war. Davis congratulated Congress for ending the complicated system of furloughs and reenlistments which had "disorganized and weakened our forces." This new plan added some troops, but it primarily converted soldiers from twelve-month service to the war. In South Carolina, for example, Davis's plan called for the number of soldiers enrolled for the war to increase from 9,349 to 18,000 men.[13]

The measure did not specifically mention a draft, leaving the means used to meet the quota up to the individual states. Several states, including Georgia, North Carolina, South Carolina, Texas, and Virginia, resorted to drafts, or at least the threat of a draft. For instance, South Carolina's executive council gave citizens until March 20 to volunteer or the state would begin conscripting soldiers. In a strategy that presaged the Confederacy's plan, South Carolina's proposed draft was intended to spur volunteering, with the idea that men preferred the honor associated with voluntary service rather than the dishonor of being labeled a conscript. A South Carolina officer worried that it would be "an everlasting disgrace" to have a draft "when the Enemy were on our own soil."

In most of the state, the strategy worked. An August 1862 military report declared that "under [the plan's] stimulus, volunteering took place with such alacrity that our skeleton organizations were rapidly filled." Mary Chesnut, whose husband served on the council, celebrated in her diary, "Conscription has waked the Rip Van Winkles." Only in Charleston did the state need to implement a draft. By the end of March, South Carolina claimed 22,064 troops enrolled for the duration of the war, a number that exceeded its quota by 4,064 (22.6 percent) and was 12,715 more than its February total.[14]

Like these South Carolinians, men across the Confederacy often enlisted in the army rather than risk the potential dishonor of being called a conscript. A Virginia officer praised his state's plan to pass a draft, for now "men are re-enlisting much more readily than I supposed they would." Commenting on recruiting in Texas, Gideon Lincecum cheered the effects of a proposed draft. He contended that anyone who loved liberty "will fight to the death," while others would volunteer, for "they hate the idea of being drafted." Writing from the home front in Alabama, a civilian observed, "People are bad scared here about a draft. Now, that will cause you to get some recruits." The extent of this stigma associated with conscription can be seen in Louisiana, where the legislature did not authorize, or even threaten, a state draft. Yet, even there, according to the *Shreveport Semi-Weekly News,* most men in that city had already joined the army, and more joined each day, "for they do not wish it said that they were drafted conscripted soldiers."[15]

Not only did men prefer to avoid being labeled conscripts, but also they recognized that volunteers might have options that conscripted soldiers did not. Generally, they got to select their own units and, at times, received bounties that draftees did not receive. Recruiting ads highlighted the multiple advantages of volunteering. A Virginia broadside urged men "Do Not Wait to Be Drafted, but Volunteer!!" It offered a $50 bounty plus $25 for clothes for men who passed a medical examination. As the Confederate Congress debated conscription, an advertisement in the Atlanta *Southern Confederacy,* "Recruits Wanted for the Bartow Invincibles," warned, "This is about the last chance that you will have to volunteer," and promised a $50 bounty. It added that men should defend their state: "Georgians! Our country is in peril! It is invaded on all sides." Finally, it concluded by stressing the importance of demonstrating one's commitment to the combination of liberty, manliness, and race. "'Tis better to die freemen than live as slaves. Show your manhood."[16]

Living in a slave society, white southern men understood this distinction, and they contrasted their own manhood and liberty with that of enslaved African Americans. In *For Cause and Comrades,* James McPherson convincingly demonstrates that Confederate soldiers fought for their liberty and against their own enslavement by the North. Encapsulating southerners' worst fears, a Louisiana officer assured his father, "Never, never shall our mothers & sisters & fathers & brothers be the slaves of the Yankees." Antebellum southern democracy celebrated white male liberty in advancing the idea that all white men were equal and held a status higher than the South's mudsill—African American slaves. The former had choices, whereas the latter acted under compulsion. Or, to put it in military terms, in their daily lives, white men volunteered, while slaves were drafted. In April, North Carolina Colonel Zebulon Vance, who would soon be the state's governor, made this comparison explicit when he urged potential conscripts to "fill up their companies like white men" rather than face the prospect of the sheriff bringing them in as a slave patrol would.[17]

Many white southerners considered defending their liberty to be intertwined with defending their homes and families—an idea which resonated across the Confederacy. A Louisiana volunteer reminded his wife that his love for his family "makes me want to fight," and "It is for you that I have come to defend." In February 1862, Confederates agreed that protecting their households required more soldiers in the field. An officer expressed his astonishment that any man could remain at home when "duty, honor, and . . . love of country is beckoning them to assist in defending their homes from the depredations of our northern enemies." Two Georgians concurred. One contended that the "time has emphatically arrived when nearly every man capable of bearing arms . . . should be in the field," with the South "pressed on every hand . . . by overwhelming forces." The other stressed that with his state "invaded by a vandal foe whose only aim is subjection to the tyrant's rule," it was time for "the patriotic young men of Georgia . . . to volunteer to rush to their country's call."[18]

If "patriotic young men" volunteered to join the army, what did that say about southern men who remained at home? Equating military serving with masculinity, many Confederates viewed stay-at-homes as unmanly. In South Carolina, the "Ladies of Charleston" threatened to send baby dolls and hoop skirts to the men who had not departed Charleston before Valentine's Day. In Louisiana, the *Baton Rouge Gazette and Comet* called on women to present petticoats as "rewards" to young men who remained at home. For men who somehow found this suggestion too subtle, it added, "Go volunteer, at once, or forever be disgraced." A Confederate officer suggested that the "young ladies . . . do the country a service" and ask "every young man, staying at home without good visible reason, why he stands here all the day idle." In Virginia, a speaker asserted that husbands should show their devotion to their wives "by rushing to arms to defend them from pollution and dishonor!" Similarly, boyfriends should realize that "your sweethearts . . . [will] spurn you if you hesitate." A Louisiana officer agreed that under the pressure of ladies, "who would not be a soldier?" He asserted that women could influence "all who possess the slightest principle of manliness . . . to . . . offer their lives as a sacrifice upon the altar of the count[r]ies cause."[19]

As President Davis and other Confederate leaders contemplated whether they should conscript men to "offer their lives as a sacrifice," they could look to the operation of state plans and, even further back, in United States history. Examination of U.S. history provided little reason to be optimistic, for the United States had debated but never implemented national conscription. Casting themselves as equivalent to the Americans during the revolution, Confederates might have realized the disheartening nature of George Washington's experience with raising troops.

Washington advocated a draft, but the Continental Congress never heeded his suggestion. Like the Confederacy, however, it did stipulate state quotas. And while Virginia governor Thomas Jefferson railed against conscription as "the most impracticable thing that could be attempted," his state enacted a draft. Virginia leaders stepped carefully, for they realized that many of these potential soldiers possessed the ballot. If these voters disliked being drafted, they might take out their frustrations on the politicians who enacted the measure. Consequently,

Washington advised targeting "the lower class of people," and the members of Virginia's assembly agreed. They decided to conscript only noncitizens and nonvoters while allowing voters to decide for themselves whether they wished to enlist. More than eighty years later, living in a white men's democracy, Confederate legislators lacked the luxury of solely conscripting men who could not vote. They acted with the awareness that if they ran for reelection in 1863, the men they forced into the army would be casting ballots.[20]

During the War of 1812, President James Madison and Secretary of War James Monroe also tried to implement national conscription. In November 1814, after the British occupation and burning of Washington, Monroe proposed a broad-based national conscription exempting only the president and governors. Monroe's conscription proposal raised two questions that would later bedevil Confederate officials: How can national necessity and individual liberty be balanced? and How is "equal" service defined?

On one hand, the administration's voice, the *National Intelligencer,* argued, "Making every man a soldier . . . is the only plan which readily, equally, and economically secures the safety of the nation." On the other hand, a Massachusetts representative objected to the measure on the ground that it threatened liberty, contending that Madison planned "to kidnap the people as you would slaves." Conscription bills narrowly passed both the Senate and the House, but they differed, so they were sent to a conference committee. The war ended, however, before the committee could meet. Viewing themselves as heirs to these Virginia Founding Fathers, Confederates paid attention to these lessons. Joseph Davis would make the connection explicit when he later congratulated his brother, President Davis: "I am gratified to hear of the passage of the conscription law in this you are more fortunate than Mr. Monroe in Mr. Madison's administration."[21]

Between the War of 1812 and the Civil War, Congress never broached conscription. So, in searching for historical precedents, Confederates looked beyond the borders of the United States, with Napoleon Bonaparte's France serving as the classic example. Not wanting a Napoleon, many southerners preferred not to emulate his policies. On April 4, as Congress debated the president's proposal, the *Georgia Weekly Telegraph* published a letter to the editor that proclaimed conscription, which has its modern origins in 1798 in France, to be "*a tremendous engine of military despotism.* It is in truth the devil's own invention for the subjection of liberty." Later in the month, a Baton Rouge newspaper echoed this concern in claiming modern conscription had its roots with the "blood-thirsty despot" Napoleon. Similarly, the *Memphis Daily Appeal* warned its readers that Napoleon's conscription "carried misery into every cottage and bathed with tears every mother in France."[22]

While these newspapers worried about the lack of liberty in France, for the Augusta *Daily Constitutionalist,* Napoleon's results vindicated his methods. Within an elaborate proconscription article, its editor argued that Bonaparte used conscription to maintain "the best army in the world." The *Charleston Mercury,* in calling for conscription to supply the men for a two-pronged invasion of the North, pointed out that "Bonaparte repeatedly raised immense armies by conscription in as short a time from an exhausted state." Its editor called on Confederate leaders to be bold enough in "adapting means to ends," for victory over Union forces would provide all the justification needed for conscription.[23]

In his March 28 call for conscription, President Davis, despite his awareness of these precedents, mentioned neither the War of 1812, France, nor even Confederate state conscriptions. According to prominent Davis biographer William Cooper, the president paradoxically acted "boldly and timidly" at the same time. Underestimating the potential challenges the policy faced, he provided only the briefest explanation for the need for conscription. Davis operated under three assumptions that not all Confederates shared. First, he possessed a total commitment to independence, and he mistakenly presumed that all other Confederates would unhesitatingly join him in supporting all measures that led to that goal. Second, while championing states' rights, Davis did not believe it applied in this case. He viewed national defense as important exception to the doctrine. For him, the Constitution unequivocally sanctioned conscription when it granted Congress the power "to raise armies." Third, having no desire to seize dictatorial powers, the president continually took the seriousness of fears of military despotism too lightly.[24]

Davis's concise request for a conscript act hid the revolutionary nature of the measure, which challenged many of his countrymen's most sacrosanct ideals. It put national priorities ahead of states' rights, put the Confederacy's needs ahead of individual liberty, and sharply prescribed a single path—army service—for southern men to show their loyalty to the cause. With the president offering little justification, southerners had to interpret on their own its necessity and constitutionality. In a May letter attacking conscription's violation of the Confederacy's constitution and its creation of "a military despotism," Georgia governor Joseph Brown sarcastically assessed Davis's rhetorical strategy. He groused to Vice

President Alexander Stephens, a fellow Georgian who shared Brown's antipathy toward conscription, that the president had not even bothered with "the tyrant's plea of necessity for the passage of the act."[25]

Irrespective of whether Davis should have constructed a more effective proconscription argument, Congress now had the ball in its court. Over the next two weeks, congressmen debated conscription, but most of this debate occurred in secret sessions. During open sessions, the two senators from Texas—Louis T. Wigfall and Williamson S. Oldham—provided the only real public sparks on the issue. A staunch secessionist, Wigfall endorsed conscription, for he considered no sacrifice too great for independence. Admonishing his states' rights colleagues to "cease this child's play," he reminded them that great leaders such as George Washington had favored a draft. Wigfall argued that "there was no limitation on [congressional] power" to raise armies. He added, "No man has any individual rights, which are in conflict with the welfare of the country." The Confederacy's reliance on volunteering had left it without an adequate army. The senator posed the dilemma as "We need a large army. How are you going to get it?" He offered an easy answer: conscript men into existing regiments. "The safety of our liberty and our homes requires that we shall do this." Wigfall concluded, "It will not do to talk about the justice of our cause . . . We must have heavy battalions."[26]

Oldham offered a different view of both the present situation and of Confederate liberty. For this Texan, conscription violated the fundamental theory of Confederate government, and he asserted that victory could be achieved without such an infringement. The voluntary and quota system had not failed, for the Confederacy had continually produced more soldiers than the nation could arm. For Oldham, a conscription law would give the impression that the government lacked confidence in the people. Rather than preserving liberty, the senator maintained that conscription "would be destructive of the liberties of the people." In his postbellum memoirs, the senator complained that conscription converted Davis from a "constitutional president" into a "despot with unlimited powers." Oldham also condemned Wigfall's efforts to wrap himself in the cloak of Washington, for in doing so, he employed the deplorable debating tactic of using "great names . . . to sanction great sins." Plus, Oldham claimed that Washington, along with all other good republicans, would oppose conscription as something more befitting "the despotisms of Europe" than an American republic.[27]

While Oldham and Wigfall debated constitutional theories and definitions of liberty, other legislators focused on the pressing needs of the Confederacy. Louisianan Edward Sparrow cheered the "energy of purpose" in Davis's message. Senator John Clark of Missouri bluntly declared, "In times like these the sovereignty of the States must be secondary to the sovereignty of the people." Although fearing the measure would "inaugurate a strong military government," Congressman Thomas Ashe reluctantly supported the measure as the "only means of saving the country." In a diary entry from later that summer, Texas Congressman Franklin Sexton recounted that he "voted for the conscript law with some doubt as to its constitutionality—& with regret," but he "believe[d] that it had save[d] the country." A large majority of the Senate and the House shared the view that military needs required conscription. After two weeks of debate, the act passed the Senate in a 19 to 5 vote and the House with a 54 to 26 vote. The leading scholars on the Confederate Congress contend that no exact formula determined how a congressman voted on conscription. In their assessment, personal considerations played a role, with the measure's supporters tending to be prewar Democrats who had favored secession.[28]

Highlighting the demand for action, the measure's preamble stressed "the absolute necessity of keeping in the service our gallant Army, and of placing in the field a large additional force to meet the advancing columns of enemy." In an effort to emphasize need and downplay any constitutional fears, Congress entitled the law "An Act to Further Provide for the Public Defence," intentionally avoiding the use of either *conscription* or *draft* in its name or anywhere else in the act. Careful wording, however, did not change its groundbreaking effect. It authorized President Davis to call out "all white men who are residents of the Confederate States," between the ages of eighteen and thirty-five, to serve "for three years, unless the war shall have been sooner ended." The law stipulated that twelve-month men between eighteen and thirty-five currently in the army were required to serve two more years or until the end of the war. After quickly and succinctly changing armed service from voluntary to compulsory, the bulk of the measure addressed bureaucratic issues such as furloughs, bounties, and unit reorganization.[29]

Extant evidence does not offer a clear verdict on who authored the administration's proposal or how Congress modified it. In his memoirs, General Robert E. Lee's aide-de-camp, Charles Marshall, claims that Lee drafted the bill and had Marshall present it to Secretary of State Benjamin, who in turn provided it to Congress. Yet, while Lee had established himself as Davis's most important advisor in March, Marshall's memoirs demonstrate an unreliable memory. They have an implausible timeline—he asserts that these exchanges took place in April, which was too late—and he wrongly claims the act contained a measure exempting overseers.

In his study of the Confederate cabinet, Rembert Patrick claims that Benjamin collaborated on the act before his move from the War Department to the State Department in mid-March, while Archer Jones credits Benjamin's successor, George W. Randolph, with authorship of the measure. According to Jones, Randolph employed the 1861 Virginia militia conscription act, which he had written, as a model for the Confederate act. Additionally, in its secret sessions, Congress undoubtedly altered the proposal. Jones maintains that President Davis objected to the measure's retention of one-year volunteers in the army, and Marshall claims that Lee despised its provision that soldiers could elect new officers. Regardless of the act's precise mix of authors, the available evidence supports a conclusion that both Davis and Lee endorsed the bill, even if they had trivial misgivings. In his official response to Congress, the president only criticized a few minor sections, which he found contradictory.[30]

Many southerners had greater concerns than the president. They immediately recognized conscription's revolutionary nature and its impact on almost every family in the South. It forced them to decide how much loyalty they owed to the Confederacy. Robert Magill, a prospective conscript, later depicted the "three horns to the dilemma." First, one could volunteer and be given the chance to select his own unit. Second, a man could "be conscripted and placed in a company not of your own choosing and bear the odious name of conscript." Third, he could "attempt to go North, turning [his] back on the home of [his] childhood and a widowed mother, and run a risk of ten to one of being captured and shot as a traitor to the Southern cause." In 1862, very few men chose this final option. Only one year into the war, southerners still anticipated victory. Even for those who might be inclined to flee, Union lines were often too far away to make this option viable. More likely, men who dodged enrolling officers hid in barns, cellars, woods, and marshes near their homes. A North Carolinian heard rumors of men who planned to dodge conscription by "tak[ing] there fare with mockisons & Bull frogs in the widest and thickest swamps they can find."[31]

More important, Magill, who wrote long after the war ended, conflates opposition to conscription with opposition to the Confederacy. Fleeing to the enemy meant rejecting the Confederacy. However, in 1862, a southerner's dislike of conscription did not equate to an abandonment of their new nation. In fact, some Confederates rejected conscription precisely because they felt the measure itself violated their country's ideals. In his study of Confederate politics, George Rable argues that for these opponents, "condemning conscription became the patriot's highest duty." As loyal Confederates, they were obligated to oppose anti-Confederate measures that endangered the country's commitment to individual liberty and to states' rights. Placing tremendous power in the hands of Davis, the War Department, and the army, conscription epitomized this threat.[32]

Magill also leaves out a fourth option. Conscription potentially left families and communities defenseless. Many southern men, who considered both serving in the army and fleeing to enemy lines to be unpalatable, sought a compromise option. They strove to be loyal both to their families and to their nation by finding a way to comply with the conscription law yet remain home legally. In the first year of the war, individuals, families, and communities had been able to create their own definitions of Confederate loyalty. That fealty did not have to include army service. Although "very warm in [his] southern feelings," a secessionist decided against enlisting because he viewed the war as a conflict between Black Republicans and slaveholders, and "I will leave them to fight it out." This former slaveholder added that he would "under no circumstances join the federal army."[33]

More generally, prior to conscription, a family could choose to provide three brothers to the army and keep one at home to take care of the family's dependents. A community could send two doctors into the army and have another serve on the home front. A plantation owner could retain his overseer to police the slaves working in his fields. In turn, this slave force grew more vital food for the army or the community than it would have with the overseer in the army. Now, Congress had made "southerner" and "Confederate soldier" synonyms for white men between eighteen and thirty-five. In doing so, the act defined exactly what loyalty to the Confederacy meant.

Writing to the *Richmond Daily Dispatch,* a soldier contended that the volunteer system allowed communities to sort out who could best remain at home, while conscription's supposed equality could prove "detrimental to the welfare and prosperity of the country." In other words, the equal service conscription demanded on the battlefront did not translate into equal impact on families and communities. Some men could be more easily spared from the home front than others. Conscription eliminated any flexibility in duty to the Confederacy. As written, the act sent every white man of military age into the army, and therefore it took the decision for what type of service constituted loyalty from the hands of the people and put it in the hands of the government. In the cases noted previously, for instance, it would force the last brother, the only doctor, and the needed overseer into the army if they were of conscription age, regardless of how important these men were to their families and communities.[34]

The letters of Lieutenant George Huntley of North Carolina demonstrate how southerners viewed Confederate service and loyalty on their own terms. He and his correspondents thought of service from the perspectives of family and community, not of individuals. Huntley urged his friends not to volunteer but to "stay at home and make all [the crops] you can." In particular, he wanted to keep his father out of the army. He instructed him to "stay at home and take care of the rest" and requested that his friends "tell Pap not to volunteer." Nevertheless, Huntley neither opposed the war nor regretted his own enlistment. Instead, he insisted that if he were at home he would volunteer and that he planned to reenlist and collect a $50 bounty. His service proved his family's commitment to the Confederacy, so they did not need to send anyone else.

In viewing his community as a whole, Huntley offered a sharp distinction between who should and who should not join the army. He warned that men at home "that has nothing to hinder them" would "repent it some day" if they did not enlist. These men without dependents should join the army, according to Huntley, as "men of families ought to be the ones that stays at home, as someone will have to stay." Huntley's letters recognize that the number of both dependents at home and family members in the war should affect a man's service. The conscription act made no such distinctions.[35]

Like Huntley, other Confederates maintained seemingly contradictory views. On one hand, they could make the sweeping generalization that everyone should volunteer to demonstrate their patriotism. On the other hand, they could grant more latitude when addressing specific men, for they recognized that the home front needed men, too. Telling his father to stay home and care for their family, a Georgian declared, "I will fight for both of us." While he considered his service to be meeting his family's obligation, he did not think that others at home had done their share. He added, "Send the young men here." A Louisiana soldier sent a letter home stating, "I don't want you and Henry to leave home [and enlist] if there is any other chance." From Tennessee, Joseph Offield wrote his father, "I was sorry to hear of James enlisting for I know he cannot stand the fatigue of a camp-life . . . I don't want you to let him go." Thomas Goree took a different view. He did not see his service as counting for his whole family. Goree told his mother that "I think it best that you should no longer keep [his brother] Bob at home. . . . It is a sacrifice you will have to make." A planter's daughter, in a single diary entry, offered sharply different assessments of two men who enlisted under the threat of conscription. She sympathized with Mr. Valentine, who "would have gone long ago but for his father's persuasions," but condemned Mr. Catlin, for "nothing but necessity could start him."[36]

At the same time that some southerners objected to conscription's mandate that all serve, others celebrated this very provision of the act. The antebellum South posited itself as a democracy, with all white men politically and socially equal. Conscription proponents contended the act followed that logic. According to the *Charleston Mercury,* it "operates equally on all, and puts the high and the low, the rich and the poor on the same footing." Major James Griffin used almost the exact same words in asserting that the draft was "about the most equitable way after all—it places all on the same footing." From Atlanta, the *Southern Confederacy* described a militia muster where only two groups of men volunteered: those physically unfit for duty and those with numerous dependents who had no other support. In the meantime, physically fit men, who "could go with but little inconvenience to themselves or the country," refused to budge. For this editor, a draft would ensure fairness by making all these men serve. A South Carolina officer concurred that the "bill compels all to espouse their independence," not just "a few willing hearts."[37]

Not only did conscription contribute to a debate over equality; it also engendered a debate over Confederate ideology. Die-hard states' rights advocates immediately complained that the policy could destroy the states, especially the initial act, which did not even exempt state government officials. Governors led this charge, with Georgia's Joseph Brown carrying the standard at the forefront of the assault. He alleged that conscription policy "strikes at the very foundation" of the doctrines that justified secession. The governor attacked conscription as a "consolidation of all the military power of the State in the hands of one man." In a May 1862 message to his state legislature, Virginia's Governor John Letcher declared that he considered conscription to be an unconstitutional violation of states' rights. North Carolina governor Henry Clark called the act "very distasteful to our people" and noted that "doubts about its constitutionality have been raised." Farther west, Alabama governor John Gill Shorter claimed the Confederacy's resort to conscription made him "despair of our ultimate triumph."[38]

Nevertheless, in the spring of 1862, governors' barks exceeded their bites. Despite lambasting the measure, Governor Letcher "urge[d] upon the people [of Virginia] a prompt and cheerful response." Letcher stressed patience, for "we can mark clearly and distinctly the line between state and confederate authority, after the enemy is driven from our soil and our independence established." Governor Clark informed the secretary of war that he would "carry out the Conscription Act fairly" and—recognizing the impact of his words on his constituents—told the president that he "cannot allow myself to be represented as opposed or even neutral towards it." Even Governor Brown, the measure's harshest critic, initially offered some encouraging words. On the day the act passed, he reminded Georgia troops that the "Country is now in great peril," so regardless of their opinions of the constitutionality of conscription, "it behooves us all as Georgians and patriots to sacrifice our personal interests . . . upon the altar of our common country."[39]

In addition to governors, other southerners feared the act violated the very states' rights principles they had seceded to protect. They deemed the act more fitting for the oppressive Union government than the liberty-protecting Confederate nation. Branding Congress a "corrupt body of men," a Mississippi private carped that men "haven't much choice now between the C.S.A. and the North." Several North Carolinians came to the same conclusion. One soldier complained that secession occurred because "Lincoln denied the principle of state sovereignty," and now a year later, our government "repudiates this very same principle of State Rights." Another worried that the Confederacy had evolved into "worse than a monarch government," with a third agreeing that it is "one grand step to monarchy." He denounced the measure as "striking at the foundations of all we hold dear or that is worth fighting for." R. C. Puryear wrote to Governor Clark that the measure was "unnecessary, unequal, unjust, and tyrannical," for with it, states' rights were "repudiated and trodden underfoot." Even after conceding that his father had persuaded him of conscription's constitutionality, Charles Hutson did not sound convinced. He repeated, "Are you sure?" and worried about the "*evil* precedent" it set.[40]

The editor of the Augusta *Daily Constitutionalist* offered an elaborate response to most of the objections to conscription, including these states' rights concerns. Like President Davis, he concisely asserted that "no flagrant violation of State rights" existed. First, he asked his readers to trust their leaders. He contended that one year earlier, voters had elected President Davis and Congress to protect their rights. These politicians adhered to states' rights and would not have passed the measure if it infringed on those rights. Second, the national government had the constitutional power to raise armies and to call out men if necessary to defend the country. That time had clearly come. Admitting that volunteering might have worked in 1861, he explained that "'Heavy battalions' must now decide our cause." In the editor's opinion, only conscription could create those battalions; it was time for "every one . . . to be a soldier." He added that, in contrast to volunteering, conscription had the additional positive effect of putting men into established units, which would accelerate their training and improve the army's effectiveness.

In asserting the fairness of the act, the editor anticipated attacks upon it and acknowledged that some would have to make greater sacrifices than others, and that it would be impossible to resolve this discrepancy through legislation. "Exact equality of circumstances cannot be found in any instance." For instance, he speculated that one might think that married men should remain at home while bachelors serve in the army. Yet what about the poor bachelor who was uncle to several orphaned boys and girls, in comparison to a married man who had the resources to care for his family in his absence? Asserting a standard of patriotism perhaps greater than some of his readers possessed, the editor stressed that in wartime, "a man's *first* duty . . . is to his country, his *second* being to his family."[41]

The editor had raised—and immediately and unequivocally answered—an important question: How did a man reconcile the needs of his country and his family in wartime? Some soldiers agreed with the editor. In November 1861, a South Carolinian wrote to his daughter that with his home state invaded, "I would be disgraced if I staid at home." Four months later, he elaborated, explaining that after Confederate independence, "it will be pride to you to know" that the only man in the family volunteered to fight. He equated country and family in declaring, "A man who will not offer up his life for his family . . . does dishonor to his wife and children." A North Carolinian expressed the same sentiment to his fiancé: "My first duties are to my country and then to you." Arkansas soldier W. C. Porter recorded in his diary that only his "love of country" could keep him from his family, and he believed that men should bear all hardships—the worst being separation from family—for the Confederate cause. Similarly, a Louisiana private explained to his wife that "It is for you that I have come to defend" and that his love for his family "makes me want to fight." In other words, for the Augusta editor and these soldiers, one fulfilled his duty to family by putting his country first.[42]

Others would contend that these men had their priorities reversed. Louisiana Sergeant Edwin Fay made this point explicit, telling his wife, "I hold that my first duty is to my family, my country is secondary." In the view of men like Fay, soldiers provided service in exchange for an implicit promise that their government would take care of their families. In their minds, a prolonged service in

Virginia did not necessarily protect their families in Georgia, Alabama, or Louisiana. If they felt that their families needed them to return home, they would try to do so. Another Louisianan expressed this same family-first sentiment. After hearing of conscription, he declared, "I am willing to sacrifice all that I have got to get back home with you all" and later added that he was "all most crasey to get back home." A North Carolina officer, whose business and private affairs had suffered in his absence, "felt it my duty to myself & others to retire." Visible at the onset of conscription, this sentiment intensified as the distress caused by the war and by shortages of food and supplies increased.[43]

Many of these letter writers represented the group of men perhaps most affected by conscription—the soldiers who had to stay in the army. In military camps across the Confederacy, the volunteers of 1861 debated the wisdom of the measure that not only brought new men into the army but also forced them to remain in the ranks. Having enlisted for twelve months, these soldiers anticipated leaving the army in May, June, or July of 1862. Instead, the act had extended their service two more years and generally denied them even the opportunity to return home briefly to visit their loved ones. Learning from the mistakes of their December act, Congress did not grant wholesale furloughs in its April measure. It did permit furloughs for soldiers who had not received one previously, but only "at such time and in such numbers as the Secretary of War may deem most compatible with the public interest." Given the dire military situation in 1862, the army did not deem it "compatible with the public interest" to issue many furloughs.[44]

The inability to reunite with their loved ones frustrated soldiers as much as their additional time in the army. One soldier complained that conscription was "a nough to make you twelve months volunteers rebel if they don't let you come home." Alabama Private J. M. Tate heard "that sum has laid down their guns and say they wont fight," and he predicted soldiers "will rebell against it." A Mississippian heard a similar rumor and feared that "a great many of our regiments swear they will throw down their guns." A quartermaster from the same state recorded in his diary that soldiers were "very much disappointed. . . . and some even say they will disregard it and go home." A South Carolina officer speculated that "almost every man would be willing to enlist for the war—if he could be allowed to spend a month at home."[45]

While furloughs existed in theory more than reality, the law did provide current soldiers a few minor concessions, including participation in the election of new officers. When units formed in 1861, soldiers elected their officers, generally community leaders. Conscription stipulated that they could now hold new elections. While Congress may have considered this provision to be a boon for soldiers, it troubled some of them. Reporting to President Davis that conscription in Alabama "has worked most disastrously in this army," Colonel W. P. Johnston offered the extension of soldiers' terms of service and the election of new officers as the two examples that proved his contention. In his view, officer elections often replaced experienced officers with "grossly incompetent" men.[46]

Other soldiers agreed. South Carolinian James B. Griffin feared that "a good many of the old officers will be turned out, and worse ones put in their stead." Officers who have "allowed most privileges, and have been least efficient, are the men who will be elected." One Georgian felt the election of a new colonel "was the greatest calamity" that his regiment could face. Private John Kinyoun concurred that the election of officers made for an inefficient army. Only "the lowest demagogues" participated, while "honorable gentlem[e]n" declined to enter the races. For South Carolinian Charles Hutson, this "ill-judged feature in the bill" only "sowed discord & dissatisfaction."[47]

Hutson also epitomized Col. Johnston's first contention: soldiers disliked the extensions of their terms. He lamented that it "falls more heavily upon those who were prompt to respond . . . than upon the laggards." In this view, the law unfairly punished men who had volunteered for service, in contrast to men at home shirking their duty. An enraged Virginian wondered why Congress targeted men who had already provided a year of service to the Confederacy. He complained, "The papers make a huge fuss about re-enlisting," when their focus should be on the "idle lazy loons [who] remain at home." Charles Liebermann, who had twice excitedly written his wife in March that their reunion was imminent, saw these hopes dashed. He excoriated the law, which "has had a very demoralizing effect over our whole regiment," for it singled out men like him who had "nobly responded to the first call" by forcing them to stay two extra years without even allowing them a furlough. In declining to reenlist in January, a South Carolina soldier explained, "Let those who are at home come next, and I will take turns with them." These men had shown their loyalty to the Confederate cause and now planned to step aside and allow others to take their chance at the front. Or, as a Raleigh editor had predicted that same month, "Our present soldiers would like to see these [loafers] driven to duty. But they do not wish to be driven themselves."[48]

The idea that military service equated to patriotism, as well its converse—that staying at home was unpatriotic—resonates throughout the words of those who praised conscription. Charles Truehart, a Virginian, expressed no surprise at the dissatisfaction of men without true hearts who now faced conscription. "Nothing better could have been expected of such men," he informed his sisters. They had remained at home "and le[ft] their countrymen to defend their common liberties and property." Earlier in April, a doctor describing men who pretended to be saltpeter makers to avoid the state draft complained, "There is no patriotism in men who are able to go into service & will seek subterfuge to keep out of it." Serving in Stonewall Jackson's army, the doctor emphasized that men who had dodged the draft "deserved to live in a land of serfdom with a tyrant to govern them." He singled out the childless J. M. Thomas as a shirker whose "heart is as barren as he is barren of children. There is no patriotism in his nature." A lieutenant praised conscription as "the very thing for the occasion," since it would enroll "men who have been shirking the cause." Without acknowledging any irony, another officer exclaimed, "If our people wont volunteer to fight for their Liberty . . . they ought to be made to do it."[49]

Some conscription proponents asserted that the men at home not only lacked patriotism but also should be considered cowards or dishonorable opportunists. James Holloway contended that healthy men who remained at home should be "subject[ed] to censure," and later wished these "stout young men . . . could all be branded—so that their children might know what part they have taken in this struggle for independence." One Georgian predicted the conscription law would "put many a coward to his wits." In Virginia, a Confederate complained that the "journey men stay at home, sell whisky to the soldiers, trade horses and groan and complain" whenever they are expected to perform militia service. Another Virginian declared, "every man that is now at home is for his self and they take every advantage of them that is now in the army." Previously having wondered "how can a man rest quietly at home" during "these troublous times," Kate Stone joyfully recorded in her diary that "conscription has caused a great commotion and great consternation among the shirking stay-at-homes . . . We earnestly hope these coward souls will be made to go."[50]

Regardless of one's impression of men who remained at home, the idea that they "will be made to go" troubled southerners. Compelling men to join or to remain in the army sparked one of the most frequent complaints against conscription—that it created "a military despotism" which destroyed individual liberty. A soldier claimed coercing men to fight for their liberty struck "at the foundation of all we hold dear" and it would most likely "damn the government it intended to save." Another dramatically complained, "A more oppressive law was never enacted in the most uncivilized country or by the worst of despots." A disillusioned William L. Sullivan lamented that conscription "have shoen there tyranny military despotism . . . it is worse than a monarch government." Writing from an encampment in Virginia, a North Carolinian, who had expected to be discharged on April 24, 1862, claimed that conscription deserved "the hearty condemnation of every free man," for it was "an act of military despotism in violation of every republican principle." As Congress debated the act, another soldier conveyed to his wife the same sentiment in fewer words. The men in his unit thought it was "not justice."[51]

To deflect arguments about the justice of conscription, its defenders claimed that necessity trumped these concerns. As if to underscore the pressing need for heavier battalions, during the midst of the congressional debate over conscription, the Confederate army lost a battle at Shiloh, Tennessee (twenty miles north of the vital Corinth, Mississippi, railroad junction) on April 6–7, 1862. Although overshadowed by later Civil War battles, Shiloh, at the time, stood as the largest conflict in United States history, with approximately 60,000 Union troops fighting 40,000 Confederates. Recognizing the imperative need for troops, the *Richmond Enquirer* declared that the Confederacy had to "*whip our enemies and save our homes;*—we can attend to questions of theory afterwards." In advocating conscription to one of his state's Confederate senators, an Alabama colonel averred that "our people . . . must temporarily submit to absolute discipline as part of the price of permanent civil liberty."[52]

On April 1, the *Richmond Dispatch,* in responding to critics of the proposed law, asserted, "If the Yankees overrun us, they will leave us no rights at all either State or personal. We shall be the veriest slaves in all Christendom." This newspaper editor preferred the risk of creating a southern despot to the certainty of life under a Yankee despot. Four days later, William Holden, the states' rights editor of the *Raleigh Standard,* responded directly to the *Dispatch*'s editorial. Contending "we will not have a despot of any stamp," he denied that the Confederacy could be saved "by the establishment of a great military consolidation." In contrast, he urged Congress to check this tendency to "military consolidation and military despotism."[53]

In their exchange, the two editors touched on another debate over conscription: Was it really necessary? In April 1862, despite the grumblings about the ideological threats posed by national conscription, most southerners supported the measure on the grounds of necessity. Four months after the measure's passage, the secretary of war would claim that in April 1862, with 148 regiments' terms due to expire, "it was obvious that conscription alone could save us." Many Confederates shared his assessment of the pressing need for the law. They would temporarily sacrifice some liberty to achieve the larger goal of independence. Georgian G. W. Bolton wrote that the soldiers in his unit "are generally satisfied. They are willing to stay here if the country needs them." A Mississippi soldier agreed on the "great necessity for all of us to remain in service," and he expected that his unit "will submit quietly and do their duty as soldiers fighting in a just and righteous cause." In North Carolina, Governor Clark stressed that his state's populace had misgivings about the law and had only accepted it "as a necessity of our welfare."[54]

The manifest need for conscription led some southerners to wonder why the Confederacy had waited so long to pass the measure. Surprisingly, the *Charleston Mercury,* one of the South's leading states' rights newspapers, only voiced two complaints against President Davis's call for conscription: that he should have done it sooner and that its upper age limit should be forty-five rather than thirty-five. The *Richmond Examiner* concurred. Contending that the Confederacy should have used conscription to put an "invincible army" of 750,000 men in the field the previous summer, the nation instead relied on a "wretched shift" of twelve-month volunteers and militia. Thus, the newspaper's editor was relieved that the government had finally implemented measures that it should have employed ten months earlier. A Georgian agreed that he "wish[ed] it had been passed sooner." Sharing this sentiment, a South Carolinian went even further and grandiosely proclaimed the law "one of the best things ever passed by a supreme body."[55]

Many southerners disputed this superlative, and some would even dispute the measure's necessity. In announcing the passage of the act, the *Wilmington Journal* conceded that people would sacrifice some of their rights when necessary, but the editor remained unconvinced that the Confederacy had reached that point. Earlier in the year, the anticonscription editor William Holden had declared that proconscription attitudes were based on an "assumption as uncomplimentary to our people as it is unsustained by the facts." An April 16 letter published in his newspaper complained that since volunteering had not failed, conscription "proposes to coerce the people to do that which they are ready to do willingly." Critics, including this letter writer, pointed out the individual states had never failed to meet any Confederate quotas. They added that throughout the first year of the conflict, the army had a harder time finding weapons than finding soldiers. In an argument that he would use for the duration of the war, Governor Brown declared, "The difficulty has never been to get men. If the guns and provisions can be had the states will furnish enough men without conscription." In a letter to President Davis, he frankly stated, "The plea of necessity, so far . . . as [Georgia] is concerned cannot be set up in defence of the Conscription Act." In other words, these critics maintained that the current system worked. Given that, why would the government change it to a system which threatened liberty?[56]

In April 1862, most southerners rejected these calamitous warnings and accepted the idea that the end—a larger army that would produce a swift Confederate victory—justified the means—conscription and its potential, temporary infringement on their liberties. The Executive Council of South Carolina exemplified this view. One member wrote President Davis asserting that "Your Conscription Law is the right thing—we will give it cheerful hearty support." As a whole, the council recognized that military necessity could trump constitutional scruples. It declared that it was "induced to waive, for the present, all objections to the measure, and to give it a cheerful and energetic support upon the ground of imperious necessity." The phrase "for the present" left the door open for future objections, but in April the council stood loyally with national conscription. Across the Confederacy, most southerners, like these South Carolinians, accepted conscription "for the present."[57]

The council's actions, however, demonstrated an area where problems would soon arise. In acquiescing to the draft, it specified an exception that put South Carolina on a collision course with the federal government. The council insisted on being able to control the list of who would be exempt from conscription in their state. Having the power to declare whether men were eligible or exempt from conscription was tantamount to controlling the process entirely. One could dismiss or enroll whole classes of men, whether farmers, fathers with three or more children, state militia officers, overseers, or doctors. In theory, with this power, South Carolina could exempt its entire white population. The idea of allowing each state to provide its own list of exemptions would defeat President Davis's plan to use conscription to maximize the army's size, to make military service equal across the Confederacy, and to replace confusing and contradictory recruiting legislation. In sum, whoever controlled the list of exemptions truly controlled conscription, and President Davis and the Confederate Congress had no intention of turning that power over to the states.[58]

The Executive Council's concern over exemptions was tied to conscription's unsolvable puzzle: how to perfectly balance the needs of the battlefront and the home front. While conscription rested on the broad idea that a draft was fair because it made all men serve—regardless of their wealth or occupation—this theory quickly crashed into the reality that all men could not serve in the army. In reacting to conscription, Georgian William Daniel Dixon, on April 22, 1862, scribbled in his diary, "Everyone now has got to do duty." Everyone's duty, however, could not be military service. Some men had to remain at home. A home front of old men, young boys, and women could not sustain itself, let alone sustain the army, too. On the day conscription passed in Congress, the Shreveport *South-Western* reported that "a great consternation prevails in certain circles," since the conscription law made no mention of "lawyers, doctors, or druggists" being exempt from the law. Realizing the difficulties of trying to enumerate exempt occupations, the editor saw "no reason why they should have preference over printers and blacksmiths." This discussion foreshadowed a war-long debate over what the duty of every adult white male would be in the Confederacy. Within a week of the law's passage, Congress would pass the first list of exemptions. That list would not resolve the issue but represented just the opening round in the contest over the meaning of duty to the Confederacy.[59]

The issue of exemptions was only one of the many issues that remained unresolved in April 1862. The conscription act had passed quickly, without a national debate. While some had complained about its threats to liberty, a general recognition of the need for more troops subsumed this opposition. Nonetheless, an acceptance of conscription on paper did not equate to an acceptance of conscription in operation. Many questions remained: Could states' rights advocates truly accept this nationalistic legislation? What would happen when areas with high concentrations of slaves lost their white male populations? What would happen in regions where white men were needed for the harvest? Could conscription undermine the alliance of slaveholders and nonslaveholders? Could service truly be equal? Would men in the army accept the Confederate argument that conscription provided the best means for protecting their homes, even as their homes faced the threat or reality of Union army occupation? Southerners' answers to these questions shaped their attitudes toward conscription, and each southerner's answer depended on a variety of factors, including where they lived, how the war had affected their family and community, and how the government responded to their concerns.

CHAPTER 2

# The First Efforts to Manage Conscription, April–August 1862

The day after the conscription bill passed, John Conrad, a North Carolina lieutenant, wrote to his wife and offered a mixed assessment of the measure. On the one hand, Conrad contended, "I am not in favor of the law," but on the other hand, he recognized that "it will bring out a great many men that ought to be out." Even if these men "ought to be out," the lieutenant worried that "it will take rather many men from home." He feared that "unless [conscription] is managed very well and the cotton states plant all corn the people through the country as well as the soldiers will suffer for provisions."[1]

Conrad's letter recognized that the army could not enroll every adult, white male in the South. Some men would have to remain at home. Both soldiers and civilians needed doctors, blacksmiths, millers, ministers, and other professionals. Both groups also needed to be fed. If all men entered the army, a North Carolina legislator worried, "famine is inevitable," and a farmer from that state justified his desire to remain home by contending, "It is impossible for men to fight unless they have something to eat." A wholesale removal of men from the home front would lead to the collapse of the Confederacy. Confederate political and military leaders had to find a way to balance these competing needs. For Conrad, and for other southerners, the key to their attitude toward conscription would come down to whether they felt it was "managed very well."[2]

In his call for conscription, President Davis did not offer much of a plan for managing enrollment. Instead, he requested a "plain and simple method," and in its April 16 act, Congress had obliged. In that measure, the only way that a healthy, white southern man of conscription age could legally avoid entering the army would be to travel to a camp of instruction and present a substitute to serve in his place. Substitutes had to be medically fit men ineligible for conscription, a category including men outside the age range, foreigners, or residents of states that had not seceded. Five days later, Congress, in its first effort to oversee conscription, added a list of occupational exemptions. This list included government officials; mail carriers; teachers; nurses; newspaper employees; apothecaries; ministers; employees in mines, furnaces, and foundries; and men working on railroads.[3]

Substitution and occupational exemptions represented the acknowledgment that some men would fight and some would remain home. Congress adjourned the same day it passed its list of exemptions, and it would not reconvene for four months. Thus, the summer of 1862 provided the opportunity to see if conscription worked in practice. Would it increase the size of the army? Would it thwart the Union's invasion of Confederate territory? Would it keep enough men at home to supply both the army and civilians? Were the occupational exemptions appropriate or were others needed? Did the right men go into the army and the right men stay at home? Would southerners accept substitution and exemption as fair to all classes? Did these policies alter the balance among competing duties to nation, community, and family? In short, the summer allowed southerners to decide if the legislative and executive branches had successfully managed conscription.

Many historians give the Confederate government a failing grade for its administration of conscription. In his seminal 1924 work on the measure, Albert Burton Moore condemned it as "not only contrary to the spirit of the people but [also] to the genius of the Confederate political system." Twenty-six years later, E. Merton Coulter lamented that "conscription had been a failure" as its lack of "workability" undermined the support of the people and the state governments. Paul Escott directly blamed the mismanagement of the policy for turning the yeoman class against the Confederacy. He contended, "Inequities in the administration of the conscription and exemption laws produced disastrous results." In his study of desertion, Mark Weitz succinctly judged the 1862 act "a failure." He asserted that while it brought some men into the service, it pushed others away from both the army and the Confederacy. James McPherson branded conscription as "the most unpopular act of the Confederate government."[4]

In their negative assessments of the law, scholars highlight its substitution provision. Decrying substitution as "the most lamentable feature of the conscription system," Moore contended it received no support on either battlefront or the home front. Escott concurred, labeling it "one of the greatest causes of discontent." Bell Wiley, in *The Life of Johnny Reb,* goes even further in arguing that substitution was a "shameful reflection on Confederate patriotism." Mary L. Wilson entitled her article on substitution in Texas "Profiles in Evasion," which highlights principals' avoidance of service. Armstead Robinson denounced it as "a blatant concession to wealth and privilege," painting a sinister portrait of legislators meeting in secret session, who "tucked [substitution] away near the end of the legislation." In a 1970 *Civil War Times Illustrated* article, Lowell H. Harrison captured the spirit of this standard view of substitution, stating both that it "obviously favored the rich" and that it "probably caused more resentment than conscription itself."[5]

The conclusion that the substitution clause demonstrates that Confederates leaders managed conscription poorly is easily accepted, since the idea of someone paying another man to take his place in the military (and possibly die as part of the bargain) challenges twenty-first-century sensibilities. These descriptions, however, inaccurately characterize southerners' view of conscription in the summer of 1862. Most Confederates approved of the government's administration of conscription during its initial months of operation. At that time, substitution was not a divisive topic, and the mere fact that a man purchased one neither automatically marked him a coward nor always earned him censure at home. In supplying a substitute, these men obeyed a Confederate law—neither an unpatriotic act nor an example of evasion. In a continuum of reactions to conscription, which included willingly entering the army, pleading for a medical release, seeking an occupational exemption, truly evading enrolling officers, fleeing to Union lines, or armed resistance, substitution fell much closer to enlistment than to resistance.

Historian Patrick J. Doyle has shown that substitution reveals much more about Confederates' "understandings of citizenship and its inherent duties" than about class tensions or Confederate loyalty. He convincingly demonstrates that "substitution was not perceived as inherently incompatible with the duties of citizenship in the South." Substitution specifically, and conscription itself more generally, fostered a debate over the obligations southern men owed to their nation and their families, rather than proving loyalty or disloyalty. If a man served the "public interest," his staying home was defensible. Of course, defining "public interest" was not simple, and the assessment of a man's home front contribution often varied in the eye of the beholder. Regardless, what most historians consider to be opposition to conscription and the Confederacy in 1862 really involved men trying to work within the law to remain home and to balance the needs of their family and their nation. With conscription, this balancing act had become more precarious, but it still seemed possible.[6]

When Armstead Robinson portrays legislators sneaking substitution into the law, he points out that President Davis had not mentioned substitution in his initial call for conscription, nor did any congressman or newspaper editor suggest such a provision. Their silence is telling, but not because it proves disreputable motives. Simply put, substitution was uncontroversial. More likely, Confederate leaders did not engage in lengthy debates, act duplicitously, or craft elaborate justifications for substitution because they assumed its inclusion in the bill. It had a long history in United States military service. During the American Revolution, the Continental Army accepted substitutes. In the local militia musters that routinely occurred throughout the nation in the years preceding the Civil War, wealthy men often supplied substitutes to take their places. Compulsory antebellum slave patrols also often allowed for the option of providing a substitute to serve in one's stead. With substitution being part of traditional military culture, the provision likely entered the Confederate law without a second thought.[7]

In fact, in the Confederacy, substitution actually preceded conscription. In October 1861, Secretary of War Judah Benjamin proposed regulations regarding the acceptance of substitutes into the army, stipulating that principals—the term for a man who provided the substitute—needed written permission to provide a substitute, that substitutes must enlist for the war, and that each company would accept only one per month. In preconscription substitution, men who wished to demonstrate their support for the Confederacy, but who preferred not to fight for reasons such as poor health, family needs, or old age, offered their services through surrogates. These men did not truly substitute for their principal, who was neither in the army nor under obligation to serve. Instead, these principals' payments created a privately funded bounty to aid in recruiting. Substitution also appeared in the 1862 state drafts. In Virginia, advertisements for and from substitutes filled the Richmond *Daily Dispatch*. The South Carolina draft provided for substitution if the principal provided "an able-bodied man, well clothed." According to draft records, 117 Charlestonians took advantage of this provision.[8]

In all cases, substitution represented a contract between a substitute and a principal. The terms of the contract varied by individual, by location, and over time. As a purchasable item, substitutes had a cost based at least partly on supply and demand. Negotiating a contract with a substitute did not end the process. The replacement soldier had to be accepted into the army. Some officers proved reluctant to take on a man who seemed to be joining the army solely to secure a financial gain, especially if the man was replacing a soldier already in the ranks. According to the terms of the April law, both new recruits and veteran soldiers could provide substitutes, but the army greatly restricted this process for the latter group.

The Confederacy's main objective in enacting conscription was to increase the size and quality of the army, and its substitution policy exemplified this goal. It made it much harder for the 200,000 soldiers in the ranks to exit the army than for a man on the home front to avoid entering the army in the first place. While every new conscript could provide a substitute, units in the field would only accept one substitute per month for men in already in the army. Regardless of this regulation, some officers refused to accept any substitutes. One soldier complained that his colonel refused to add "green men" to "the best drilled company in the country." Another maintained, "Our Officers do not care about taking in substitutes," an attitude which left a recently married fellow soldier seeking to provide one out of luck.[9]

The army's exemption policy discriminated even more against men already in the army. All prospective conscripts could claim a legal exemption if they worked in a designated occupation. Soldiers in the ranks, however, could not receive exemptions. Even if a soldier were a teacher, editor, or preacher, he was ineligible for an occupational exemption. According to the army, by definition, a man could only be "exempt" from service if he was not in the service; he could not be "exempt" from a task he was already performing. In other words, the army made a sharp distinction between an exemption (allowed) and a discharge (not allowed). By volunteering, even if for only one year, soldiers had forfeited their right to claim exemption. In denying soldiers' exemptions, the commandant of conscription in North Carolina repeatedly reminded applicants that exemption is "*prospective* in its operation" and not applicable to men already in the army. This distinction frustrated soldiers who felt this provision unfairly penalized loyal men who had volunteered in 1861 while seemingly favoring those less loyal men who had remained at home during the war's first year.[10]

Another group struggled to exit the army: one-year volunteers younger than eighteen or older than thirty-five. While not subject to conscription, they could not simply walk away from the army. Regulations stipulated that these men would be released on July 16. As this day approached, forty-three-year-old Charles Friend fretted that the government would deny his release. With the Confederacy losing potential conscripts from Union-occupied areas in Texas, Arkansas, and Louisiana, Friend worried that the army would "be very strict" and he "fear[ed] she will not be able to comply with her promise or will be very rigid in holding on to all she can." Friend was right. The army did delay their departures, moving them from July 16 to ninety days after these soldiers' terms of service expired, thereby converting twelve-month men into fifteen-month men. These regulations also clarified that men who had enlisted for the war previously would not be released, regardless of their age. Thus, if a thirty-eight-year-old father had volunteered for the war in 1861, with his eighteen-year-old son remaining at home to take care of the family farm, both men now would be responsible for service. They could not simply swap places.[11]

Soldiers outside of conscription age resented these provisions. In August, a group of men over thirty-five referring to themselves as "non-conscripts"—a phrase which highlighted both that they had volunteered for service and that they did not fall within conscription's age range—petitioned Congress that these measures violated "a solemn legislative compact with the States and society." They had left home "*to fight as freemen in the army of freemen*" and were "prepared to sacrifice everything but their honor and manhood." Three weeks past their anticipated July 16 discharge date, the petitioners wondered whether they lived under a constitutional or unlimited government and whether the people were free or the executive was supreme.

A month later, twenty-eight Louisiana privates sent their governor a protest, which copied much of the language used by those "non-conscripts." Concerned about the "ministerial caprice" that had unconstitutionally altered Confederate law, the men—all over thirty-five years of age—petitioned both as "citizens of Louisiana" and as "ardent supporters of the doctrine of States rights." As such, they appealed to their governor to intercede on their behalf to get the army to grant their immediate discharge. With a relative on the other end of the age spectrum, another Louisiana family worried that "despite of law justice and right," the army was trying to keep their seventeen-year-old in its clutches, only giving up because they feared Congress.[12]

While men outside of conscription's age range could seek legal remedies to return home, soldiers of conscription age possessed very few options. Desertions increased during the summer of 1862. Historian Mark Weitz shows that conscription helped fuel these desertions, as soldiers found the pull of home stronger than the force of Confederate laws. Contending that soldiers enlisted to protect their families and homes, Weitz demonstrates that, for many, this family loyalty overcame national loyalty. Thus, if they felt that the Confederacy had abandoned their families, soldiers might in response desert to relieve suffering on the home front.

Nevertheless, desertion, even if just to return home to take care of one's family, implied disloyalty. Most soldiers who had volunteered to fight for the Confederacy in the first year of the conflict remained loyal to the Confederacy even if its conscription policy infuriated them. Instead, they sought legal methods to reconcile the needs of their family and their country. Ineligible for exemptions, these soldiers needed to find substitutes if they wished to exit the army and return home. In doing so, they had to invoke the help and support of their family and home community.[13]

The efforts of Edwin Fay, Grant Taylor, and Abner Ford reveal a great deal about how conscription contributed to struggles in balancing family needs, national loyalty, and a sense of honor. Suspecting that conscription legislation was imminent, on April 4, 1862, Louisianan Edwin Fay, preferring to fight alongside his friends rather than strangers, and in a saddle rather than on his feet, volunteered for one year of service in the Minden Rangers, a cavalry company. He enlisted not only just prior to the passage of the conscription law, which immediately extended the length of his service, but also just prior to the passage of the exemption provisions, which might have allowed him to remain home as a schoolteacher.

Serving in Mississippi, Fay almost immediately sought a legal method to return to Minden to be with his wife and their one- and five-year-old boys. In order to do so, the thirty-year-old Fay simultaneously pursued claiming an exemption as a teacher and procuring a substitute. Despite his efforts, he failed to secure his exit from the army. His letters demonstrate the complex considerations connected to conscription. In making his decisions, he considered material factors—money and his family's living conditions—as well as nonmaterial factors—honor and identity. Also, his missives reveal that the decision was not his alone. He repeatedly sought his wife's help and approval, and he also took into account how others would view his actions.[14]

On May 20, Fay told his wife that he was considering claiming exemption as a teacher, and he wanted to know if she approved. In that same letter, and in another letter five days later, he proposed an alternative: offering $400 per year plus a horse, a bridle, and a saddle for a man to serve in his place. In later defending his plan to purchase a substitute, he explained, "If I furnish a soldier to the services as good as myself, that would not otherwise be in it, I am in fact actually fighting for my country myself." This rationale—that the army lost nothing by accepting substitutes—was a common refrain among principals, as was Fay's contention that he could "serve the country better [at home] . . . than in the field."

In looking for a replacement, Fay suggested targeting a boy under the age of eighteen, for he believed that a young man would cost less than a man over thirty-five. While he contemplated how much to pay, fellow soldiers found substitutes. Their success, however, meant that his unit stopped accepting them. By the end of the year, Fay clung to the idea of claiming exemption as a schoolteacher. "A little squirt of a captain," however, informed him that by volunteering he had "relinquished [his] right to claim exemption." The "little squirt" was correct. Nevertheless, Fay hoped that if his former school filed a petition with the secretary of war, the army might relent in his case. Fay told his wife that he would even be willing to write the petition himself if the school would endorse it.[15]

While yearning to return home, Fay also worried about how people would view his departure from the army. In proposing to secure a substitute, he reminded his wife (and perhaps himself) that there was "nothing dishonorable about it." Regardless, he feared that if he returned home, he would have to "brave the the stings and taunts of outraged women" whose husbands remained in the army. After repeated letters obliquely asking his wife for some assurance that she agreed with his decision, he finally asked her point blank, "Do you think it contemptible for me to come home?" While he wanted to come back to his family, he would not "forfeit her good opinion" to do so.

Apparently, she endorsed his decision, and perhaps this endorsement, coupled with his increasing frustration with army life, led Fay to declare that he no longer cared how the community felt. In his view, he had already proven his loyalty by joining the army, even if only for a few months. If necessary, he would honor his commitment and spend a year in the ranks, but he did not want to spend any more time away from home than that. Also, he believed that his neighbors' concerns might be assuaged as he planned to join a home guard unit in Minden, for "there will be a need of an army" in Louisiana, too.[16]

Like Edwin Fay, Grant Taylor, an Alabama soldier, sought a substitute, and he also consulted his wife. The letters between Grant and his wife, Malinda, reveal that Confederate conscription caused a shift in both gender and class roles in southern society. A thirty-four-year-old nonslaveholding farmer, Taylor, again similar to Fay, was a reluctant rebel, having volunteered for the army—in his case, taking a $40 bounty rather than face conscription. During the summer of 1862, Taylor sought to acquire a substitute and return home to his wife and four children. Since he could not go home to find one himself, Grant needed Malinda's help. The Taylors targeted James Riley as a prospective substitute, and Grant repeatedly urged his wife "to see old Rily." Through the first two weeks of July 1862, the Taylors negotiated with Riley. Grant wanted Malinda to offer his land (though he never articulated a specific amount of land or its value) and, if that did not work, to sweeten the pot with an additional $50 per year.

However, Malinda found negotiating with Riley to be exasperating. While she was inclined to "give the land, houses and all if he would go," Riley refused to declare his price. By mid-July, Malinda discovered the reason for Riley's coyness. When she stopped by his house, she found a man there trying to hire Riley to go in someone else's place and discovered that "There is 1 or 2 after him evry day." At that point, Riley, perhaps delighting in the attention and in his power over his wealthier suitors, rejected all offers, stating "when he went it would bee in his own place."[17]

The Taylors retreated and reconsidered their strategy. Malinda tried to dissuade Grant from seeking a substitute, claiming it was a waste of money. She insisted that "almost evry one says tha [they] would not do it . . . That peace will bee made soon." Perhaps chary of instructing her husband about what to do or appearing as if she did not want him to come home, Malinda immediately backtracked and reminded him that "I would freely give all we posess for a substitute to take your place." On the home front, she relied on advice from others, particularly family friend Miles Leatherwood. She returned to Riley with a contract that Leatherwood had drawn up. It offered Riley $800—including $600 in land and crops, $130 in cattle, $30 in hogs, $6 in beehives, and $4 in shoes—to serve as Grant's substitute. On August 6, Grant wrote that he did not like this offer, for he preferred that Malinda offer more land and less livestock. He also worried that Riley was taking advantage of Malinda, and he urged her to make sure to have Leatherwood help her price things and witness the trade. Nonetheless, Grant realized, his absence from the situation undermined his power to instruct his wife, for in the same letter in which he issued these directives, he twice stated, "Make the best trade with him you can." Two days later, he reiterated that she should have Leatherwood help but that she should "make the best bargain with [Riley] that you can."[18]

In a postscript, Grant emphasized that he did not trust Riley. The process of substitution required careful negotiations, so he wanted to make sure not only that she "let no one see this" but also that she would "be careful that [Riley] does not find out that you doubt him." Grant's doubts were justified, as Riley backed out of the deal at the last minute. The Taylors had had enough. Grant urged his wife to "spurn [Riley] from your presence and have nothing more to do with him in any way." Malinda had come to the same conclusion. She informed her husband, "I have not seen him since I was thare nor I don't care if I never do again." Ten days later, Malinda followed up with the infuriating news that "Old Rily is gon to the ware in a big mans place." The "big mans" offer exceeded the Taylors' bid for Riley's services. According to Malinda,

Riley received "a fine horse" and $1,000; $500 of which Riley used to purchase a house for his family.[19]

Early the next year, Abner Ford, a thirty-three-year-old Virginian who had enlisted in May 1862, tried to secure a substitute. Like Taylor and Fay, he employed the help of his wife (Mollie), and he experienced a similar disappointment. Ford, who "want[ed] to get home very badly," suggested that Mollie sell their slaves if necessary, and he grew increasingly annoyed by her failure to respond promptly to his letters and her inability or unwillingness to sell them. Deciding on this course of action led to the question of which of their slaves to part with and to whom the Fords should sell them. Most likely lacking experience in such transactions, Mollie quickly turned to her father as a prospective buyer. Abner disagreed with this decision. While he was willing to "sell them lower to your Papa than any body else," if that provided enough money to get a substitute, his information indicated that she could get higher prices in Richmond (without specifying how he expected his wife to travel more than eighty miles to the capital).

Three days later, he had another plan, which would take the onus completely off Mollie's shoulders. He suggested that she instead borrow the money to buy a substitute. When he returned home, he would sell the slaves himself and then pay off the loan. But, like Grant Taylor, he realized that serving in the army both restricted his ability to make all the family decisions and limited his understanding of his ever-changing home community. After offering these recommendations, he acknowledged, "You all can sell the Negroes & do as you like," and urged that she "do as you all think best."[20]

From February to September of 1863, Abner's letters grew increasingly desperate. He feared that his wife acted too slowly, believing that the price of substitutes was increasing at a faster rate than she could raise the money. In March, he urged Mollie to "sell all our things" to get him a substitute, and he whined, "I haven't a friend in the world that will take interest enofe to get me out of the army." In April, Abner "hope[d] you have sold the negroes buy [*sic*] this time if not sell them as soon as you can." One month later, his melodramatic tone reached a crescendo as he complained that no one had really tried to get him a substitute. "You all don't want me to come home," he griped, and then added that "no one cares any thing for me but my dear children."

Reflecting on this letter, he concluded either that its tone was too offensive or that insults would not motivate Mollie to help him. Three days after penning it, he wrote again, vainly hoping that Mollie had not gotten the vituperative letter, for "I aught not to have riten you such a letter but was very much out of sorts that everything had gone rong." Perhaps as a penance, for the next two months he did not send any letters mentioning substitution. In July, however, he returned to his theme of "I am willing to give most any price," and in August he implored Molly, "Don't stop trying." In September, however, even he finally admitted, "That is all played out. I will have to stay until the war ends."[21]

Grant Taylor, Edwin Fay, Abner Ford had much in common. First, despite their efforts, none of them succeeded in acquiring a substitute. Coincidentally, however, all three men survived the war and lived at least into the 1890s. Second, while they clearly desired to leave the army, none of them deserted. Fay admitted that "I think strong about [desertion] sometimes," but he had "sworn to support the Confederate states." Even while carping about army life, Taylor acknowledged that he "ought not to grumble for I believe that it is for our good." Taylor and Fay did not moan that they were fighting for a losing cause, did not hope to rejoin the Union, and did not advocate disloyalty. While Fay had misgivings about some of the Confederate government's decisions, these paled in comparison to his absolute "hatred" of northerners, which led him to bombastically conclude that he expected "to murder every Yankee I ever meet" after the war. These men simply wanted to go home to their families, and in their fealty calculations, family trumped country. "A man's family," according to Fay, "is dearer to him than anything in the world . . . & 40 Confederacies may go to the Devil if I am going to be kept away."[22]

Third, unexpectedly, none of these men fit the classic definition of southern wealth—a planter owning twenty or more slaves—but that simple statement is deceptive. According to the 1860 census, Edwin Fay, a teacher, possessed no slaves but surprisingly had a personal estate worth $10,000. His letters, however, indicate that he did own slaves, including one who accompanied him into the army. This discrepancy—and his unusual wealth—can most likely be explained by the fact that Fay's father, in Alabama, owned twenty-five slaves and his father-in-law, in Minden, owned four slaves (and a personal estate of $35,000). With $4,400 in personal wealth, Abner Ford fell just outside the planter designation in 1860, owning nineteen slaves. Unlike Fay or Ford, Grant Taylor did not have much money to spend on a substitute. He owned no slaves and had $500 in real estate and $825 in his personal estate. Perhaps the Taylors were relying on their neighbor Miles Leatherwood for more than just advice, as he owned almost $10,000 in property and six slaves.[23]

Finally, their letters also demonstrate the dramatic impact of conscription on southern families and their dynamics. The three men wanted their wives' approval and needed their help. In seeking substitutes for their husbands, Malinda Taylor, Sarah Fay, and Mollie Ford had to step outside their traditional family roles. Potentially, they had to negotiate contracts, sell slaves, and assess the value of land, and it was unlikely that they had experience in these types of transactions. While their husbands tried to provide them with precise instructions or general guidance, the situation on the home front changed too rapidly even for men who, like Fay and Taylor, had recently departed. Decisions had to be made at a pace faster than letters could travel back and forth. Although he never stopped inundating Mollie with advice, Abner Ford confessed his impotence, as he wrote, "Do all you can for me I can't do anything for my self." And, from the very start of his efforts to escape the army, Fay acknowledged to his wife that "I shall in a great measure be governed by you."[24]

Any man considering purchasing a substitute had to take into account not only his wife's opinion, but also the attitudes of the wider community. Potential principals, such as Edwin Fay, feared being branded as unmasculine cowards, a stigma that might permanently smear their family name. In June 1862, North Carolinian Lewis Warlick took umbrage when his girlfriend suggested that he hire a substitute. He claimed that he did not know where to get one, and even if he could find such a man, he would not do it. Warlick could not bear the thought that people would "throw up to my relations" that he, in unmanly fashion, "hired a substitute to be shot at in my stead." He preferred "death before dishonor" for himself and for his descendants. John Williams, serving in a Virginia artillery battalion in May 1862, concurred. Telling his sister that two comrades had found men to serve in their places, he declared, "I think it is the wrong time for substitutes," most likely alluding to the presence of the Union army on the Virginia Peninsula, menacing Richmond. A month later, the nineteen-year-old expressed relief that his father had not secured him one, for "I am ashamed to have one as young as I am."[25]

In contrast to these attitudes, other Confederates did not find substitution a disreputable or disloyal way to leave the army, especially in comparison to other methods. Instead, they considered a wide range of variables, including age, health, family situation, and community need, when assessing whether to acquire a substitute or judging those who had acquired one. In October 1862, A. J. Gilkeson advised his brother Hugh to remain home. A. J. hoped Hugh could gain an occupational exemption, but if not, he suggested that Hugh acquire a substitute. A. J. felt that his brother could not withstand the rigors of service and was needed to take care of his family. In rendering this advice, A. J. declared, "A man must be governed by the circumstances of the case," and if health and family needs demand it "then by all means employ a substitute."

An elderly Virginian feared his son Norborn would "disgrace our family" and "bring my gray hairs down to the grave in sorrow" by hiding from conscription. To avoid this shame, the father described two alternatives: Norborn should turn himself over to the enrolling officer or he should provide a substitute. If he chose the latter route, the father would do his best to help him secure one. For this Virginia father, draft dodging equated to disloyalty but providing a substitute did not. Similarly, a soldier, who desperately "wanted to get out of this place" offered $5,000 and "almost . . . the shirt off my back." However, despite his desperation, he did not contemplate breaking the law. If he was unable to find a substitute, the soldier planned to "stay as long as any body els."[26]

In many instances, southerners considered "the circumstances of the case" when viewing principals. In his diary, Louisiana private William R. King condemned substitution generally, but when his friend J. R. Cavett provided one and left the army, King praised the action. Cavett's family needed him at home, and King admitted, "I am glad of it in this case." In replacing the sickly Cavett with a healthy substitute, King believed his unit benefited as well. While King supported Cavett's departure, he wanted to see ardent secessionists, who talked big but remained home, forced in the army: "Conscription is just what they deserve." Like King, James Marcom, who professed to oppose substitution "in toto," accepted it for specific individuals. When Sergeant Long provided a substitute, Marcom wrote in his diary that he would rather see Long, "a nice man [and] a perfect gentleman," secure one than anyone else.

In other cases, after evaluating circumstances, people concluded that some men should not take advantage of substitution. Edgar Richardson, a Georgia soldier, hoped two men in his company would fail to acquire substitutes. He considered one to be "the ugliest, roughest soldier" he had ever seen. However, ugly and rough did not mean incapable. Additionally, Richardson felt soldiering would be good for a second man. When both procured substitutes, Richardson thought it "should be an everlasting disgrace" for these "big healthy lazy men" to return home when the army needed them.[27]

Like the aforementioned men, other southerners possessed a nuanced view of substitution and conscription, considering age, family status, and community needs. Pulled by both country and home, men considered how much their family and community needed them before looking for a replacement. While frantically trying to escape the army, Edwin Fay maintained, "If I had no family I would not give ten cents for a substitute." Virginian William Larue recognized that a single man faced greater censure for providing a substitute than a married man did. In an incredibly unromantic marriage proposal, he wrote to his girlfriend, "If you will promise to marry me very soon after I get off then I will try to get a substitute." Larue believed that a marriage "will be a good excuse, [and] nothing would be thought of" his efforts to leave the army. While Larue's sweetheart did eventually become his wife, there is no evidence whether she accepted this "good excuse" to get married, or if he found a substitute. Regardless, Larue knew that society did not view all principals in the same light.[28]

Also aware of community opinion, Samuel Burney, a Georgian who had volunteered in 1861, struggled over whether to hire a substitute. On June 22, 1862, he confessed to his wife that he had asked his father to inquire about finding him one. Burney pleaded with her to "keep this to yourself," for he knew "that a man that gets a substitute is not generally thought well of." While insisting this sentiment "makes no difference to him," Burney's letter belies this notion, as he begged her "not to let anyone know of my intention. Nobody!" Three days later, he wrote again, referring to this "matter of secrecy" and "anxious to hear what you both [his wife and his father] think of it." In this letter, he explained that he desired to leave his company both because its officers were fighting and because he wanted to see her. Over the next several weeks, he discussed his plan with some of his fellow soldiers. He maintained that many of them felt he was doing the right thing, but he returned to his contention that their opinions did not mean too much, for "when I make up my mind . . . it is a trifling consideration with me what this man or that man says." He contended that he based his decision on his family's needs, asserting, "If I had no wife & child I would stay in this war until the last shot was fired."[29]

Potential principals also faced the accusation that they were rich men using their wealth to avoid service while poor men fought and died in their places. As part of litany of complaints about the conscription law, North Carolina private Charles Liebermann lambasted the substitution provision as proving "this law is more for the rich than the poor." Liebermann focused on family needs. He contended that the substitution process allocated the Confederacy's manpower resources backwards. It allowed men whose families needed them least to stay home. While the rich could hire a replacement, "the poor man," according Liebermann, who "cannot afford to pay three or four hundred dollars, but whose family is solely dependent on him must go out and expose his body as a mark to the enemies bullets."

Only a year into the war, Liebermann's class-based rhetoric was the exception, as very few men criticized substitution on these grounds, and principals did not worry too much about this charge. In 1862, the "rich man's war, poor man's fight" complaint most likely did not resonate both because substitution was part of traditional military culture and because suffering on the home front was not as dire as it would later become. Plus, Liebermann unintentionally points out another reason that not too many southerners shared his fear. He put the price of substitutes at $300 to $400, an amount that was still within the realm of possibility for many southerners outside of the elite class.[30]

Regardless of their wealth, principals offered another defense: their actions made both the army and the home front stronger. Thus, principals posited themselves as loyal Confederates with their nation doubly benefitting from their actions. First, the home front received a benefit from the valuable service they would provide upon their return. They would feed their family and others or offer some other useful service to their community. Second, the army received a man as capable, or more capable, of bearing arms. In this view, if the army received a healthy twenty-seven-year-old Irishman in exchange for a thirty-five-year-old sick man, how could anyone view substitution negatively? How could it be harmful if a father returned home to take care of a family filled with helpless dependents while a poor, single seventeen-year-old received a $800 bonus to enter the army? Many of these men, such as Edwin Fay, also maintained that they would join the militia or home guard and thereby continue to shoulder weapons for the Confederacy. Given these rationales, they wondered how anyone could question their loyalty to their country.

As if to prove this fealty, substitution, in some cases, actually provided a net gain to the army as men *not* required to serve provided substitutes anyway. For example, men with legal exemptions, such as a forty-three-year-old or a state legislator, could show their loyalty by paying a proxy to serve in the army. In 1861, prior to national conscription, men had hired substitutes to enable their local companies to meet army-mandated quotas or to demonstrate their commitment to the cause. In March 1862, during Virginia's state conscription, the Richmond *Daily Dispatch* encouraged men over forty-five years of age (the upper age limit for the state draft) to enter the army or to hire a substitute, for "many poor men are ready to go if you will assist them."

This sentiment did not end after the passage of the conscription law. In February 1863, a Virginia captain wanted to enroll four substitutes at the same time. He explained that the army should suspend its prohibition against the receipt of more than one substitute per company per month, since the principals in question were not liable to conscription. When pedantic war department bureaucrats declined to modify their rules, General Gabriel James Rains, the head of the Bureau of Conscription, directed them to reconsider the request. Assuming that the officials had misunderstood the captain's appeal, Rains reiterated, "It is not a matter of substitutes for persons *in* the provisional army but *out* of it." Thus, if the transaction was legitimate, the army would have a net gain of four men.[31]

Confederate officials not only had to analyze the legitimacy of substitute transactions but also had to sort out exemption claims. The law's enumerated list of exempt occupations engendered criticism from those who felt that it encouraged fraud. Congress intended conscription to increase the ranks of the army not the ranks of the ministry or teaching professions. In a letter to his governor, a North Carolinian chided men who "got little mail contracts & Schools to keep them out of the war." Since the war was "a common cause . . . I think able bodeyed men ought to make common sacrifices, without resorting to evry little means to evade the law." If men in these occupations could escape service, "I think it time that the common citizen should be excused." He contended that men outside of conscription's age range could serve in these jobs. Another Tar Heel echoed this view. He also knew sham postmasters, men pretending to make saltpeter, and men falsely claiming to run government shops, all of whom should be in the army. Wanting to "correct these abuses," he hoped that "patriotic men in office" would punish "men trying to avoid doing their duty to our common country."[32]

When Grant Taylor sought a substitute, his wife complained that "Washington Leatherwood has got up a little school to keep from going into the army." This exemption especially galled the Taylors, both because they were in the midst of unsuccessful substitute negotiations with "Old Rily" and because Grant had previously taught school but had quit prior to the war. A Virginian wondered why Dr. Bagby and Tom Dudley remained at home. While the soldier acknowledged that "the Dr. in his sphere may be serving the State; Tom is not." He considered Dudley "remiss," since he was "young healthy unembarrassed by his wife, with money enough."[33]

Overall, for many of these critics, exemption policies, when loosely enforced, allowed dishonest men to remain at home while forcing honest men into the Confederate ranks. In other words, if one of President Davis's goals for conscription was to ensure that the burdens of armed service did not fall only on the "ardent and patriotic," many southerners felt that the exemption policy did not achieve this goal. While perhaps sharing the anxiety about abuse, others expressed more concern that Congress, in assembling its initial exemption list, had forgotten key occupations. These critics disagreed, however, on which occupations should be added. Less than a month after the passage of the conscription act, Secretary of War Randolph admitted that the list was "manifestly very incomplete" and that it "will doubtless receive the attention of Congress at its next session."[34] The next session, however, would not commence until August 18, so in the meantime southerners pleaded for exceptions to the exemption policy while making suggestions for occupations to be added to the list when Congress reconvened.

The War Department and President Davis steadfastly maintained that they could not alter the exemption categories. Nevertheless, they did have the ability to detail men. Men who received a detail were mustered into the army but then assigned to unpaid service in a specified occupation on the home front. While, technically, these men served the army, soldiers and civilians generally viewed a detail as equivalent to an exemption.

From the inception of conscription, people complained about the wrong occupations being exempt and about the lack of clarity in the law. North Carolina legislator Jonathan Worth, the brother of the state's salt commissioner, contended that men engaged in salt-making "ought to be relieved from military service in preference to judges, mail-carriers, [and] postmasters." In the same letter, Worth added that people repeatedly asked him whether the law exempted sheriffs and clerks of courts. Later, he received a letter from a hatter, who claimed that his occupation needed an exemption, and offered as evidence the dubious claim that he had heard many soldiers "say[ing] that he had rather go Barefooted than Bare Headed." The secretary of war received a petition from Atlanta avowing that "our manufactory of Gold Foil and dental material is *the only one* of the kind in the whole Confederacy" and therefore its employees needed exemptions. The plea enclosed a letter from a congressman endorsing the factory owners as "true to our cause."[35]

More commonly, petitions with numerous signatures flooded local exemption boards, the war department, and President Davis's office. In Carroll County, Mississippi, more than 250 people petitioned to have two doctors detailed to take care of all the white women, children, and African American slaves in their county. In their case, they highlighted the fact that their county "has done its duty nobly," sending twenty companies into the army, and that one of the doctors was "physically incompetent to do the duties of the field." In Charlotte County, Virginia, during the state draft, sixteen people signed a petition urging Daniel Ramsey's exemption as a blacksmith, fifty-four people signed one to exempt Dr. Spencer as a physician, and sixteen others wanted Dr. McClary exempted in the same category, especially since there were no other doctors exempt within eight to ten miles of their homes. Seventy-five people, including at least twenty-five women, wanted Dr. J. O. Snell released from duty. They stressed that he would "attend upon soldiers families, gratis, in their absence." Some of the women stressed both their Confederate loyalty and need by writing "husband in service" next to their names. Historian Stephanie McCurry convincingly posits these 1862 petitions as the beginning of a new and important political constituency in the Confederacy—soldiers' wives. As conscription produced soldiers, it correspondingly produced soldiers' wives who demanded a quid pro quo: the government must provide services for the home front in exchange for the services their husbands provided on the battlefront.[36]

In 1862, in addition to requesting doctors, women (and men) also repeatedly pleaded for overseers to remain home, a request that reveals much about the Confederacy. The withdrawal of slave supervisors from the southern countryside engendered both fears of starvation—as crops withered in the fields—and of slave-initiated violence. A frightened Louisianan wrote a letter to his congressman alleging that "The negroes . . . are giving *a great deal* of *trouble,*" with runaway slaves planning "to kill the *women* & *children.*" Another Louisianan complained to President Davis that "a deep seated anxiety in regard to *negroes*" was keeping men from joining the Confederate army. In North Carolina, the "Ladies of Halifax County" petitioned the governor to have J. C. Randolph exempted from service because, in their community, there was "no man to protect us." Writing from Mississippi, a state where slaves comprised a majority of the population and where forty slaves were hanged in 1861 in connection with a slave conspiracy near Natchez, General Daniel Ruggles warned the war department "that fears are entertained of some serious disturbance in the sections most densely populated by the servile race." W. B. Overstreet alerted Georgia's governor that slaves were "choosing out the young damsel[s] for wives," for "they will rise as soon as the men are taken away."[37]

While some southerners feared slave rebellion and rape, others worried that, in the absence of overseers, slaves would not work and therefore food production would suffer. A South Carolina Executive Council member complained that without the crops provided by overseers, "not only our people but our armies would perish." Immediately after the passage of the conscription act, Georgia's Governor Brown advised President Davis about both slave control and crop production. Brown cautioned that the failure to exempt overseers left thousands of slaves without any supervision. This omission hampered "the production of provisions and supplies for our armies," and "the peace and safety of helpless women and children must be imperiled for want of protection against bands of idle slaves, who must be left to roam over the country without restraint."[38]

The April 1862 conscription act did not provide an exemption for overseers. In responding to the anxieties of Mississippi's Governor Pettus, President Davis enclosed the response of Secretary of War Randolph. The secretary admitted "applications of a similar character have been very numerous" but stated that his department had no authority to override congressional acts. Davis suggested that a combination of men over conscription's age range, men who had not yet enrolled, and principals who had supplied substitutes and returned to their homes could replace conscripted overseers.[39] This answer reveals another reason for the presence of a substitute clause in the original measure. It provided an indirect method for resolving any flaws in the exemption list. If a man was important at home but his occupation was not on the exempt list, the family or community could hire a replacement soldier and he could remain—or return—home.

The concern about overseer exemptions again emphasizes the fact that conscription's impact extended well beyond drafted men. Though it was intended to bring individuals into the army, conscription—through seemingly straightforward, unambiguous provisions such as substitution and exemption—also had a dramatic impact on families and communities. In November 1862, North Carolinian David Siler sent his governor a remarkable letter that revealed how southerners viewed the policy from a community perspective and how they sought to balance the needs of their families and the state. When Siler penned his letter, the Confederacy had raised the upper age limit for conscription to forty-five, thus forcing Siler into the army. He wrote to the governor that he and several other men on whose behalf he spoke desired to enter a local unit, presumably home guards or Partisan Rangers, rather than enroll in the regular army. They felt "it is our duty to stay here and provide for the helpless," for they would have previously enrolled "had it not been for the earnest appeals of brothers who have fallen in service." In his neighborhood, "consultations were held and it was agreed in family councils who should go & what one should stay." Alluding to the perception that men on the home front shirked their responsibilities, he alleged that being selected to stay at home was not a prize, as these men "in many instances made the greater sacrifice of feeling."

Siler then reminded the governor that his community did not oppose the Confederacy. They shared the nation's goals: "We are opposed to negro equality." Their loyalty, however, had limits. It was only one of several loyalties they possessed, and in this case, it conflicted with family and community loyalty. His neighborhood would "spare the last man down to the point where women & children begin to suffer for food & clothing," but when "these begin to suffer or die," community loyalty would trump Confederate fealty.[40]

Siler's letter depicts the complications of multiple loyalties—family, community, and Confederacy—which could demand contradictory courses of action. Again, like men in the army seeking substitutes to come home, Siler was not opposed the Confederacy. Instead, speaking as a Confederate, he wanted to ensure that politicians remembered the home front in their conscription deliberations. Obligations were reciprocal. As the community had to send soldiers into the army to defend the nation, the Confederacy had to ensure these communities had adequate food and supplies.

The term *community* could mean "neighborhood," but it also could include people sharing the same religion. Within the Confederacy, conscription especially troubled pacifist denominations such as Quakers, Mennonites, and Dunkers. Like other southerners, they faced competing demands from their multiple loyalties, but there was no ambiguity for them. As pacifists, they rejected armed service, and their religious beliefs superseded national loyalty. For instance, one Quaker supposedly declared, "I would prefer to see the South victorious," even as he suffered imprisonment and beatings for refusing accept conscription.[41]

The Confederacy possessed forty-two Quaker, thirty-seven Dunker, and five Mennonite churches with combined seating capacities of 15,980, 18,925, and 2,150, respectively. These relatively small denominations—in contrast, the Confederacy housed 5,666 Baptist churches with a seating capacity of 1,864,283—were concentrated in the Appalachian region, with all eighty-four of the churches located in Virginia (fifty-two), North Carolina (twenty-four), or Tennessee (eight). General Stonewall Jackson acknowledged the problem with drafting members of these denominations, pointing out that while surely they "can be made to fire . . . they can very easily take bad aim." Private Christ Good concurred with Jackson's assertion. When asked by his captain why he had not fired his gun in a battle, this Mennonite succinctly confessed, "We don't shoot people."[42]

When Virginia began its state militia draft in 1861, Mennonites, Quakers, and

Dunkers wished to be considered conscientious objectors. By March 1862, the Virginia legislature had granted this request, allowing them to pay $500 plus 2 percent of the value of their assessed property to stay out of the militia. Unfortunately for them, the Confederate conscription act, passed less than a month later, included no provisions for conscientious objectors. Thus, in the summer of 1862, members of these denominations either had to accept conscription, pay for a substitute, flee to the North on "an underground railroad," hide from the army, or accept imprisonment in Richmond's Castle Thunder. Some congregants chose one of these routes, while others worked on securing conscientious objector status in the Confederacy. The Confederacy proposed a compromise, with the secretary of war having "no objection" to assigning pacifists to duties "not repugnant to their belief." General Jackson endorsed this arrangement, and he persuaded some pacifists to serve the army in noncombatant teamster roles. Others rejected any association with the army. One man hid under his barn for eighteen months to avoid enrolling officers. Reaching conscription age during the war, a Mennonite, who described the 1861 state militia draft as the "period of hiding," kept his age a secret.[43]

The denominations disagreed on the morality of purchasing substitutes. The Quakers rejected this option but the Mennonites and Dunkers had no specific policies against the practice. Mennonite Historian Samuel Horst maintains that hiring proxy soldiers "was quite common among Mennonites as well as Dunkers." Throughout the summer of 1862, families and congregations raised money to help them. Horst recounts Jacob Geil paying $600 for a six-month substitute, George Brunk paying a man $50 per month, and Henry Rhodes's employer providing him a replacement soldier. In Rockingham County, Virginia, one of the few Confederate counties with both extant substitution records and a significant Dunker population, several Dunkers provided substitutes. When substitution ended in early 1864, the enrolling officer assessed the principals' eligibility for service, and in fourteen cases he scribbled "Exempt as Dunker" next to their names.[44]

Some men who worshipped at a different altar—the political altar of states' rights—also found conscription repugnant to their belief system. From its inception, conscription crashed head-on into this doctrine. First, the operation of conscription could infringe on state laws. For instance, South Carolina's state draft exempted both overseers and students in military academies, while Confederate conscription called both groups into the army. In South Carolina as well as in several other southern states, laws required plantations to have a white male present for the purposes of slave control. The state's executive council stressed the importance of providing either an exemption or detail for overseers, who were vital to food production.

In their creative, states' rights reading of the Confederate conscription act, members of the South Carolina Executive Council saw no conflict between state and federal provisions. They determined that Confederate conscription implicitly exempted all men exempted by state law. In reality, not only was the act completely silent on this issue, but also such a reading violated one of the main rationales behind the measure—the creation of uniform laws across the South. In June 1862, when South Carolina turned over its state draft records to the national government, it omitted the names of men exempt by state law, regardless of whether or not they were exempt from Confederate conscription.[45]

More likely, vocal states' righters insisted that the measure itself, regardless of its precise provisions, violated states' rights. Throughout the war, Georgia's Governor Joseph Brown served as the most outspoken proponent of this view. He initially claimed that he would accept conscription despite his misgivings, but that acceptance lasted only a few weeks. Throughout the summer of 1862, Brown and President Davis engaged in a bitter, extremely quotable epistolary debate over conscription's constitutionality. While Brown and Davis might have differed on the legality of the measure, they agreed on the importance of getting the last word in a debate, so what could have been a simple exchange of letters ballooned into a lengthy correspondence. The president and the governor wrote not only to each other but also to the southern public, and Davis had their letters published in pamphlet form during the summer. While Brown expressed his surprise and disappointment at this "hasty" and "informal" publication, he added an additional letter and wanted it published as well.[46]

In this exchange, Governor Brown, who saw himself as a states' rights scholar in the mold of Thomas Jefferson and James Madison, wrote longer letters, and he wrote more often. He maintained that conscription unlawfully gave the national government power "to destroy her State Government." When Davis objected to that characterization, the governor reiterated that the question involved "the very existence of State Government" and that conscription was "at war with all principles for the support of which Georgia entered into this revolution." If Brown posited himself as Jefferson, he portrayed the president in the mold of Alexander Hamilton, the classic symbol of the federal government seizing power from the states. While stating that he was willing to postpone discussion of conscription's constitutionality until a time when "it may less seriously embarrass the Confederacy," Governor Brown then repeatedly maintained that he found the act both unconstitutional and unnecessary, especially as Georgia had provided the Confederate government all the men it requested, without resorting to a draft.[47]

Although Davis insisted that "it was no part of my intention to enter into a protracted discussion," the president, notorious for his need to be recognized as correct, never backed down from a written challenge. In this case, Davis believed that ignoring Brown's assault involved "consequences . . . too momentous to permit me to leave your objections unanswered." The president could not resist the chance to instruct Brown about both the constitutionality and the necessity of the act. First, in every letter of the exchange, Davis reminded the governor that the power to conscript did not come from the power to call out the militia (which is where Brown insisted it lay) but instead stemmed from the power to raise armies, with Congress possessing the prerogative to decide what methods to use. Second, as for its constitutionality, the president pointed out that a large majority of both houses of Congress and every cabinet member, including the attorney general, endorsed the measure.[48]

In May 1862, Attorney General Thomas Watts provided Davis a written explanation of his view of conscription. He prefaced his opinion with a discussion of states' rights, asserting that "a strict construction of the constitution is essential to the preservation of the rights of the States," but Watts found no violation of the Constitution in the conscription act. The Constitution granted Congress the power "to raise and support armies." Since the Constitution did not specify how armies should be raised, it "left to the wise discretion of Congress to adopt *any* mode of raising and supporting armies" as long as their chosen method did not violate any other constitutional terms.[49]

Watts's opinion merely reinforced Davis's own view of conscription. The president found the law to be both necessary and proper. In fact, for Davis, it was more than necessary, "it was absolutely indispensable." He concluded his final missive included in the pamphlet with a reminder that he, too, adhered to the doctrine of states' rights. The right of states to monitor the federal government's usurpation of power "is too familiar and well settled a principle to admit discussion," but Davis could "not share the alarm and concern about State rights . . . which to me seem quite unfounded." For the decade prior to the war, southerners had considered Davis to be one of the South's foremost states' rights spokespersons in Washington, but even then he had consistently considered national defense as an exception to the doctrine. As president, he maintained this stance. In fact, never grasping why conscription so offended states' rights advocates, the president did not do very much to get critics on board with the measure. Nevertheless, Davis would have been gratified to read a letter to the editor in the Atlanta *Southern Confederacy,* which agreed with his interpretation regarding Congress's power to raise an army and concluded, "Davis is the right man in the right place."[50]

Regardless of the president's emphatic stance, some southerners, especially Brown's constituents in Georgia, subscribed to his alarm regarding the threat to state sovereignty. From Pike County, the governor received assurance "that a large majority of the Citizens of this County sustain your course and views," for the conscription act "is certainly subversive of state sovereignty." In his endorsement on the back of the letter, Brown reiterated that "I will do all in my power to maintain the sovereignty of the state." Another Georgia soldier considered Brown's letter to the president to be "a noble document," and he believed it "will be endorsed by nearly every soldier in the field, as well as the friends of States Rights at home." He even drew the extreme and flattering conclusion that "it would be a great deal better if we have Old Joe at the head of our government in the place of Jeff Davis." The Confederacy's most prominent Georgian, Vice President Alexander Stephens, shared Brown's misgivings. Concern over the expansion of federal government power led Stephens to spend most of the war away from Richmond, at his Georgia plantation. Stephens and Brown wanted independence, but not at the cost of the nation's core principles.[51]

Even southern politicians who accepted the constitutionality of conscription often butted heads with the federal government with regard to state defense. On the same day Congress passed the exemption law, it also passed a measure allowing for the creation of units of Partisan Rangers intended for local defense. Congress envisioned that these groups, whose members were exempt from conscription, would serve briefly and on very specific missions, and it stipulated that the president or secretary of war had to approve their creation. Ranger units generally had less discipline than the regular army, served closer to the home front, and rode horses rather than marched. Consequently, the units' popularity greatly exceeded the demand for these irregular troops. Across the Confederacy, enrollment in Partisan Ranger units became a common and ostensibly legal method to avoid conscription into the regular army.

Disliking his officers and tired of his current position, Miller Francis told his father that he wanted to join a regiment of rangers, since he understood that men "from all classes whether the conscript law applies to them or not" would be accepted. With Francis serving in the medical department on the Virginia

Peninsula, the Confederacy probably would rather have had him remain there than return to Alabama. In Georgia, a man who had completed one year of volunteer service in the army now sought double-barreled shotguns and sabers for his already organized Partisan Ranger corps. If the governor provided the weapons, he would "give any security required." He hoped Governor Brown would oblige, for it was his "only chance except conscription."[52]

Heading the conscript bureau in North Carolina, Colonel Peter Mallett found the presence of Partisan Ranger units a constant headache. In July, he warned Adjutant General Samuel Cooper that "we are losing a very large number of able bodied men who have joined 'Partizan Rangers.'" Mallett saw no value in these companies "formed to stay at home to avoid conscription, doing no service whatever." His complaints regarding the rangers included the fact that they illegally enrolled men after his soldiers had conscripted them and that the units offered the men false promises that they would never have to leave their counties. He also expressed frustration over the difficulty in distinguishing authorized from unauthorized units. In Burke County, his men had enrolled 250 conscripts, but only fifteen came to camp. The county's sheriff maintained that the rest were part of a ranger unit, and Mallet could not determine the veracity of this claim. Overall, in the colonel's assessment, Partisan Rangers "have greatly impeded my efforts and reduced the number of conscripts."[53]

Surprisingly, North Carolina governor Henry T. Clark sided with Mallett and the national government over his constituents. He informed the secretary of war that "the eagerness of our conscripts to avoid enrollment by enlistment in those independent corps of partisan rangers sadly conflict with the progress of the enrolling officers." Clark's letter reflects the confusing interrelationship between Partisan Rangers and conscription. In his endorsement of the letter, Secretary of War Randolph reminded the governor that all ranger companies must have official authorization. The assistant secretary of war continually pointed out that men could not transfer from the regular army to the Partisan Rangers because it "would be impossible to keep up the line." General Henry Heth had predicted this result. During Virginia's state draft, he blasted ranger units there as "organized bands of robbers and plunders" and decried the system as "a loophole through which hundreds are escaping draft and in fact all service." On July 31, 1862, the war department tried to clear up any confusion with General Order 53, which declared that "persons who are liable to conscription . . . will not be taken into service as partisan rangers," and to ensure this result, stipulated that rangers must be over thirty-five years of age.[54]

On the other side of the Confederacy and occupying a civilian office, Louisiana's Governor Thomas Overton Moore viewed the rangers differently. He saw them as a valuable solution in managing conscription, to provide local defense and balance state and Confederate needs. As Moore repeatedly explained to both Randolph and Davis, "A literal enforcement of the Conscript Law will take away all our conscripts." The law required conscripts to fill existing state units. In the summer of 1862, in the wake of the fall of New Orleans and the Confederate army's subsequent evacuation of Louisiana, no units served within its borders. Thus, an adherence to the letter of the law would send every conscript away from the state.

Located on the periphery of the Confederacy, far from Richmond, Governor Moore decided it was better to ask for forgiveness than permission. By July, he had authorized nine companies of Partisan Rangers. On July 3, he received a letter from Randolph declaring that the formation of these units "has been greatly overdone in Louisiana." The secretary explained that Partisan Rangers were effective only when used in tandem with an army, for otherwise their lack of discipline undermined their efficacy. Randolph invoked the argument that service in the Confederate army, even if in Virginia, best defended Louisiana homes and communities. According to the secretary of war, "the greatest evil of the [Partisan Ranger] system" was that it undermined conscription, for it left Louisiana's thirty regiments serving elsewhere in the Confederacy below strength and unable to contribute to the "great and decisive operations [in the eastern theater] which alone can terminate the war."[55]

Randolph emphasized a key way to judge conscription's success: Did it add men into the army to fill these skeleton regiments? Determining the exact number of conscripts enrolled in the summer of 1862 is impossible. The records do not exist. Moreover, Confederate leaders did not seek conscripts, they sought soldiers, thereby viewing conscription's goals as keeping the twelve-month volunteers in the army and obtaining new men. Whether these new men volunteered or were conscripted did not matter. Plus, no sharp line divided volunteers and conscripts. How would one consider Jordan Council, for instance? On April 27, 1862, Council wrote his wife, "I have joined the reglers and has gote $50 bounty but I can say to you that it was against my will but I had to go in or do with[out] it." He told her that men who waited would be conscripted, thereby losing both their bounties and their choice of units. In short, Council—like Edwin Fay and Grant Taylor—volunteered, but only because he feared the passage of the conscription act. In assessing the act, a Georgia lieutenant agreed that many men had volunteered under "the pressure of the Conscript Act" filling up "our decimated ranks—although not by men who would be technically known as conscripts." In other words, merely counting conscripts tells an incomplete story of the impact of conscription.[56]

Instead, it is best just to look at the total size of the Confederate army. When assessed in this fashion, the initial conscription act could be viewed a success, as the Confederate army grew substantially during 1862. In February, the army possessed 333,250 men, with 240,475 having their enlistments scheduled to expire during the summer. By the end of the year, it included at least 449,439 men. Given that it suffered 75,000 casualties, the gain attributed to conscription would include almost 200,000 new men plus the retention of a substantial number of twelve-month volunteers. The reinvigorated army achieved results, especially in relieving the threat against Richmond, as it pushed McClellan's army off the Virginia Peninsula in June 1862. In the western theater, Confederate armies did not fare as well, but they did prevent the Union from severing the Confederacy at the Mississippi River. Thus, in the succinct judgment of the *Charleston Mercury,* conscription "saved the country." Zebulon Vance, North Carolina's new governor, agreed. In his September inaugural address, while criticizing the law as "harsh" and possibly unconstitutional, he admitted that it "was passed and the country was saved."[57]

National government officials concurred with the assessments of Vance and the *Mercury.* Calling conscription "a wise measure," former attorney general Thomas Bragg posited, "We should have no army but for the bill." On August 12, 1862, Secretary of War Randolph, in preparation for the reconvening of Congress, presented President Davis with a report on conscription that, for the most part, confirmed the *Mercury*'s encomium. Reminding the president that back in April "it was obvious that conscription alone could save us," Randolph celebrated its achievements as "the present condition of the Army and of the country sufficiently proves its wisdom." Due to conscription, the army had gone from "retiring, weak, and disorganized" to "advancing, with increased numbers, improving organization, and renewed courage." Consequently, Randolph claimed, conscription should be "cherished and perfected," explicitly citing the substitution and exemption policies as areas that needed to be "perfected." In other words, the secretary believed that the Confederacy had managed conscription very well in the summer but there remained room for improvement. Convening six days later, on August 18, the new Congress would have a chance to do just that.[58]

CHAPTER 3

# Revising Conscription, August–December 1862

As the summer came to a close, Peter Mallett, the Confederate officer in charge of conscription in North Carolina, reflected on the measure. He declared that the "first great rush is over," and he hoped that now "the business can be done with more system and dispatch and with much less expense to the Government." When the Confederate Congress reconvened in Richmond on August 18, 1862, tweaking the conscription system topped its agenda. In his opening message to Congress, President Davis called for some modifications. He acknowledged that conscription had received "unexpected criticism," particularly with regard to state versus national power. These complaints had reduced the measure's efficiency, but he optimistically asserted that in all states the "popular mind" favored conscription. Davis still felt that it did not threaten states' rights, but he deferred to the legislators, "thoroughly imbued with the feelings and sentiments of the people," to make the best decisions to preserve harmony between the state and Confederate governments. The president urged Congress to heed the requests made in the secretary of war's report, which proposed ending abuses in the substitution system and increasing the number of exempt occupations. Davis provided only one additional recommendation. In response to Lincoln's recent call for more Union troops, Davis endorsed the expansion of the upper age limit from thirty-five to forty-five.[1]

Davis could speak optimistically because the Confederacy's fortunes—at least in the eastern theater—had improved dramatically since his initial call for conscription. In April, congressmen had debated while Union troops assembled at Fortress Monroe, less than eighty miles away from the capital. Since then, the war in Virginia had gone the Confederacy's way. In May, Stonewall Jackson had dazzled the Confederacy with his Shenandoah Valley campaign . In the following month, the newly appointed commander of the Army of Northern Virginia, General Robert E. Lee, had led his men to victory in the Seven Days Battles, which pushed the Army of the Potomac off the Virginia Peninsula, thereby removing the immediate threat to Richmond. Within the first two weeks of the congressional session, Lee and Jackson would combine to defeat Union General John Pope at the Second Battle of Bull Run. The Army of Northern Virginia would then march north into Maryland with grandiose goals. They hoped to garner recruits, to gain European recognition for the Confederacy, and to influence the North's upcoming congressional elections.[2]

In April, given the desperate military situation, legislators had hurriedly passed conscription out of necessity and without any time to consult with their districts. Since then, these politicians had traveled home, met with their constituents, received letters detailing the measure's effect on families and communities, and read newspaper articles discussing the measure. When the legislators returned to Richmond, they were ready to debate. And debate they did. During the next two months, they spent more time on deliberating conscription than on any other topic. One senator claimed that the discussion over the list of exempt occupations comprised "the most extended debate that had yet taken place in the Senate."

In their speeches, the lawmakers repeatedly referenced their consultations with voters. Mississippi representative Ethelbert Barksdale claimed to have heard no voices opposed to measure in his state. Fellow Mississippian Otho Singleton concurred, describing a "universal sentiment" in favor of the bill, which was met by "acclamation[s] of joy." According to Alabama's Edmund Dargan, the proconscription spirit in his state fell just short of the unanimity of its neighbor as he had heard of "only one man . . . who had any doubt about the law."[3]

No one took these hyperbolic evaluations literally. The speeches in Congress nevertheless exhibited an awareness that ordinary southerners were paying attention to the debates in Richmond. They were. Newspapers published frequent—almost daily—articles on the measure. A Georgia soldier reminded his wife to "tell Pa to keep up with Congress in regard to the law regarding substitutes." More pointedly, an angry Texas soldier complained that his congressman, William Wright, had lied about his interactions with his constituents. During the congressional debate, Wright admitted that he had not been in Texas since his October 1861 election, but he claimed to have met with tens of thousands of Texans while spending the summer at Tupelo, Mississippi. While Wright favored conscription, the soldier, stationed in Tupelo, opposed the measure and questioned whether Wright had "ever been at Tupola [*sic*] a single *hour,* to say nothing of three months."[4]

The extensive congressional deliberations frustrated observers who wanted action. The annoyed editor of the *Richmond Daily Dispatch* described the situation. He explained that some legislators wanted to abandon conscription and replace it with a call on the states for quotas of men; others questioned the measure's constitutionality; "a third has a scheme which he is assured is much better than any yet devised; and a fourth has another scheme still better than this." In August, the editor fretted that the legislators were "wasting precious time, in making speeches" while the enemy put more troops in the field, and a month later, he railed against "the orators who have imperiled a nation's independence for the sake of airing their vapid eloquence." The *Charleston Mercury* echoed these sentiments, declaring that Congress squandered "precious time. . . . in idle talk" rather than preparing for the onslaught of "Northern barbarians."[5]

Undoubtedly, legislators agreed that their time was valuable, but they felt equally passionate about the importance of deliberating conscription. In the fall of 1862, debates over conscription continued to touch upon key aspects of Confederate ideology. Southerners still challenged the act's perceived assault on states' rights. State judges joined legislators and governors in offering opinions on the constitutionality of the measure. Also, southerners continued to worry about balancing the competing needs of the army and the home front. Congress expanded the number of exemptions, but Confederates could not achieve a consensus on how best to use the exemption policy to achieve equity among national, state, local, and family requirements.

In one of its most significant alterations of the policy, Confederates considered the need to control the nation's slave population. In contemplating whether plantations merited exemptions, the discussion touched on the relationship between wealthy slaveholders and nonslaveholders. An overseer exemption, coupled with substitution, raised the prospect of class animosity, but in 1862, the opposition to these measures consisted more of angry talk than action. That fall, the majority of southerners, even if disputing specific aspects of the conscription, still accepted the policy as necessary to win the war.

As historian George Rable points out, congressional debate "increasingly centered on the operation rather than the legitimacy of the draft." Yet Congress did contain a vocal anticonscription minority. While proponents celebrated it as ensuring Confederate survival, these legislators offered a counterargument. Texas Senator Williamson S. Oldham, who had opposed the April bill, scoffed at those who considered it "the salvation of our country." He maintained that the retention of the twelve-month volunteers, and not the drafting of new soldiers, had led to summer victories. Keeping these soldiers in the army had not required conscription. For Oldham, the military triumphs did not change the fact that conscription "reduce[s] our soldiers and armies down to . . . mere machines, not citizens." He warned that "no act . . . could possibly have a more deleterious effect" than conscription, which destroyed the liberties of the citizens and turned them into slaves. In his view, the Confederate army would improve if it was composed only of "intelligent thinking men, freemen, who have a country to love." Oldham also contended that conscription destroyed the fragile equilibrium between home and battlefront. He cautioned his fellow lawmakers that "the population at home must be provided for, the industrial pursuits of the country must be carried on, supplies for the army in the field must be raised and furnished."[6]

Trying to balance community and army needs meant debating modifications to the list of exemptions. Everyone could agree that the original exemption list, hastily put together in the final days of the April session, was incomplete. They disagreed, however, on what occupations should be added. In their analysis of this debate, historians Thomas Alexander and Richard Beringer contend that "almost every congressman seemed to have a pet type of exemption providing an excellent logrolling opportunity." Millers, tanners, and physicians were among the most frequently proposed additions to the exemption list. The debate also crossed over into the more controversial topics of class and states' rights. Did planters need an exemption for their overseers? All agreed that state officers should be exempt, but they disagreed on what positions counted as state office. Did this provision apply to sheriffs, justices of the peace, tax collectors, and militia officers? States' rights ideologues feared that without a broad exemption for all state officers, the Confederacy jeopardized its very foundations. Taking this theory to its extreme, Oldham, who believed that each state should decide its own exemption policy, boycotted these deliberations entirely, retreating to a sofa outside the Senate chamber.[7]

In the house, Henry Foote, a hot-headed congressman from Tennessee, also railed against the measure. Foote's conduct in Congress, according to a recent biography, "seemed almost completely driven by his hatred for Jefferson Davis." The two men had a long-standing, mutual enmity stemming from the 1840s, when they bitterly opposed each other in Mississippi politics. This conflict involved partisan politics, specifically Foote's defeat of Davis in a gubernatorial race, as well as a fistfight and a narrowly averted duel. In opposing nearly every administrative measure, Foote wrapped himself in the cloak of states' rights, which, in his view, must be maintained "at all hazards." He also chided those who portrayed conscription as overwhelmingly popular in April, incorrectly asserting that only a small majority had supported it then and they had done so "painfully." Throughout the session, he harped on states' rights and the idea that the precedent set by conscription's violation of the Constitution would endanger the nation's future. In particular, he cautioned his colleagues that the measure could lead to the establishment of a "military despotism" under President Davis.[8]

A few other lawmakers joined Foote and Oldham in fearing that conscription destroyed states' rights. Several legislators expressed anxiety that the government intended to conscript state officers, which, according to Senator Thomas J. Semmes of Louisiana, would "result in the destruction of the Confederate government." In their view, any line of reasoning that allowed the Confederacy to conscript one state officer would logically allow it to conscript all of them, including state legislators, state supreme court justices, and even governors. Texas representative Caleb Herbert expressed a different states' rights apprehension. He denounced conscription for leaving his state without an adequate defense against Native American attacks, concluding his speech with the classic states' rights response: secession. If conscription tried to take too many Texans, Herbert warned his colleagues, his state would be compelled "to raise 'the Lone Star' standard again."[9]

Alabama Senator William Yancey best epitomizes the conundrum that Confederates faced in balancing states' rights and national needs and loyalties. In April, he had reluctantly voted for conscription out of necessity, but with southern armies on the advance, Yancey now argued that the necessity no longer existed. So he proposed instead to call on each state for a quota of men in lieu of expanding national conscription. At the same time, Yancey nevertheless admitted that conscription was constitutional, and he warned his fellow senators against states' rights extremism. Alluding to governors whose actions weakened the military, such as Georgia's Joseph Brown, he argued that if too much emphasis was put on states' rights at the expense of the army, "the strongest [point], may yet become the weakest point in our organic system." At times, Yancey sounded as if he were debating himself. While he accepted the constitutionality of conscription, he vehemently opposed the conscription of state officers. In doing so, he made the bold states' rights claim that "the Confederacy is a not a Sovereign State" and warned that the Richmond government was following "the very footsteps of Lincoln despotism." If the Confederacy were to end up with a dictator, Yancey preferred one imposed as the result of losing a war rather than a self-imposed one. Nevertheless, hedging his bets once again, he admitted that he did not believe that President Davis had dictatorial ambitions.[10]

Not sharing the misgivings of Foote, Yancey, and Oldham, the majority proconscription legislators alleged that these critics wasted time crying wolf. They singled out the acerbic Foote as especially exasperating. Former attorney general Thomas Bragg lamented that the "political Charlatan Foote day in and day out is talking." Bragg feared that this "cry of 'State rights'" would "destroy the Gov't of the Con. States. . . . If the doctrines of some prevail the Gov't will be emasculated completely & will not be worth preserving." He worried that the northern army grew stronger while states' rights legislators in the Confederacy blathered ad nauseam about political theory. Some congressmen shared Bragg's frustration with Foote. On August 19, Franklin Sexton of Texas recorded in his diary that Foote "tire[d] everybody," and three days later he again derided Foote for "consum[ing] nearly the whole day in useless discussion of the Conscript Act." Otho Singleton of Mississippi protested that there was "nothing new" in one of Foote's speeches. It was merely an unproductive "rehash of his former speech on the law."[11]

Conscription proponents such as Bragg, Sexton, and Singleton preferred to focus on the clear and present military danger rather than on hypothetical constitutional dangers. A "well endorsed remark" making the rounds of Confederate newspapers articulated their view. It contended that "the question of State rights can be easily adjusted, after we shall have *established the right to have States."* They reminded their listeners that independence required a strong army, and a strong army required a strong central government. In supporting an expanded conscription, Mississippi representative Ethelbert Barksdale took the most radical view, expressing his willingness "to throw aside the constitution" if necessary to win the war. William Porcher Miles of South Carolina reminded listeners that while he "yielded to no one on the sovereignty of States rights," in the wake of invasion it was "the duty of the States to yield to any measure which was designed to serve the country." Tennessee's Meredith Gentry considered states' rights objections to be based on confused priorities. They were akin to a shortsighted man doing nothing as his house burned down because he feared that using water to fight the fire would damage the paintings inside. In short, these members of Confederate Congress would temporarily sacrifice the limb of states' rights to save the life of the Confederacy. For them, national preservation superseded any abstract discourses on political theory.[12]

A twist on the states' rights debate stemmed from original act's provision that men could only be conscripted in their state of residence. This created a scenario whereby men could avoid enrollment simply by crossing state lines. Stationed in Alabama, General John Forney complained to Florida governor John Milton that

Floridians "are evading [conscription] by loitering about near the [state] line." State borders served as a bizarre revolving door of evasion, for as Floridians could escape to Alabama, Alabamans simultaneously fled to Florida. Governor Milton, in turn, protested to the secretary of war that hundreds of "fugitives from other States to avoid the Conscript Acts" dwelt in West Florida.[13]

Lawmakers personally witnessed evidence of this type of circumvention every day. In the streets and hotels of Richmond, they routinely encountered men from across the Confederacy who were ineligible for conscription solely because they were not citizens of Virginia. Texas Senator Louis Wigfall had no sympathy for men "dodging about from one place to another to avoid military duty," and he wanted to conscript "every vagabond" from elsewhere loitering in the capital. In his August report, Secretary of War Randolph condemned this abuse. He defined military service as "a debt due to the Confederacy," which "should not depend on the accident of place." Randolph had addressed the crux of the issue. Did men owe service as citizens of the Confederate nation or as citizens of one of the states composing the Confederacy?[14]

While Randolph believed it was the former, others viewed military service as a debt due only to their state. Consequently, they considered the provision requiring conscription within their home states to be a vital protection of states' rights, especially since it ensured that these men would serve in state units, as provided for in the original conscription act. Senator James Orr of South Carolina worried that repealing this provision would allow the army to harass loyal citizens as they traveled across the Confederacy on legitimate business. In a caustic response to Wigfall, Missouri Senator John Clark asserted that residents of his state could more easily avoid conscription by remaining at home than by traveling to Richmond. If the Confederacy wanted Missourians, he added, it should send an army to Missouri. That army could conscript men there while in turn defending these soldiers' currently undefended homes.[15]

Secretary of War Randolph also called on Congress to change another aspect of the conscription system. Believing that substitution should only be allowed where it benefited the community, he decried substitution "founded merely on considerations of private interest." In debating whether to alter this provision, legislators addressed class, home front conditions, and Confederate loyalty. Louisiana Senator Thomas Semmes, who wanted substitution abolished completely, emphasized that "every man, high or low, rich or poor, should be forced to go into the army for the defence of the country." Legislators focused on the poor quality of substitutes, recounting anecdotal evidence that one man had sold himself twenty times and that substitutes made up 90 percent of deserters. South Carolina senator Robert Barnwell succinctly summed up the antisubstitute view, considering them "in all respects inferior" to regular troops. Several congressmen proposed to resolve part of the mercenary aspect of substitution by making principals responsible for the loyalty of their substitute. If the substitute deserted, the principal would face conscription.[16]

Other legislators focused on Randolph's concern about the services that the principal provided at home. Ideally, substitution provided a net gain to both the army and the principal's community—the army enrolled a soldier and the community kept a vital producer at home. The Senate Military Committee's report advocated making this ideal into law. It urged limiting substitution to situations where the principal "is skilled, and actually employed in some mechanical art or public utility, or is the only white male adult on a farm or plantation having thereon not less than fifty slaves." Barnwell emphasized this point, urging the limitation to situations where "the Secretary of War should say a man would be more serviceable working at his trade than in the ranks." In stressing the utility of principals on the home front, Barnwell touched on another sensitive subject: the subjugation of slaves. He numbered large slaveholders among those who should be allowed to provide substitutes. Although "he did not wish to favour" planters, he recognized that slaves needed supervision.[17]

Congressmen debating alterations in conscription policy did not work in a vacuum. Military actions influenced political decisions. In this case, events in Maryland provided a further impetus both for an expanded conscription and for an exemption for overseers. On September 17, Robert E. Lee's Army of Northern Virginia fought the Union Army of the Potomac at Antietam Creek. While outnumbered, Lee's men held their lines on the bloodiest day of the Civil War. Nevertheless, in the absence of a secure supply line, the Confederates had to withdraw from the field and return south into Virginia. In the wake of this battle, General Lee requested more troops. He pleaded to President Davis that recruiting was "of paramount importance" and that conscripts "would add greatly to our strength." In a letter to the commander of the defense of Richmond, Lee called for "a better system" of bringing men into the army, contending "there never was a more urgent necessity." While his letters focused primarily on concerns about the current act ("I hear of no conscripts coming from the South") and on returning stragglers to the ranks, a request for more troops by the Confederacy's foremost general benefited legislators who supported an expanded conscription.[18]

A simple way to enlarge the army would be to broaden conscription's age range. The April act called out men from eighteen to thirty-five, but many people felt that the upper limit should be increased to forty-five. President Davis endorsed this alteration in his opening address to Congress. Two months later, the secretary of war estimated that that such an expansion would add approximately 145,000 men to the army. He contended that the addition of just men up to forty years old would allow the South to put almost 500,000 troops in the field, which in his view was almost the maximum number of men that could be supplied. Less concerned with logistics, a Virginia soldier simply claimed that they would "whip old Abe's men" if conscription embraced a broader age range. Predicting more battles in the fall, a Georgian agreed that the age limit needed to be expanded, for "we are going to need [more soldiers]." Lamenting that the Confederate army had not been able to follow up on their summer victories, the *Charleston Mercury* concurred that raising the upper age limit would bring in mature men who "are more endurable—more reliable—and more unconquerable." Two months later, it urged that "no time should be lost" in making this alteration. Despite considering the conscript law unrepublican, a Louisiana soldier approved an expanded age range as equalizing burdens by forcing into the army older men who had stayed home and "speculate[d] on the necessities of soldiers, & their wives & children."[19]

In letters to their governor, two North Carolina civilians disagreed about the utility of increasing the age range. Revealingly, both Confederates emphasized the proposal's impact on the home front rather than its impact on the size of the army. A supporter of the alteration suggested to Governor Vance that "all should bear their part," contending "there is enough over forty five to do all the business that is wanting." He knew that an extension would cause pain on the home front, but he explained that "we must expect to suffer much before we get our Independence." The other Tar Heel disagreed. Believing that there would not be enough men to do all the business at home, he feared that the age expansion would encourage slave revolt and armed opposition from anti-Confederate whites. He warned Governor Vance that this provision "would complete the ruin of [Bertie] County." More ominous for the Confederacy, Georgia's Governor Brown shared this opinion. He had begrudgingly submitted to the April act because he felt that men over thirty-five could defend Georgia. Now he harangued President Davis that this expanded age range would effectively *"disband and destroy* all military organization in this State." He refused to accept such a threat to Georgia's defenses and its sovereignty.[20]

Ironically, while news from Antietam might have inspired lawmakers to put more men in the army, it also supported keeping one group of men at home. Following the battle, the need for an overseer exemption received a stimulus. President Lincoln had been waiting for a Union victory to strike a blow against slavery, and Lee's return to Virginia after Antietam provided the semblance of one. On September 22, Lincoln issued the preliminary Emancipation Proclamation, calling for the end of slavery in any state that remained in rebellion on January 1, 1863. Southerners attacked the proclamation as designed to provoke insurrection, servile war, murder, and rape. Confederate congressmen denounced its terrifying consequences: "massacre of families," "indiscriminate slaughter, of all ages," and "unspeakable horrors." Historian Chandra Manning contends that the measure united the South, for "no internal tensions . . . could outweigh the danger of imminent abolition or the terrifying prospect of armed slaves." A Confederate diarist denounced "Mr. Lincoln's Emancipation act," declaring that in its wake "it will not do to remove all the owners from the plantations."[21]

With these anxieties in mind, Confederate congressmen addressed overseer exemption in October 1862. Allowing planters to supply a substitute indirectly allowed them to keep an overseer at home, but if slave control required overseers, then it made more sense to provide a specific exemption for them. These discussions reveal worries that the measure would be perceived as unfair class legislation. During the legislative debate, Senator Wigfall lectured his colleagues that a plantation owner would gain an exemption "not because he might be a rich man, but because it was deemed imprudent for the public service to leave the slaves without someone to keep them in subjection." Similarly, Senator Yancey proclaimed that while he "eschewed class legislation," he supported overseer exemptions as an absolute necessity. Another senator felt that it was "important to the prosperity of the country" for slave owners to remain on their plantations and keep their "slaves in subjection." Retaining some white men on the home front helped both to protect and to feed Confederate families, and considerations such as these led to the passage of a provision exempting one man on each plantation without the presence of an exempt man on its premises. The exemption applied to plantations with at least twenty slaves (or two farms within five miles of each other with a combination of twenty or more slaves), and consequently, southerners commonly referred to it as the "Twenty Negro Law."[22]

The overseer exemption was only one part of an overhauled exemption policy. Congress listened to all the petitions and the reminders that the Confederacy could not have an "army of consumers with not even a corporal's guard of producers." The list of exemptions approved in October was more than six times longer than the original April list. Referring to this expansion a few months later, a diarist derisively claimed that the Bureau of Conscription "ought to be called the Bureau of Exemption." The most significant alterations included the aforementioned overseer exemption plus provisions allowing doctors, editors, and religious objectors. The list also gave preference to men in war-related industries such as iron manufactories, railroads, telegraphy, and textile mills. It acknowledged other key home front needs by including river pilots, shoemakers, tanners, blacksmiths, millers, and apothecaries.[23]

In an effort to reduce fraud and ensure that men permitted to remain home benefited their communities, Congress attached conditions to many of the exemptions. Tradesmen's exemptions came with the condition that they had to be producing for, rather than speculating on the needs of, civilians. They had to be "actually employed at their regular vocation" and to swear an oath that they would sell their product at a fixed price (generally 75 percent above the cost of materials) or face conscription. Doctors had to have five years'experience, while teachers had to have two years leading a class. Ministers needed to be "in the regular discharge of ministerial duties" and conscientious objectors had to either provide a substitute or pay a $500 fee. State officers had to be exempt from militia duty. Manufacturing establishments that padded their employee roles just to shield prospective conscripts could lose the exemption for all their employees.[24]

Increasing the number of exemptions did not mean that Congress retreated from a commitment to conscription. When the debate was over and the votes were counted, champions of a centralized conscription continued their triumph over states' rights proponents. Only two senators, including the beleaguered Oldham, voted against the measure. Reacting to the revisions, a soldier's wife exaggerated, "All has to go that has got two legs and two arms so says the law." Conscription remained the prerogative of the national government, and in a separate bill, Congress expanded the age range to embrace those up to forty-five years old. For the moment, however, Davis only called for men up to forty. Crossing state lines no longer protected potential conscripts. Floridians could be conscripted in Alabama and Missourians in Richmond. Substitution remained unaltered. Nevertheless, advocates of an expanded army did not win every battle. In addition to the increased exemption policy, states could designate which of their officials to exempt. Even with the stipulation that these men needed to be exempt from militia duty, this amendment tipped the scales of federalism slightly back toward the states, thereby appeasing some states' rights critics.[25]

The new act also acknowledged that the difficulties engendered by conscription did not fall evenly across the South. In the only specific mention of a state, Congress permitted Texas to retain one regiment to defend the frontier against Native Americans. And, to allow for some flexibility in responding to other crises, the act authorized the president to halt the enforcement of the measure where he considered suspension necessary. In some states, the issue was not stopping enforcement but starting it. By June, camps of instruction had only been established in Virginia, North Carolina, South Carolina, and Louisiana. In January 1863, a report from the secretary of war cryptically declared that in every state at least one camp of instruction "has been, or is being established," without announcing how many camps were still "being established" more than eight months after the passage of the original act. Regarding suspension, Davis received requests from East Tennessee to halt conscription due to a combination of the Unionist proclivities of the population and to a fear of starvation. Louisiana's senators received an appeal to suspend conscription, for it was "a waste of time," as potential conscripts could hide in the state's bayous. In this latter case, the secretary of war relented and suspended conscription in part of Louisiana in October.[26]

Perhaps alluding to this suspension, the *Opelousas* (La.) *Courier* cheered the new act, for its "liberal provisions and wise discriminations" would "secure its popularity with all classes of citizens." Support, however, was far from unanimous. The age range expansion put an even greater strain on the home front. Rural communities already suffering from a labor shortage could ill afford to lose even more men. Louisiana's governor received a petition from his home parish, where conscription had not been suspended, explaining that the April act had left only five "efficient men" to serve ninety-six "indigent and destitute familys." The new measure cut even deeper—reducing the number of caretakers from five to two—and "deprives the families of their only hope." Therefore, the applicants requested that the governor exempt five more men from conscription. Western North Carolina faced an identical predicament—a home front devoid of providers. A resident suggested to Governor Vance that "for every able bodied man taken from this county, there ought to be an able bodied man retained . . . Deprive us of that labor & the innocent & helpless must perish."[27]

The expanded exemption list retained many men on the home front, and these exemptions in turn engendered charges of favoritism. Much of this venom focused on the Twenty Negro Law. The overseer exemption remains one of the most misunderstood aspects of Confederate conscription. It is referenced in every study arguing that internal divisions doomed the Confederacy, with Armstead Robinson taking the most extreme view. He boldly declares that with its passage, "The War for Southern independence was, in consequence, effectively lost." At face value, the exemption appears to be irrefutable proof that tin-eared planter-politicians callously exploited their nonslaveholding neighbors. The law did engender complaints. However, these complaints tell only part of the story. They do not reflect the fact that the overseer exemption itself tried to balance the army's need for soldiers with the home front's need for slave control. Instead of being simply an example of class favoritism, the overseer exemption is actually an example of the almost impossible challenge in trying to create an equitable conscription policy satisfactory to all Confederates.[28]

Some southerners vociferously objected to the exemption. A soldier's father complained to Vice President Stephens that "It does look hard to exempt a man because he has 20 Negroes they say it is a rich man's war and a poor man's fight." An angry Mississippian reported to his governor that the Twenty Negro Law was "the handle at which most of the malcontents grind." Disgruntled soldiers from North Carolina and Georgia voiced almost the exact same concern about the fairness of the law. They wondered why the poor should fight when the "rich man because he owns twenty negroes is permitted to stay at home" and when "the rich are allowed to remain at home at enjoy ease and pleasure." A Louisianan justified his desertion by declaring that the Confederacy had "always made laws to oppress the poor," and he listed the Twenty Negro Law as his first example. While acknowledging that the "unfortunate clause" was designed to "guard against servile insurrection," novelist Augusta Evans worried that starving soldiers complained that they suffered while slaveholders "remain[ed] in quiet enjoyment of luxurious ease."[29]

North Carolina legislators condemned the law for making an "unjust discrimination between [planters] and their less fortunate fellow citizens, contrary to the spirit of our institutions." They called on their representatives and senators to work for the law's speedy repeal. The law also sparked a reaction in soldiers' wives. Historian Stephanie McCurry depicts soldiers' wives increasing their political voices in denouncing the law and appealing to have their relatives discharged. One asked President Davis, "If widows ladies overseers are released . . . why not release a poor man to his suffering family." Another informed the governor of South Carolina that plain folk did not like the law. She suggested an improvement: amend it to have planters pay $1,000 to poor soldiers' wives in order to secure their overseer's exemption. Mississippi Senator James Phelan admonished Jefferson Davis, "Never did a law meet with more universal odium than the exemption of slave owners." Writing two months after the measure's passage, Phelan, who had voted against the exemption and planned to propose a new law rescinding it, contended that even planters recognized its "gross injustice" and that "its influence on the poor is most calamitous."[30]

Too frequently, historians have adopted Phelan's view uncritically, but the senator's stance did not coincide with the reality of the military situation in December 1862. His condemnation lost some of its luster when he added that the Confederate army stood on the verge of disintegration, with most soldiers only looking for someone to lead the mutiny. It was not. The actions of Sam Watkins, whose memoir is also among the most cited criticisms of the measure, are telling. Watkins proclaimed that with the passage of the Twenty Negro Law, "the boys were . . . whipped" and "the war might as well have ended." Yet, despite his harsh censure, Watkins and most of these "boys" loyally served two and a half more years, until the end of the conflict. Similarly, an officer in Lee's army excoriated the law as "conferring a special privilege upon a favoured class," and he noted that it was "severely commented upon in the army."[31]

Severe comments, however, are a far cry from mutiny, desertion, and defeatism. Historian Colin Woodward makes a similar point in his study of race and Confederate soldiers. He quotes a Louisiana artillerist, who alleged that the overseer exemption was "about to caus a rebellion in camps." As Woodward succinctly notes, "No such rebellion occurred." In other words, the rhetoric against the overseer exemption demonstrated frustration with a government policy but not an abandonment or rejection of the Confederate cause.[32]

Politicians had attempted to preempt this potential dissatisfaction and mitigate class bias in their measure. The law stipulated that it only applied to plantations that did not have a nondraftable white man already on its premises. In other words, a forty-six-year-old planter or a state legislator who lived on a plantation could not gain an exemption for their son or anyone else as an overseer. Both owners were "nondraftable," and therefore the law assumed that they could direct the plantation's operations themselves. Elected by the Georgia legislature to the Confederate Senate in December 1862, Herschel V. Johnson experienced this restriction. Despite the senator's ownership of 115 slaves, Assistant Secretary of War John Campbell denied Johnson's request to have his overseer exempted. Probably enjoying the chance to use strict construction against Georgia's strict constructionists, Campbell explained that at the time of the law's passage, Johnson—prior to his Senate election—lived on his plantation. The fifty-year-old Johnson qualified as a nondraftable man. Therefore, his plantation did not merit an overseer exemption. According to the War Department, Johnson's subsequent election and move to Richmond could not provide an ex post facto exemption for his overseer.[33]

Also, the enforcement of the law had even more restrictions. It allowed only one exemption per plantation, not, despite some historians' claims to the contrary, an exemption for every twenty slaves owned. In other words, a plantation with one hundred slaves merited only one exemption, not five. Colonel Mallett, directing conscription in North Carolina, created additional obstacles. While the October 1862 iteration of the law was silent with regard to the experience required for an exemption, Mallett contended that the law applied only "to those who were employed [as overseers] at the passage of the law." In rejecting a different application, he again defined its object very narrowly, maintaining that it was only for "those who are actually engaged in overseeing." In his interpretation, owners could not simply designate one of their sons or themselves as an overseer. In May 1863, the Confederate Congress would make Mallett's policy into law. An amendment would specify that only men who had prior experience as overseers qualified for an exemption.[34]

Also, the law was an exemption, not a discharge from active service, so planters, their children, or overseers already in the army could not return home based on this act. Mallett rejected an appeal, reminding the applicant that overseer exemption, like all other exemptions, "does not apply to persons in the service." He informed a different soldier that the measure was "*prospective* in its operation and not applicable to persons enrolled under the first act." Appealing to his governor for a discharge, a North Carolina planter, who had an overseer but wished to go home to take that man's place, also learned of this restriction. The endorsement on the letter indicated that Governor Vance considered the overseer law "unjust & unfair." Therefore, the governor offered no sympathy in informing the planter that "the law does not operate to discharge a man already in the service." In his January 1863 report, the secretary of war rejected the view that any exemptions—including the Twenty Negro Law—could be used to discharge men from the army. He contended that "no foundation can be found in the law" for such an interpretation.[35]

A letter from North Carolina legislator Jonathan Worth to his son David G. Worth demonstrates an awareness of community sensitivity regarding the overseer exemption. In the fall of 1862, David's substitute was about to turn eighteen years old. This birthday would make the boy eligible for conscription and thus end David's exemption as a principal. Worth tried to persuade his son to claim exemption as an overseer. According to the elder Worth, "If I felt there was anything disagreeable in it I would not advise it." He wanted David out of the army, but not if it meant using "disreputable" means. In this case, he believed that the community (or at least "intelligent opinion") would be aware that David began overseeing before the passage of the overseer law, when "it did not carry corruption with it." Worth concluded, "I have heard of no one being blamed for obtaining exemption by any lawful means who had a family to protect and was not an original secessionist."[36]

The letter reveals the multiple variables involved in southerners' assessment of a potential conscript's behavior: Did he have a family? Was he a fire-eater? Did he take a position solely to receive an exemption? Revealingly, in a letter consumed by a concern for public opinion, Worth does not even broach the idea that David's current status as a principal would be considered "disreputable." Although Worth's argument apparently persuaded his son, David never applied for an overseer exemption. While engaged in this debate, David tracked down evidence proving that his substitute was still too young to be conscripted. This kept David out of the army for another year without having to apply for an overseer exemption.

If the Twenty Negro Law frustrated yeomen soldiers and their families, it did so more in theory than in practice. Fears that rich planters would easily avoid service using this exemption were misplaced. While Confederate conscription records are notoriously incomplete, the available evidence clearly belies historians' assertions such as "the infamous twenty-slave law . . . virtually excused planters outright from the draft." The most commonly cited figure suggests that 4,000 men received an overseer exemption. This number represents only 4 percent of the total number of exemptions granted and fewer than 10 percent of the more than 43,000 plantations in the Confederacy. And, given the stipulation in the May 1863 law that overseers had to be employed as such prior to April 1862, one can assume that many if not most of the 4,000 exempted men were not part of the Confederacy's upper crust but instead were members of the yeoman class.[37]

More precise state-level figures buttress this contention and suggest that even the 4,000 figure is an exaggeration. For instance, Virginia records list 12,045 men exempt from service on November 1, 1863. Of these, only two hundred (1.6 percent) are listed as overseers. Numbers from elsewhere in the Confederacy support the relative infrequency of overseer exemption. According to a December 1863 report, overseer exemptions in North Carolina, South Carolina, and Georgia totaled only 622. This number represents a small fraction of these states' plantations (3.96 percent of their 15,719 plantations) and only 1.4 percent of the total exemptions recorded for the three states. On the opposite side of the Confederacy, relatively more Louisiana planters took advantage of this exemption. An incomplete set of enrollment statistics from twenty-four parishes in 1865 specifies that 210 men had obtained overseer exemptions. Even in this case, these 210 overseers represented only 5.3 percent of the planters living in the state in 1860. Thus, across the Confederacy, evidence indicates that probably more than 90 percent—and perhaps as much as 95 percent—of plantation owners did not employ this method of exemption for their sons or overseers, whether for reasons of patriotism or from an inability to qualify for the exemption.[38]

Critics of the October law did not limit themselves to class-based attacks. They advanced on multiple fronts. Some Confederates still maintained that the entire measure was an unconstitutional violation of states' rights. President Davis vehemently defended conscription's constitutionality but never contended that this decision was solely his. He agreed that the courts had a say in the matter, and in the Confederacy, which lacked a national supreme court, this view would come from the state court systems. In a November letter to North Carolina's governor, Davis expressed hope that state judiciaries would resolve concerns about conscription. He focused his attention on the court in Georgia—home of the Confederacy's most obstreperous governor. Davis claimed that he did not fret over that body's decision. "Having full confidence in the constitutionality of the law," the president hoped that a proconscription decision would resolve the tension between the federal and state governments. By the end month, the Georgia Supreme Court had proven Davis half right. He got his decision, but it did not end the controversy there.[39]

During the final months of 1862, Georgia was on everyone's minds. The front lines of the states' rights conflict over conscription had moved from the summer's epistolary and pamphlet battle between Davis and Brown to the other branches of the Georgia government. Desiring both to keep control over Georgia's soldiers and to prove conscription unconstitutional, Brown looked to the state courts and legislature for support for his position. While awaiting the legislative session, Brown declared that he would "do all in my power to maintain the sovereignty of the State," and he postponed any enforcement of the measure.[40]

Georgians, however, did not line up uniformly behind Brown. In the Confederate Senate, Texan Louis Wigfall reminded Georgia Senator Benjamin Hill of that fact. He chastised the Georgian for falsely equating Governor Brown's opinions with the opinion of all Georgians. Two Georgia newspapers provided support for Wigfall's stance. The *Savannah Republican* asserted that Brown's "heart is fixed upon himself" while Davis strives "for the deliverance of his country." J. Henley Smith, the editor of the *Southern Confederacy,* concurred. He denounced the "cranky" and "unsafe" Brown as motivated by "vindictiveness," "bad impulses," a desire for votes, and the need to be *"contrary,"* rather than by any coherent doctrine of states' rights.[41]

The editor branded Brown as inconsistent because of the governor's attempts to shield militia officers from conscription. Considering them state officials, Brown had forbidden their conscription while allowing the enlistment of men in the militia's ranks. Smith considered that to be a "ridiculous" position, for any argument that would shield the former group should also shield the latter. A letter from "Georgia" in the *Daily Constitutionalist* made a similar point, contending that debate over conscription of particular state officials missed the point: conscription was either constitutional or unconstitutional. According to this anonymous author, whom politically astute Georgians recognized as Vice President Stephens, either no man or all men could be conscripted. Stephens believed it was the former—no member of the militia (or anyone else) should be subject to conscription. Despite the governor's inconsistency, the Confederate government acquiesced and did not conscript militia officers. Former attorney general Thomas Bragg lamented, "Gov. Brown of Geo. bullies and threatens" and the Confederate government yields.[42]

In looking for allies in his dispute with Richmond, Governor Brown turned to the state courts. He received support when a lower Georgia court ruled conscription unconstitutional in September. Its decision equated the acceptance of liberty-threatening conscription to "commit[ting] suicide to avoid personal danger." The true test, however, would come in the state supreme court in the case of *Jeffers v. Fair.* In the wake of the September act, which expanded conscription's age range, Confederate officer John Fair had conscripted thirty-seven-year-old Asa Jeffers. At the behest of Brown, who advised Jeffers's attorneys to the point of editing their briefs, the case went to the Georgia Supreme Court. In *Jeffers v. Fair,* the court dealt the governor a stunning blow as it echoed Davis's view that "compulsory enrollment is a proper incident of the power to raise armies." When the judges searched the Constitution for any restrictions on this power, they found none. Even if that were not the case, they added, the "necessary and proper clause" sanctioned conscription. Otherwise, the Confederacy would be but "a shadow of a government."

The *Jeffers* decision acknowledged states' rights only in limiting who could be conscripted. It precluded drafting state officials and interfering with states acting "in the exercise of their proper functions." In other words, as long as conscription did not destroy state government, it was constitutional. President Davis rejoiced "that the decision of the supreme court of Georgia may be regarded as conclusive on the constitutional question." He enjoyed this "good news" from Governor Brown's own court, particularly as it had reached its decision unanimously and "without any lingering doubt."[43]

Across the Confederacy, other state supreme court justices might have possessed more lingering doubts than the Georgia justices, but no state court ever ruled conscription unconstitutional. In each state, the justices unequivocally endorsed President Davis's position and rejected Governor Brown's. In Alabama, in *Ex Parte Hill,* the court ruled that "The Confederate government . . . has the unquestioned right to call the male residents of the Confederacy into service." The court declared the Confederate Constitution to be "the supreme law of the land" and implored citizens to "respect and obey [its laws] as such." In Mississippi, in *Simmons v. Miller,* the judges addressed the potential flaws in allowing any state interference with conscription. If a governor or legislature could exempt one citizen, then they could exempt all citizens. Accepting state interference would be "absolutely and totally contradictory" to the Constitution and would, in effect, "paralyze the war-power of the Confederate government."[44]

In Texas, the *Ex Parte Coupland* decision, which preceded the Georgia court's judgment, declared that the framers of the Constitution could not have "intended to leave the government dependent upon the will either of the citizen or the state to carry [the power to raise armies] into effect." For the Texas court, the necessity of the present crisis easily eclipsed the arguments of "over zealous advocates of states rights." The court then, undoubtedly to the chagrin of many of these overzealous advocates, proceeded to deny that the Confederacy was based on an ideology of states' rights. The *Coupland* decision emphasized the federal nature of the Confederacy, comprising both national and state governments, with "neither of these governments . . . inferior or superior to the other." Judge James H. Bell, who had opposed secession, offered a vigorous dissent. According to Bell, the Constitution granted the power to raise armies but not the power to use conscription. Necessity could not transform an illegal act into a legal one. The judge's anticonscription stance led a Texas lawyer to accuse him of lacking "the proper feelings of a patriot" and "indulg[ing] in personal considerations and resentments."[45]

Like Bell, Governor Brown faced accusations that he lacked patriotism. These conscription opponents, however, portrayed themselves as Confederate patriots defending their states against despotic encroachments. Brown maintained that the misguided *Jeffers* judgment was "rendered under heavy outside pressure." His allies concurred. Linton Stephens ranted to his half brother Alexander Stephens that the decision was "a *sham* . . . entitled to no respect," especially since these proconscription judges had previously considered the measure unconstitutional, with one branding it an "*outrage*." Linton viewed conscription as part of a conspiratorial plot designed to establish a military despotism, claiming that any arguments for the necessity of the measure were manufactured, and were done so "not negligently but *intentionally*." Later in the year, Stephens, in urging the legislature to pass a resolution condemning conscription, branded it "the very embodiment of Lincolnism."[46]

Did the Georgia Supreme Court have the final word? The Augusta *Daily Constitutionalist* insisted it did, stating the decision "settles this question so far as Georgia is concerned." Linton Stephens and the ever-obstinate Governor Brown disagreed. As a Brown biographer has noted, "No one ever won an argument with Brown for he never stopped arguing." Brown continued the dispute by attempting to discredit the judges, calling out the militia to forestall conscription, and urging the state legislature to act against the measure. One Georgian praised the governor's "unselfish and patriotic course" and informed the state's adjutant general that he had "never been convinced by the puerile and absurd opinion delivered by the Supreme Court." The adjutant general followed Brown's dictates, declaring that the "governor of this State refuses to have anything to do with [conscription's] execution," so state officers would not participate in its enforcement. Having lost on the judicial front, conscription opponents moved their efforts to the state legislature. In their view, "until action has been taken by that body a definite answer cannot be given."[47]

On the opening day of the legislative session, which preceded the *Jeffers* decision, Governor Brown delivered a passionate anticonscription diatribe. He reminded legislators that even though states' rights had formed the basis of their revolution, state citizens were now treated like "vassals" and "chattels" of a central power. He claimed that defenders of conscription found it either constitutional or unconstitutional but necessary. For Brown, it was neither. He asked the legislature to answer the vital question: "Shall we continue to have States, or shall we . . . have a consolidated military despotism?" One week later, after the *Jeffers* decision, Brown called upon the General Assembly, which "represent[ed] the sovereign people of the State," to provide him with advice and direction. J. Henly Smith, the editor of the *Southern Confederacy*, belittled this action as "ludicrous." Smith maintained that while he had previously considered conscription unconstitutional, the state court's decision had resolved the issue. For the editor, Brown's attempt to undermine a judicial verdict ironically placed him in the same position as northern abolitionists in the 1850s, whose undercutting of the Supreme Court's Dred Scott decision and the fugitive slave law had led to southern secession.[48]

In response to Brown's call, the Georgia legislature delivered a mixed message that must have infuriated the governor. At first glance, the majority report of its Committee on Confederate Relations appeared to support Brown. It declared conscription without a state's consent to be "incompatible with both the sovereignty and safety of the States" and therefore unconstitutional. Yet, after its strong rebuff of the *Jeffers* decision, the report's final resolution rejected immediate nullification. Admitting that "while the foregoing resolutions express our convictions, we are still willing to leave the conscript acts undisturbed in their operation, reserving to the State such rightful remedies as may be demanded by future exigencies." In contrast, the minority report simply endorsed the *Jeffers* verdict and affirmed conscription's constitutionality. The two reports thus embodied the governor's worst fears: the minority viewed the measure as constitutional, while the majority considered it unconstitutional yet accepted it regardless. Neither document indicated that the legislature would support Brown's defiance of the Confederate government.[49]

In Georgia's state senate, George Gordon gave a speech, disseminated as a broadside, that reflected the ambivalence many southerners felt toward conscription. Gordon spent the bulk of his oration examining the constitutional and congressional debates of the Founding Fathers. For him, this analysis clearly revealed the unconstitutionality of the measure. Nevertheless, after paying homage to the doctrine of states' rights and the "sacred ground" of the principles articulated in the Virginia and Kentucky resolutions of 1798, he concluded on a different note, unenthusiastically urging Georgians to accept conscription as loyal Confederates. In his role as senator, he had to protest, but "as a citizen I am willing to submit to much more than this to bring this war to a successful close." He also tried to ease the tension between Governor Brown and President Davis. Alluding to the president, Gordon maintained that his speech did not besmirch "the pure patriot" as "we should perceive the sadness, with which he forced himself to sacrifice on the altar of his country the principles of a life time." Gordon further exonerated Davis by making the implausible contention that in the spring the president had actually recommended state conscription (a policy Governor Brown would accept), but that when Congress passed national conscription, the president yielded despite his misgivings.[50]

In looking at the federal relationship, many historians, particularly those who contend that states' rights doomed the Confederacy, concentrate on Brown. In his study of conscription, Albert Burton Moore devotes almost half his pages on Confederate governors to the Georgia executive. Sounding almost like Brown, Moore finds conscription to be anathema to Confederates, arguing that it violated the Confederacy's core political philosophy—states' rights. The dean of the "Died of States' Rights" school, Frank Owsley, argues that conscription would have worked much better "if it had not been opposed so bitterly by the state-rights leaders." For Owsley, a needless tug-of-war between Richmond and state governments contributed "very materially to the defeat of the Confederacy." Twenty-five years later, E. Merton Coulter, in *The Confederate States of America,* echoed Owsley and contended that conscription destroyed the Confederacy's best weapon: "the cooperation of the state governments and their people."[51]

Scholars have successfully challenged this Brown-centric view. In his 1961 study of Confederate federalism, Curtis Amlund downplays the threat posed by states' rights. He sees the actions of Brown regarding conscription as posturing for his constituents, and he views Brown as an exception. W. Buck Yearns concurs that most Confederate governors followed hasty protests with cooperation. Thus, one should be wary of condemning them for their words when their deeds did not indicate animosity toward the national government. In their 1986 work *Why the South Lost the Civil War,* Richard Beringer and his coauthors offer a devastating rebuke of the "Died of States' Rights" school of historians. They argue that conscription policy "proved effective" in operation, with opposition rhetoric serving as a Confederate safety valve rather than a true challenge to policy. Michael Powell characterizes this give-and-take between Richmond and the governors as "negotiated federalism." Nonetheless, the states' rights theory persists. In 2006, David Eicher portrayed the fall 1862 congressional session as a time when the conflict over states' rights came to a head over issues such as conscription. He concludes that with these threats to their sovereignty, "most states by now were feeling an increasing separation from the Richmond government."[52]

Events in the fall of 1862 support those scholars who downplay the idea that conscription foundered on the shoals of states' rights. Brown was not representative of Confederate governors, and conscription did not shatter the relationship between Richmond and the states. Brown even recognized his isolation. He complained to his ally Vice President Stephens that "no other governor seems to raise these questions [of states' rights.]" In 1862, other governors did not clash with Davis but cooperated with him. Even while expressing misgivings, they endorsed conscription. Governor John Gil Shorter of Alabama urged all men between eighteen and forty-five to join the army. He relied on public opinion to effect this enrollment. "Every community owes it to its own reputation and to the country" to put men into the service. Shorter called upon "all good and patriotic citizens . . . to constrain those persons into the path of duty and patriotism." In his message to the legislature, Texas governor Francis Lubbock sounded like the antithesis of Brown. Rather than tightly holding on to his population, he favored sending soldiers out of the Lone Star state, instructing his legislature that "Each battle fought in Virginia, Tennessee, Mississippi, or Arkansas is a battle for the freedom of Texas."[53]

If one examines Davis's correspondence with North Carolina's Governor Zebulon Vance, often portrayed as the Confederacy's second most obstructionist governor, a greater sense of compromise emerges. Elected in September 1862, Vance, like Davis, recognized the competing claims that nation, state, and community had on southern men, and their letters reveal a desire to compromise. Unlike his Georgia counterpart, Vance realized that obstinacy was not the best policy with Davis. Getting concessions from the president involved finesse and compromise. Vance placed his demands to tweak conscription in a larger context of winning the war, and this strategy often worked with Davis.

In November, Davis responded to Vance's concerns regarding how conscripts would be assigned to units. Vance wanted to give conscripts a greater choice, arguing that such a policy would cause more men to accept conscription. Davis first thanked the governor for his help and then explained that conscription was the best "means equitable to distribute the burthen of public defence." He believed that, aside from isolated cases, the reaction to it had been positive as "popular sentiment . . . supports any measures necessary to . . . secure our political independence." After defending the popularity, equity, and legality of conscription, Davis proceeded to grant Vance's request.[54]

While Brown represented the most extreme attack on conscription, Davis tried to assuage his concerns as well. After the *Jeffers* decision, Davis sent his aide-de-camp, Colonel William Browne, to confer with the governor and gain his cooperation. A month later, after several fruitless meetings with Brown, the colonel sent the president a twenty-three-page report addressing the depressing status of conscription in Georgia. Browne wanted to get the governor to "aid actively" in conscription, but the "slippery gentleman" insisted that the *Jeffers* decision had not changed his mind about conscription's unconstitutionality. The governor refused to help enlistment, but he agreed not to impose any obstacles.

In a letter to his close friend General Howell Cobb, Browne, most likely referring to the Stephens family, blamed "designing men" for trying to "bring Joe Brown into open rebellion."

Overall, the governor's negative attitude poisoned the atmosphere surrounding enrollment in Georgia. It led people to defy enrolling officials, which, in turn, contributed to unprofessional behavior among these officers who, according to the report, asserted their authority "by insulting and defying the Governor." The colonel recounted a flawed system, which included using threats to bring men "in irons" into the army. Overall, he found enrolling officers in Georgia "arbitrary, unnecessarily harsh . . . [and] offensive not only to the men concerned but to society in general." In his view, an enrollment based on mutual trust with a cooperative governor and more sympathetic officials would yield between 10,000 and 15,000 additional soldiers.[55]

Cognizant of concerns regarding the harshness and perceived inequality of conscription in Georgia and elsewhere, President Davis tried to address them. Davis, however, faced an insurmountable task, for it was impossible to make conscription universally popular. By definition, conscription demanded sacrifice, and these burdens could never fall evenly across every southern family. The president struggled to convey this message, and his efforts reveal both the extent of this challenge and his inability to inspire the public.

In December 1862, Davis traveled across the Confederacy to his home state of Mississippi. In a well-publicized speech to its legislature, he offered a lengthy defense of conscription. The president maintained that the April act did justice to those in the army, who were willing to stay in the field as long the stay-at-homes, "who had thus far been sluggards in the cause," should be forced to join them. Strangely, within the same paragraph that Davis smears these men as "sluggards," he changes his tune and, without much explanation, declares that "it is no disgrace to be brought into the army by conscription." Davis regretted that the conscription act had suffered from "erroneous" and "harsher criticism than it deserves." Alluding to his dispute with Governor Brown, he added, "Let it never be said that there is a conflict between the States and the Confederate government, by which a blow may be inflicted on the common cause." Unlike Georgia, Mississippi and the Richmond government had a harmonious relationship, and he hoped that this trend would continue.[56]

Next, Davis turned his attention to the exemptions enumerated in the October 1862 revision of the conscription act. He lectured his audience that exemptions kept at home men whose services on the home front would be more useful to the country and to the government than their service in the army. Lamenting that critics of the policy in general, and the overseer exemption in particular, had resorted to class-based attacks, he reminded his listeners of the simple lesson that throughout history "the poor do, indeed, fight the battles of the country." At the same time, however, he added that "most of the wealthiest and most distinguished families of the South have representatives in the ranks." According to the president, the objective of the overseer exemption was "not to draw any distinction of classes, but simply to provide a force, in the nature of a police force, sufficient to keep our negroes in control. This was the sole object of the clause." After defending even the most controversial parts of the conscription act, Davis paradoxically ended his discussion of the measure on a different note, predicting that "the Exemption act . . . will probably be made the subject of revision and amendment."[57]

Earlier in December, Senator William L. Yancey preached a similar message about the overseer exemption, to his constituents in Alabama. Yancey's widely publicized efforts offered none of the ambiguity of his prior congressional speeches. First, he asserted that the law was better termed a *detail* rather than an exemption. In a detail, the man still worked for the government, just on the home front, and if he chose not to work for the Confederacy, he would be forced into the army. In this case, the law directed that these overseers supervise slaves, "the great and peculiar strength of the South in the war," so that their labor benefited both the army and civilians.

Second, he framed the law simply as a response to the question "Is the exemption of someone competent to manage slaves demanded by the interests of the army and the community?" To Yancey, that answer was an obvious yes. He pointed out that even during peacetime, all southern legislatures that had debated the importance of overseers on plantations had enacted measures requiring their presence. If such laws made sense in peacetime, they made even more sense during wartime.

Third, he compared the amount of produce a nonslaveholding farmer could produce to the surplus that a plantation yielded. An overseer managing twenty or more slaves could feed many families, whereas a nonslaveholding farmer could feed only his own family. The editor of the Augusta (Ga.) *Daily Constitutionalist* concurred. In his view, if the exemption favored affluent slaveholders, it was only because the requirements of the Confederacy and the planter coincided.[58]

In the wake of Davis's and Yancey's speeches, the new secretary of war, James Seddon, in a report to Congress, offered a glowing endorsement of conscription, which had "wrought our salvation from destruction or infamous thralldom." He recognized that the measure had demanded sacrifices but "the results worthily rewarded such sacrifices." Seddon noted only two problems. The first was the mistaken opinion that "has strangely prevailed," equating an exemption and a discharge. Exemptions never sent men home from the army. Soldiers who remained in the army would "feel the gravest discontent and indignation" if the measure discharged their comrades. According to the report, "Exemption implies freedom from a call to be made, not discharge from existing service." The second problem was concerns over the fairness of the twenty-slave law, which provide an exemption for one class of southerners while not providing for the care of "helpless children or females." Thus, in order to "promote equity and the public good," he suggested that, rather than eliminating the exemption, in cases where eight to ten helpless white women and children requested aid, a potential conscript should be allowed to stay home to care for them.[59]

The final months of 1862 had reinforced the Confederacy's commitment to conscription. In his report, Seddon barely addressed the need for conscription or its constitutionality. Those questions were settled for the time being. Most Confederates either endorsed the measure wholeheartedly or at least accepted its necessity. During the congressional debate, Governor Brown had grumbled to the vice president that "we have much more to apprehend from military despotism than from subjugation by the enemy."[60] He, however, represented a minority of southerners. Most Confederates considered the scenario from the opposite perspective. Fearing subjugation by the enemy much more than by their own government, they recognized the need for more troops and therefore accepted an expanded conscription. Nevertheless, they still disagreed on how to balance the potentially competing needs of army and home, slaveholder and nonslaveholder, and states and federal government.

President Davis's Mississippi speech epitomized this dispute. Were men at home "sluggards" or were they just serving the Confederacy in a different manner? Were the current exemptions acceptable or in need of changing? With Davis's words offering support to both answers to each of these questions, Confederates understandably held mixed views on the measure. So, while conscription's first great rush was over, there remained plenty of work to do as the Confederacy entered 1863.

CHAPTER 4

# The Herculean Task Facing Enrolling Officers

In 1863, Lieutenant Leonidas L. Polk served as a Confederate enrolling officer in eastern North Carolina. He recounted to his wife the "sad & unpleasant task" he faced in searching for conscripts. His unit would ride up to a house where a man stood with his "loving wife & sunny-faced children," and ten minutes later they would depart with the husband, leaving the "doors on the road crowded with the faces of frightened & crying & helpless women." His misgivings led Polk to wonder, "What have we gained by this trip?" Performing the same task in Louisiana, Captain John David Workman probably asked himself the same question. After not hearing back from his cousin, he halfheartedly joked that he was beginning to think that his relatives had "concluded to cut our acquaintance because we were engaged in conscript hunting." In this letter, he described surrounding a church to capture the men inside. When women emerged from the service and saw armed soldiers, they "were a little frightened at first, .. [but] they approved our course." Despite this supposed endorsement, Workman worried that "my heart is not hard enough to treat [conscripts] with the harshness they deserve. It is a very disagreeable business and one which I dislike much." Conscripting men in Georgia, Lieutenant Charles C. Jones concurred in the distasteful nature of this work with civilians terrified of enrolling officers, whom they considered "the terrors and the bugbears of the present day."[1]

At face value, the jobs of conscript officers such as Polk, Workman, and Jones appeared very simple. They just needed to use Confederate regulations to separate men in their assigned districts into two groups—those who would serve their country in the army and those who would serve it on the home front. They asked potential conscripts their age, inquired about their health, decided if they were residents, and judged if they merited occupational exemptions. If these queries established that the man was eligible for conscription, he would either enroll in the army or provide a substitute. Conscripted soldiers went to camps of instruction, where enrolling officers trained them and then sent them out to replenish understrength regiments from their home state.

The actual operations of their offices, however, belied any notion of simplicity. It was based on three false premises: first, that people truthfully answered these queries; second, that the Confederacy had clear, unambiguous conscription regulations; and third, that men willingly turned out when enrolling officers called for them. In reality, people lied, regulations were contradictory and constantly shifting, and men often failed to show up as required. Acknowledging that he had made an incorrect decision regarding a conscript's exemption, one officer explained, "In this region of the country it is exceedingly difficult to arrive at the correctness of anything, and what we accept as truth today we hear contradicted tomorrow." He told his superior, Colonel Mallett, that "the public sentiment of this community" and "neighborhood feuds" made it nearly impossible to discover the facts of any case. Mallett assuredly sympathized, for he had previously groused that his own superior in Richmond had "but a faint conception of the Herculean task and complicated duties devolving upon me."[2]

This chapter will examine "the Herculean task and complicated duties" that the men charged with administering conscription encountered and will look at the policy from the perspective of those trying to enforce it. If Confederate leaders intended conscription to achieve a perfect balance of men in the army and men on the home front, they charged enrolling officers with aspiring to this perfection. While few complete Confederate conscription records are extant, two large collections from North Carolina still exist—the records of the Seventh Congressional District and the records of Colonel Peter Mallett, the state's commandant of conscripts—along with a smaller but still significant set of Virginia records. Less complete collections from other Confederate states can supplement these records.

Regardless of location, these soldiers tell a similar story of a painstaking but frustrating pursuit of an unachievable goal. In March 1864, General John Preston, the superintendent of the Bureau of Conscription, pessimistically asserted, "From one end of the Confederacy to the other, every constituted authority, every officer, every man and woman is engaged in opposing the enrolling officer in the execution of his duties." If enrolling officers read this report, they undoubtedly would have nodded their heads in agreement. Moreover, they probably would have added that the ever-changing regulations sent from Preston's office in Richmond exacerbated their problems.[3]

At its most extreme, enrolling officers faced coordinated armed resistance, but few draftees chose that option, and the Confederacy experienced nothing like the draft riots in Union cities.[4] Instead, opposition fell somewhere along a spectrum that included hiding out in the woods, faking an illness, lying about one's age, fraudulently claiming an exemption, obtaining a government job, or merely claiming that one was more needed at home than in the army. For those trying to avoid joining the army, gray beards and baby faces with smooth chins became badges of honor, and state political offices became a hot commodity. The ministry, teaching, and other "bombproof" professions surged in popularity. Creative bookkeeping was employed to increase the size of slaveholdings and qualify for overseer exemptions. Men offered bribes to accept ineligible substitutes, or they feigned illness when they arrived at camps of instruction. Some men employed more than one plan to avoid conscription. According to an enrolling officer, Green Bynum first claimed to be a minister of the gospel. When this approach failed, the "rather young looking" Bynum suddenly remembered that he was too old to be drafted. Bynum's ploy failed, as did many others with one officer maintaining that "[one] hundred [requests] are refused weekly."[5]

The job of the enrolling officer was to determine each man's true status, but in the mid-nineteenth century, even determining a basic fact such as age could be challenging. At the onset of the policy, conscripts needed to be between eighteen and thirty-five, and by the end of war this range had expanded to encompass ages seventeen to fifty. Official birth certificates did not exist, so no government documents proved whether someone fell within or without these ages. Birthdates could come from church documents, neighborhood recollections, or unofficial records such as a listing of births inside the front cover of a family Bible. In 1863, in an effort to clarify how it determined ages, the conscription bureau stipulated that it accepted sworn testimony from relatives or friends, written family records, a general reputation of one's age, and, only if no other evidence was available, an affidavit from the conscript himself. For instance, when George Lucas provided his son John as a substitute, the enrolling officer determined the boy was too young for the draft (and thus eligible to be a substitute) because "he is of respectable parents, who I feel sure would not make any statement that is not true."[6]

Not all parents were as respectable as the Lucases, and most officers were not so easily swayed. To determine John King's age, an officer interviewed Ms. Mary Hill, a midwife and "one of the most respectable ladies of this town." She swore that King was over eighteen and probably close to twenty-one years old. In October 1863, an officer sent a list of prisoners with notations such as "He claims to be under 18 but it can be proven that he is 18 or over," and "His parents claim that he is under 18, but Alfred Warren Esqr. and others say he is over 18." In Louisiana, the Fortners presented a family record of ages showing their son Elisha to be seventeen, but Lieutenant Davenport discovered "that a portion of the record had been mutilated," with "the figures 1846 . . . made with a different colored ink and very new." Elisha's admission to Davenport that he had spent the previous three nights in the woods, evading conscription, coupled with his father's reputation as a "Union Man" further weakened his case.[7]

While neighbors might have an accurate sense of whether boys such as John Lucas, John King, and Elisha Fortner had reached seventeen or eighteen, recollections became foggier when assessing conscription's upper age limit. In 1863, with the draft targeting men up to forty-five years old, officers needed to distinguish between men born in 1817 (ineligible) and those born in 1818 (eligible). In October, the enrolling officers of the Seventh Congressional District investigated a number of these applications. Horace Sinbury struggled to prove that he was too old. Sinbury's neighbors maintained that his deceased parents had been illiterate and thus kept no family records. They agreed that Horace had been born the same week as John Wood, but this evidentiary trail led to a dead end as the Bible in which Wood's family had recorded birth dates had burned thirty years earlier. The fact that Wood was simultaneously trying to claim exemption himself further complicated matters.

In an analogous incident, John Hancock's mother swore that her son was over forty-six, but "she and her husband being totally ignorant . . . prevented them from keeping a record." In Hancock's case, his actions spoke louder than words. Similar to the situation of the young Elisha Fortner, Hancock's hiding in the woods undermined his claim for exemption. One state to the north and one year later, with the upper age limit now fifty years old, a Virginia enrolling officer reported examining a suspicious Bible where someone had altered a birthdate from 1817 to 1807.[8]

The Confederacy lacked not only birth certificates but also any paperwork to determine whether aliens—foreign-born noncitizens—could be drafted. The conscription law emphasized domicile. In short, enrolling officers had to judge whether an alien intended to remain in the Confederacy or planned to return home. Determining whether an immigrant intended to go back to his native land proved difficult in practice. The whim of army officials, who might not have spoken the same language as potential conscripts, often replaced codified rules. Historian Gary B. Mills contends that in Louisiana, for instance, despite the rules of international law, conscription of aliens "was almost routine." W. C. Corsan found that his British passport did not prevent a conscript officer from removing him from a train there, though subsequently another officer discharged him. Serving approximately one hundred miles east in Mobile, Alabama, a British consul warned of an enrolling officer in the far reaches of his jurisdiction who "defies all British protection" in conscripting foreigners.[9]

Closer to the East Coast, which housed more Confederate officials, more army officers, and more diplomats, a man's claim to exemption as an alien had a greater chance of success. Virginia enrolling officers allowed "a poor man, [who] owns no property, never voted nor paid taxes" to return to Ireland and permitted another European without "real or personal estate" who had at no time "declared [his] intention of becoming a citizen" to leave for Prussia. The army called for "a most rigid investigation" into these petitions. The regulations stipulated that marrying, voting, taking an oath of allegiance to the Confederacy, and owning real estate could make an alien liable to conscription, but even this evidence was not necessarily conclusive. They added that "Declarations of a party of his intention to return to his native country, if made since the passage of the first Conscript law, are entitled to no weight whatever." In South Carolina, a judge rejected such a claim, especially since the petitioner had volunteered for a militia company and "participated . . . in the reduction of Fort Sumter."[10]

Enrolling officers considered suffrage to be the key factor. In most states, one did not have to be a citizen to vote but had to declare one's intention to become a citizen in order to do so. Such a declaration made a man eligible for the draft. A Confederate officer maintained that Patrick Welsh and James Burdett forfeited British protection, as the former admitted "he has voted once" and the latter acknowledged "he has voted several times." In writing to a British diplomat, Colonel Mallett explained that he had conscripted two men who claimed to be British based on that rationale. They were "engaged in business and enjoying all the rights and privileges of Citizens of the Confederate States." One had definitely voted, while an enrolling officer maintained the other had voted as well. Other cases were not as clear-cut. In 1864, a captain recommended conscripting Thomas Langley. Langley had married a North Carolina woman, and since "he was allowed a certain time to leave the Confederacy & took no advantage," the officer considered him a domiciled foreigner.[11]

With Confederates courting British recognition, they sought to avoid the international incident that could come with pressing British men into the army. Georgia's adjutant general acknowledged that the "delicacy of our position with

Europe" would influence his governor's actions. This policy initially held true across much of the Confederacy, with an adjutant general in the conscript bureau advising that "cases of foreigners are required to be handled with caution." Even in a case where Mallett knew a man had voted, he assured the British vice consul, "If they are British, I apologize . . . I respectfully disclaim any intention of pressing them into service." Exemplifying this caution, the army, partly to avoid such conflicts, decided to stop taking foreigners as substitutes less than four months after the passage of the initial conscription law. While this directive was not always followed, in reducing the amount of alien substitutes, it correspondingly reduced the potential for diplomatic incidents.[12]

Consuls often tried to intercede on the behalf of aliens. Allan Fullarton, the British vice consul at Savannah, received numerous requests from men who claimed to be British subjects and wanted his protection from conscription. Among them was a man who alleged that army officers had threatened him with death if he refused to take an oath of allegiance and two men who hoped he could provide them with protection even though they had resided in the South since 1833.[13]

In October and November 1862, Georgia lieutenant John Weems, Secretary of War Randolph, and Fullarton debated this delicate issue. Weems agreed that aliens should not be conscripted, but he rejected claims where the alien's testimony was the sole evidence indicating that the man planned to return to Europe. For him, the fact that a conscript had lived in Georgia for many years, had enjoyed the protection of its government, and had several business investments trumped his self-serving claim that he intended to return to England. Nevertheless, Secretary of War Randolph ordered Weems to suspend the enrollment of any foreigners until he could craft a general order. Following up on this case, Randolph reminded Fullarton that the Confederacy had previously honored, and would continue to honor, its policy of not drafting aliens, but the vice consul must recognize that "mistakes will occur."[14]

British officials' repeated efforts to exempt prospective conscripts contributed to the deterioration in the relationship between the Confederacy and Britain. When the war began, the British did not recognize the Confederacy as a sovereign nation but kept their consuls at several cities. Nevertheless, while present in the Confederacy, these men had not presented their credentials and had no legal standing in the new nation. As noted, Confederate officials, in an effort to encourage British recognition, generally gave these consuls the benefit of the doubt when they requested that men be released from the army. Secretary of

State Benjamin, however, grew increasingly frustrated, both because consuls came to regard these certificates as guarantees of exemption rather than just one piece of evidence enrolling officers would consider and because "these certificates were freely issued" to anyone who requested one. The tipping point came when Consul George Moore, stationed in Richmond, claimed exemption for two men who had lived in Virginia for eight years, owned land there, and had voted in state elections. Benjamin objected to Moore's interference in this case, for he contended that it was "difficult to conceive a case presenting stronger proofs of the renunciation of native allegiance." When Benjamin later heard that Fullarton supposedly had advised aliens to throw down their weapons rather than fight, the die was cast. In October 1863, the Confederate cabinet, declaring that consuls had tried to undermine Confederate sovereignty, dismissed them from their offices and sent them home.[15]

With regard to conscripting citizens of other nations, in June 1864, Colonel Mallett faced a puzzling dilemma. Two potential conscripts claimed exemption as citizens of a foreign country—the United States of America. The men, who considered themselves Confederate sympathizers, maintained that threats and violence had driven from their northern homes. Despite their sympathy with the Confederacy, they had "no intention of becoming residents . . . [and] are *among* us involuntarily." Mallett sought advice from his superiors, fearing that allowing this type of exemption would open the door "to a vast amount of fraud & corruption" as such claims would be hard to disprove.

These men did not specify their home state. In general, however, Marylanders were the most common group of northerners to cross the paths of enrolling officers. The question of whether Marylanders could serve as substitutes, meaning they were ineligible for conscription, repeatedly came up, particularly in Virginia. In 1862 and 1863, conscription officers consistently answered that they could be substitutes, thereby implying they were ineligible to be drafted. Just three days before Mallett wrote, however, the army had changed its mind and authorized the conscription of Marylanders.[16]

If determining age and nationality proved troublesome, occupational exemptions provided the most headaches for enrolling officers. In Georgia, Lieutenant Jones described his superior as besieged "amid a thousand and one questions reiterated by each newcomer." Regulations could not address every possible permutation: If newspaper employees were exempt, what constituted a newspaper? Did it depend on the frequency of its publication or its contents? Was a poorhouse that provided medical services a hospital? Were dentists covered by an exemption for doctors? If a man owned a farm and made shoes, was he a farmer (not exempt) or a shoemaker (exempt)? What if a man facing conscription fled and while avoiding capture got a "bombproof" government job in the Nitre and Mining Bureau? What happened to a doctor conscripted in September 1862 when his profession became exempt the following month? This last issue—could a man serving in the army claim an exemption when his occupation, whether doctor, overseer, or tanner, entered the exemption list—often appeared in correspondence. To the confusion and disappointment of many soldiers, new exemptions did not discharge men from the army.[17]

At times, conscription officers, such as John Coke in Virginia, admitted that even they could not comprehend the complex regulations. Coke encountered a case that sounded like a brainteaser from a logic test. In 1862, John Curry provided German native Charles Cook as his substitute. In joining the army, Cook had admitted his intention to renounce his allegiance to any foreign state and eventually become a Confederate citizen. This declaration, most likely uttered to show that he would be a loyal substitute, actually made Cook liable to conscription himself. Enrolling officials apparently did not catch on to this declaration until February 1863. In the meantime, Cook had died. Normally, if a substitute died, the principal remained exempt (as if he had died himself). However, considering Curry's status, Coke wondered whether the error in allowing his initial substitution in the army changed that provision. He wrote his superiors in Richmond, "His substitute is dead. If living he would be liable to duty . . . Does his death alter the case?" The conscription bureau called for Curry's conscription, declaring, "The principal is exempt only so long as the substitute is not liable to duty if he were living."[18]

In North Carolina, the application of Jas. Jordan similarly baffled Captain Haughton. Jordan made shoes and was a minister, although he had only started the latter position in 1862. Haughton could not figure out which part of the law applied to Jordan, so he forwarded the petition to Richmond for advice. In July 1864, an officer enforcing the collection of beef from plantations with exempt overseers admitted that the law had stumped his office. Unable to come to a conclusion at the local level, he had to send an inquiry to Richmond for clarification. A Louisiana officer who inadvertently accepted an ineligible substitute confessed, "I was totally ignorant of the [amended] order . . . I was absent from the army at the time it was passed."[19]

If army officers could not keep up with the ever-changing and at times conflicting regulations, how could an ordinary Confederate? Lawyers offered to help. Aware that "thousands in the Confederate States . . . are so mystified as to their real duties," Thomas Jones, a Raleigh attorney, offered his expertise. In Virginia, Frank Thompson offered attorney Francis Smith $250 immediately and then another $750 if Smith secured an exemption for Thompson and a friend. Apparently, Smith did not like Confederate currency, as the final contract stipulated two 500-pound bales of cotton instead.[20]

Despite the complexity in conscription laws, some occupational exemptions appeared straightforward, such as the one for teachers with twenty or more students. Nonetheless, even this concise definition created controversy. In Virginia, Captain Coke received an anonymous letter complaining that a man exempt as a teacher taught less than two hours per day, had just started teaching in the past two weeks, and had bribed a preacher to obtain his position. Given examples like that, Mallett reminded officers that the law distinguished between experienced teachers and "those having gotten up schools as an '*expedient*' to stay at home." As he sarcastically pointed out, "The object of the law is not to establish new schools, but to prevent schools already established from being broken up." Two months later, Mallett defended his conscription of self-described teacher Duncan Steward by branding his instructing as "of no consequence." Steward taught only three months a year and, if not for the chance he could qualify for an exemption, would not be teaching in the summer. Mallett informed Secretary of War Randolph, "There are great many such cases, some of them teaching for a mere trifle, while others teach for nothing save exemption from conscription."[21]

As evidenced by Mallett's look into Steward's teaching credentials, conscription officers, though understaffed, in the midst of a war, and living during a time when the national government stayed out of people's private affairs, often thoroughly investigated exemption claims. A simple glance at tax or census records did not produce the information they needed. Instead, they had to interview conscripts, family, friends, and coworkers and investigate places of business. Officers might need to determine how much a mill produced, how many people worked there, and how long a prospective conscript had held his position there. In June 1864, discussing the detailing of agriculturalists, Captain Jones directed an enrolling officer to "ascertain who are producers, their ability to produce, and whether they would be of more service to the Govt. as producers than as soldiers."[22]

That same month, Jones meticulously researched a claim to have R. C. Burgess exempted as a miller. In marking the application "Disapproved," he concluded, "The mill is a small corn mill and does not run from the want of something to grind . . . The carding machine . . . is not indispensably necessary, there being one about three miles off." Based on his inquiries, Jones added that the applicant had questionable motives, for "party bought this mill for the purpose of securing himself" an exemption, and "his family will not suffer in his absence." Considering wool carding to be the prerogative of women, Jones decided that "no great loss to the public will occur" with Burgess's enrollment. Like Burgess, Cicero Holmes failed to gain an exemption. His mother hoped to have him stay home to manage her slave workforce. An officer, however, decided that she was a better overseer than he was, and that Cicero's brother, although not currently on speaking terms with his mother, would take care of her farm, since he stood to inherit it.[23]

A man who was both a harness maker and a tanner also failed to secure an exemption, after the enrolling officer decided he was "not *absolutely* necessary" to his business. His father, who was too old to be conscripted, owned the shop and could operate it without the son. Another tanner suffered a similar fate. Enrollment officers decided that J. B. York, who had requested his son's exemption, exaggerated the extent of their business. They determined that the Yorks, who owned a farm in addition to their tanning yard, had gone to "very extra pains" to make themselves appear to be prominent tanners. Despite the Yorks' efforts, the officers believed that "one hand & perhaps one small boy" could run the tannery. Similarly, S. W. Swain's blacksmith petition did not pass muster. While Swain managed the shop, conscript officers concluded that hired slaves and men outside of conscription's range did the work. Plus, Swain charged "almost exorbitant prices" and the community had an abundance of mechanics exempted already. At times, officers' extensive research on a petition could change a decision. Initially, they held a favorable view of the exemption of a man named Hinshaw, considering him to be loyal, ill, the sole laborer on his farm, and a member of the Society of Friends. In overturning this recommendation, a superior officer's investigation revealed that "he is supposed to be a disloyal man," his "father is well able to take care of them," and he "has recently found the Quakers to avoid the army."[24]

In October 1862, Congress had granted members of pacifistic denominations, such as Quakers, the right to pay $500 in lieu of conscription. In the case of Hinshaw, enrolling officers had to decide on the sincerity of his conversion. More commonly, petitioners, who claimed to be aligned with the Society of Friends but had not officially joined the church pleaded for leniency. Elwood Moore's mother vainly hoped the fact that he was "brought up among 'friends'" would be sufficient. Alpheus Mendenhall, who had been a member of the Society of Friends until being "disowned for accomplishing his marriage contrary to discipline," asked if his retention of Quaker principles still entitled him to pay for an exemption. Similarly, a Quaker advocated for his brother, who "has attended Friends meetings" and "is as much opposed to war as we are," asking that he might pay the $500, even though the brother never officially joined the church.[25]

In investigating religious or occupational exemptions, enrolling officers provided the community a voice in this process. They took testimony from friends, neighbors, and relatives, and they read petitions signed by lengthy lists of supporters. John C. Smith, a doctor in Anson County, offered one signed by "*every* man in neighborhood." To obtain community input to enforce the draft in Clarendon, South Carolina, William Elliott relied on an informal set of "three elderly gentlemen who I've styled 'Conscript Fathers.' They are substantial farmers and knowing the district can tell who should or should not be exempt."

Conscription officers, however, recognized that neighbors' testimony could be biased, especially if they wished to help a friend, relative, business partner, or prospective voter avoid military service. While Elliott might have relied on local help in Clarendon, he had not trusted civilians while previously stationed in Greenville, South Carolina. There, he complained his "bloods up" because men "will make oath to any thing & magistrates who will countenance them and advocate their case to make money or get votes." In Greenville, he used his sergeant, an outsider like himself, to investigate the claims and canceled all those "given upon false statements." In North Carolina, upon scrutinizing the case of a man who sought a detail as a miller, an officer concluded, "The circumstances were misrepresented to me by designing parties."[26]

In looking into the application of John Morgan, Captain Pearson found similar misrepresentations. Morgan worked at his father's mill, but Pearson learned that he had only started there in 1863, after his father dismissed an employee to create a position for his son. The captain was "satisfied that [Morgan's] son would never have gone into the mill but for the extension of the conscript law." However, he warned his superior, Colonel Mallett, that since Morgan was "one of the most wealthy men in the county . . . he can get a large number of good men to certify to anything that would be calculated to exempt his son." Mallett took umbrage at Pearson's report, for in his view it implied that gentlemen were predisposed to lie, whereas Mallett felt just the opposite. He had the application sent back to Pearson for a more thorough investigation. Pearson had the mill's employment history over the previous ten years analyzed. When he refiled his report, he noted that he did not mean for his initial decision to imply that wealthy men would likely perjure themselves. Instead, he only meant that he found it suspicious that a wealthy planter's son was an "ordinary miller." After his thorough reinvestigation, he concluded his instincts had been accurate, for "it is difficult to conceive a stronger case of an effort to evade the law than this."[27]

In an 1864 report, Adjutant General Samuel Cooper described the laborious investigative process. Three or four officers could consider and sign a petition, with some analyzing it more than once as it went up and then back down the chain of command. A county enrolling officer, a district enrolling officer, the state commandant of conscripts, and an officer in Richmond (plus members of their staffs) might investigate the application. Given such circumstances, Cooper's report lamented, "Let no one be surprised that cases should be found pending from six to twelve months." In the meantime, the prospective soldier generally remained at home rather than in the army. At times, the applicant moved or switched jobs (or conscription rules changed), which further complicated the process. Cooper recommended simplifying the system, and he finished the report with an extra note explaining that in just two months, the Virginia commandant of conscripts' records filled six hundred pages.[28]

After all of their investigations, enrolling officers still sometimes had to make judgment calls, and they often made their decisions based on the answer to the question "Would this man be more valuable in the army or at home?" In analyzing John Smith's application, the officer decided, "I am at a loss to know how his services are necessary at home," since his father-in-law was one of the county's wealthiest men. In assessing Ambrose Beck, Captain Little concluded that the family, living in a wealthy area, "would suffer very little if any." The officer rejected the very next application as well. He concluded that James Holt, a bank cashier, "could better serve his country in the field." Holding a negative view of the state militia, Little happily disallowed a militia colonel's request that his overseer receive a detail. He suggested that the colonel resign his militia office instead and return to his farm, "where no doubt he would do more good to his country." In denying a petition for a blacksmith, an officer first looked at community needs and determined that they had several blacksmiths but needed only one. He pointed out this was "a young man and can go into the service without injury to any one. There are too many smiths . . . and such as can be best spared should go to army."[29]

Paradoxically, the presence of too many or too few slaves in the community could impact an enrolling officer's decision. Too many slaves necessitated someone to control them. Too few slaves meant the community could have a difficult time feeding itself if totally stripped of its male population. In western North Carolina, it was most often the latter situation. As one investigator noted on an appeal of a detail, "This case like a great many others in this county is a meritorious one from the fact there are so few slaves to the number of whites." In Randolph County, a petition for a miller noted that almost all of the white men in the neighborhood had left for the army, and "there are very few slaves in that section" to support the soldiers' wives and daughters at home. Chatham County had similar demographics. There, an officer approved an application, for it "is not a large a slaveholding county . . . Labor is scarce as most of the white population is in the army."[30]

The decisions in other cases hinged on the abundance of slaves in a community. Prior to October 1862, such decisions required a detail. From then to the end of the war, overseers could receive an exemption through the Twenty Negro Law, though this exemption's guidelines became more stringent over time. Supporters of William Dawson's exemption stressed that four hundred to five hundred slaves lived in a five-mile radius of his farm. They added that Dawson was a "very efficient man in the management of negroes," for they "all fear him." In trying to secure the exemption of his grandson, Elias Brooks, the eighty-six-year-old Benjamin Harris worried that his twenty slaves would be "left entirely uncontrolled" and that the neighborhood would "suffer from [the slaves'] depredation" if Brooks entered the army. Captain Thornburg approved a trio of details in May 1864 on the basis that the men were needed for slave control. Without E. J. Bell as an overseer, "the negroes become demoralized and worthless"; the community required B. F. Lambeth's presence for "subduing the negroes in the neighborhood"; and Augustus Alston served as an overseer in a neighborhood where slaves represented almost the entire population.[31]

Conscription officers read petition after petition recounting the extensive sacrifices and misery on the home front. Trying to keep Thomas Clark at home, supporters stressed that he had planted a crop that would die in the field if he was not allowed to harvest it, he had a broken femur, his wife was dying, and he was "an ignorant, simple fellow." William Long's situation might have been even worse. Forty-nine years old with "a feeble constitution," this "good & loyal citizen" had nineteen people depending on him. In addition to taking care of his wife and six children, he had responsibility for his seventy-six-year-old mother; his dead brother's widow (with two children); another brother, described as a widower "prostrated and at the point of death with consumption"; and this widower's seven children. William Moore lacked a strong constitution, his wife was ill, and he had six young children at home. Four of these children were nieces and nephews, as Moore's brother had died in the army, and catastrophically his brother's wife had died at home the same day. To top off this tale of woe, Moore was a "very poor man."[32]

Even if they were sympathetic to this never-ending series of petitions detailing suffering, officers, never forgetting the goal of conscription, still sent many of these men into the army. In rejecting Jonathan Cox's petition based on family hardship and multiple dependents, Colonel Little scribbled on the back, "The district is inhabited mostly by very poor men with large families & if you exempt one of them you must exempt hundreds of others." Another official denied exemption for the only white man on a farm with a wife, two slave women, five white children, and seven slave children. Despite all twelve children being ten years of age or younger, the officer stated, "The demand for men is too great to grant indulgence." Likewise citing the "great demand for men," another officer refused to allow James Smith to remain at home to take care of his sick father, notwithstanding the fact that James's seven brothers had all volunteered to serve in the Confederate army.[33]

In disallowing Jesse Richardson's petition, an officer hit on the crux of the issue. He admitted, "If we grant exemption to all who . . . make sacrifices . . . by going in the service, our army will not be recruited." To achieve its independence, the Confederacy needed to enlist every man possible, and obtaining them meant families would suffer. This duty, however, could be viewed from the opposite perspective as well. Assistant Secretary of War James Campbell, serving in Richmond as the final appeal in the process, endorsed one exemption with the declaration, "The family must be maintained for the preservation of the state and this family has contributed its fair proportion to the common defense." As families had obligations to the nation, the nation had obligations to the family as well. Unfortunately, in some districts—and possibly in the Confederacy as a whole—there were not enough men to satisfy both of these competing demands. Enrolling officers had to combine the law with their personal judgment to balance these needs.[34]

When the precise circumstances remained in doubt, or when determining which of the flood of similar petitions to accept, officers weighed the Confederate loyalty of a man or his neighborhood. While no iteration of the conscription law ever mentioned loyalty, enrolling officers repeatedly considered it to be a key—if not *the* key—factor in their decisions. In a case where a man sought a detail as a farmer, the investigator made a favorable recommendation as "party is considered and [*sic*] honest upright man. True to his country." In allowing a widow's son to remain at home, an officer noted, "She has given two of her sons [who volunteered in the first year] and I recommend that the third son be detailed to aid his mother." In seeking a detail as an overseer, Duncan Niven hoped that living in a community that was "loyal, true, liberal, & patriotic" would help, particularly since he supervised slaves for "ladies whose husbands and sons have gone into service." In requesting that an ill man be detailed for service in the conscription bureau rather than being sent to the army in Virginia, an officer described him as "a true southerner." In seeking an exemption, William Bell, who had three brothers serve in the army, one of whom had died, hoped the fact that he was "a true and loyal citizen to the Southern Confederacy" would persuade the conscription officer to allow him to remain at home.[35]

The Confederate loyalty of Isaac Pragg, a Mexican War veteran who had volunteered in 1861 but later provided a substitute, swayed Captain Reucher. Pragg stressed that "his application for exemption results from no want of patriotism . . . nor from skulking cowardice that actuates many to pray for exemption." Pragg's devotion persuaded Reucher, who noted, "This is the only petition I have ever signed recommending executive clemency." A different officer endorsed an exemption request partially because the petitioner "lives in a patriotic portion of the county where not only conscripts but those who are not liable have gone into service." Exemptions based on Confederate devotion, however, had their limits. On the back of an application based on "patriotic contribution," Secretary of War James Seddon scribbled, "The party alluded to has enjoyed exemption long enough for such display of patriotism. He ought not now to object to displaying the same quality in the field."[36]

Officers not only rewarded loyal areas but also tried to keep some Confederates in disloyal areas. In Louisiana, W. S. McIntosh urged a conscript officer to leave some men at home to protect soldiers' families. Otherwise, "if all the good active citizens are taken out of the Parish, the country will be preyed upon by thieves until our country will be entirely devastated." In North Carolina, John Graffenedt justified his exemption on the grounds that he farmed in an area that "has long been deeply impregnated with abolition feeling." Thus, "it was imperative that a loyal Confederate such as himself stay home" to combat this traitorous behavior. The enrolling officers in his county might have agreed with his assessment. In the same month that Graffenedt made his appeal, they denied John Pike's claim for a blacksmith exemption on the grounds that he was "a Black Republican in sentiment" and "most of the neighborhood are of the same stamp."[37]

If Confederate loyalty could keep men out of the army, an absence of loyalty might guarantee one's enrollment. Like John Pike, other conscripts saw their petitions denied not because of the letter of the law but because officers judged them lacking in sufficient enthusiasm for the cause. An officer rejected R. L. Griffin's claim for a detail to make saltpeter, for "undoubted authority" had declared him "a rank abolitionist." The same official expressed concern about a man named Munson whose leather prices were "very expensive." Elsewhere, two men who sold yarn "at enormous prices" stood no chance of escaping conscription. James Covington, despite having seven brothers in the army, saw his application for detail initially denied since he was "not as liberal as he should be in support of the government." Captain Thornburg rebuffed Alvis Snipes's application because Snipes "had not manifested that desire for our success" that victory demanded. Likewise, Captain Pearson denied the exemption request of William Hill, a shoemaker, who "is disloyal to our cause and would be the cause of much harm if allowed to remain at home."[38]

In enforcing conscription, enrolling officers interacted not only with prospective soldiers but also with state officials. The original 1862 conscription act stipulated the use of state militias to enforce it. This requirement soon proved impractical, as states provided no men—or men who proved unable or unwilling to accomplish the task. Thus, the Bureau of Conscription used Confederate soldiers to enforce conscription. In implementing a policy that brushed up against, and in some minds crossed, the line of states' rights, understaffed conscription officers needed to tread carefully to keep the support of (or least prevent the outright opposition of) governors, legislators, judges, and the militia. In North Carolina, Governor Vance, while trying to secure a favor, subtly threatened Colonel Mallett that if his state chose to be "unaccommodating, I fancy you would find the task of enrolling . . . quite a different job."

Keeping state officials "accommodating" often meant that, in questionable cases, conscription officers tried to avoid antagonizing governors. For instance, the army debated conscripting men on election day. Instead of seeking men out, this plan efficiently waited until they appeared in public. Enrolling officers, however, contrasted the despotic image of uniformed soldiers seizing men as they cast ballots with the ease of gaining them. Aware that this scenario would infuriate state officials, the bureau wisely decided against it, "so that it may not said that the polls have been controlled by an armed force."[39]

The quarrels with state governments most frequently stemmed from the exemption of state officials. The army and state politicians concurred that state officials were exempt, but they disagreed on what constituted a state office. The act certainly included governors, legislators, and state judges, but what about militia officers, justices of the peace, tobacco inspectors, and deputy sheriffs? Georgia's Governor Brown presented the greatest challenge, as he defined "state official" in its broadest extent, including all militia officers and a broad array of judicial positions. According to a February 1865 report, the governor claimed that each one of Georgia's 132 counties required a surveyor, coroner, tax receiver, sheriff, deputy sheriff, constable, superior court clerk, superior court deputy clerk, ordinary, and deputy ordinary, as well as two inferior court deputy clerks and five justices of inferior court. Additionally, the state required slightly more than ten justices of the peace per county (1,350 total), the same number of tax collectors per county, and about twenty militia officers per county (2,751). Altogether, Georgia exempted 8,229 state officers from service in the ranks of the Confederate army. Only North Carolina (5,589) came close to approaching this total, with Virginia (1,894), South Carolina (307), and Alabama (1,333) reaching only a fraction of Georgia's sum.[40]

Enrolling officers could run afoul not only of states but also of state-sponsored businesses. In North Carolina, conscription agents struggled with men who worked in the niter and saltpeter industry. Generally, these companies' contracts with the government specified that their employees were exempt from conscription. Conscription officers, however, often felt that these employers hired some men just to shield them from conscription. Therefore, on many occasions, they arrested employees, only to have the employer use their government connections to have the men released. To clarify things, General Order 32 stipulated that the army could not "remove or interfere with workmen or employees" working under government contracts. Consequently, when conscript officers seized two men working on saltpeter works, the Confederate Nitre and Mining Bureau reminded them that they committed "a great error" in "interfering . . . with a vital interest of the government." In October 1864, Josiah Gorgas, the Confederacy's chief of ordnance, called for a greater emphasis on the exemption of skilled workmen to put into his bureau. He reminded the War Department that these men were not "disaffected or unpatriotic." The government had simply decided that they better served the Confederacy in their machine shops than in the army. Therefore, enrolling officers needed to let them work unmolested.[41]

As he did in individual cases, Captain Pearson in North Carolina judged details and exemptions in war-related industries based on the company's Confederate loyalty. For instance, he approved a series of details to a factory with a government contract specifically because it worked with the conscription department. Despite "strong inducements," the factory had never taken in a man "for the purpose of screening him from the service." In fact, he contended that it had "been rigid in refusing to take in hands" solely seeking a detail. Most conscription officers would have considered this factory to be an anomaly. More commonly, they made complaints such as "The number of employees between 18 & 45 . . . excessive." Based on their assessment of the North Carolina Railroad Shops, enrolling officers desired that its president sharply decrease that number and make "constant efforts . . . to substitute with persons not liable to duty in the armies."[42]

Unexpectedly, conscription officers sometimes even viewed the Confederate army as interfering in the enrolling process. Most often, this dispute stemmed from army officers trying to recruit men for their depleted units outside the official conscription process. After July 1862, men of conscription age lost the privilege of volunteering, but this stipulation did not prevent North Carolina regiments from recruiting across the state. In January 1864, a captain in Moore County, in complaining to Colonel Mallett that a unit had accepted a volunteer, insisted, "The interference of officers of the army with the conscription service produces great confusion & should not be tolerated." Mallett assuredly sympathized, for his own 1863 correspondence reveals constant fights with Partisan Ranger units over men and constant requests from North Carolina units demanding that conscripts be sent to them. In Louisiana, an enrolling officer maintained, "I alone had a right to conscript enrolled men in Morehouse Parish," yet when he arrived there, he discovered that three other officers had already taken some men and driven others into the woods.[43]

When enrolling officers overcame all of these obstacles and succeeded in finding eligible men, they still faced one more hurdle before they could put the men into the Confederate army: the men needed to be healthy enough to march and fight. From the start, conscription officers feared that local physicians would prove too sympathetic to their neighbors. For instance, during his state's March 1862 draft, Virginia's governor complained that allowing family physicians to perform medical examinations had produced a "startling" number of medical exemptions. In some cases, reports to the governor indicated that doctors had not even met with the prospective soldiers they supposedly examined. In Mississippi, an officer claimed that the medical board in Brookhaven discharged more than 70 percent of the men conscripted there as unfit for duty. Across the border in Louisiana, an enrolling officer sought to stop a doctor who was "constantly engaged in endeavors to exempt men from the service."[44]

In North Carolina, concerns like these led Mallett, in the summer of 1862, to enforce an army directive asserting that men could be exempted only at the camp of instruction. Thus, he insisted that men claiming medical exemption had to travel to his camp to prove their illness. Not surprisingly, he found himself repeatedly granting permission for them to remain at home until their health improved enough for them to travel to the camp. Alarmed that many men received improper medical certificates, whether at home or in a camp, the army declared that these exemptions did not relieve a man for the entire war. Instead, the army could recall medically unfit men for reexamination whenever they deemed it necessary.[45]

People recognized the inefficiency and absurdity in requiring unhealthy men to travel to the army—potentially several times—to prove that they were too sick to fight. A Georgian pointed out that the policy directly contradicted conscription's goal of balancing battlefront and home front. Not only did the army have to spend money to bring men to camp and house and feed them, but from the time these men left home until they returned, the Confederacy "los[t] the products of their farms and soldiers service also." Recognizing the "lose-lose" nature of that plan, by the end of 1862 the army set up regulations for a three-member medical board in each congressional district. To avoid localism, the board would include an army physician, a doctor from within the district, and a doctor from outside the district. With the Confederacy chronically short of the physicians, this new policy worked better on paper than in reality. By 1864, an enrolling officer complained to Mallett that it was "impossible to properly [execute] the conscript law without the presence of a medical officer." He had "been without a surgeon two thirds of the time." Consequently, many men are "lost to the government service for the want of a physician to examine them."[46]

Medical boards and enrolling officers had to decide on the veracity of claims of poor health. In Virginia, Dr. Harvey Black was "besieged all day by applicants . . . some entitled and a good many are not." In North Carolina, Eli Sinberry suffered from a "chronic affliction of the stomach and liver," Zebulon Pearce possessed "a feeble constitution," and John Cassady had "very little use of his left hand, and is also diseased." Reilly Johnson, a forty-six-year-old farmer, was "a weakly man" who was "totally blind in one eye." While "a very loyal man," he was "not the least calculated to make an efficient soldier." Frederick Nims described his forty-seven-year-old brother Horice, whom he had taken care of for the previous fourteen years, as suffering from repeated spells of sickness, including typhoid fever. In Frederick's assessment, Horice's health was "greatly delicate and his constitution frail." He added, "I think him consumptive" and "I consider him entirely unfitted for the service." Three men in Alabama, not wanting to risk entering the service, created their own disability by shooting off one or two of their fingers. Willis Crawford hoped his dyspepsia would exempt him, but a board of investigation decided that "he will make a good soldier and camp life will no doubt cure him."[47]

As in Willis Crawford's case, the army did not simply rubber stamp medical exemptions. Instead, enrollment officers possessed a healthy skepticism regarding the self-proclaimed unhealthy. A soldier interviewing these applicants found it "no pleasant work . . . to listen to their *ten thousand 'Ailments.'*" In his diary, a Louisiana officer recollected with amusement the reactions of conscripts as army physicians pronounced "the dreaded words 'fit for duty.'" He contrasts the despair of this event with the happy scene when "the man has simply been told, that nothing is left him but to go home and die in peace! But he is not in the army—and therefore he is happy." Similarly, a Virginia woman described a conscript "rejoicing" at being pronounced too "mentally inept" to be a soldier. His real malady, according to her, was that he was "constitutionally a coward." Charles C. Jones, a Georgia officer, sarcastically commented that taking conscripts' medical complaints at face value would lead one to believe that "you never saw such a collection of sick men in your life." In Jones's summation, each man the board examined possessed "some woeful disorder," which he expected to gain him exemption, yet "these selfsame fellows find ample strength to loaf from year to year and attend to their own interests at home."[48]

The Confederate army's 1864 *Manual of Military Surgery* recognized the propensity for soldiers to fake illnesses or injuries. It added a final section entitled "Malingering" to "offer . . . a few suggestions regarding the frauds daily practiced upon medical officers by impostors who feign illness . . . to escape military duty." This work, addressing both current soldiers and conscripts, advises surgeons to flush out false claims of pain, rheumatism, deafness, and impaired vision. In all cases, it directs surgeons to be sentinels looking out for symptoms that do not correspond to the diseases that patients claim. The manual suggests an array of ploys to discover feigned diseases, such as offering uncomfortable remedies to those in pain, making sudden loud noises near a "deaf" man, tickling a man who claims paralysis of the arm, threatening to put alcohol or turpentine in the eye of a man claiming epilepsy, and applying chloroform gas to make a "dumb" man speak. The section concludes that surgeons must be prepared to use "all the means, both morally and medically, which their ingenuity would suggest, to detect and punish the malingerer."[49]

Paradoxically, while worrying about malingerers dodging service, the *Manual of Military Surgery* simultaneously underscored the opposite concern: that the conscript net ensnared too many ill men. The manual indicted conscription as creating an army comprised not of physically fit specimens but instead of all but the most ill. It feared the conscript act brought men into the army only to put them right into the hospital, thereby costing the home front a farmer or mechanic and adding to the army's responsibilities, but not increasing its fighting force. A Louisiana soldier, commenting on the conscription of a man "diseased throughout his entire system," asked the rhetorical question, "Won't he make a good soldier?" Kate Cumming, a Confederate nurse, recounted meeting a mother whose son, despite suffering from a cancer that had "eaten out" one of his eyes, had been conscripted. This story did not surprise Cumming, for she had "known conscript officers to take men from their homes whom the surgeons had discharged many times," only to have "them die in our hospital before reaching the army."[50]

The August 1864 records of the Examining Board in North Carolina's Seventh Congressional District supports the contention that the army took too many unhealthy men. Fifty-three men appeared before the medical board that month. Of those, thirty-six did not receive an exemption, eight received either a full or temporary exemption, and nine results were unclear. Those failing to secure exemption included men with "functional heart disease," epilepsy, rheumatism, deafness ("not excessive"), kidney problems, and chronic pneumonia. A man diagnosed with "mental derangement" received only a thirty-day exemption, as did one with "chronic and debilitating diarrhea." Full exemptions were reserved for three men with phthisis pulmonalis (also known as consumption and now called tuberculosis) and others with chronic bronchitis, heart disease, and prostate disease.[51]

Judging whether a man met all of the age, occupation, and health criteria for conscription assumed that the man had presented himself at camp when called out. When men did not turn out, conscription officers headed out to locate them. From Camp Holmes, Mallett sent out squads to find recusant conscripts, but he worried about the effect it might have on the community. As he advised a fellow officer, "It is my desire that the men be brought into camp without the use of force if possible." Nevertheless, Mallett recognized that that not all men would respond to such a call. In that case, "If they persist in opposition to the execution of the law, force will be applied." In order to keep peace with the community and to avoid trampling on the sensitivities of civil authorities, he instructed his officers that they had the authority to arrest only recusant conscripts and deserters, but not anyone who aided and abetted their hiding.[52]

The plans to find recusant conscripts often read like military operations in enemy territory. In November 1862, conscript hunters headed toward Wilkes County, North Carolina, a notorious haven for deserters and draft dodgers. On the first of the month, Mallett wrote to Lieutenant Thomas Robards that he was sending him two weeks' rations for the clandestine operation. He stressed that Robards must keep his precise route "perfectly secret" and reminded him to "be ready to march at any time." Two days later, Mallett added more instructions: "On Thursday morning you will commence operations." Planning the offensive, he ordered Robards "to drive the whole country" and "arrest all men between 18 and 35 who have not satisfactory papers." After entering Chatham County, Robards should "incline toward the left, so as to form a junction with [me] on Friday or Saturday." Fearing armed opposition, Mallett counseled, "Do not send off squads of less than ten men." And, in an effort to win the hearts and minds of civilians, he told Robards to "instruct your men to be kind to every one." This final statement contradicts the tone of the rest of the order but exemplifies the difficulties in enforcing conscription.[53]

In June 1864, writing from Montgomery County, Captain Haughton also viewed his job as more of a military operation than a simple enrollment. Haughton begged for help, and his plea demonstrated the odds against enrolling officers in the battle to capture conscripts. The conscripts he had called out had not appeared. He had requested the aid of the home guard, but he did not expect to receive any help from these local, nonprofessional soldiers. Ten days later, his expectations were confirmed, as the guard had not captured any conscripts, leaving Haughton to conclude that they were "afraid to hunt them up!" Thus, without more men, he felt conscription would be "a dead letter" in Montgomery. The harried Haughton continued, "It is utterly useless to try to enforce the law here without some force . . . I am greatly in need of ammunition." His frustration was understandable. He estimated that approximately two hundred deserters and conscripts were lying in the woods. In contrast, he had only eighteen men and only about one round of ammunition per man. Haughton hoped that a "good active force" would not only round up conscripts but have "a beneficial effect upon the loyalty of the citizens," which he found "not of the most exalted character."[54]

Haughton celebrated the Fourth of July with the seizure of two conscripts. His joy, however, was tempered, as he heard rumors that his life had been threated. Consequently, he was "getting a little nervous." Based on incidents elsewhere in North Carolina, Haughton's anxiety might have been warranted. A year earlier, the three Dial brothers sent an ominous letter to a man who was presumably enforcing conscription. It included a drawing of a pistol in the upper left corner and threatened, "If yo ever hunt for us a gin I will put lead in yo god dam your hell fired soll." Two months later, a report on conscription in western North Carolina indicated that in Randolph County, which bordered Haughton's Montgomery headquarters, three hundred to four hundred men, "having just put to death yet another of our enrolling officers," would continue to fight conscription.[55]

Possibly in an effort to come to a compromise with the community and to save his life, Haughton suggested detailing some older conscripts for agricultural duty. Feeling besieged, the captain's panic grew daily as he continued to hear reports that an attack on his outnumbered force was imminent. A week later, he sent five conscripts to the camp of instruction, along with a plan to catch fifty more men and "reinforce Genl Lee with these rascals." All he needed was one hundred troops. On July 14, he followed up, requesting "*as soon as possible . . .* men who know how to obey an order and fight." If he did not get this force, he would evacuate Montgomery, where "two thirds of the county are Lincoln men." Fighting for his life, Haughton probably did not recognize his faulty logic. The captain's math did not add up. In pledging to catch fifty conscripts with one hundred men, his proposal would take one hundred quality soldiers from the army and replace them with fifty potentially unwilling conscripts.[56]

While Haughton might not have recognized that every soldier serving in the conscription bureau drained a man from the front lines, others in the army, and civilians, were well aware that each soldier enforcing conscription could serve as an argument against the policy itself. In their eyes, conscription officers serving on the home front dodged the very draft they were tasked with enforcing. One critic described them as "poppinjays" [*sic*] who "delight in harassing and putting to expense everybody," and another grumbled that "their main business was to keep from going to the front themselves." Confronted by an enrolling officer, a Louisiana soldier on parole lambasted men who refused to see combat but who instead find a "higher sphere . . . [to] see that others do not remain at home." Assessing conscription efforts in Georgia, Alabama, and Mississippi as "almost worthless," an officer speculated that sending all men engaged in conscription to the front lines would be more productive than having conscription continue in these states.[57]

County statistics from North Carolina provide support for this contention. There is not much county-level data in the state's conscription records, but there are some records for six counties in central North Carolina for the summer of 1864. At this point, there should not have been many prospective conscripts still home. With the last revision of the law five months earlier, officers should have already enrolled all eligible men. In April, the head of the Bureau of Conscription had moaned that "fresh material for the armies" no longer existed. The county statistics bear this out. In July 1864, the six counties produced only fifty-two conscripts, seventy-three light-duty men, and five volunteers. In contrast, they had 811 men exempt for physical disabilities and 598 state employees. In terms of detailed occupations, their lists included more shoemakers (117), blacksmiths (130), and millers (130) than conscripts. While verifying illnesses and occupations kept enrolling officers busy, one could easily conclude that, by 1864, enlisting all men connected to army enrollment would have a greater numerical impact than having them repeatedly try to harvest the same picked-over field.[58]

The conscription bureau tried to rectify this problem by having men unfit for the front lines enforce conscription, and by keeping the units as lean as possible. That policy would have worked if enrolling officers simply signed men up, but clearly their tasks were much more complicated and arduous than that. The longest letter in Mallett's letterbook details the many responsibilities that commandants of conscription camps faced. Captain Lucius Johnson wrote the letter detailing the "deplorable condition" in which he found the camp after temporarily taking over command from Mallett. Johnson did not blame his predecessor. The Confederate army had ordered Mallett and most of his soldiers away from the camp to participate in an operation designed to stop a Union advance at the Battle of Kinston on December 14, 1862.

According to Johnson, Mallett's departure occurred at a particularly vulnerable time for the camp. It served to confirm rumors that the Confederacy was planning to shut down the camp and "the conscription business in N.C. was at an end." Johnson found the number of troops under his command to be completely inadequate to enforce the policy. In describing the situation, the irritable captain reminded his superiors in Richmond of soldiers' multitude of duties in the conscription bureau. They did not merely enroll men into the army, which, given the complexities of finding men and determining the validity of exemption claims, was a full-time job. They also had to "guard safely the camp property, deserters, conscripts in camp, negroes—men, women, and little children—sent to camp to be taken care of, political prisoners sent by state authority, prisoners of war and traitors caught in arms against the Confederate States." Also, as Mallett had just experienced, they could be ordered into battle when needed.[59]

Adding to challenges such as those Captain Johnson described, the army sent its best soldiers to the front lines, not to enrolling offices. In December 1862, Senator James Phelan told President Davis that he considered conscription "a farce," and he based his assessment partially on the "young men . . . whom nobody fears, for whom nobody cares" serving as enrolling officers. Confederate leaders did not listen to these concerns, and instead, as a matter of policy, usually sent men unfit for field duty to serve in these posts. In 1864, the head of conscription complained that his seventy best officers had been reassigned to the field. In their place, the army assigned men to serve in the conscription service, "in consequence of disability from wounds." Later, the war department ordered another soldier to conscript duty with the notation, "belongs to Invalid Corps." In recounting the escape of fourteen deserters from his camp of instruction, Colonel Mallett maintained, "It is not a matter of surprise . . . when they know their guard is composed of men who cannot 'double quick' fifty (50) yards or offer much resistance."[60]

Conscription officers and their small, unfit staffs also often had tempestuous relationships with the Bureau of Conscription in Richmond. On one hand, local enrolling offices complained that they did not always receive prompt directives when policies changed. In October 1862, after Congress significantly revised the exemption law, officers waited for instructions from Richmond. This revision exempted physicians, but two weeks after its passage, Mallett still had not received any information on how to implement this clause. On the final day of the month, he pleaded with General Cooper for "instructions at the earliest convenience" for "I am daily receiving inquiries as to the constructions of the new law." At other times, Mallett informed Richmond of a multitude of complications: that he did not have enough soldiers to enforce the law, that he had conscripts in his camp but no transportation to send them to the front, and that unclear orders made it impossible to know to which units he was to send the conscripts.[61]

On the other hand, conscription officials in Richmond felt the enrolling officers did not always put the army's needs at the forefront. Allegations abounded that bribes could secure an exemption and that some enrolling officers extorted money by threatening to conscript men legitimately at home. In Georgia, a board of inquiry investigated charges that an enrolling officer sold exemptions for $1,000 apiece. In a February 1864 circular, the bureau called for a reevaluation of everyone's exemption papers to see if they represented genuine exemptions. The next month a South Carolina officer informed his mother that the War Department planned to rotate enrolling officers as "Errors, Fraud, and abuses are known to exist & they mean to make a clean sweep of us all—the innocent suffering with the guilty." General Preston hoped that having a new set of eyes audit the exemptions would lead to the revocation of fraudulent and erroneous ones. In doing so, the plan remained the same: "that every man should be in the field . . . who ought to be there."[62]

Given all the stress they faced, it is not surprising that conscription officers occasionally cracked under the pressure. In June 1864, one enrolling officer complained to Captain Pearson, "I am completely overwhelmed in the flood of petitions. Every man in the county [Wadesboro] has put in some plea to remain at home." Pearson shared this frustration. During the spring of 1864, he started to dismiss applications without any investigation. When he simply wrote "disapproved" on an application, however, his superior, Captain Jones, rebuked him, writing that such an endorsement was "improper and should not be repeated," for applicants had the right to appeal. Even if Pearson found their petitions of "little merit," he was required to forward them "with a full and impartial report."

A month later, Jones wrote to Pearson, addressing that reprimand and Pearson's response. In this letter, his tone softened. He emphasized that he was not filing a complaint but just impressing upon Pearson "the importance of removing, so far as in your power, every cause for such complaint." Jones provided Pearson with some straightforward advice: "Let vigilance, promptness, and courtesy characterize your course, and the Comdt. has no fears of the result." Jones's succinct instructions, however, provided no guidance about how one could practice "vigilance," when constantly understaffed; "promptness," when everyone, including prospective conscripts, state officials, and even Confederate officials, seemingly did their best to delay the process; or "courtesy," when the job involved seizing men from their homes.[63]

On December 9, 1863, enrolling officers in Louisiana received General Order 1, which revealed that the western theater shared the same elusive goals in enforcing conscription. The order encouraged officers to "visit every portion of the parish . . . to promote a general understanding with the citizens" and admonished them that "it is not intended to unnecessarily harass those who are clearly unfit for service." At the same time that these officers were to treat citizens with kid gloves, however, they also were reminded that "no one need expect to escape service who should be in the field" and that they could apply to headquarters for cavalry reinforcements "to arrest those conscripts who persist in evading military service."[64] In other words, like Captain Jones in North Carolina, superiors in Louisiana hoped that conscript officers there could accomplish the nearly impossible task of rounding up 100 percent of the eligible soldiers in their district while not touching a hair on the head of a single ineligible man or angering the community.

Similarly, in April 1864, C. D. Melton, the commandant in charge of conscription in South Carolina, issued circular no. 6. Two years after President Davis had called for a plain and simple method, it exemplifies both the continued unfeasibility of his plan and the complexities that enrolling officers faced. Intended to explain how to enforce conscription policies, this directive is neither plain nor simple: it comprises nineteen pages and includes more than 7,000 words divided into sixty-one sections. The circular instructed officers to grant exemptions "only after careful and thorough inquiry," basing their decisions on "information solicited of persons not connected with the application."

Ostensibly, the officers simply applied a straightforward law, but the circular recognized a great deal of nuance. They should "inquire into the past conduct of the individual in reference to the public interest," allowing unselfish men to remain at home while conscripting speculators. Also, these soldiers needed to remember that some men had to stay home, for "the production of grain and provisions for the army is, moreover, equally as essential as the furnishing of men." The fifty-ninth section reminded them of the delicate nature of their work, which involved "the separation of husbands and fathers from their families, and of sons from their parents." Given that, they must "avoid all petulance and harshness, and . . . patiently and courteously listen to and investigate all such claims."[65]

As the circular indicates, enrolling officers did face a Herculean task. The Confederacy relied on conscript officers such as these men in South Carolina—Mallett, Pearson, and Jones—to maintain the precarious balance between battlefront and home front. Jones instructed Captain Little that it was both "necessary to keep an army in the field for the maintenance of our rights and the achievement of our independence" and "equally necessary that the army should be supported" at home. While they served on the home front, these enrolling officers found themselves on the front lines of this effort to balance military and civilian needs.

Unfortunately, despite the many directives urging conscript officers to treat southerners gently, this mission still led to scenes such as "the heart-rendering sight of men torn away from their families by the strong arm of the law; heads of families, surrounded by weeping women and children, are forced into the army." Confederate officials recognized that "harsh treatment to conscripts" could "prejudice the cause of the Confederate States, by encouraging opposition to the acts of conscription." They needed conscription officers to bring men into the army, not to turn southerners away from the Confederacy. In order to do so, they would continually seek to improve the process throughout the entire war to try to achieve the chimerical goal of putting all the appropriate men into army while ensuring that all on the home front remained Confederates.[66]

CHAPTER 5

# Confederate Conscription Policy in 1863

When President Davis spoke to the Mississippi legislature in December 1862, he pledged to call for changes in conscription. When Congress reconvened a month later, Davis made good on this promise. Overall, he praised the measure, declaring, "The wisdom and efficacy of these acts have been approved by results." Nevertheless, Davis encouraged Congress to revise the exemption law, since he had heard "serious complaints" from "eminent and patriotic citizens whose opinions merit great consideration." His charge to the body, however, made apparent the near impossibility of such a task. Davis presented the supposedly simple request: "that some means will be devised for leaving at home a sufficient local police without making discriminations, always to be deprecated, between different classes of citizens." He offered no suggestions as to how this goal could be met and ignored the unlikelihood of devising a policy fair to all southerners. By definition, allowing some men to remain at home while the army conscripted others involved discrimination, or at the least the appearance of discrimination.[1]

Possibly because of the difficulty of this instruction, the president did not suggest, nor did Congress pass, any major alterations to conscription. According to one representative, "the people had got accustomed" to the current law, so changing it would only disrupt the balance in place.[2] Also, since exemptions did not discharge men, adding more occupations to the list would not have much impact. For instance, even if Congress passed an exemption for dentists or for farmers with six or more dependents, such a change would not affect dentists or farmers between eighteen and forty already in the ranks.

In amending the measure, legislators focused on the Twenty Negro Law—the provision that had engendered the most complaints. Lawmakers tightened up this exemption by stipulating that it now applied only to plantations owned by a minor, someone of unsound mind, a *femme sole* (a woman living by herself on a plantation), or a soldier in the field. These owners would have to pay a $500 annual fee for this privilege, and they had to sign an affidavit indicating that they could not obtain the services of anyone ineligible for armed service.

Congress made two additional efforts to decrease class animus by simultaneously making it harder for rich men and easier for poor men to stay home. The new overseer law specified that only men who had served as overseers prior to April 1862 could receive an exemption, and that the president could now detail men in areas "deprived of white or slave labor indispensable to the production of grain or provisions necessary for the support of the population remaining at home."[3]

In an effort to increase the efficiency of conscription, the government also made bureaucratic changes. On December 30, 1862, Secretary of War James Seddon transferred control of the policy from the adjutant and inspector general to its own bureau. He appointed General Gabriel J. Rains to lead the new Bureau of Conscription. Rains had gained a formidable reputation for his development of land mines and his performance at the Battle of Seven Pines in the Peninsula Campaign, where he was wounded. Seddon assigned lieutenant colonels A. C. Jones and George Lay to assist Rains. This bureau would be in charge of processing all future recruits. Ideally, this arrangement would help make conscription more uniform across the Confederacy, clarify contradictory regulations, and improve the response time on requests for exemptions and on puzzling cases.[4]

The government did not make any radical changes to conscription because by 1863 almost all Confederates accepted it. Regardless of whether they had celebrated its passage, begrudgingly acceded to it, or protested it as unconstitutional, they now viewed it as necessary and saw no alternative path to victory. Historians, particularly Gary Gallagher, have argued that as the war continued, Confederate nationalism changed its emphasis from an abstract ideology to a concrete connection to the armies in the field, especially to Lee's Army of Northern Virginia. With the army forming the nucleus of nationalism, Confederates wanted to see it strengthened rather than weakened. Consequently, the debate over conscription evolved. In 1862, the emphasis was often on whether the law violated individual or states' rights or created a military despotism. Now, legislators sought to improve it, and southerners wanted everyone to do their share to achieve victory. An April 1863 report indicates that conscription was progressing toward that goal, as it listed 498,169 soldiers in the Confederate army—the highest figure for the entire war.[5]

In 1863, Confederates focused on how to make the measure more equitable and how to bring more soldiers into the ranks while simultaneously taking care of the home front. Southerners carefully studied military-age men at home, looking for any evidence of a lack of commitment to the cause. In particular, they hunted for speculators who took advantage of soldiers' families and warily eyed antebellum secessionists whose shameful efforts to avoid the army belied their prewar bellicosity. Alleging that the civilian bureau allowed too many men to remain home, the army tried to seize control of conscription in 1863. It fought a battle with the Bureau of Conscription over whether a purely military conscription could improve results.

In the fall congressional elections, candidates echoed the need for an improved policy. They did not champion a repeal of conscription but instead competed to demonstrate that they favored the most equitable plan. Challengers denounced incumbents for allowing too many exemptions, with the Twenty Negro Law serving as the most glaring example. Though muted, opposition to conscription did not completely disappear. The most vocal and ardent foe of conscription, Richmond Pearson, sat on the North Carolina Supreme Court. While Pearson's isolated voice failed to garner much support across the South, he proved a thorn in the Richmond government's side, reminding his countrymen that the act, regardless of its necessity, violated individual liberty and states' rights.

As the year opened, Mississippi soldier John Lewis made the succinct assessment, "I think if all the men in the Confederacy were in the army, there is no doubt as to the result [of the war]." A North Carolinian concurred, informing his governor that soldiers wanted the conscript act "rigidly executed and enforced." While these men counted only soldiers on the battlefront, most southerners recognized that his ostensibly straightforward solution completely overlooked the other side of the coin—the home front. As if responding to Lewis, the *Macon Daily Telegraph* proposed that "for each man in the ranks one was needed at home." Otherwise, within a month, soldiers would be "a shoeless and unclad rabble" with "nothing to eat." J. F. Morton pointed out that "common sense" dictated that his community would not survive another year "if we are all to . . . go into the army." Away from the front lines and from the political battles of Richmond, the debate over conscription continued to involve potentially competing loyalties to family, community, and nation. According to Morton, "Men feel it to be their first duty to take care of their families, the country next," but others continued to disagree on his ranking of priorities or disputed the best method to safeguard their families. They believed that only military victory shielded their families from abolitionist Yankee invaders.[6]

Two years into the war, the tension among these fidelities intensified as strains on both the army and the home front increased. The army needed to replace casualties after it suffered costly defeats at Gettysburg and Vicksburg. Plus, the opposing Union army grew as it began enforcing its own draft in 1863. In response, Confederate conscription expanded its reach. In October 1862, Congress had authorized President Davis to conscript men up to forty-five years old, but he had only called out men up to forty. In the summer of 1863, Davis increased the upper limit to forty-five.

Meanwhile, wartime devastation, inflation, and food shortages stalked the South. Confederates' attitudes toward conscription, exempts, draft dodgers, and principals depended upon a combination of practical issues and ideology. Some southerners condemned all men at home. More likely, however, people judged their neighbors on their behavior. Were these men home legitimately or illegitimately? Did they serve or exploit their communities? Were other families suffering while these nonconscripts enjoyed a life of ease?

Confederates increasingly hurled the epithet "speculators" at draft-age men who remained at home but undermined rather than supported the cause. While most likely rich, speculators raised animus not solely for their wealth but also because they took advantage of soldiers' families, charging them more for goods than they could afford. A Georgia soldier defined speculators as "the vile product of these times that try men's souls" who "monopolize everything and resell at enormous profit." On one hand, a sharp rise in prices simply aligned with inflation. On the other hand, soldiers' families felt a disproportionate brunt of these increases because soldiers' pay had not risen with inflation, instead remaining at a paltry $11 per month. Additionally, Confederates felt that speculating stay-at-homes had broken a promise—they had exchanged service in the army for service to their community. For some men, this agreement was implicit, but the October 1862 conscription law had made it explicit for others. The act prohibited many exempt men from selling their goods for more than the cost of production plus 75 percent.[7]

The presence of selfish rich men at home extorting their families infuriated soldiers. A letter in the Atlanta *Southern Confederacy* decried "the ill treatment of his family by the very men who are . . . exempt from duty." A poem in the *Montgomery Weekly Advertiser* entitled "A Soldier's Reflections," drew a sharp distinction between men who helped their neighbors and speculators who abused them. The author pointed out that some exempts had done their duty. However, he chastised those who demand "the last dollar for a scrap of meat, pound or two of flour or a few ounces of sugar." By heaping vituperation on these "stay at home vampires" who exploited soldiers' families, this Alabama soldier judged men on their behavior rather than simply on their class. In a satirical "military catechism" in the *Southern Literary Messenger,* the southern people's supposed first duty was "to keep out of the army," while their second was "to make all the money they can out of the Government and the soldiers."[8]

Many Confederates did not find the joke amusing. To them, these "stay at home vampires" doubly weakened the Confederacy. Their unwillingness to enlist or accept conscription hurt the army, and their disloyal conduct weakened morale, especially when soldiers' families suffered as a result of their avarice. In a letter to the president, a Mississippian complained of these "engines of oppression." In his opinion, "If speculation and extortion are not put down speedily . . . our country will be completely ruined." A North Carolinian sent his governor a list of men at home improperly, including a supposed mechanic who was "no mechanic . . . but purely a speculator" and an overseer who did not manage slaves but only "attends to speculating." Elsewhere, a Louisiana officer denounced the "army of speculators now infesting society." More ominously for the Confederacy, a South Carolina enrolling officer claimed that a group of men in the mountains resisted conscription because they considered the Confederacy doomed to defeat due to "speculations and extortions." He grimly added that their "argument is unfortunately too true."[9]

Confederates criticized those who abused the exemption system by either pretending to engage in exempt occupations or bribing enrolling officers. "Astonished at the way people are acting in trying to keep out of the servis of their country," Private John Harris complained about these dishonest men. He cited examples of rich men who had employed poor men to supervise their slaves prior to the war but now considered themselves to be the "best of overseers" and of men who had never touched an awl who professed to be shoemakers. A Mississippi congressman feared that in creating a list of exempt occupations, the Confederate government had inadvertently "exempted a set of extortioners," singling out millers who received exemptions to grind corn but who instead "grind the faces of the poor." A Richmond bureaucrat grumbled that the conscript bureau was "granting a fearful number of exemptions daily"—some obtained "for a price"—and predicted that an end to all exemptions would add 200,000 men to the army.[10]

These moans about improper exemptions resonated across the Confederacy. Claiming to know men "pretending to carry on Government shops" and others "pretending to make salt petre," a North Carolinian ranted that "there is a Screw loose in the government Waggon some where." A Texan complained about preachers without flocks, suggesting that if they needed a congregation of sinners, they could easily find one by enlisting. General D. H. Hill called out "cowardly" men, proclaiming that "when our independence is won, the most trifling soldier in the ranks, will be more respected . . . than an army of these skulking exempts." Tennessee officers maintained that "the whole system of exemption is based upon a false assumption"—that the home front should not suffer during the war. Consequently, "all those vocations are crowded which afford exemptions, while the ranks of the Army are daily becoming thinner." A North Carolinian stationed in Richmond believed that "only one class ought to stay at home viz. those necessary to make bread & clothing material & materials of war," but regrettably he found military-age speculators, gamblers, and liquor sellers living in the capital.[11]

Generally, men did not brag about extorting the last penny from their neighbors or admit that they schemed for an exemption. Some men, however, did admit factoring future profits into their decision to purchase a substitute. In trying to amass $1,000 to $1,500 to pay a replacement, D. W. Hood predicted that "if I was out of the war I could myty soon make the money back," without explaining how he planned to quickly earn the funds. Similarly, G. W. Poindexter, serving in Virginia, offered the following advice with regard to a relative considering a substitute: "Let it cost what it will for [he] can make it back in a short time." In North Carolina, a man working in a machine shop informed his parents, "I have been compelled to adopt the trade of a mechanic to avoid the conscript law & consider my mechanical proclivities the greatest blessing God has conferred on me." Seeking an exempt position in the magistrate's office, a Georgian urged his friend "to maneuver to get me in that position as it will exempt me from conscription." Another man confessed that he sought "as soft a place as possible," so he might have been disappointed to find out that a Virginian discovered "getting an easy berth is ten times harder than I had any conception of."[12]

Confederates logically assumed that ardent secessionists would be among the most willing to sacrifice for independence. Consequently, antebellum fire-eaters who tried to avoid service comprised another category that incensed southerners. These secessionists had bellicosely championed war, but apparently not a war in which they would fight. George Guess ranted about a man who "would have eaten his way to Old Abe through an army of Yankees" but turned out to be "all talk and pushing off others to the war." Home on a furlough, William King complained about men who felt "too patriotic to go to war" but nevertheless had the audacity to make sure that he did not overstay his authorized leave. William Speer decried secessionists who, "when danger stares them in the face, back down from what they did & said, [they] are not fit to be called cowards." Theophilus Holmes concurred. He reminded his wife, who had chastised him for condemning all men who did not serve in the army, that he did not denounce everyone at home. Instead, Holmes directed his wrath on "the rabid violent secessionist who . . . ought to have shouldered his gun at the beginning of the war."[13]

Confederates reserved some of their greatest contempt for stay-at-homes who doubly sinned: secessionist speculators. Holmes carped that these "ardent hypocrites" had "whipp[ed] the reluctant youths of the land off to War." Now they "ignobly speculated upon the necessities of the soldier and his family" while "skulk[ing] away from dangers themselves." He did not advocate a draft, but if it brought these skulkers into the army, he supported one. Gideon Lincecum found these men "far more damaging to our cause" than "Lincolnites." These "greatest encouragers of the war . . . have made shift to crawfish out." In the meantime, these "heartless speculators" were "bloodsuckers . . . amass[ing] to themselves immense wealth." Considering them worse than deserters, General D. H. Hill fumed against anyone who "breath[ed] nothing but threatening & slaughter before the war & now contents himself with military criticism in his parlor . . . or still worse in making fortunes upon the miseries of the country."[14]

While many judged men at home by their conduct, others resented all eligible men who did not serve in the army. Present from the onset of conscription, this sentiment increased as the war dragged on. Soldiers who had served for a year or more in harsh conditions with low pay understandably felt bitter toward men who slept comfortably in their own beds. Edwin Fay referred to them as "stay at home patriots" who seemingly had more rights than soldiers did. He worried about the South's future, since all children born during wartime would be offspring of these cowards who had refused to fight for their country. Alabama troops marching through Richmond "had a good deal of amusement" as they "jeered & taunted the men on the streets who ought to be in the Army" but instead "are dressed up & playing the dandy." Even though he acknowledged some men could better serve their country at home, Peter Alexander asked, "Are men worthy of liberty who will not themselves strike for it?" A week later, he answered his own question: "The man who is able, and yet unwilling to serve his country in the field, is unfit to serve it anywhere."[15]

Alexander and others hoped to enlist women, who had spurred enlistment in 1861, to now serve as conscript hunters. He wanted "heroic, self-sacrificing women" to apply "the last of their indignant scorn" to the "croakers and cowards" remaining at home. Considering women to be the South's "bravest defenders," John Lewis hoped that they would aid the army by "spurn[ing] from among them such men as are able to bear arms." This action would guarantee that "the enemy can never hold our territory."[16]

Mollie Wendel's conduct exemplified Lewis's and Alexander's desires. She objected to boyfriend Jeremiah Gage's plan to obtain a substitute. Serving in the Army of Northern Virginia, Gage's patriotism had "well nigh played out." But neither Mollie nor Jeremiah's sister Mary wanted him to buy his way out of the army. "I dislike for you to think of getting a substitute" declared Mollie. "I have always spoken in such contemptuous way of men who are able to fight themselves and getting another man to do it." Similarly, Mary Davis declared, "If I had a son in the army I would rather see him fall on the altar of his country than have him skulking from duty." She decried the "great quantity of young men that are now at home engaged in speculation and our poor country bleeding at every pore."[17]

While women like Mollie Wendel and Mary Davis wanted all men in the army, others wanted their relatives to return home. The correspondence between Will Neblett and his wife, Lizzie, reveals the continuing complications regarding the competing loyalties between country and family. Whereas Edwin Fay, Grant Taylor, and Abner Ford had all worked with their wives in the search for substitutes, this Texas family fought over the propriety of hiring one. Two of Lizzie's brothers (Garrett and Jim) volunteered in 1861, while both Will and Lizzie's third brother, John, stayed home. A thirty-six-year-old prosecession lawyer with four children under the age of ten, Will owned $12,500 in real estate, $14,500 in personal property, and eleven slaves. Along with his brother-in-law, John, Will enlisted in April 1863, and the family quickly divided over whether he should seek a substitute. Putting family duty ahead of country, Lizzie—pregnant with the couple's fifth child—and her brothers Jim and John Scott thought it an acceptable decision. By 1863, Jim had purchased a substitute, and John was seeking one. In contrast, Will, who put country and honor ahead of family, found paying a man to take one's place in the army shameful.[18]

Overwhelmed by the demands at home, Lizzie pleaded with Will to secure a substitute "even if it takes half we have." The cost did not to matter to her, for "what would the world full of money be to me if you were dead." Four months later, she suggested doubling this fictional proposal, now offering all they had to purchase a substitute. If necessary, they could then move to another country.

One week later, she repeated that he should give up everything "for God's sake" to come home to "the rescue of your family."

Will opposed this course. He disapproved of substitutes, considering them "almost entirely worthless." He also disagreed on the best means of protecting his family. In response to Lizzie's request, he defended his reluctance by appealing to the larger cause: "We should recollect who we are contending for—for our families and their safety & liberty." In his mind, "men of property" such as himself bore a greater responsibility, as it demoralized poor men in the ranks to see their wealthy neighbors return home when they could not. In short, the spouses agreed it was Will's duty to protect his family but disagreed on whether he could do that better on the front lines or at home.[19]

For Lizzie, Will's refusal to come home compared unfavorably to her brother John's course. While Will despised substitution, John Scott actively sought a man to take his place in the ranks. Having read John's letters to his wife, Susan, a frustrated Lizzie needled Will that not only did her brother endorse substitution but that he was much more "lover like in his letters than you are." In Lizzie's view, John's letters (and presumably his efforts to acquire a substitute) revealed a "fondness for his wife." In her opinion, neither Will's words nor his actions showed the same fondness. Will objected not only to substitution but also to this comparison. Having already explained that his service in the army demonstrated his love for his family, he now added that his inferior writing skills did not mean that he lacked the loving sentiment of his brother-in-law.[20]

John Scott's efforts revealed another facet of substitution in 1863—the skyrocketing price. In 1862, men generally paid $1,000 or less. The next year, the cost seemingly climbed faster than potential principals could raise the money. Two factors explain the increase. The first was the shrinking pool of substitutes, who had to be ineligible for conscription themselves. By summer, conscription embraced men up to forty-five years old, thereby eliminating men between thirty-six and forty-five as possible substitutes. With regulations also barring substitutes from other countries, the demand easily outstripped the supply of potential replacements.

The second issue was Confederate inflation. With Confederate currency rapidly declining in value, John Scott discovered that one potential substitute "won't talk about Confederate money," and another offered two prices: a lower one for livestock and an interest-bearing loan and a higher one for Confederate money. Supposedly, a broker offered to find Scott a substitute for $4,600, but that did not pan out. A week after that deal fizzled, Lizzie wrote to Will that a man had declined John's offer of $5,000 in favor of another soldier's offer of $6,000. Two days later, a man who had offered to go for $6,500 raised his price to $7,500. By November, Lizzie had heard that substitutes cost as much as $12,000.[21]

Other principals shared the experience of the Scotts and Nebletts. In Richmond, a government clerk tracked the rise in prices. In November 1862, he observed that the cost had already increased from $100 to $2,000. Eight months later, that price doubled, and by the following November he claimed it had reached $6,000. In Louisiana, Samuel Davis paid $3,000 in January and Gustave Favrot paid $3,800 in March. When the conscription age range expanded in July, a Georgian predicted that substitutes would cost $8,000 to $10,000. In October, Sarah Wadley's brother found a man willing to serve for in excess of $10,000, but an officer rejected him, asserting that the army would no longer take substitutes for men physically able to bear arms. Even Sarah, who despised substitution, found that response "ridiculous." Such a policy effectively made substitution a dead letter, since men medically unable to serve did not need substitutes. They could simply gain a medical exemption.[22]

Jim Scott, Lizzie's other brother, faced his own challenges regarding substitution, Confederate loyalty, and familial resentment. Jim wished to stay home, but his sister-in-law Susan Scott (John's wife) disrupted this transaction. Jim had provided a substitute, but it appeared that his replacement might face conscription himself. The substitute's age was unknown, but if he was eligible for conscription, Jim would lose his exemption. A friend suggested that Jim offer the man $1,000 to swear that he was over forty-five years old, and the substitute himself offered to do so for $100 in specie. Some combination of the absence of specie and the presence of integrity made Jim forego this route. Instead, he entered into negotiations with a new potential substitute named Dowdy. Angry that her husband, John, had failed in his own negotiations with Dowdy, Susan spitefully tried to get the would-be substitute to refuse Jim's deal. She offered to feed both Dowdy and his horse for a year if he rejected Jim's offer. Unsurprisingly, all of these machinations offended the antisubstitution Will Neblett. Even Lizzie agreed that the Scott brothers might have their eagerness to procure substitutes "thrown up to them" when the war ended.[23]

Like Will Neblett, other Confederates continued to find the entire process of substitution distasteful. General D. H. Hill branded principals as "poor dogs" who acted "as though money could pay the service every man owes his country." A Louisianan who considered himself one of the best shots in the army refused to consider hiring a replacement. He worried that "it would disgrace my own dear children for me to hire a substitute." He feared that "people would say 'there father hired a substitute; was afraid to see a yankee much less smell there powder.'" When she heard that her brother sought a substitute, Sarah Wadley was dumbfounded that he would pursue such an unpatriotic course. She confided in her diary that if he obtained one, "it would be the saddest sorrow I have ever known." She later referred to the idea of purchasing a substitute as "a stain." She refused to speak of his attempt "and cannot think of it without pain."[24]

If some Confederates disliked principals for seeking a substitute, they often disliked—or at least distrusted—substitutes even more. Confederates considered them mercenaries lacking in loyalty and more prone to run away than to fight. In a November 1862 report, Colonel John C. Shields, the commandant of conscripts in Virginia, complained that four-fifths of the 140 deserters from his camp were substitutes who had fled the army within twenty-four hours of their enlistment. A North Carolina soldier reported that an Irishman who had repeatedly hired himself out and then deserted was slated for execution. A Virginian complained that substitutes represented "the paupers and discarded of creation." The editor of his town's newspaper, in explaining why he believed a man's death was a suicide and not a murder, listed serving as a substitute alongside alcoholism and domestic difficulties as character flaws making suicide more likely.[25]

Another Virginia newspaper decried the entire process of substitution as "one vast fraud upon the Government and the country," and although they disagreed that the entire system was corrupt, Bureau of Conscription officials expressed their frustration that they could not control its flaws. Lieutenant Colonel George Lay presented a report on the process to the secretary of war. In it, testimony from a man cryptically described as "Secret Detective Greenwall" detailed substitution agents and army officers partnering in deceit. Not only did the bureau lack jurisdiction to punish these improprieties but also, an angry Lay explained, investigations ran up against principals protesting their innocence, lawyers working to keep men out of the army, and local officials and friends lying to abet their neighbors' shameful course. Even when caught, the parties often escaped punishment by pleading ignorance of substitution regulations. To solve these problems, Lay suggested only allowing substitution transactions at camps of instruction, so bureau officials could verify their legitimacy.[26]

In Virginia, an enrolling officer preserved the regulations coming from Lay's bureau, and they demonstrate the constant vigilance needed to discover abuses in the system. Orders instructed enrolling officers that substitutes could not enter Partisan Ranger companies, that units could only accept one substitute per month, and that, by May 1863, no one ranked lower than a general could authorize a substitution. In February 1863, the Bureau of Conscription alerted officers to the "large number of irregular and bogus substitute papers in circulation." Seven months later, the admonition was more specific. Warning that "the evil of fraudulent substitution" had deprived the army of many soldiers, it advised officers to be on the alert for papers bearing the signatures of officers killed in battle. In October, more letters arrived, listing specific regiments whose substitution papers should not be trusted. Ultimately, in effort to end fraud, the bureau directed enrolling officers to collect documentation from all principals and to forward these items to Richmond so the conscript office could authenticate each case individually. Because of this reexamination, the superintendent of conscription's year-end recap stated that his office was investigating as many as 15,000 substitution cases.[27]

A Mississippian attacked substitution as "a great evil in many cases." His use of *many* rather than *all* is important. My examination of substitution in Rockingham County, Virginia, emphasizes that categorizations of principals as evaders and cowards who should be considered alongside deserters and Unionists are flawed or at least overly simplistic. At its basic level, wealthier men paid poorer men to serve in their places, but the community did not reflexively judge these men as disloyal or selfish. If they provided a community service, principals' presence at home did not disqualify them from being considered loyal Confederates. Indeed, they could be farmers feeding the community, tradesmen helping soldiers' families, men whose religious scruples kept them out of the army, or men who had other exemptions but wished to contribute to the Confederate army. The postwar Southern Claims Commission, which judged petitions of southerners claiming loyalty to the United States government, contrasted principals with men who harbored deserters, hid in the woods to avoid conscription, or found other methods to truly evade service. The commission rejected the claims of anyone who had employed a substitute. In disallowing one petition, it equated principals with loyal Confederates, maintaining that "furnishing a substitute to the service was of precisely the same nature and character" as serving in the army.[28]

While southerners undoubtedly did not view principals and soldiers as providing "precisely the same" service to the Confederacy, the case of Fields Fox further demonstrates the flaw in automatic assumptions that men providing substitutes lacked fidelity to the Confederate cause. In March 1862, during North Carolina's state draft, Fox provided William Pike as a substitute. With the onset of Confederate conscription a month later, Pike remained in the army in

Fox's place. The Fox family had eight sons. Seven volunteered for the army before conscription began, while Fields remained home to farm and take care of the family's aged parents and his brothers' families. While Pike served as a "good and faithful soldier," Fox farmed 127 acres of bottomland, producing more than twenty barrels of flour per year, providing large quantities of pork to his community, raising cattle and sheep, and harvesting wheat and oats. Not only did he feed his extended family, but also a "great many soldier families . . . depended on him for food."

In 1864, Fox petitioned to remain on his farm, claiming he was "willing to do anything he can to aid his country in its struggle for liberty and independence." Endorsed by his neighbors, his request also received the approval of the county enrolling officer, who considered it "a meritorious case." While his actions were not precisely equivalent to serving in the army, Fields Fox (and the Fox family generally), despite engaging in substitution, demonstrated support for the war effort and fidelity to the Confederacy.[29]

In July 1863, regardless of the loyalty of individual principals such as Fox, rumors spread that the president planned to call Congress into a special session to repeal all substitution and exemption laws. Even while admitting that substitution "has done much harm and been prolific of crime," however, President Davis declined to call Congress back to Richmond and instead urged that the current regulations be more strictly enforced. He maintained that the new bureau had already begun this process by diligently applying rules limiting who could serve as substitutes and reducing abuses. This improved administration negated the need for Congress to intervene immediately.[30]

Davis did feel pressure to reinforce the army after Confederate losses at Gettysburg and Vicksburg, but he did so by raising the upper age for conscription to forty-five. The October 1862 conscription law had provided authorization for this expansion, but at that time, Davis had chosen only to conscript men up to age forty. Now, to "drive back the invaders," Davis requested all men between eighteen and forty-five, unless otherwise exempted. Hopeful Confederates predicted that this alteration could add another 75,000 men to the army. Harriet Holmes, whose husband already served in the army, faced the loss of a cousin and five uncles. She expressed the thought running through the minds of many Confederates: "When will it end?"[31]

Supposedly, bureau rules dictated the end point of conscription, but they were not always clear. In assessing potential modifications of the substitution law, the *Daily Constitutionalist* complained that "in the mass of bungling, mismanagement and change . . . it is difficult to determine what the rules and regulations actually are." The piecemeal implementation of conscription did lead to an incredible array of unforeseen scenarios that defied easy answers. The most common questions included: If the substitute deserted, did the principal owe service? What happened if a substitute died? Did this make the principal immediately eligible for conscription or did it end his obligation to the government (as if he had died himself)? Fearing the conscription of his brother, a Louisianan groused, "Nothing was said about the principal having to stand good for death or desertion." What happened if the substitute became eligible for conscription? For instance, if a planter hired a forty-two-year-old, did the planter become eligible for conscription when President Davis extended the call to include men up to forty-five years of age? Implicit in all these questions was the issue of whether providing a substitute made the principal exempt for the entire war or the government could later add stipulations that would make a principal eligible for service.[32]

Officials in the Bureau of Conscription tried to answer these questions, but, adding to the confusion, their answers changed over the course of the war. In February 1863, a circular addressed the liability of the principal when his substitute deserted. Desertion itself did not automatically end the principal's exemption. But, if the principal had engaged in fraud to get his replacement in the army or abetted the fugitive, then desertion made the principal liable. Also, if the deserter faced conscription (for example, if they were forty-two years old), then the principal would face conscription. By July, the bureau simplified this policy. It now declared that if the army lost the service of a substitute through any cause other than as a casualty of war, the principal's exemption ended.

Regardless of bureau instructions, individual officers created their own policies. Louisiana private William King complained that the army even tried "to resurrect the dead" by conscripting principals whose substitutes had died. In a separate case, he heard of a wealthy principal allowed to remain home even after the conscription of his substitute. With both decisions arbitrarily violating official policy, King moaned about fighting for freedom from a government that ignored its own laws only to serve another one which did the same thing.[33]

State judges saw themselves, not the Bureau of Conscription, as the ultimate arbiters of the legality of conscription policies. Richmond Pearson, one of three judges on the North Carolina Supreme Court, continually attempted to thwart any changes in the substitution provisions that made a principal eligible for service. From the summer of 1863 until the end of the war, Pearson proved to be the biggest judicial obstacle to the enforcement of conscription. A Whig politician, Pearson had become chief justice in 1858. He had opposed North Carolina's secession but supported the Confederacy. Much like Georgia's Governor Brown, Judge Pearson considered himself to be a loyal Confederate unwilling to sacrifice the nation's ideals to save its army. He placed great emphasis on individual liberty and thus ran headlong into policies such as conscription which centralized power in Richmond. Due to the judge's stubborn and vocal opposition to the national government, historian Mark Neely calls him "the single most important member of the bench in Confederate history."[34]

In the cases of *In re Irvin* and *In re Bryan,* Pearson overruled the Bureau of Conscription's substitution rules. He declared that, regardless of army regulations, a principal did not become liable for service simply because the army conscripted his substitute. In the summer of 1862, John Irvin and J. C. Bryan provided men between the ages of thirty-five and forty to serve in their places. When conscription's age range expanded, both men's substitutes became eligible for conscription, so Confederate enrolling officers conscripted Irvin and Bryan (since they no longer had substitutes). In separate cases, Pearson issued writs of habeas corpus demanding their release from the army. The judge contended that the army had enlisted substitutes for the duration of the war. The revised conscription acts did not apply to either them or their principals. Principals had entered into a contract with the government, and the government could not unilaterally alter that contract. In Pearson's view, much as exemptions were prospective and did not impact men in the service, neither did changes in substitution policy. Substitute soldiers, according to this logic, continued to be the proxy of their principals for the war, regardless of future policy changes.[35]

In other cases, Pearson issued writs to release men he felt should have received exemptions. The men whose attorneys sought relief from Pearson had a variety of complicated issues, generally stemming from the timing of conscription policies and when enrolling officers found them. For example, if a twenty-five-year-old should have been conscripted under the April 1862 act but had not enrolled before the October 1862 expansion in exemptions, could he take advantage of the changes in the law? In his decisions, Judge Pearson zealously favored a Confederate identity based upon individual liberty. He consistently placed this principle ahead of national needs. Critics contended that he granted writs of habeas corpus and discharges whenever uncertainty existed about a man's eligibility. He had no doubt such power lay in his hands and not in the army's. For the judge, the "construction of the conscription and exemption act . . . so far as they concern the rights of a citizen . . . is a matter for the courts." Pearson assumed "the principle of constitutional law is so clear that I suppose it will be conceded by every one."[36]

The Confederate government did not concede this principle, and it rejected Pearson's decisions. Assistant Secretary of War John Campbell eagerly responded to the legal challenge. Having served eight years on the U.S. Supreme Court, Campbell knew something about constitutional law himself. He instructed the head of conscription in North Carolina that the judge's opinion "is not regarded by the Department as a sound exposition of the act of Congress, and you will not regard it in your official action as such." Suggesting that Pearson's motives were not as pure as he avowed, Campbell decried judges who kept out of the army wealthy men "who above all others are interested in the revolution." After all, Pearson only issued writs to men who could afford an attorney. Poor men generally did not appear in his court. Historian David Carlson finds a similar scenario in Georgia, where local judges liberally used the writ of habeas corpus to keep the planter elite (but not plain folk) out of the army. The secretary of war also contended that Pearson's decisions rested on faulty logic. He likened Pearson's use of habeas corpus to antebellum decisions of abolitionist judges who employed the doctrine to thwart the fugitive slave law. Responding to this claim in a separate decision, Pearson sarcastically retorted, "Who made the Secretary of War a judge?"[37]

Considering Pearson's release of principals "wrong," a North Carolina officer pointed out that "it was well understood (in the army at least) that if the conscript age would be extended the principal would become liable." The officer claimed he had always informed men of this policy. A Georgia principal shared this understanding. After paying $2,500 for a forty-six-year-old rather than the fifty-three-year-old he preferred, he worried that if Congress extended conscription to embrace his substitute, "I suppose I should again become liable." In the view of the Bureau of Conscription, the army had not entered into a contract with the principal. The principal and the substitute most likely signed a contract, but the government was not party to this agreement. Instead, calling principals into the army was no different than other alterations in conscription, such as expanding the age range or adding exemptions.[38]

The touchiness of both Pearson and Confederate officials stemmed from their mutual realization that bigger issues were at stake than the eligibility of a few men in North Carolina. For the moment, Pearson did not address the issue of whether the Confederate Congress could pass a law ending substitution and making all principals liable for service. Firing a warning shot, Pearson made his view on that issue very clear, declaring such a law "would violate natural justice and shock the moral sense." Also, Pearson never offered an opinion on conscription's constitutionality, though an officer insisted, "He is itching to pronounce it unconstitutional." While the judge never rendered such a verdict, Governor Vance informed the president that rumors containing "a very exaggerated and ridiculous form" of Pearson's decisions had encouraged men to believe he had declared the measure unconstitutional. This gossip had led some to resist the draft and others to desert. Even one of Pearson's friends warned the judge that "the construction put upon your decision[s] is greatly injuring the army." Regardless, Pearson, a judicial Don Quixote, did not serve as the vanguard of a state judiciary arrayed against the federal government any more than Joseph Brown epitomized Confederate governors. Even in North Carolina, Pearson's two fellow state judges generally rejected his anticonscription stance, and across the Confederacy no other state supreme court justices endorsed, cited, or copied his decisions.[39]

While Pearson's decisions did not indicate widespread judicial hostility toward conscription, they did increase the strain between North Carolina's Governor Vance and Confederate authorities. Like most Confederate officials, Vance disagreed with Pearson, and they exchanged a series of quarrelsome letters debating the merits of the judge's decisions. In his official capacity as governor of North Carolina, however, Vance, regardless of his own opinion, felt obligated to follow the decision of the chief justice of his state's highest tribunal. He chided Confederate officials that the absence of a national supreme court exacerbated the problem. Without such a court, each state's judiciary had the last word on constitutionality. Serving in an elective position, Vance had to delicately position himself between his constituents and the national government. By 1863, the Conservative Party, a coalition of former Whigs, antisecessionists, and Unionists, comprised the majority of North Carolina voters. Frustrated with Confederate policies, they desired peace. They had elected Vance in 1862, and he wanted to maintain their support. To do so, he could not publicly side with the Confederate government over his state's judiciary.[40]

Tensions between Vance and Richmond also simmered over conscription's stipulation that a governor could exempt all necessary state officials, provided that they were exempt from state militia service as well. Some governors protected only a select few officials, while others used the law to shield thousands. Vance interpreted the law broadly to include justices of the peace, constables, and "police organizations" in North Carolina's towns and cities. The governor took the liberty of assuming that President Davis respected states' rights too much to conscribe "a few officers who could do little toward increasing the ranks" but were needed at home.

Davis took three months to respond to this request. He optimistically hoped that in the meantime his instruction to conscription officers to defer to the governor whenever possible within the confines of the law had resolved the conflict. In reality, conscription officials struggled to both honor Vance's wishes and enforce the law. General Rains admonished the governor that "there are no means, short of supernatural power" for enrolling officers to know precisely which employees Vance wanted to exempt. Taking umbrage to the tone of this letter, Vance reminded Rains of his past cooperation, in contrast to those politicians—no doubt alluding to Governor Brown—"who made the 'night (and day) hideous' with cries for *State rights*."[41]

With conscription not always meshing well with provisions in state law, Vance solicited information from other governors with regard to the protection of state officials. The act said that governors could only exempt state officials if they were exempt from militia service. North Carolina law, however, stipulated that in cases of invasion or slave insurrection, no one was exempt from militia service. Adding to the confusion, during these emergencies, the officials could only be required to serve in their own county. So, in theory, every North Carolina official could be conscripted but perhaps not forced to leave their home counties. Such a literal interpretation benefited no one. In responding to Vance, Governor Brown explained that Georgia faced a similar dilemma with all its civil officers eligible for militia service. Its legislature, however, solved this problem by passing a new law exempting judges, justices of the peace, sheriffs, deputies, clerks of courts, and ordinaries from militia duty and thereby from conscription.[42]

With most governors fighting over the exemption of state officials but accepting conscription generally, perhaps the most heated dispute in 1863, ironically, pitted the bureau against the army. The bureau enforced conscription unevenly across the Confederacy. While the correlation was not precise, generally the farther one moved away from the East Coast, the less likely one was to see an effective conscription force. In June, General Edmund Kirby-Smith, who had taken command of the Trans-Mississippi Department (Arkansas, western Louisiana, and Texas), reported that its conscript bureau was "defective [and] has been under no general supervision." Elsewhere, army officers chafed at the civilian safeguards which, in their view, allowed too many men to escape the army. In their opinion, a combination of exemptions, details, and illnesses (real or fabricated) meant that the majority of men who interacted with enrolling officers never went into the ranks. According to this line of argument, this proportion was high because men with exemptions always came when called out, while men being forced into ranks were more likely to delay their arrival. Plus, enrolling officers or the militia members aiding them often knew potential conscripts, and thus they were inclined to bend the rules in their neighbors' favor. As the need for soldiers grew, both the leniency in and the abuse of the system increasingly frustrated generals, who needed a full army.[43]

In 1863, these smoldering tensions came to a head as the Army of Tennessee openly competed with the bureau in enrolling troops. In January, Adjutant General Samuel Cooper, citing the "great necessity which now exists for strenuous exertions in securing men to fill up the commands," issued a circular permitting the detailing of officers to go to sections where their regiments had been raised to recruit men. In his plan, units could send prominent community members home to use peer pressure to convince recusant conscripts to enlist. Cooper's strategy intended to use "kind treatment" and convincing arguments addressed to "patriotism and sense of duty" to persuade heretofore reluctant men to enlist and fight alongside their neighbors. In short, Cooper wanted to improve rather than overhaul or eliminate the current process. Nevertheless, Cooper's orders unintentionally allowed the army to bypass the Bureau of Conscription. Most significantly, regular soldiers, rather than enrolling officers, enforced the policy, and they sent men directly to units rather to than camps of instructions. Without enrolling officers and camps of instruction, the conscripts enlisted using this method had no place to appeal their enlistment.[44]

Regardless of the policy's intent, in northern Alabama and middle Tennessee, generals Gideon Pillow and Braxton Bragg chose to interpret the order very broadly. They used it as a pretext to enact military conscription outside of, and in competition with, the civilian bureau. On January 16, Bragg appointed Pillow to organize a "volunteer and conscript recruiting bureau." Two days later, Pillow announced his plan to enroll conscripts and capture deserters wherever he encountered them. In his reading of the law, his officers could seize any southern man, regardless of whether they had a connection to the conscript's community or not. Though he preferred to succeed without violence, through "a proper appeal to [the country's] patriotism," he was willing to use force to make Confederates defend their homes. Since his involvement in the surrender of Fort Donelson in February 1862, Pillow had sought to restore his reputation. Not the greatest military general, Pillow found his calling in this new post. In his study of the Army of Tennessee, Thomas Connelly calls conscription Pillow's "finest hour," with the task dovetailing with "his pedantic, tin-soldier nature."[45]

Pillow's plan netted conscripts. General Bragg told the president that Pillow brought in men quicker than they could be armed. In his first six weeks, Pillow, according to Bragg, had "zealously and efficiently" accomplished "ten times as much to strengthen the army" as all the enrolling officers in the vicinity. Pillow himself maintained that he had brought in 12,000 men in a single month, in sharp contrast to "how little is being done by conscript officers." Operating under the assumption that all men belonged in the army, Pillow and his men meticulously reviewed exemption papers. In their view, this reexamination revealed extensive abuses and frauds within the current system. Sympathetic doctors granted medical exemptions, and officers (one of whom he described as a "drunken worthless man") took bribes to give occupational exemptions. Even in the rare cases where local enrolling officers determined men were liable for duty, Pillow's men discovered that these officers often immediately granted their friends furloughs to remain at home. For Pillow, all of these duplicitous actions justified a reliance on coercion. Without a threat of compulsion, he considered conscription a "dead letter," but with it, he expected to enroll 100,000 men.[46]

Pillow's plan also netted complaints. His actions offended many Confederates, who perceived him as operating an unconstitutional press gang, which, in strong-arming men into his infantry, ignored legitimate exemptions and civilian control of the process. Even while singing his own praises, Pillow admitted that his soldiers relied on force and that consequently the task was "most distasteful and repugnant to [his] feelings." Responding to rumors of "disorder" in western North Carolina, Governor Vance instructed the secretary of war that "the illegal seizure of Conscripts by Genl. Pillow's Independent Conscript Bureau" represented the only threat there. The anger of politicians paled in comparison to the anger of the Bureau of Conscription itself. Regarding the seizing of a shoemaker, an enrolling officer noted that "many proceedings under Genl Pillow's orders have been reported to me as in conflict with law & General Orders . . . but . . . I have no power to exercise any control over him." General Rains agreed that this shoemaker's case deserved redress. After reviewing other cases, Rains sent the secretary of war a letter, complete with eleven enclosures and several subenclosures, articulating numerous complaints against Pillow.[47]

Rains objected to Pillow inaccurately describing himself as chief of a conscript bureau, but more significantly he charged that Pillow's actions undermined the authority of the real bureau. Rains also warned that a short-term, results-oriented analysis of Pillow's recruitment led to an erroneous conclusion. While the general's "extreme measures" had brought men into the army, they had also engendered a "spirit of hatred and resistance to the very name of conscription" and they had rendered camps of instruction useless. If Pillow had the authority to decide the legitimacy of exemptions (and to reject almost all of them), what role did the Bureau of Conscription have? By the end of the month, the bureau would issue a circular condemning the general's "hasty action," which compelled men into service "in every way subversive of the true interests of recruiting." If critics had worried that conscription equated to military despotism, Pillow's actions provided all the evidence they needed.[48]

Secretary of War James Seddon sided with Rains and the bureau. He declared that from conscription's inception, a key component of the program was civilian control. Congress created a conscription policy, which, while it may have used soldiers, existed outside the regular army and allowed for appeals to civil authorities. Therefore, the Army of Tennessee's bureau was "incompatible with the system" and had "no authority whatsoever." In April, the bureau won its first round against Pillow as the War Department ordered General Bragg to shut down Pillow's unsanctioned interference with conscription. Military reverses in the summer, particularly the surrender of Vicksburg, however, underscored the need for more troops and provided Pillow with a second chance in the conscription business. In July, the secretary of war offered General Joseph E. Johnston the opportunity to take over conscription in Alabama, Mississippi, and Tennessee. Johnston accepted and immediately turned recruitment back over to Pillow. This time, the general had even greater power, as the Confederate government removed any ambiguity by explicitly putting the conscription bureaus in these states under his authority.[49]

The firm Pillow again got results. In September and October, he claimed to have brought as many as 18,000 men into the army. These included recusant conscripts, stragglers, and deserters. He even targeted men who had joined the state cavalry to escape conscription. Finding them useless on horseback, Pillow's bureau forced them into the infantry. Pillow insisted that if his organization encompassed every state, the Confederate army would gain 30,000 men per month and soon double in size. Believing the ends justified the means, many Confederates endorsed Pillow's course. The *Richmond Daily Dispatch* printed a letter praising the general for cutting through the red tape: "His plans are so well laid, and his orders so rigidly enforced, that none can escape." Senator James

Phelan and General Leonidas Polk both urged President Davis to put Pillow and his "iron policy" in charge of national conscription, with Phelan stressing that success required men to realize "the *impossibility* of escape." The governor of Tennessee agreed that Pillow should run national conscription, for he had fixed "a defective system," doing more in a few months than it had accomplished in over a year.[50]

Heady with success, Pillow sought to expand his conscription empire. Ideally, he wanted to recruit across the entire Confederacy, but in the short run, adding Georgia made the most sense. In the wake of the Union invasion of eastern Tennessee, the general had moved his headquarters from Chattanooga to Marietta, creating the unusual scenario in which he supervised troops in three states (Alabama, Tennessee, and Mississippi) while stationed in a fourth (Georgia). He hungrily eyed the Peach State, speculating that it contained as many as 30,000 "able-bodied men, who have slipped through the hands of Government." The War Department informed Pillow that political considerations prevented him from conscripting Georgians. If Pillow's aggressive methods were to put him on a collision course with any state executive, Governor Brown, given his sensitivity regarding states' rights, seemed the most likely candidate. Surprisingly, however, Brown, while declaring he still found conscription unconstitutional, supported Pillow. This approach allowed the governor to maintain his populist championing of the farmer in the ranks over the rich man at home and also helped him fend off accusations of not supporting the military in his fall reelection campaign. Nonetheless, even with Brown's backing of Pillow, the Confederate government stood its ground, refusing to allow the general to expand his operations.[51]

While Brown and others endorsed General Pillow's actions, the Bureau of Conscription continued to oppose strenuously his challenge to their bailiwick. General John Preston, who had run conscription in South Carolina, was appointed head of the bureau at the same time Pillow began his second foray into conscription. Earlier in 1863, Preston had predicted that conscription run by the army would be a "system of impressment" producing "infinite discontent." After witnessing this policy in action, his opinion had not changed. Overall, he considered Pillow's plan a drawback rather than an asset in putting men in the army. An enrolling officer in Alabama agreed that conscription needed to be "executed not only with vigor but with discretion." In this officer's view, Pillow's lack of discretion trumped his vigor. In particular, Pillow's reference to his "arrest" of conscripts epitomized the conflict between the general and the bureau. The bureau enrolled men. It did not arrest them. Arresting men undermined efforts to make the system palatable and eliminate any stigma attached to the term *conscript*.[52]

Secretary of War James Seddon praised Pillow's "promptitude and efficiency," but he, too, worried about the consequences of the general's actions. Seddon concluded that Pillow's infringement on individual rights increased dissatisfaction on the home front and ultimately "operate[d] most disastrously to the Confederacy." In October, the secretary ordered Pillow to Richmond to explain his actions. While generals Pillow and Johnston believed that the army had full power over conscription, officials in Richmond still asserted that potential conscripts had the right to appeal to the secretary of war and the president. A furious Johnston ranted that this interpretation "virtually annul[led] the authority" granted to his department. In November, Seddon provided President Davis a report on the state of the military. He took the opportunity to lobby for the bureau, whose use of "prestige and the sanction of public sentiment" to enforce the measure had been sufficient. Alluding to Pillow's actions, the secretary declared "the appearance of compulsion . . . unnecessary and revolting."[53]

Seddon's description highlighted the difference between the conscription philosophies of the bureau and Pillow and Johnston. In the field, the generals had come to the opposite conclusions—compulsion was necessary and the presence of eligible men at home was revolting. They contended that the Bureau of Conscription naively believed that "the *moral obligation* created by the law will be sufficient." The reality of a year and a half of enforcement, however, had revealed "the *fallacy* of this theory." Reluctant conscripts needed to be compelled, and sometimes, regrettably, public sentiment endorsed resistance to rather than compliance with the law. Later, Preston framed the debate as between those who wanted the army to run conscription, which he considered a "military despotism," or "whether [conscription] is a law covering and protecting civil and personal rights."

By December, the status quo could not hold. Pillow maintained that because of his successful recruiting, the region under his command could yield no more men. Therefore, either his authority had to expand to a larger area, or he needed another assignment. Unfortunately for the general, Seddon and bureau officials had greater access to the president's ear. Plus, Davis shared their vision of a nation of Confederates who willingly accepted conscription in order to achieve military victory. Consequently, General Preston and the Bureau of Conscription held on to their power, and Pillow was reassigned to a field command.[54]

The Pillow fight represented the military's first main efforts to seize control of conscription, eliminate all evasions, and favor the battlefront over the home front. Confederates diverged on their judgments of Pillow's actions. Regardless of how they viewed Pillow's cure, many Confederates agreed with his diagnosis. Too many healthy men slipped through the cracks and remained at home as principals, in exempt occupations, or claiming an illness. While Pillow advocated solving these problems by strictly enforcing (or possibly ignoring) conscription guidelines, other Confederates preferred changing those guidelines to eliminate the fissures in the policy's foundation. Congress was scheduled to meet in December 1863 to once again allow lawmakers the chance to tweak conscription and make sure that it enrolled the men that it needed to enroll. Before this session met, however, Confederate voters, in the fall congressional elections, would get to weigh in with their opinions on how to correct the unfairness, abuses, and ambiguities of the measure.[55]

The 1863 congressional elections—the Confederacy's only wartime national elections—gave conscription's critics an opportunity to put their support behind politicians who shared their frustration. The elections defy easy analysis. First, they were nonpartisan. Confederates generally decried a two-party system as unrepublican, and the system had collapsed in much of the South in the decade prior to the Civil War. Second, wartime complications further undermine their study; many newspapers had ceased publication, Union occupation prevented regular campaigning, and in some states general elections replaced district contests. Turnout was light, and local issues often eclipsed national concerns.

Historian George Rable describes the elections as "a crazy quilt of idiosyncratic, almost apolitical contests conducted before a largely apathetic though sometimes angry electorate." Other scholars concur that the elections do not provide a simple referendum on Davis's policies. John B. Robbins contends that, across the Confederacy, they hinged on "war weariness" and an anti-incumbent sentiment rather than on specific issues. In his study of ten races in Georgia, Rob Andrew echoes this war weariness theme and adds that candidates who had served in the army—and therefore represented the themes of shared sacrifices and martial values—won regardless of their specific platforms.[56]

On the topic of conscription, a pattern does emerge. Regardless of their stance on the measure's constitutionality, candidates did not call for its repeal, and none suggested an alternate mode of raising troops. Eighteen months into conscription, with hundreds of thousands of men already impacted, scrapping conscription was an impossibility. In his January 1863 message to Congress, President Davis had called for elimination of the discrimination among classes. Candidates vowed to do just that. Congressional aspirants pledged to eliminate loopholes, thereby forcing speculators, secessionists, and exempts into the army. In Louisiana, two candidates championed equality with their platforms, declaring "opposition to exemptions from military service, especially exemptions based on property . . . [and] opposition to the principle of substitution in the army." Historian Armstead Robinson asserts that "voters responded to the inequities of conscription," with incumbents being charged with favoring the wealthy in the Twenty Negro Law, substitution, and exemption provisions. Generally, these incumbents responded defensively to these attacks, making promises to amend the act.[57]

North Carolina and Georgia—two states where conscription was effectively enforced and competitive elections took place—offer the best evidence of conscription's impact. In North Carolina, a loosely defined coalition dubbed Conservatives dominated; winning nine of ten seats. These politicians agreed that the Confederacy's policies had threatened their liberties. They wanted peace but divided over whether it should come from negotiations with the Union (and a reunion with the North) or from military victory and independence.

Even the candidates who championed peace and individual liberty did not call for conscription's repeal. Citing its "doubtful constitutionality," James G. Ramsay said he would not have voted for it. However, he not only did not propose its repeal but in fact "advise[d] a prompt and cheerful acquiescence." Conservative challengers, such as Ramsay, proposed that all men, regardless of wealth or occupation, should share in the sacrifices needed to achieve Confederate independence. While his opponent, incumbent William Lander, considered conscription constitutional, their platforms on the issue, nevertheless, mirrored each another. Neither wanted to repeal the act, and both vowed to eliminate unjust exemptions.[58]

James Leach, another Conservative challenger in North Carolina, expressed his opposition to the "principle of exemption in every shape," highlighting the "odious twenty negro feature." Yet, Leach, like Ramsay, did not seek the elimination of conscription. He just wanted to make sure that all physically and mentally fit men, regardless of class, served. In a different district, A. H. Arrington, an incumbent Democrat, struggled in vain to defend his vote for the Twenty Negro Law. He claimed to have supported it for "the safety of the families of our soldiers," as he feared insurrection in the wake of the Emancipation Proclamation. Admitting that this dreaded scenario had not materialized, Arrington now tried to distance himself from his vote. He made the unprovable claim that, in the spring 1863 session, he had championed repeal of the overseer exemption, only to see his effort die in a conference committee. Arrington lost his reelection bid. Yet his campaign, too, demonstrates the increasing consensus on conscription policy in North Carolina in 1863.[59]

In the fall of 1863, Georgia held congressional elections in all ten of its districts, along with a gubernatorial election. Georgia candidates sounded a lot like North Carolina politicians. In his analysis of these elections, Rob Andrew considers them as "a critique, not a rejection, of the Davis government," reflecting "frustration that some were having it harder than others." According to Andrew, "Many Georgians believe that the time had come for all men—rich, poor, old, and young—to do their time at the front," and the candidates' stances on conscription support this contention. They critiqued but did not reject conscription and emphasized that all must share in the burdens of the war. In the Second District, incumbent C. J. Munnerlyn called conscription "harsh, but . . . essential." He denied charges that he voted for expanded exemptions, claiming to be home sick in Georgia when these measures passed. Nevertheless, Munnerlyn reminded voters that exemptions, including the Twenty Negro Law, had been passed with a "patriotic desire" to take care of the home front. That being said, he agreed the exemption was "impolitic" and advocated its repeal.[60]

Other candidates—both incumbents and challengers—concurred that the army needed men and that conscription was necessary to provide these men. Rather than advocating its elimination, they urged its expansion. One branded all hindrances to raising an army, including appeals to states' rights, as "unwise and unpatriotic." J. W. Trawick declared, "I am not willing to disturb the conscription act, but the exemption act needs revising." While not referencing any specific policies, William E. Smith alluded to conscription when he declared that those who opposed the Confederate government "aid[ed] the invader in his work of subjugation." Warren Akin requested that voters elect only candidates, such as himself, who supported the commander in chief in all his efforts to win the war. W. W. Clark wanted to add more men to the army by getting into the ranks able-bodied men currently on details in the quartermaster and commissary departments. Another candidate took this extension one step further, stating that he wanted conscription to embrace all southerners with the exception of congressmen. This type of stance was endorsed by a letter from a soldier who urged voters to cast their ballots only for men in favor of "repeal of the odious exemption provisions."[61]

The concurrent gubernatorial election further demonstrates the breadth of the commitment to conscription in 1863. Timothy Furlow and his supporters tried to capitalize on Brown's long-standing antipathy to the measure. In a letter allowing his name to be put forward, the obscure Furlow declared that Confederate independence necessitated sending all able-bodied men into the army. Contrasting himself with Brown, he announced, "If elected Governor, I shall throw no official protection around any citizen within the embrace of the Conscript Law." Brown's attempt to defy the state supreme court's endorsement of conscription, and his efforts to bully the legislature into endorsing his anti-Richmond stance, made him potentially vulnerable on this point. In supporting Furlow, the Milledgeville *Southern Recorder* declared that "the Conscription Act alone saved the South" and repeatedly harped on Brown's hostility toward conscription and his misguided efforts to bring the Davis government into disrepute.[62]

Although Brown had little to fear from the challenge of the unknown Furlow, these accusations apparently hit a nerve. Throughout 1862, Brown had proudly trumpeted his anticonscription views. A year later, in an electoral climate more likely to attach nationalism to the army than to states' rights, the governor recognized that this opinion could stigmatize him as unpatriotic. By the end of 1863, Brown joined the chorus of Confederates championing shared sacrifice, declaring, "If every wealthy man would do his duty . . . but few complaints would be heard from the poor." This stance had led him to endorse General Pillow's military-run conscription a few months earlier. Not only did the governor shy away from his previous anticonscription pronouncements but also some of his proponents' revisionist history portrayed Brown and Davis as longtime allies. During the campaign, the Atlanta *Daily Intelligencer,* a pro-Brown organ, kept a quote from a letter from President Davis to Brown atop its editorial page. In this quote, Davis acknowledges Brown's debt in defending the country and praises the governor for his "prompt, cordial, and effective co-operation" and for Georgia's ability to raise men without resorting to conscription.[63]

Furlow backers justly claimed that the newspaper used this quote, which appeared as a polite conclusion at the end of a May 1862 letter, out of context. In the body of the missive, President Davis had not sounded so friendly to the governor. Instead, he had sternly lectured Brown on the constitutional justification for conscription. Plus, even in the unlikely event the two politicians had an amicable relationship that May, their subsequent letters undermined it. Through the rest of 1862, Brown continued to vocally defy both President Davis and his own state supreme court in challenging conscription's constitutionality, thereby making a portrayal of the men as allies a far-fetched scenario. Nevertheless, the attacks on Brown and his stance toward conscription, regardless of their truth, had little impact, as Brown easily won reelection. The dark horse Furlow could not outdo Brown's popularity among Georgia's yeomen. Furlow finished a distant third behind both Brown and Joshua Hill—a peace candidate who made no statements regarding conscription.[64]

In his analysis of the 1863 congressional elections, Wilford Buck Yearns contends that conscription was a key issue in these campaigns and that "some elections turned on this issue almost alone." Evidence supports the first part but not the second part of his assertion. While the measure frequently appears in candidates' public statements, their stances depict more of a consensus than a cacophony of voices. Election results did not hinge on an issue upon which candidates agreed. No candidates called for the end of conscription. Nor did any candidates call for an expansion of the exemption list. They wanted exemptions, especially those favoring certain classes, ended. The most effective charge against incumbents was not that they favored conscription but that they favored these unfair exemptions. Incumbents recognized the potency of this assertion and generally expressed a willingness to repeal the very exemptions that they had voted into place just a year earlier. By this time, most Confederates agreed that independence called for military victory, that victory depended upon a large army, and that creating a large army depended upon conscripting as many men as possible. Given the incredible stress that such a policy put on the home front, it was also imperative that special privileges, or even measures perceived as special privileges, did not allow too many men to remain home.[65]

In August 1863, Reuben Davis privately offered President Davis a candid assessment of conscription, which was similar to that of these congressional candidates. Reuben Davis had served in Congress but had resigned to run for the Mississippi governorship. He declared that "Every man says that every other man ought to fight in this war, and if all go, he will go." In an effort to make sure that all went, and to minimize class-based concerns, Reuben Davis advocated the repeal of exemption and substitution laws. This action "would have a salutary effect and perhaps save us from subjugation."[66]

This view epitomizes the conscription climate at the end of 1863. Confederates had moved from a debate over whether conscription should exist. It existed. Instead, they struggled over how to make it more equitable. Men and women at home could easily point out others, whether speculators, secessionists, recusant conscripts, principals, or fraudulent exempts, who should be conscripted.

Nevertheless, regardless of this view, not every man could be in the army. In fact, Reuben Davis recognized that President Davis could make a compelling counterargument to honor exemptions and substitutions. Individual interests supported those exceptions, but in the midst of war, "they must yield." After more than two years of sacrifice, victory rested in the army; thus, when in doubt, Confederates—civilians, politicians, and soldiers alike—favored putting more men into the ranks. Reuben Davis made this argument in dramatic fashion, declaring, "Unless the conscript act is extended, and the substitute and exemption laws repealed, the *Cause* is in its last agonies, and will soon expire; never, never to be revived."[67] While Davis lost his bid to be Mississippi's governor, his assessment of the people's demands was accurate. They wanted all to serve, and Congress, which would convene again in December 1863, had another chance to amend conscription policy to eliminate these perceived special privileges, bring even more men into the army, and prevent Confederate defeat.

CHAPTER 6

# The Iron Goes Deep

## *Conscription Policy in 1864*

When Congress reconvened at the end of 1863, the Confederacy was battered but still standing. Optimists could point out that the Union army was no closer to capturing Richmond than it had been at the onset of conscription. Pessimists, however, looked to Tennessee, where General William Sherman's Army of the West had just captured Chattanooga. More daunting, General Ulysses S. Grant had assumed command of the Union army. In conjunction with President Lincoln, Grant planned to use the North's superiority in numbers to wear down the Confederate armies. The general wanted the Army of the Potomac to apply continuous pressure to General Robert E. Lee's Army of Northern Virginia. At the same time, he ordered Sherman to thrust into Georgia, with other generals launching smaller offensives on the fringes of the Confederacy. In Lincoln's colorful language, those not skinning could hold a leg. In other words, Grant and Lincoln believed that the Union's victory could come down to simple math—a constant application of the North's numerical dominance would force the Confederacy to surrender.[1]

Southerners could count just as well as their northern brethren. Outnumbered, Confederates struggled for ways to add more men to the army, which meant mobilizing an even higher proportion of their population than they had done previously. Looking toward the 1864 campaign, Lee called for an expansion of the army to "embrac[e] the whole population capable of bearing arms." In schools, pupils learned this lesson from the *Confederate Speller and Reader:* "Let all who are able, take up arms to drive [the invaders] back."[2]

While increasing the size of the army appeared to be a straightforward solution even children could grasp, in reality, there were few avenues to add new troops. At the start of year, army rosters included 464,646 soldiers, which was only 15,000 more than a year earlier. The secretary of war, however, credited conscription with bringing in 80,000 to 100,000 troops in 1863, a total offset by the year's extensive casualties. In terms of conscription, the three most discussed options to add more soldiers included drafting men who had provided substitutes, reducing or eliminating exemptions, and expanding the age range to include boys under eighteen and men over forty-five. Lee focused on an overhaul of the nation's exemption policy, contending it was "open to much abuse, and many escape service . . . who are only nominally within the provisions of the law." Later, the general declared to the secretary of war, "The emergency requires the sacrifice of every other consideration to the vital question of the public safety." Agreeing with Lee, Confederates buttressed the army by acting on all three of these fronts in 1864.[3]

In the Senate, Louis Wigfall succinctly stressed the Confederacy's prevailing philosophy in 1864: "The army was the country and the country was the army."[4] To defend the country, Confederates made every effort to add men to the army. Listening to concerns about special privileges and witnessing the results of the 1863 congressional elections, legislators ended substitution and conscripted principals. They also shrank the exemption list. Some officials, including President Davis, embraced the concept of replacing exemptions with details to put more men into the army.

These plans to denude the home front of men and to tilt the balance of federalism even more in favor of the national government reinvigorated fears of the creation of a military despotism subverting the Confederate tenets of states' rights and individual liberty. Predictably, North Carolina's Judge Pearson and Georgia's Governor Brown most ardently voiced these misgivings. Despite these concerns, in 1864, the proponents of putting the national emergency ahead of all other considerations triumphed. By the end of the year, however, their victories looked Pyrrhic, as Confederate math simply did not add up. The ever-challenging puzzle of finding enough men to fight the Union army while keeping them and their families fed and clothed began to appear unsolvable.

As legislators met in December 1863, they recognized that ending substitution and compelling principals to join the army had popular backing across the South. A senator bluntly declared, "The country demands it," and he claimed to have heard no opposition to the bill. It would both add men to the ranks and respond to criticisms that the rich had not done their share. The congressmen and senators making these decisions had been elected in 1861, and many of these lawmakers were finishing up lame duck terms. Nevertheless, they had paid attention to the results of the November elections, in which voters had chosen candidates who had attacked special privileges and emphasized a commitment to shared sacrifice. Gauging the congressional mood, a Virginia diarist asserted that lawmakers "wish to thrust every man, woman, and child into [the army]," scornfully adding, "except themselves."[5]

Throughout 1863, many Confederate leaders had pleaded for the end to substitution. In May, Florida's Governor John Milton, who rarely challenged Confederate policies, told President Davis that he considered substitution "a most unfortunate blunder" that enabled "tens of thousands" of unscrupulous men to use "money and vile Artifices upon the ignorant" to shirk their duty. Governor Milledge Bonham of South Carolina also wanted to end this practice that benefited the class which had the greatest interest in the success of the Confederate cause. Mississippi legislators passed a resolution instructing their representatives to vote for the measure's repeal. Georgia's Governor Brown shared this sentiment. Looking at the policy in his favorite terms of class and constitutionality, he could find no objection to rescinding this law. Contending that "private rights must yield to the public good," the governor believed that the government could force principals into the army. Even the contrarian Senator Henry Foote, who seemingly detested every Davis-endorsed measure, urged that substitution, which had "given rise to nothing but discontent," should be abolished.[6]

Soldiers saw eye to eye with these officials. A North Carolinian predicted that "the best law in the South . . . is about to pass," for the ending of substitution would "bring all the Rich men in the service." A South Carolina cavalryman hoped for the conscription of principals, for Congress "must do something to fill up our ranks." He believed that 75,000 to 80,000 men had provided substitutes. Their entry into army could turn back the Yankee invaders. Another soldier put the number at 100,000. As their conflicting estimates demonstrate, no one knew how many men would be impacted. Congressmen continued to express their frustration that the conscription bureau could not provide accurate numbers. Trying to extrapolate from the data they had, their estimates ranged from 20,000 to 30,000 on the low end to 100,000 on the high end. A Texas soldier accepted the highest estimate. Believing that "the army must be recruited at all hazards," he optimistically projected the addition of 100,000 new soldiers to the ranks.[7]

The Texan expressed one concern. He worried that the change represented a "breach of faith." Similarly, a Virginian found it "very unjust" to conscript principals without refunding their expenditures. The primary, maybe the only, argument against enlisting principals stemmed from the stance that it was an illegal or unfair "breach of faith," violating a contract. They had paid significant sums of money—maybe as much as $5,000 to $10,000—to stay home. Principals had given up their land, their slaves, and possibly their life savings in exchange for being exempt for the entire war. Some argued that the government could not—or should not—violate this contract without at least providing financial redress. Even while calling for their enrollment, Governor Brown insisted that the government had a responsibility to provide some compensation for principals' financial injury. According to this logic, if a man had paid $5,000 for a substitute for the duration of the war, he deserved at least a partial refund if the government now conscripted him. In some cases, this contention stemmed from sympathy toward principals, but for other Confederates, such as Brown, it stemmed more from their strict legalistic tendencies. South Carolina senator James Orr exemplified this ambivalence when he maintained the government had an obligation "even to this odious class."[8]

Without rendering any judgment on principals' character, President Davis felt the time had come for them to join the ranks. In a message to Congress, he called for an end to substitution and for the conscription of all principals. To defeat the Yankee invaders, the Confederacy needed every available man in the army. President Davis later lamented that "the spirit which rendered volunteering so general . . . at the beginning of the war" was no longer present, so an expanded conscription was the only alternative. Unlike Brown, the president did not see a need to compensate men who had hitherto avoided army life. He and other supporters of the amendment viewed substitution as a special privilege, not a binding contract. The Confederacy had previously altered its enlistment commitments. For example, in 1862, Congress had made twelve-month volunteers remain in the army. If it could force these patriotic men to remain in the ranks, it could compel men who had stayed home to join them. Since then, the government had altered conscription's age range and its exemptions several times. From this perspective, making principals join the army was simply another change in an almost two-year fine-tuning of conscription.[9]

Davis could call for changes, but Congress controlled conscription legislation. Senator Albert G. Brown of Mississippi made one of the most influential speeches in favor of taking conscription to its limits. Published as a pamphlet, his oration urged an end to substitution and to all exemptions, thereby putting the entire adult male population in the army. In supporting his proposal, he emphasized the theme that all Confederates must do their part and reiterated many of the key arguments that conscription proponents had advanced during the preceding two years. Fashioning himself a "strict constructionist," Brown nevertheless found the measure constitutional. The founders of the Confederacy, according to the senator, gave Congress the power to fight the war and certainly did not intend to drive the nation to commit suicide by limiting this power. The Confederate army had consistently won victories, but it had failed to follow up on them for want of a sufficient number of troops. For Senator Brown, the only question that now mattered was whether a measure strengthened the army. Given that, he maintained that "the addition of every available man is one of those self-evident propositions that calls for no elucidation."[10]

Regardless of whether his proposal called for elucidation, Senator Brown provided one. Despite admitting "I never supposed it possible, Mr. President, for the entire male population of a country to go into the army at once," he offered few methods to avoid serving. He wanted "heartless and unblushing extortioners"—exempts and principals who had consistently broken the implied promise to take care of soldiers' families—to come to the front lines.

While calling all men into the army, Brown simultaneously requested that the national government "make provision for feeding and clothing the destitute families of soldiers in the field." If the government had the right to draft male family members, in his view, it had the responsibility to take care of their dependents. In order to do so, Brown supported the detailing of soldiers. In contrast to exemptions, details "insure[d] fidelity and responsibility, and crush[ed] down the spirit of extortion." Since detailed men were in the army but serving on the home front, behavior rather than occupation served as the barometer of whether a man could remain at home. A detailed man knew that if he grew cotton instead of corn or charged exorbitant prices, his detail would end. Senator Brown concluded his proconscription message with a reminder of the goal: "My great desire is to see the army strengthened, and I will embrace any plan that will effect that object and do it speedily."[11]

Brown's colleagues agreed with him. Echoing the theme of common sacrifice, a Louisiana congressman called for "young and old, rich and poor" to "take up arms and drive the enemy from our soil." According to a cynical soldier, Congress "will never be satisfied till every body is in the army." On December 28, 1863, legislators ended substitution and kept current substitutes in the army. Eight days later, they made principals liable for conscription, without any provisions for compensating them. As usual, most soldiers praised any measure that compelled men to join them. A Texan claimed it "afford[ed] infinite satisfaction" to men in the ranks, and a Mississippian praised Congress for doing "one good thing" in passing these measures. General Thomas Hindman claimed the end of substitution helped convince two of his regiments to unanimously reenlist. In Virginia, Abner Ford's misery looked forward to company. Having failed in his own repeated efforts to acquire a substitute, Ford sounded gleeful in telling his wife that principals would have to "leave there pretty wives a crying," adding, "You can tell them their pretty husbands wont come to see them until the war ends."[12]

In addition to targeting substitution, Senator Brown had criticized excessive exemptions, and other Confederates shared his desire to make that procedure more effective. To them, the policy suffered from both inefficiency and fraud. An assistant adjutant general considered it "unfair, unjust to exempt a man from the service of his country because he happens to be a shoemaker." Others might substitute *minister, miller, Quaker,* or *blacksmith* in that sentence. Rather than exempting certain categories, the secretary of war, like Senator Brown, suggested conscripting all men within the age ranges and then detailing them as needed. W. L. Cunningham urged the president to "make a clean sweep" in replacing all exemptions with community-selected details. For many Confederates, a system of details appeared to be the best method to increase the size of the army. Details offered the perfect panacea for balancing home and army. This true conscription granted the government precise control in allocating manpower. If a community needed two millers, then precisely two millers—no more, no less—would be kept home. Details had the added benefit of ensuring that jobs that could be accomplished by older men, disabled soldiers, slaves, or free Blacks would not be used to shield healthy twenty-five-year-olds from conscription.[13]

To put the entire population on war footing, President Davis also wanted details to replace exemptions. He reminded Congress that the goal of the exemption policy was not to privilege specific occupations but to keep valuable labor at home, and details provided a better method to allocate scarce southern manpower resources. According to the president, "Considerable numbers are believed to be now exempted . . . who are not needful to the public in their civil vocation." In other words, no group—whether teachers, preachers, printers, or overseers—should merit automatic exemptions. Later in the year, Davis stressed that the most important responsibility of citizens was preserving their home and country. The main method of defense was serving in the army, and only truly necessary men should remain home. In the president's opinion, details also eliminated the problem of fraud. People pretending to be shoemakers, overseers, or preachers stood no chance of gaining details. Davis explained that "nothing can be more invidious than an unequal distribution of duties or obligations," and the president maintained that details prevented this inequality better than exemptions did.[14]

Congress rejected the idea of replacing all exemptions with details. Some legislators worried than relying solely on details put the entire male population under the control of the president and the army. Granting the executive branch the power to decide the status of every adult, white male in the South represented the very military despotism that liberty-sensitive Confederates had feared since the passage of the initial conscription act in April 1862. A Virginia newspaper highlighted the distinction between exempts and details, describing the former as "a citizen" and the latter as "a subservient creature of a bureau." Speaking to the Georgia legislature, Vice President Stephens asked, "Could dictatorial powers be more complete?" Two congressmen contended that details did make the president's authority absolute. One claimed such a system would clothe Davis with more power than any living European monarch, and another extended this comparison back in time, stating that the president's autocratic rule would even exceed Napoleon's. The latter also argued that details created a greater chance for favoritism than exemptions did. Enrolling officers decided which two millers or one blacksmith received details, and they undoubtedly would select their friends or relatives. According to this argument, in the limited detail system already in place, influence, fraud, corruption, and bribery had prevailed.[15]

Other legislators supported the reduction of exemptions in theory but balked when it came to eliminating specific occupations. After much debate, Congress finally passed an exemption bill on February 17, 1864, the final day of its session. The new law created a hybrid system combining exemptions and details. This bill had a truncated exemption list composed solely of state and federal officers, ministers, editors, printers, apothecaries, doctors, overseers, teachers, and conscientious objectors. Numerous occupations, including shoemakers, blacksmiths, and millers, lost their exemptions. To remain home, these men and others, most significantly farmers, had to receive details.

President Davis's opposition to exemptions would be revealed when Congress tried to remove some of the ambiguity in this list. Upon its reconvention in April, Congress passed a joint resolution requesting that the exemption for newspaper editors be clarified to specifically include the editors of periodicals. Davis vetoed the measure, reminding Congress, "When our lives, our liberty, and our independence are threatened . . . every citizen capable of bearing arms ought to be found in the ranks."[16]

For those exemptions that remained, the law often increased the connection between exemption and behavior. Most important, Congress again modified the Twenty Negro Law, making it the "fifteen–field hand law," as the number of field hands was more closely correlated to crop production. Anyone laying claim to the exemption had to provide the government with one hundred pounds of bacon or pork and an equivalent amount of beef per field hand. In his study of Virginia, William Blair contends that this amendment transformed plantation owners into "government growers." They had to provide their "marketable surplus of provisions and grain now on hand" to the government or to soldiers' families at fixed prices, which were about 50 percent below the free market price. These prices enabled soldiers' families to purchase food at half the cost paid by families without male relatives in the ranks. Additionally, in the same section of the new conscription act, Congress gave the secretary of war the power to exempt or detail men—with no specific slaveholding requirements—whom he thought would help "to insure the production of grain and provisions for the Army and the families of soldiers." The law stipulated that the exemption for all of these agriculturalists would cease if they violated these terms.[17]

A report on the distribution of Robert Edmond's crop provides a sense of one grower's contribution to the Confederacy. An owner of more than fifteen field hands, Edmond received an exemption for his overseer. In return, his plantation, which produced six hundred barrels of corn, gave sixty barrels for the government's 10 percent tax-in-kind, fifty to Henrico County to feed the poor, and eight to soldiers' families. He also sold 150 at fixed prices to the Confederacy and traded forty-three barrels for cotton, farm equipment, and shoes. Edmond grumbled that these contributions left him with less than the 350 barrels his farm usually consumed. Similarly, he divided his 1,250 bushels of wheat as follows: 150 for the tax-in-kind; 704 sold to the government; one hundred sold at fixed prices to a local manufactory that employed detailed soldiers; forty given to his son ("an enrolled soldier"); and seven allocated to poor families (four at fixed prices and three free). Much of his potato crop also went to the tax-in-kind or the manufactory, with another 40 percent traded to the Virginia penitentiary for shoes, clothing, and wagon repair. His records show a similar distribution of his oats, hay, bacon, and beef. In short, Edmond and his overseer might not have joined the army, but they did contribute to the Confederacy.[18]

In order to leave no potential soldier unfound, legislators tweaked some other aspects of conscription as well. Conscription's age range expanded, now encompassing all white men between seventeen and fifty years old. Congress, however, did not send seventeen-year-olds and men from forty-six to fifty to the front. Instead, the young and old provided a reserve corps stationed at home, only to be activated as needed. The same measure enrolled all men, including those already in the army, for the duration of the war. The original conscription act called for three years of service. Men who had enlisted for twelve months in 1861 were now approaching their third anniversary in the army, but they would not be sent home in 1864. This provision surprised no one. While lengthening service in 1862 provoked anger and debate, two years later, no southerner operated under the illusion that the Confederacy planned to release large numbers of soldiers from its clutches. Congress also forced independent Partisan Ranger organizations into the regular army. Demonstrating their commitment to enlist every possible soldier, Confederate leaders even tried to expand their geographic reach. By the middle of the summer, even as the nation's borders shrank, the Bureau of Conscription ironically expanded its definition of "Confederates," declaring Marylanders subject to conscription for the first time.[19]

Not all southerners celebrated these changes. Private William King, who had continually complained of the privileges extended to the wealthy, still managed to moan about the ending of substitution, which "violate[d] a sacred contract." He carped that when soldiers changed their minds, it was "treason, desertion, &c.," but when Davis and legislators reversed their opinions, it became law. In addition, the ever-pessimistic King believed that the change would only affect men who had paid all their savings for a substitute. Truly rich men would find another "loop hole through which to get out." Fellow Louisianan Edwin Fay agreed with King. Alleging "bad faith" on the part of the Confederate government, he worried that the "Yankees cannot conquer us, but we are fast conquering ourselves." Across the Confederacy in Virginia, Henry Waddell shared the sentiment, finding the measure both "bad faith" and "miserably impolitic."[20]

Waddell wondered how the Confederacy planned to feed and clothe these new conscripts, as "there will be no body left . . . to cultivate the fields." Conscription had always favored the battlefront over the home front, and the 1864 law tipped the scales even further toward the army. A senator contended that this new plan was based on what he called the "popular fallacy of putting every man in the army," and a congressman reminded his fellow legislators that the "fighting interest" and the "provision interest" were "mutually dependent." Putting all into the army affected both industry and farms. Requesting that more men be detailed to his line, a North Carolina railroad official reminded an enrolling officer that the government had a choice: "Either have the men and let the road and Army suffer, or leave the men alone and let the road be worked as advantageously as possible." Virginia railroad officers agreed that the expanded conscription plan was "the idle dream of theorists." They remonstrated against the legislative proposal to conscript their employees and replace them with disabled soldiers as "nothing is more certain than that men unfit for military service are wholly unfit for the employment on railroads." Josiah Gorgas, the chief of the Bureau of Ordnance, expressed a similar opinion in defending the exemption of skilled laborers. Gorgas bluntly asserted that "workmen will not fight and work both."[21]

Pressing conscription too far left farms, and farm families, too lean. Many Confederates shared the sentiments of a letter supporting a detail: "I don't know what new orders have been issued," the writer acknowledged, "but if the army is to be fed" the Confederacy needed more men detailed as farmers. A Georgia congressman asked, "If we force every man in the ranks, who is to make the food of the country?" His governor had the same question. Brown compared producers and fighting men and concluded, "The one is as indispensable as the other." The president of the University of North Carolina warned of "danger, if not of actual starvation, of destitution bordering upon it." Elsewhere in the Tar Heel State, a petition signed by ten men and fifty women ("wives and members of soldiers families") requested a detail for a miller, for these loyal Confederate families had no other way to get their grain milled. Hearing appeal after appeal denied, a government official maintained, "The iron is gone deep into the heart of society." Even the Bureau of Conscription recognized that the policy cut deep, reminding its officers that "the production of grain and provisions for the army is, moreover, equally as essential as the furnishing of men"—without giving them any instructions on how to accomplish both of these goals.[22]

Men at home were indispensable, but skeptics continued to worry that they would be the wrong men. In particular, Confederates feared that former principals would find new methods to escape service. While one principal maintained that going into the army did not bother him, he knew others who "would much rather go to the gallows then return to the army." Some principals preferred fleeing to Union lines. A soldier heard rumors that "a great many of them" were "going to the Yankees," and a Richmond newspaper predicted that "scores of speculators" were "preparing the run the blockade." More commonly, however, former principals searched for legal ways to avoid the front lines, with "every ingenuity . . . resorted to." From Alabama, the president received a complaint that the change "will be of little benefit . . . since every man who can has and is still getting [government] contracts." A South Carolina soldier wondered about the machinations of a former principal who sought another avenue to avoid the army: "Is he fixing to go in the service or is he going to try and get an exemption as an overseer or miller?" A civilian from the same state sadly portrayed "substitute men . . . hurrying in, all wanting offices." The Bureau of Conscription instructed enrolling officers to screen men carefully, declaring that supplying a substitute was "prima facie evidence that the principal has no other claim for exemption." Even with this scrutiny, the bureau, in a pessimistic April report, fretted that a "general effort to keep . . . principals out of the army" had resulted in a disappointing number of new recruits.[23]

Sam Richards, a Georgia principal, exemplified the men trying to avoid army life. He had closely followed the debate on ending substitution. He considered any change in the law to be "a flagrant breach of faith" or, put more simply, "a regular cheating!" When he discovered that the measure had passed, he lamented that in "a grand Government Swindle" his "$2500 Substitute becomes worthless." He immediately sought a different method to avoid enrolling. While at home, Richards had joined the staff of a religious newspaper, *The Soldier's Friend,* and he hoped to gain an exemption or detail based on his editorial occupation. In January and February, in preparation for applying for a detail, he collected signatures of clergy and officers on a petition, which stated the value of his newspaper. Fortunately for Richards, he never had to send the petition to Richmond, as the February 17 conscription law maintained an exemption for newspaper editors and therefore enrolling officers let him remain home.[24]

Principals ranged across a spectrum of Confederate loyalty. Men who fled to Union lines, those who hid from enrolling officers, and those who sought fraudulent exemptions represented one end. Someone like Richards, a healthy man who legally tried to avoid the army, might fall in the middle. A Bureau of Conscription report described the other end: patriotic principals. These men had always had legal exemptions, but they provided substitutes regardless. Many planters, wealthy manufacturers, and mechanics who had legitimate exemption claims, whether occupational or age-related, supplied replacement soldiers.

While acknowledging that some principals shirked their duty, General Howell Cobb offered a passionate defense of others, reminding the secretary of war that "there were large numbers who were as brave and patriotic as any who went into the service." He offered examples of families that kept one male behind while the others served, businessmen who provided supplies to the army, and plantation owners who helped feed soldiers' families. Additionally, the class of principals included "many patriotic persons of feeble health" who now merited medical exemptions. A Virginia officer wrote a testimonial on behalf of such a principal from his unit. The man had volunteered in 1861, reenlisted in 1862, and then was shot in the chest. At that point, the wounded soldier, who had never previously considered providing a substitute, hired a replacement, who was still serving in 1864. A North Carolinian wrote of a similar situation. His weakly son had enlisted in 1861 and served until his health gave out; only then did he employ a substitute. In both cases, the letters implied that medical boards would have exempted these men, but instead the unhealthy Confederates paid for others to serve in their places.[25]

Some legislators shared Cobb's view of patriotic principals. A congressman lectured his colleagues that they had to "soften the law." He suggested distinguishing between loyal principals—those who had a legitimate reason to remain home, such as growing food or those whose substitutes remained in the army—and disloyal principals—speculators and those who hired known bounty jumpers. The House passed an amendment drawing this distinction, but senators never voted on it. Their decision most likely rested on a combination of a commitment to the ideal that all must serve and a realization of the impossibility of trying to sort out which principals had acted loyally and which had acted opportunistically. One senator pessimistically envisioned such an amendment resulting in 90 percent of principals keeping out of the army, with loyal and disloyal principals alike claiming it applied to them.[26]

The evidence from the records of a North Carolina enrolling officer further demonstrates the difficulty in drawing hasty conclusions about principals' motivations. The officer kept a list of seventy-five principals in his district who were now eligible for service. In a column entitled "Now Exempt As," the officer had made notations for twenty-nine of the men. The list included four millers, four men with disabilities, three home guards, two constables, two blacksmiths, and two men in the Nitre and Mining Bureau. In contrast, in the "Now Conscribed" column, it listed notations of "fit for service" for only two of the men. Forty-four men had no notations whatsoever, but it is unclear if they had left the county, dodged conscript officers, or simply had not yet turned themselves in.

On one hand, this evidence could support a view that principals lacked loyalty to the Confederacy, since the overwhelming majority appeared to continue to avoid army life despite the new law. On the other hand, it also supports a contention that some principals possessed Confederate loyalty, since many of them had provided a man to serve in their place even though they might not have faced conscription. Most clearly, the presence of three men over the age of forty-five in the "Now Exempt As" category provides indisputable evidence that at least a few men had provided substitutes even though they had not faced conscription themselves. Additionally, if these men were truly disabled, blacksmiths, state officials, or millers, they—depending on the timing of their conscription—could have claimed exemptions in these categories without purchasing a substitute.[27]

For almost all of the men, the list also includes the name of their substitute and a column headed "Why Not in Service." The information there adds to the difficulty in making concrete judgments about substitution. While this column's title presumes that substitutes were no longer in the army, the notations within the column contradict this supposition. In fact, it lists twenty-five substitutes as "in service," four as dead, and three as discharged. In contrast, only one was labeled "not in service" with four others classified as deserters with an additional two having possibly deserted. The remaining men had no notations whatsoever. While a lack of comments for almost half the men undermines the ability to make conclusive judgments, the presence of only four to six deserters in a list of seventy-five substitutes would have surprised many Confederates. Critics often assumed that the overwhelming majority of substitutes quickly deserted, but, in this case, at least one-third—and potentially many more—of these replacement soldiers had already served for two years.[28]

Rather than seeking exemptions, some former principals sought protection from the judiciary to avoid conscription. Praising the end of substitution as "one of the best things that could be done," a soldier expressed the caveat that "there is little doubt but it will be tested all over the country." He was correct. Principals argued that they had entered into a contract and the government should be compelled to honor its terms, which usually stipulated exemption for the duration of the war. The government disagreed. Just as Congress could amend the conscription laws to end the exemption for teachers, preachers, or forty-year-olds, so too could it end the exemption for principals. Moreover, not being a party to the contract between principals and substitutes, the government could not be bound by its provisions. Judges would make the final decision, and a congressman worried about that scenario. He fretted that "the country should be lost because of the opinion of every petty judge."[29]

Congress and the Bureau of Conscription correctly anticipated that they had to worry about one petty judge in particular. This legal challenge achieved its greatest traction in the chambers of North Carolina's Judge Pearson, who had previously thwarted the conscription of principals whose substitutes had been enrolled in the army. Pearson had a well-deserved reputation for consistently releasing men from enrolling officers. Supposedly, the judge considered conscription unconstitutional, and in 1863, while releasing individual principals from service, had warned that he considered the idea of conscripting all principals to be anathema to the law. When asked about this possibility of Pearson negating the new measure, the secretary of war reportedly said, "I will not hesitate a moment to arrest [him]." Another official offered a rationale for such a drastic action, branding Pearson "a traitor, if not open at least at heart."[30]

In February, partly in an effort to thwart Pearson's traitorous judicial challenge to conscription, President Davis requested—and Congress authorized—the suspension of the writ of habeas corpus in conscription cases. In their view, disloyal judges used the writ to help disloyal men escape their military obligations. In some cases, the mere prospect of having to travel a long distance and neglect their other responsibilities caused overworked enrolling officers to release these men without a fight. In other cases, even when the officers appeared, judges disregarded Confederate law and dismissed the men from the army. In sum, when abused, the writ completely undermined conscription. The army needed men now, and it could not afford to face lengthy legal challenges in civilian courts. Suspending the writ kept the power to decide whether a man belonged in the army securely within the Bureau of Conscription, for judges could no longer force enrolling officers to bring conscripts to court.

The 1864 habeas corpus law enumerated thirteen categories under which the writ could be suspended, including cases of "attempts to avoid military service." Davis felt that this draconian remedy was necessary to ensure that conscription worked. The president maintained that "loyal citizens will not feel the danger, and the disloyal must be made to fear it." In short, Confederates who accepted conscription regulations had no reason to fear the suspension, especially because it still permitted appeals within military channels and stipulated punishments for officers who impressed men illegally. The *Savannah Republican* parroted this argument contending that "only bad men should disapprove of [the suspension]."[31]

In contrast, the measure confirmed the suspicions of southerners who had always seen the potential for despotism in conscription. Critics mocked the cry that suspension was necessary, calling it a "fatal delusion" and contending that if liberty and independence were not reconcilable now, they would not be after the war, either. A North Carolina newspaper reminded its readers, "Dark as the situation of the country is . . . let it not be said of us that we threw off one tyranny only to build up another at home." The Georgia legislature condemned suspension as an unconstitutional measure that amounted to government-sanctioned kidnapping. Governor Brown claimed that it bestowed "the powers of a monarch" upon Davis, and he urged "every state in the Confederacy" to "denounce and condemn this wicked act." Robert Toombs hoped Brown would defy the law, which "subverts all rights," and an editor shrieked, "Our freedom is now gone!" In Richmond, a war department official worried that the suspension made "the executive absolute to every intent and purpose," and a clerk insisted that the measures clothed Davis with "DICTATORIAL POWERS."[32]

Judge Pearson did his best to use the bench to block the development of a military tyranny in the Confederacy. The full North Carolina court did not meet until June. In the meantime, each of the three judges heard cases independently in chambers, with their individual decisions binding until they met together. When Edward Walton, a principal who faced conscription, appealed to Pearson, the judge decided that enrolling officers had no right to conscript him. The judge maintained that if Congress could change this law, it could repudiate its bonds or conscript state officials. Such logic would "put an end to 'State Rights,' and erect on the ruins a 'consolidated military despotism,'" all in the name of raising an army. While Pearson decided Walton's case before the suspension of habeas corpus, he would later argue that the suspension did not apply to men who appeared in his court. It specifically pertained to men trying "to avoid military service." According to Pearson, any man who appealed to the judicial system was by definition not trying to avoid military service. People avoiding service hid in the woods or fled to the enemy's lines. They did not seek legal remedies. He also added that the suspension should apply only to criminal cases, not to civil cases. Consequently, in his own mind, Pearson, as in his previous decisions, did not strike a blow against the Confederacy but instead acted as a loyal citizen enforcing an ideology that protected individual liberty.[33]

The judge's ruling astonished no one. The *Wilmington Journal* remarked that with Pearson adjudicating, "no matter what the case may be, the public are always prepared for the same result—a decision against the Confederate government." One general advised declaring martial law in North Carolina to forestall the judge's efforts. Secretary of War Seddon lamented that "Judge Pearson is still, I fear, bent on mischief," and he later alluded to Pearson in decrying the "injurious efforts of some judges" who believed "that by diminishing the Army and obstructing the authority of Congress they are performing a public duty."

Pearson undoubtedly maintained that he was performing a public duty. The judge also tried to add some levity to the confrontation. He explained to a friend that he did not always decide against the army. In fact, he had a stack of rejected cases on his desk, and he expected that his enemies might "be surprised to learn I have such a bundle." Whether one regarded Pearson as a traitor or a patriot, his decision regarding Walton was binding until the full court met in June. In the meantime, Governor Vance informed Confederate officials that "there is no escape from th[e] conclusion" that he was obligated to honor Pearson's decision.[34]

While allowing Pearson's decision to stand for Walton, Confederate leaders refused to view it as a precedent applicable to other cases. They had a variety of reasons for taking this course. First, Confederates considered the law constitutional, so they branded Pearson's judgment as "strange and clearly incorrect." As one government lawyer grandiosely argued, the idea of Congress passing an unamendable bill keeping men out of the army forever "would have been an act of madness unparalleled in the annals of time!" Second, the army needed men immediately; it could not afford to wait until after a lengthy judicial appeals process. Third, Confederate leaders believed that conscripting principals improved morale in the ranks and at home. They did not want to lose this benefit. Fourth, Pearson had decided the Walton case before the suspension of the writ of habeas corpus. Now, with the writ suspended, Pearson did not have the authority to hear additional cases. Undoubtedly, Pearson disagreed with all these arguments, but most important, he continued to issue writs (perhaps as many as 120), stubbornly insisting that the suspension did not apply to his actions.[35]

When the full North Carolina court met in June, Confederates nervously awaited the results. In the middle of the month, the head of conscription in North Carolina anxiously wrote to a lawyer acting on the government's behalf, wondering if he had a sense of the "probable action." The court's decision relieved his anxiety. In *Gatlin v. Walton,* Pearson's two counterparts, judges William Battle and Matthias Manly, voted against him, ruling that abolishing substitution and making principals liable for service was constitutional. For them, congressional war power was almost absolute and substitution was a "personal privilege," not a contract. Pearson's minority opinion worried that the majority decision resisted upon the unanswerable—and liberty-threatening—doctrine that "necessity knows no law." He concluded that, sadly, the wartime crisis had caused rule of law to disappear. Regardless of the accuracy of that assessment, the judge's power over conscription had disappeared. In the summer of 1864, in a series of 2 to 1 decisions, Pearson's generous use of the writ was repeatedly reversed by the full court.[36]

Rulings in Georgia and Virginia also upheld the conscription of principals, with the latter declaring that the national government "is charged with the whole military strength of the nation" and that substitution was only allowed "as an act of grace and favor." In rendering their opinion in *Burroughs v. Peyton,* the judges on the Virginia Supreme Court emphatically declared that the power to conscript is "so far from being inconsistent with liberty, it is essential to its preservation." In Georgia, Superior Court Judge O. A. Lochrane, in *Fitzgerald v. Harris,* also took a strong pro-government stance. In his opinion, substitution only existed when the interest of the principal and the Confederacy coincided. Once their interests diverged, the nation's welfare took priority. Simply put, when public and private interests differed, the latter must yield. Taking a swipe at obstructionist judges like Pearson, he concluded, "*No nation will die by contract.*" His state's supreme court concurred, calling interpretations like Pearson's "a novelty in jurisprudence."[37]

If habeas corpus cases tested the government's patience, details tested its administrative capabilities. The 1864 law allowed executive branch–granted details to supplement exemptions to assign the Confederacy's manpower more efficiently. The clause allowed more men, families, and communities to appeal their cases to government officials. Every conscript could request a detail, and at times it appeared that every conscript did. An officer inspecting North Carolina's camp of instruction found much abuse in this system. He believed "applications for detail are almost as numerous as the persons enrolled," with more than one hundred received each day. He later explained that men put in "sham petition[s]" simply to get a few extra months at home as they awaited the results of their appeal. In taking over conscription in South Carolina, James Chesnut worried that the flood of applications for exemptions and details were "so numerous" that "I will be unable to give them the examination necessary" to make proper decisions. Virginia officials undoubtedly shared his concerns, as they had 25,000 applications for details pending in July.[38]

Decisions on detail applications often hinged on Confederate loyalty. A seventy-five-year-old mill owner in Randolph County, North Carolina, requested the detail of one of his employees, arguing that the man had done this job for sixteen years, that he had "never speculated," and that most of his 156 customers were poor women. The week before, that county's board of investigation endorsed two details, describing a shoemaker as "a good & loyal citizen" and a farmer as an "honest upright man. True to his country." In Virginia, James Saunders emphasized both his need and his suffering for the cause. His dependents included his wife, four small children, his widowed mother, three nieces, and two young slave children. The Yankees had taken his other twenty-eight slaves and destroyed his mill and farm equipment. He then expressed the standard claim that "those dependent on him will greatly suffer and add much more distress to the community than his person & single presence in the army can possibly do good."[39]

Elsewhere, an Alabaman described the other side of the coin: men who sought details simply to escape from the army. He portrayed a scenario with "more pushing [and] shoving than you ever saw to git details." To push and shove to the front of the line, a Virginia soldier hoped to have his congressman, John Goode, help him. Initially, his application was denied, but Goode assured him that he could help him, since it was the intention of Congress to detail all who "could furnish the meat & make something for the Government." This definition exemplifies one of the main problems with details. If the policy truly intended to detail all men who "could furnish meat & make something," almost every conscript could claim it applied to them.[40]

James Holloway, a Virginia soldier, denounced the maneuverings of his friend Jimmie Balfour. On July 23, Holloway heard that Balfour had failed to get a detail. While Holloway had hoped that Balfour would succeed, he now "advise[d] him to join a company and take his musket." He did, however, admit that Balfour's "patriotism is not sufficiently strong for such a sacrifice." Two days later, he talked to Balfour, who "presented a dozen prospective schemes . . . all of which will keep him out of the ranks." While Holloway considered Balfour to be desperately "clutching at straws," he underestimated either his fellow soldier's determination or his connections. After another two days passed, Balfour headed home with "an exemption of 40 days from the President." Holloway did not mention the grounds for this temporary exemption (which was more likely a detail), but he recognized that "one thing is uppermost in [Balfour's] thought—namely—to escape and keep out of the army." Holloway found Balfour's actions unbecoming and pointed out, "One cant help thinking how much better it would look—if he would enter the ranks."[41]

In criticizing the excessive number of healthy men avoiding combat, some Confederates considered the government to be part of the problem. Many southerners protested the presence of healthy, military-age men serving in rear echelon jobs in government bureaus. A Louisiana private decried these men as "dead heads." A colonel suggested that the best solution for defeating the Yankees was to put all the able-bodied men in the "peace departments" in the army and replace them with "disabled officers & men." The president endorsed this plan, and a supporter praised it, adding that women could also fill some of these positions. A July 1863 order had already required healthy men in these bureaus be sent to the front lines, but it had not been strictly enforced. In January 1864, Congress requested information on how many soldiers in the quartermaster and commissary bureaus had been replaced by disabled officers, and the February act threatened officers with court martial if they shielded men. The bureaus could not provide specific totals but insisted they were doing their best to honor this policy. Despite these efforts, critics continued to complain that the presence of "fat, sleek, well-dressed able-bodied men" in these departments mocked the president's declaration that all men should be in the ranks.[42]

In Georgia, an officer venting to Governor Brown summed up these frustrations. Even with Sherman's army threatening Atlanta, the officer complained of "a good many men hanging around the various towns doing no good . . . speculating on honest people." In his view, "Every one should be of some beneficial employment," whether in the army or at home. When he returned home on furlough, his fury increased as he found conscription laws "fully abused" as if Congress had not amended the law. He listed some of the able-bodied abusers: price-gouging millers, nonessential government officials, and unpatriotic government contractors. The officer witnessed "a regular electioneering frolic" as candidates competed for positions in state government solely to get out of the service. Worst of all, local courts sadly supported these subterfuges. The officer had a simple yet drastic solution. He wanted Governor Brown to call into militia service all men under the age of fifty. If they did not appear, then the governor should have a few men shot. In matter-of-factly offering this startling advice, he voiced the standard Confederate refrain: "One man is no better than another as regards to military service."[43]

In separate letters to Secretary of War Seddon, Georgia's and Florida's governors concurred with this officer's diagnosis, though not with his cure. Brown preferred that the "almost countless swarm of young able-bodied officers" in government bureaus be forced into the army in place of farmers, who were more needed at home. Milton requested that the secretary order all draftable men in the commissary department into the army. Their presence away from the front lines demonstrated that a desire for riches "has overcome the obligations of patriotism and endangers the very existence of the Confederate States." He also wrote directly to the Commissary General complaining that most subagents of the bureau were "young able-bodied men . . . who should be in Military Service." Florida citizens were "not inclined to tolerate the practice of placing young men who have skulked military service" in positions that nonconscripts could fill. The Bureau of Conscription and the secretary of war responded to these complaints. Seddon concurred with Milton, informing the governor that "the settled policy . . . is against the employment of men fit for field service, in other capacities." The bureau sent a directive to enrolling officers reminding them that details for these bureaus should only occur if the men were absolutely necessary and if efforts had been made to find men not subject to conscription to fill the positions. In all cases, the bureaus needed to provide lists of detailed men to enrolling officers, so they could confirm compliance with the policy.[44]

The Bureau of Conscription itself also came under attack for shielding men from service in the field. Critics smugly pointed out the irony that soldiers hunting conscripts and working in camps of instruction avoided the front lines themselves. If the bureau was supposed to enforce the idea that the Confederacy needed every able-bodied man in the field, then it should start by holding a mirror up to itself. C. C. Henkel proved their point. He advised a friend to secure a position as an enrolling officer, as "in many respects it would be more desirable than being in service in the field." In areas with few eligible soldiers, some contended that the "almost worthless" bureau employed more men than it sent to the army. One Georgian complained that enrolling officers, whom he castigated as "gentlemen and their sons . . . loafing over the country, pretending to hunt conscripts," did more harm than Yankees. In his region, he believed that there were twice as many enrolling officers as conscripts. A Mississippian wrote President Davis that "old maids" could easily replace a regiment of conscription officers. Florida governor Milton suggested shutting down his state's "very expensive and perhaps entirely useless" conscript camp and transferring its soldiers to a regular command.[45]

The Bureau of Conscription responded to these complaints. Regulations stipulated that the bureau use only wounded men or those outside of conscription's age range. Since this was coming at a time when the government expected the bureau to redouble its efforts (reinspecting exemptions, investigating applications for details, enrolling potentially reluctant principals, and finding those last few men who had somehow avoided enrolling for almost two years), conscription officials fought this change. General Preston complained that his bureau faced more scrutiny than any other government office ever had. He admitted that results had not met expectations, but he blamed the "universal effort to keep men from the field" rather than his bureau. His conscientious officers made "the most laborious, patient, cautious, and intelligent investigation into the relations of every man to the public defense." They did all this when many of his best soldiers were being sent to the front lines, leaving his bureau to rely on "accidental officers" from the invalid corps, "irregularly assigned" to the conscription service. Preston predicted "utter failure" if the trend of removing capable men from his command was not reversed.[46]

The Bureau of Conscription's task, always difficult, became almost impossible in 1864. A January circular dramatically reminded these "accidental officers" of the gravity of their jobs. It asserted that nothing less than "the liberties of his country and the preservation of parents, wives, sisters, and daughters from a brutal and relentless enemy" depended upon their efforts. Consequently, if an enrolling officer neglected his duties, he would be considered "a traitor of the deepest dye." Even if such a sin went undetected, "the curse of God and his country will fall upon him." While not serving on the front lines, their service was "the most important in the public defense."

In March and April, General Preston defended his bureau. He complained to the secretary of war of the repeated problems that his officers faced in trying to wrestle men from other authorities. Army officers ignored conscription regulations and procedures, pressing men into service. Preston claimed that no officer had ever sent a conscript out of his department. Aside from the generals, "the very worst agency to have control of conscription . . . is the local civil or military authorities." In six months, according to the general, state authorities had kept thousands of men at home but had not sent any to the field. Despite all of these impediments, Preston concluded on an upbeat note: "You cannot devise a better system than the one now in operation," and he later added that the Confederacy had "just reason to be satisfied with both the system and the officers" in his bureau.[47]

At first glance, the statistical tables accompanying Preston's April report did not support the idea that the bureau was operating the best possible recruitment system. The tables, though admittedly incomplete, offered an assessment of the bureau's accomplishments through the first three months of 1864. During this period, the bureau had added just 18,144 men to the army (7,513 conscripts, 3,235 volunteers, and 8,306 returned deserters). At the same time, it had exempted 26,472 men and detailed 13,142 others.

Preston's report provided some context to explain these underwhelming numbers. First, Preston maintains that the figures represented less than half of the men who joined the army during this period. Others, under the "compulsion of the law," joined units without passing through camps of instruction. Conscription thus actually accounted for more than 36,000 additional soldiers in these three months. Second, the manpower field was almost fully harvested. Preston posited that "there are but few left whose appropriate duties . . . have not been defined." The bureau had almost completed its task, and he predicted "the functions of this Bureau may cease with the termination of the year 1864." In sum, in his view, the bureau was a victim of its own success. In his examination of Confederate Virginia, William Blair finds this assertion to be true, as he contends 93 percent of military-age Virginians were either in the army or in war-related work in 1864.[48]

Secretary of War Seddon forwarded the bureau's report to President Davis and endorsed Preston's assessment. Seddon blamed the bureau's lack of success on the excessive claims for exemptions and details, each of which had to be investigated by conscript officers, most of whom were retired or invalids. In general, the volunteering spirit of the people had declined; thus, relying "on the prestige of the law and the support of the intelligent public opinion" rather than on "military coercion" meant a sacrifice in efficiency. This sacrifice, however, helped people accept the law. The secretary reminded the president of the dire challenge that conscription posed to Confederate ideology. In passing conscription, Congress had "concentrate[d] the energy and resources and . . . the men and property of the Confederacy in larger measure than have ever been done by any government." Confederates had accepted this burden, but only with safeguards protecting their civil liberties. According to this line of reasoning, the bureau's inefficiency was a boon rather than a bane. In allowing a few potential soldiers to slip through the cracks, it inculcated a greater loyalty to the Confederacy among the masses.[49]

Though Preston had an important ally in the secretary of war, he had a powerful enemy in General Braxton Bragg. A close friend of President Davis, Bragg had failed in field command, especially at the battle of Chattanooga in December 1863. Subsequently, Davis brought Bragg to Richmond, where he served as a special advisor to the president, acting as Davis's unofficial chief of staff. Having been a staunch proponent of General Pillow's 1863 military conscription, Bragg brought with him to the capital a hostile attitude toward the Bureau of Conscription. Consequently, when Davis tasked the biased Bragg with assessing conscription, the general unsurprisingly found the "whole organization . . . defective and inefficient." When it could not provide all the reports he asked for, Bragg recommended to the president that "a complete renovation of the Bureau . . . will be indispensable." While castigating the entire bureau, he singled out two officers, Colonel T. P. August and Lieutenant Thomas Goldthwaite, for their misconduct. After August had the temerity to remind Bragg that he had no authority over the bureau, Bragg felt that the colonel should be sent to the front lines to learn "discipline and respect for his superiors." Bragg considered the twenty-four-year-old Goldthwaite to be too young and inexperienced for the important responsibilities of his job, which involved serving as the final bureau review for detail applications.[50]

Faced with this direct assault on his bureau, General Preston returned fire. First, he defended his subordinates. He argued that August had worked diligently for the bureau, and he included the medical board's report on the colonel, noting that August had already served in battle, where he received wounds that aggravated a prior medical condition. Consequently, the colonel was now "extremely liable to die at any moment" and could not last a single hour on the front lines. Preston also asserted that Goldthwaite's legal acumen negated any concerns about his age. Second, Preston defended the bureau itself. He reminded the secretary of war that Congress intentionally separated conscription from the armies in the field, and any departures from this system would be "detrimental to the service." Plus, the bureau did not simply gather and enlist men. It conducted thorough investigations to ensure that each man served in his correct position, whether at home or in the army. Despite these complicated duties, conscription had worked, doing "more to fill the armies and . . . maintain the resources of the country than any other [plan] which can be devised." Finally, the bureau accomplished these tasks despite being composed primarily of disabled and incompetent men.[51]

Preston even wrote directly to President Davis, chastising Bragg for sending "ignorant and prejudiced" agents rather than impartial inspectors to examine his bureau. He then attacked Bragg's own conscription record, reminding the president that while the Bragg–Pillow 1863 military conscription had gathered many men, it had—in violation of orders—kept them all without sending a single soldier to Lee's army, which is where Davis had wanted them. Preston therefore predicted that General Lee did not share Bragg's positive impression of military conscription. Plus, the general pointed out another complication in emulating Bragg's plan. According to Preston, if his bureau used the same proportion of men that Pillow did, it would need 6,000 officers and 36,000 soldiers, whereas an 1864 report credited the bureau with only 282 officers and a total of 3,259 men. Preston lectured Seddon that military conscription was "repulsive to . . . public sentiment." In fact, he would have found the whole concept "ludicrous" had it not been "so expensive and so disastrous."[52]

Preston and his bureau were threatened on multiple fronts. Bragg's assault led Preston to offer his resignation. The general received some solace, as Davis and Seddon refused to accept it. Yet their support did not end his challenges as the bureau's long-standing foes, states' rights ideologues, returned to the field. State leaders and enrolling officers had never seen eye to eye on conscription, and this mutual wariness reached a crescendo with the revised conscription policy and concomitant suspension of habeas corpus. The February 1864 conscription law put all men between seventeen and fifty in the army. Up until this change, state leaders could count on some of these men to make up a state militia. No one, however, could expect an adequate militia to be composed of sixteen-year-olds and men in their fifties. Historian Frank L. Owsley contends that the February law increased states' opposition to conscription, for it "proposed to divest the states of their right to maintain 'troops of war'—the sine qua non of their sovereignty." Exemplifying this hostility, the North Carolina legislature passed a resolution claiming the measure created "a consolidated military despotism" and reduced the states "to mere provincial administrations," dependent on the national government for their existence.[53]

About the only protection states had left was the exemption for state officials, and the 1864 act even threatened this right. A year earlier, a North Carolinian had lamented that the presence of tens of thousands (maybe hundreds of thousands) of men in petty offices belied "all the talk about robbing the cradle and grave." With opinions like that in mind, Congress required that states reduce their exemptions to only their most essential employees. It mandated that governors certify these exempt officers to be absolutely necessary to administer the state. Allegedly, abuses abounded, especially in North Carolina and Georgia, where governors Vance and Brown declared every minor official to be essential. One observer decried the "outrageous wrong" as 90 percent of Georgia's militia officers were within conscription's age range but were slated for exemption as state officers, despite the fact they had no militia to lead, since all the men in the ranks had been conscripted. A concerned Georgian warned Governor Brown that "young & robust men" claimed militia offices solely to evade their duty, and "cowardly rascals" claimed exemption as constables, taking refuge in these "contemptible and almost unnecessary offices." By the end of the year, the secretary of war declared that President Davis and others felt that "considerable numbers" of Georgians liable to conscription remained at large.[54]

Confederate leaders tried unsuccessfully to gauge the impact of governors' refusals to give up their state officers. A November report indicated that North Carolina's obstructionism exceeded that found elsewhere. States had exempted 18,843 officers, with North Carolina being responsible for 14,675 (77.9 percent) of them. Three months later, a new report revised North Carolina's totals downward to 5,589 and raised Georgia's total from 1,012 to 8,229. One source of discrepancies was that some enrolling officers simply reported the number of offices that were potentially exempt, regardless of whether the men in these offices claimed exemption. In this instance, if a state had fifty counties, each with a sheriff and two deputies, officials simply recorded 150 exemptions. That number, however, just represented the maximum number of exemptions possible. It did not mean that the state had shielded that many conscripts. These positions may have been vacant, filled by disabled soldiers, or held by fifty-five-year-olds. In contrast, in other states, enrolling officers just counted the men whom they had tried to conscript but who had claimed exemption as state officers. This method was employed in Mississippi; consequently, the report listed that state with only 110 exempted state officers. While the first method overcounted the number of exemptions, the second method drastically undercounted the number. In comparing the Magnolia State to others, a general declared that Mississippi "enjoys the benefits" of perhaps as many as 4,000 state exemptions "but avoids the stigma" of being labeled as an obstructionist state.[55]

Regardless of the precise numbers of its state officials, Georgia politicians objected to what they perceived as the Confederate government's effort to take control of the state's entire military-age population. Brown and Vice President Stephens publicly denounced the combination of expanded conscription and suspension of habeas corpus as "not less worthy of resistance than the Yankees." In Stephens's estimation, Davis had entered the presidency with good intentions, but his weakness, combined with his obstinacy, had "changed many of his former State's rights principles, as in case of conscription." Governor Brown agreed that Davis did not honor states' rights principles. While acknowledging that, in 1862, the Georgia courts had ruled conscription constitutional in *Jeffers v. Fair*, Brown insisted that this decision did not allow Congress to "deprive the States of the power to execute their own laws." In *Jeffers*, the court had ruled that the only restriction on the Confederacy's conscription power was that it could not prevent the state from functioning by seizing too many state officers. In Brown's opinion, that time had arrived. The current iteration of the law in conscripting all men between seventeen and fifty unconstitutionally crippled the state's ability to defend and administer itself.[56]

Believing that the *Jeffers* decision now strengthened his hand against the expanded conscription, Brown even reentered his epistolary debate on states' rights. Instead of engaging President Davis, however, he found a willing adversary in his antebellum political rival, General Howell Cobb, who commanded the Georgia reserves and who represented the planter class that Brown had long detested. Unlike Brown's 1862 debate with President Davis, which stressed constitutional interpretation, this argument emphasized personality as much as doctrine. Cobb opened the debate by denying that Congress had expected the "sweeping exemption of all civil and military officers of the State" that Georgia had pursued. The general maintained that the governor had shielded far too many sheriffs, deputies, justices of the peace, and constables. Believing that Brown illegally protected 5,000 state employees, the general complained to President Davis that Congress "never presume[ed] . . . that there would be found a Governor who would certify to such a barefaced falsehood."[57]

Brown eagerly lectured Cobb on his errors. First, he reminded the general that Georgia had always provided troops, without needing to resort to conscription. Second, and more important, Cobb had mistakenly inverted the political power in the Confederacy, maintaining that people derived their rights and powers from Congress, whereas in reality Congress derived its power from the people. After hearing reports that Cobb had denounced him as both a traitor and a Tory, supposedly even calling for the governor's hanging, Brown pronounced Cobb to be in a "crazy state of fury." The governor replied that Congress had left the decision on exemptions to the states, and that the home front needed men, too. It was better to have 250,000 well-supported troops than 500,000 "destitute of food and clothing." Brown contended that Georgians objected much more to the conscription of sick men and to the dragging of poor men away from their homes and their helpless relatives than to state officers remaining in Georgia.[58]

Unable to tolerate Brown's intransigence, Cobb sent an angry retort to the governor, highlighting again the "almost countless swarms" of state officers in Georgia. He defended his supposedly naive view that Brown intended to comply with the law and sarcastically apologized for his mistaken belief that Brown wanted to help the army rather than "those who were seeking evasion of duty." Brown quickly objected and called Cobb a speculator and merely "the pretended friend" of soldiers. The governor portrayed himself as a true friend of the men in the ranks, as he was looking after the needs of their families. In an accusation that could have applied to himself, the thin-skinned Cobb then reproached Brown for losing sight of the question at hand and instead writing "for the sole purpose of indulging in personalities."

The two Georgians subsequently took turns repeating rumors that the other had engaged in unethical antebellum financial dealings. Enjoying provoking the governor, the general then increased the rancor of their exchange by admitting that he was not too surprised at Brown's letter, since an "effort to escape . . . by the use of offensive language is quite natural for a man who has lost his temper." Brown snapped back that Cobb, with a safe position in the rear, seemed to "enjoy . . . leisure for . . . indulging in personal abuse." Cobb had had enough. The general tersely noted on the back of this letter, "This communication and the author are alike unworthy of further notice," and he forwarded the correspondence to officials in Richmond.[59]

Like General Cobb, Secretary of War Seddon also had grown tired of Governor Brown's "obstructions." After reading Brown's letters, Seddon concluded that their tone made "attempts at conciliation, harmony, and co-operation useless." Instead, he called on the bureau to act quickly and firmly in Georgia. He hoped that ignoring the governor and making examples of a few men would "strike wholesome terror and induce prompt compliance," especially since the secretary believed "the intelligence and patriotism of Georgia" supported the national government in its conflict with Brown. Seddon wanted enrolling officers to swiftly conscript principals while the suspension of the writ of habeas corpus was in effect (it would expire on July 31). He also believed that Brown sought the wrong relief. Instead of threatening armed resistance and defying the Confederacy, the governor, according to Seddon, should simply pursue a judicial solution. In 1862, the Georgia judiciary had forestalled Brown's efforts to declare conscription unconstitutional. While the potential conscription of nonessential state officers made the situation more complicated, the secretary undoubtedly hoped to see a similar result two years later.[60]

While in 1862 the conflict between Brown and the Confederacy occurred away from the main battlefields, in 1864 it had an added urgency, since it took place while Sherman's army threatened Atlanta from the north. The Confederate army and Brown dueled over who could demand the service of detailed men in the event of emergency. Seddon found Brown's actions "deplorable" and hoped loyal Georgians would reject the governor's course. Upon receiving a brief note that Cobb and Brown had settled their differences, the secretary, ever suspicious of Brown, immediately requested that Cobb provide details of this arrangement. He reminded the general that such a deal needed to follow the constitution and laws of the Confederacy. Whatever the terms of the negotiations were, Brown had not simply acquiesced, for three months later, the officer in charge of conscription in Georgia still blamed the governor for manufacturing a public opinion "not only hostile to [conscription laws'] execution but commendatory of their evasion."[61]

In North Carolina, Georgia's reputed partner in states' rights obstinacy, Governor Vance kept up his skillful balancing act between the national government and his constituents. When an officer asked the governor about the possible conscription of county officials and militia officers, Vance assured him that "he should not give them up." Earlier in the year, the governor had proclaimed to his legislature, "When the rights of the State shall exist by such a courtesy, they will cease to have any existence at all." Vance had to stand up to Confederate officials. In 1864, North Carolina contained a strong peace party. It championed the idea that, with the Confederacy "approaching a *central military* Despotism" blotting out all state lines, the time had come to end the Tar Heel State's participation in the war. In the midst of a gubernatorial race where his opponents branded him as too nationalist, Vance could ill afford to be seen as ceding his state's sovereignty. One of the governor's allies warned him that "the *only* ground of complaint against [him]" was that he "yield[ed] too much to the Richmond administration." Since his election in 1862, Vance had walked a delicate path, considering the needs of the army as well as his constituents' fears that their liberty was in jeopardy. His stance opposing the conscription of all state officials exemplifies the deft political touch that enabled Vance to win reelection.[62]

If Confederate officials considered Vance an obstinate states' rights demagogue, a letter he sent his fellow governors in September would have surprised them. After the fall of Atlanta, Vance urged his fellow Confederate governors to put national survival ahead of their political doctrines. Sounding more like President Davis than a states' rights proponent, the governor argued that "beyond all else, men must be sent to the armies of Generals Lee and Hood." He recognized that state officers made up one group at home. Some of these men were necessary, but he admitted that others had been shielded simply "because the principle of States sovereignty rendered it improper to allow the Confederate government to conscript them." Maybe the desperate nature of the times had led him to conclude that national survival had finally superseded political theory. Vance called for a meeting of all the governors to discuss which men from this latter group could be sent to the army. In October, six governors gathered in Augusta, Georgia, and passed resolutions requesting the repeal of all laws preventing state troops from being sent beyond each state's borders.[63]

The governors, however, sent a mixed message. They passed resolutions in favor of both independence and state sovereignty at a time when many argued these ideas were incompatible, at least during the war. While declaring "we will use our best exertions to increase the effective force of our armies," the governors did not cede their militia to the Confederacy; they just allowed them to be sent out of state. Also, the governors could not resist the chance to chide the Confederate government. Echoing earlier criticisms, they pointed out that the federal government also shielded men from service. Their manifesto resolved that the Confederacy should send all able-bodied men in government departments to the field. Upon his return from this meeting where he had pledged cooperation, however, Vance immediately reengaged in conflicts over state employees. Vance expressed the seemingly contradictory view that he was "willing that every man shall go" but was not willing to "break down the State of North Carolina." If the Confederacy refused his state details, the governor planned to resist any claims upon these men.[64]

Not all governors shared Vance's obstinacy. Virginia governor William "Extra Billy" Smith gave Confederates a strong ally in their efforts to conscript nonvital state officers. Smith found it "utterly impossible . . . to understand the logic which exempts State officers who are not necessary for the State government." In this case, he challenged local officials in his own state, especially those who claimed exemption as officers in counties that lay behind enemy lines. With the Union army occupying more than forty of the state's counties, Smith called on Virginians "in the name of patriotism, of our manhood, of our dear old State . . . and of our bleeding country" to join the army.

Like Governor Smith, Governor Henry Watkins Allen of Louisiana also tried to reduce the number of state employees exempt from conscription. In scaling down the state government to only its essential employees, he authorized the conscription of notary publics and justices of the peace. In doing so, he incurred the wrath of the state's judiciary. In releasing a conscripted notary public, a judge declared that the governor had overstepped his constitutional bounds. The judge expected the governor, as head of the executive branch, to enforce the laws, not to make them. In sacrificing state officers, Governor Allen sacrificed state sovereignty, making it "a laughable farce" and "put[ting] an end to our Republican system of government."[65]

The Confederate Congress, consisting of members elected in November 1863, convened a month after the governors' meeting. For legislators, President Davis, the army, and the Bureau of Conscription, state leaders' cooperation, or lack thereof, was not the greatest challenge. Their greatest foe was numbers. In his March 1864 attack on the expanded conscription, Vice President Stephens had pointed out that the act ran headlong into a "question of Arithmetic." The Confederacy could not win an arms race against the more populous Union. Plus, conscription was a zero-sum game. Every man gained by the army represented a loss to the home front. For two and a half years, the Confederacy had tweaked its conscription policy to put its entire population on war footing. In military terms, they had succeeded, particularly with the February 1864 act that emphasized details over exemptions. In *Ex Parte Tate,* the Alabama Supreme Court endorsed this power, grandly asserting that the Confederacy can "exhaust, if it becomes necessary, the entire military force of the country." It seemingly had become necessary.[66]

In fact, historians of military drafts compliment the South for putting into place the most complete conscription in American history. After the war, former Union general Emory Upton praised "the boldness" of the 1864 law, and he jealously lauded Confederate conscription as a situation in which the ends justified the means. Like Upton, Fred A. Shannon celebrated even the limited 1862 conscription as "more perfect in many respects than any similar act passed by the U.S. Congress throughout the war." Emory Thomas argues that "the wartime South became more centralized, more nationalized than her Northern enemy." Conscription showed the reach of the Confederate government not only through its ability to place men in the army but also in its ability to regulate the economy through the use of details and exemptions. For Richard Bensel, conscription served as one of the "most significant state power enhancing measures," as it enabled the Confederate government to achieve almost total control over the nation's manpower resources. More recently, Michael Brem Bonner has persuasively argued that conscription exemplified "the power of the expedient corporatist state." He explains that the measure, while similar to later drafts, developed in an ad hoc manner, intended to enable the Confederacy to survive rather than to create an intentional revolution in federalism. Nevertheless, Bonner agrees that it provided the national government control over not only the military but also the civilian labor force.[67]

Despite this praise of Confederate conscription, its success did not necessarily equate to military victory. As 1864 neared a close, the arithmetic caught up, as it appeared there were not enough Confederates to fend off the larger Union armies. The Union had mobilized a smaller proportion of its men but still significantly outnumbered the Confederate army. At the beginning of 1865, the Union's 959,460 soldiers greatly exceeded the Confederacy's 400,787.[68] Along with the Confederacy as a whole, moreover, the Bureau of Conscription teetered on the verge of collapse. Though Grant and Lincoln's multipronged simultaneous attack had not worked precisely as they had hoped, the numerical pressure the Union army applied in Virginia and Georgia had reduced the size of both the Confederacy and its armies. With Sherman marching to the sea and Grant threatening Petersburg (and consequently Richmond), the army needed every soldier it could obtain. At the same time, states, communities, and families were exhausted. They had given all the men they would and could willingly give up. Could more men be found? The newly seated Second Congress was tasked with the last-ditch effort to modify, yet again, the Confederacy's manpower formula.

CHAPTER 7

# The Collapse of Conscription and the Confederacy

During the 1864 congressional debate on conscription, Louisiana representative Charles Conrad chided his colleagues that for two years every proposed expansion of conscription had led to inaccurate predictions of "terrific, untold and unheard of calamities." These mistaken forecasts of starvation and anguish reminded the congressman of a story of an Irishman's horse. Conrad compared the misery of the Confederacy to this long-suffering horse, observing that "we had gotten so used to starving" that, like the horse, "we will be able to live on nothing." At this point, a colleague interrupted him, shouting, "The horse died." The other representatives laughed at Conrad's ill-conceived metaphor, but in retrospect, he was unintentionally on target. Conscription could not be extended forever without dealing the Confederacy a mortal blow. On Christmas Day, a government official offered a similar analysis, albeit with less colorful language. Complaining about the revocation of details, he worried, "The conscription has been pressed to its utmost limits, and beyond any reasonable ones."[1]

This final chapter will examine how Confederates pressed conscription to its limits and beyond in the last six months of the war. Some of their discussions repeated earlier disputes. In an effort to assign every Confederate to a military task—either in the army or supporting it on the home front—President Davis and Congress returned to their debate over whether exemptions or details best accomplished this goal. Meanwhile, the Bureau of Conscription and the army returned to their debate over whether the discretion of civilian leadership or the vigor of military-run conscription was more effective. In a new twist, some Confederates even advocated the controversial proposition that slaves fell within the limits of conscription. None of these options, however, prevented defeat in April 1865. In order to understand how far the limits of conscription extended, this chapter concludes with a discussion of the frustratingly incomplete and at times contradictory numbers associated with the measure, and with an overall assessment of what conscription reveals about the Confederacy.

On November 7, 1864, the first session of the Second Confederate Congress met. This body had the task of saving Conrad's horse and figuring out how far they could press the limits of conscription. A month earlier, in a speech in Augusta, Georgia, President Davis had stressed, "We are fighting for our existence," and therefore "every man able to bear arms must go to the front." While admitting that some men needed to support the cause from home, he cautioned, "There must be no pleading for exemption." His opening message to Congress repeated this theme. Yet, in contrast to the darkness and rain outside, it also gave a surprisingly positive picture of the military situation. Davis claimed that the Confederacy had regained lost ground in the Trans-Mississippi Department and had stalled the Union army's advance in Virginia. The president even shrugged off Sherman's capture of Atlanta with the assertion that the Union had secured no advantage from gaining the city. Despite his optimism, Davis acknowledged that victory required combating the North's superior numbers with even more soldiers.[2]

Along with his message to Congress, the president presented a report from Secretary of War James Seddon. It reiterated the need for the most efficient conscription possible. The secretary emphasized the principle that "every citizen must be assigned to that position and to perform that duty in which he can render the best service" and that "the country should be as one great camp." At the end of the year, Seddon pleaded, "Soldiers are our greatest necessity." To find more soldiers, the secretary suggested eliminating all exemptions and reducing the number of details given to healthy, military-age men. Having proposed the elimination of exemptions a year earlier, Davis eagerly endorsed the secretary's plan. The president believed exemptions encouraged both inefficiency and fraud.[3]

In favoring details over exemptions, Davis failed to mention a key difference between the policies: the executive branch controlled details whereas the legislative branch had power over exemptions. Legislators, nevertheless, immediately recognized his proposal as a threat to their bailiwick. A congressman reminded his colleagues that a reliance on details abdicated their responsibilities: "Congress should enact laws and the Executive should execute them." Several senators saw the president's message as a rebuke of their efforts, and they responded defensively. Senator James Orr seized upon a mistake in Davis's communication. The president had enumerated certain occupations, such as shoemaker, tanner, blacksmith, and miller, as exempt when they had lost this status in the February 1864 conscription bill. The senator angrily accused the president of attempting "to throw blame upon Congress for not doing that which it had done more than six months ago."[4]

In attacking executive control, Orr also complained about a recent military order, General Order 77, which eliminated all agricultural details. Orr believed both that this order pressed conscription beyond all limits, harming the home front, and that it demonstrated the problems with Congress deferring to the executive branch. Paradoxically, Senator Edward Sparrow approved of the order for the same reason Orr disparaged it. He viewed it as the army scolding the executive branch. To Sparrow, the revocation proved that "enormous frauds had been practiced in the matter of details." Similarly, a congressman painted a disheartening picture of details that were "depleting the army, dissatisfying the people and endangering the success of the cause." Calling conscription "a failure," Senator Henry Burnett agreed that the legislative branch should stipulate precisely who should go into the army and who should stay home, adding "no discretion on the subject should be left with the President or Secretary of War."[5]

While aware of the debate over details versus exemptions, the Bureau of Conscription was in the midst of fighting off a more significant challenge than which branch of government decided who stayed home. Even before Congress met, new conscription measures had reopened the competition between the army and the bureau. General Preston blamed Davis confidant Braxton Bragg's continued "vague and unfounded misrepresentations" as undermining the bureau, but it also suffered because the creation of a reserve force provided the army an ingress into the enrollment process. Under the February 1864 law, boys under eighteen and men between forty-six and fifty served in reserve units led by Confederate generals. They neither passed through camps of instruction nor responded to the call of enrolling officers. For these generals, it was only a short and logical step from recruiting reserves to taking over conscription entirely. Notably, when Governor Brown fought over conscription policy in Georgia in 1864, he squared off against General Howell Cobb. Cobb did not work for the Bureau of Conscription. Instead, he was responsible for Georgia's reserves.[6]

While tensions existed across the country, the conflict over reserves centered on Virginia. By late 1864, most Confederates recognized that losing Virginia meant losing the war; consequently, the need for more men there was paramount. With the Union's Army of the Potomac threatening Petersburg and Richmond, General James Kemper, in charge of the state's reserves, took over recruiting. He targeted the excessive number of detailed men—8,000, with another 25,000 applications pending. Robert Kean, serving in the war department, described the effect of Kemper's system in his diary: "The conscription is now being pressed mercilessly. It is agonizing to see and hear the cases daily brought into the War Office, appeal after appeal and *all* disallowed." A month later, he added, "No reasons or excuses being listened to and the men taken to the army as fast as a medical examination could be given to them." Describing the system as "ruthless," Kean nevertheless praised it as "marvelously efficient in putting men, and good ones too, into the army here in Virginia."[7]

Kemper's plan stepped on the bureau's toes, but seemingly it gained official sanction from General Order 73, issued on September 22, 1864. A literal reading of the order appeared to transfer total authority for conscription to the army: "The generals of reserves will hereafter control the enrolling officers and conduct the business of conscription . . . under the direction of the Secretary of War, through the Conscript Bureau." A discrepancy arose over the definitions of *control* and *conduct*. Generals, including Kemper, interpreted the directive as allowing the army to circumvent the bureau entirely. Bureau officials, however, chose to emphasize "through the Conscript Bureau." They contended that the order had just been written poorly, as *control* should only mean "watch over" rather than "take over." In making his plea to the secretary of war, Preston maintained, "My belief is that neither the President, you, nor any other competent authority ever intended such transfer."[8]

Before the government clarified the intent of General Order 73, the army issued new draconian orders (numbers 76, 77, and 81), which revoked all agricultural details and sent all these men into the army. Also, the orders required officers to reexamine anyone who had received a medical exemption. General Lee cheered these changes and optimistically predicted that in Virginia alone such a reexamination would put 10,000 more soldiers in the field. The combination of all of these new orders could effectively put the Bureau of Conscription out of business as the army assumed all its responsibilities. Preston complained to the secretary of war and the president that General Kemper had now completely taken over conscription in Virginia. Preston did not blame Kemper but instead targeted his anger at General Bragg. A war clerk concurred that the bureau was "pretty nearly demolished under [Bragg's] blows."[9]

Bruised but not beaten by Bragg's blows, Preston battled back. He hoped that the example of General Pillow's 1863 military conscription, "too recent and too sad," would prevent a return to "that fatal system." He predicted that military conscription would "chill the patriotic ardor." States would nullify it, and by the time the government fixed this mistake, it would be too late to reinforce the armies. Simply put, he found the transfer of conscription to military generals "abhorrent and futile." To correct this error, Preston drafted a revised general order, which made it clear that the reserves could aid in enforcing conscription but not direct or control it. He recognized that the army needed to be involved in conscription, as it had been since 1862, but that its involvement had to be subordinate to the civilian bureau.[10]

Preston and Kemper disagreed not only on the best means of conscripting but also on the results of Kemper's conscription policies, replaying the previous year's debate over the effects of Pillow's efforts. General Preston once more called military conscription "a failure," contending that the army had predicted 40,000 recruits but had only brought in 4,538 men. Kemper believed that the figure underestimated his success but that even the lower number represented a significant accomplishment, especially considering that, according to his sources, in the preceding year the Bureau of Conscription had only obtained 7,000 men from the entire Confederacy. For Kemper, conscription in Virginia was now "more popular" and practiced with "more vitality and vigor" than ever before. About the only thing that Preston and Kemper could agree on was that the current relationship could not continue. Officials in Richmond again had to choose one method or the other.[11]

Critics might question the results of Preston's bureau, but few could challenge his political acumen. Once more, the general—and the bureau—won their battle with the army. On the first of November, General Order 83 clarified the relationship between the generals commanding reserves and the Bureau of Conscription. Its eleventh provision revoked the confusing paragraph from General Order 73, stipulating, "All applications for exemption and detail will be transmitted to the superintendent of the Bureau of Conscription." The order mandated that copies of reports and returns be provided to the generals of reserves and allowed the generals to assign an "inspector of conscription," presumably to serve as a liaison between the army and the bureau. The new directives did not end the feud, as later that month Kemper and Preston fought over whether the bureau could send orders directly to a lieutenant colonel under Kemper's command rather than having to go through Kemper. Preston referred to the eleventh section of General Order 83 in maintaining that "this Bureau is not prepared to admit that the commandant of conscripts for the State of Virginia is subordinate of the general of reserves."[12]

In December, Adjutant General Samuel Cooper stepped into the clash and offered both constructive suggestions and a revealing description of the current process. He proposed dividing conscription's military and civilian tasks. In Cooper's view, the "greatest objection to the present system . . . is the needless complexity of its machinery," which caused multiple delays. Cooper described a disappointing scenario in which the bogged-down bureau might spend six to twelve months evaluating a single case. The general concluded, sadly, that the bureau had unintentionally made it "the hardest of all possible things to get the men into the Army." Hence, Cooper suggested streamlining the system. The general of reserves in each state would enroll soldiers, perhaps under the direction of an officer of superior rank (notably, General Preston did not fit this description). The civilian bureau would examine all applications for exemption and detail, thereby separating "the more military duties" from the "office or bureau duties." Cooper also proposed eliminating camps of instruction, which would have the double benefit of immediately sending into the field both the conscripts present in the camps and the soldiers staffing them.[13]

Month of attacks on multiple fronts exasperated General Preston. On December 18, he wrote separate letters to the president and the secretary of war. He complained of "a concerted effort" to abolish the current system, remove him from control of the bureau, and establish a purely military conscription. To congressional ally William Porcher Miles, Preston voiced his concern that some Confederates refused to grasp the simple proposition that in representative governments, "the state makes the armies, the generals fight them." Allow generals to recruit armies directly "and you establish military despotism." In his letter to the secretary of war, Preston's criticism of military conscription was more colorful. He called it "a cumbrous, confused mass of indigested regulations" and criticized its "petulant, indigested, and revolting schemes." While portraying himself as confident that his method was "the strongest which can be instituted," Preston acknowledged that the criticisms had taken their toll on him. He offered his resignation, but Davis did not accept it.[14]

Preston might have seemed paranoid, but he had plenty of enemies. Many Confederates wanted more than just his dismissal; they wanted the complete destruction of his bureau. Later, in December, a Mississippi assistant adjutant general succinctly concluded, "The department might be abolished without material injury to the service." In February 1865, a Tennessee senator complained about the seemingly ubiquitous conscription officers who did nothing more than consume rations. That same month, Congress took up a bill eliminating the bureau, camps of instruction, and the position of commandant of conscripts. In the ensuing debate, legislators lambasted the bureau. One senator complained of the "the grossest corruption" under its reign. Another reminded his colleagues that the bureau was "established without a law, with a Brigadier General at the head of it," and he claimed that in six months it had cost $2.4 million and had brought in only 13,000 troops. A congressman offered the sobering clarification that, in order to come up these few conscripts, the bureau had to examine 150,000 men. With the bureau enrolling less than 10 percent of the men it encountered, legislators concluded that the best way to increase the size of the army was to "abolish the present system of conscription." In February 1865, Congress passed a bill doing just that.[15]

John B. Jones, serving in the War Department, celebrated the measure, saying that the Confederacy "ought to have abolished it months ago—years ago." He only feared that it might be too late. A month later, Jones expressed astonishment that "the 'Bureau of Conscription' still lives notwithstanding the actions of Congress!" According to the rumors he had heard, President Davis had vetoed the bill because "the great weight (wealth) of Gen. Preston." Perhaps Preston's influence played a role, but the president primarily objected to a different section of the bill, which threatened his own control over conscription. In his veto message, Davis did not defend the bureau but instead returned to his fight with the legislative branch over details versus exemptions. He complained that the bill's elimination of details would "throw the whole machinery of Government into confusion and disorder" just to add approximately one hundred men to the army. In the final week of its session, Congress compromised with the president, allowing up to one hundred government details. By the end of March, Davis accepted this compromise and signed the bill abolishing the bureau. Thus, it predeceased the Confederacy by a matter of weeks.[16]

Eliminating the bureau did not mean the Confederacy had given up on its commitment to putting as many men as possible in the ranks. The bureau, Congress, the army, and the president all shared this end, even while disagreeing on the best means to achieve it. For example, in February, General Preston had issued a circular to enrolling officers after the secretary of war complained that eligible conscripts had avoided service and that the detail system had been abused. Preston reminded them, "After two years and a half of operation of the Conscription laws, it is certainly not creditable to the officers . . . that one single man liable to service has escaped their action." As the circular described the breadth of conscription, "There ought not to be one man in the Confederacy whose relation to the service remains undefined." In other words, every adult white male should be accounted for, whether they were in the army, medically unfit to serve, exempt, or detailed.[17]

In 1865, the main issue had not changed: the army needed men. Senator Wigfall proclaimed "a universal itching to put every man into the army." An order to enrolling officers in Georgia predicted that with renewed dedication, "thousands of young men who have hitherto held aloof from the path of patriotism" would accept conscription. Few Confederates shared this optimism. Assistant Secretary of War Campbell informed newly appointed Secretary of War John Breckinridge that "no large addition can be made from the conscript population." In Georgia, General Howell Cobb received a letter declaring, "Things look rather gloomy . . . We want more men and where are they to come from?" This question had bedeviled Confederate leaders since the war began. In 1862, the need for soldiers forced Confederates to sacrifice one of their sacred tenets: states' rights. By 1865, southerners debated whether to forsake their other core belief: African American slavery. With few white men available, Cobb's correspondent saw "but one alternative left us and that to fill up our army with negroes."[18]

General Cobb sharply disagreed. Five days later, he wrote his oft-quoted letter declaring "If slaves will make good soldiers our whole theory of slavery is wrong." He then added, "Before resorting to it, at least try every reasonable mode of getting white soldiers." Many Confederates felt that all reasonable modes had already been tried and thus looked to the nation's slave population for salvation. Two options emerged. Secretary of War Seddon had requested 20,000 slaves to be used as laborers to replace white soldiers, who could then be sent to the front lines. While this plan kept slaves in their traditional position as a source of labor, the other option was more revolutionary and more divisive: an increasing number of Confederates wanted to conscript slaves as soldiers. In January 1864, General Patrick Cleburne had controversially suggested this strategy. The Richmond government not only rejected Cleburne's proposal but also tried to suppress all records and all further discussions of it. Less than one year later, the shortage of men had remarkably transformed his suggestion from heresy to orthodoxy.[19]

Bruce Levine's *Confederate Emancipation* does a masterful job of analyzing the ideological and logistical factors associated with the issue of arming slaves. Levine clearly explains that conscripting slaves did not demonstrate any lack of commitment to slavery on behalf of the Confederacy. The purpose in the present discussion is much more limited: to show how the inability of conscription to produce enough white soldiers contributed to the South's decision to free and arm slaves. Undoubtedly, a failure to find sufficient white troops forced some Confederates to conclude that it was necessary to find another source of soldiers. According to Levine, "At the level of simple arithmetic" conscripting slaves "was a common-sense solution to the South's manpower problem." As one congressman put it, "If he was convinced that there was enough white material in the country, he would vote against negro soldiers, but he was not convinced of it." A letter to the editor of the Macon *Telegraph and Confederate* highlighted the dearth of willing white men. It endorsed the arming of slaves because prospective conscripts chose money over patriotism, with "a half million of the lazy, cowardly rascals" dodging their service.[20]

Although the majority of Cleburne's suppressed proposal focused on whether the Confederacy should arm slaves and whether those slaves would fight, he spent the opening quarter of the document addressing conscription's failures. The first weakness it highlighted was the inferior number of southern troops compared to the enemy. It then proposed ending substitution, changing the exemption laws, and reducing details. Cleburne concluded that, unfortunately, these solutions would be insufficient. He predicted that principals possessed ulterior motives "stronger than patriotism," which would cause them to continue to resist enrollment or be "unwilling and discontented soldiers." Similarly, reducing exemptions would not add to the army's strength. It would conscript vital producers and mechanics, who would then have to be returned home on details. In the best-case scenario, these changes might provide temporary equality with the enemy, but the Confederacy would find itself in a worse position a year later. Only after outlining this path to certain defeat does the proposal turn to the proposition of arming slaves.[21]

The operation of conscription in 1864 had proven Cleburne's predictions correct. Policy alterations, including ending substitution, had not provided a long-term solution to the Confederacy's manpower problem. In September, an optimistic Josiah Gorgas considered the nation to be stronger than it had been two years earlier, as "the only point against us is the Scarcity of men to fill up our armies." Of course, in wartime, a scarcity of men had the potential to be catastrophic, but Gorgas knew that "placing negroes in the ranks" provided an easy solution. Governors Allen of Louisiana and Smith of Virginia agreed. Writing the same week as Gorgas, Allen informed the secretary of war, "The time has come to put into the army every able-bodied negro man as a soldier." In December, the Virginia governor asked the legislature, "We find ourselves looking around for material to enlarge our armies. Whence is it to come?" His straightforward answer: "Our own slaves . . . are a ready and abundant stock from which to draw." In early 1865, General Lee joined this chorus, fearing that Confederates could not fight a lengthy war "without overtaxing the capacity of our white population."[22]

Freeing slaves challenged Confederate sensibilities, but proponents of the measure delighted in pointing out the irony of planters protecting their slaves while potentially sending white men to their deaths. Referring to a proposed bill's stipulation that slaves only be conscripted with their masters' consent, a general contended that owners inexplicably had a greater freedom to keep their slaves at home than they did their sons. Georgia congressman Warren Akin noted the "strange conduct" of people who "give up their sons, husbands, brothers & friends, and often without murmuring, to the army, but let one of their negroes be taken, and what a houl [*sic*] you will hear." A second Georgian ranted that "rich speculators and extortioners should be compelled to send a part of their negroes to fight." A third complained of planters who would make "more fuss" in losing their slaves "than if 1,000 white men were sacrificed."[23]

An argument could be made that slaves serving as soldiers simply extended the logic of conscription. In 1865, every man in the Confederacy—now regardless of race—must do his part. In particular, it could mollify nonslaveholders' concerns about conscription's perceived iniquities. An anonymous letter in the *Richmond Enquirer,* which Levine speculates was written by the secretary of state, makes this point explicit. It asked how, in a "war to defend slavery . . . a slaveholding Congress" could demand "that the father, the husband, the apprentice, and the minor have all been turned over to the conscript officer . . . *but that they will not disturb the right of property in a slave?*" In citing arguments in favor of the conscription of slaves, Virginia's governor made the contention more succinct: it "will effectually silence the clamor of the poor man about this being the rich man's war."[24]

Most of the opposition to African American soldiers focused on whether they would fight and whether the government had the authority to take slaves from their owners. Some opponents, however, instead emphasized that the measure was not necessary, for conscription had not yet failed. In his November 1864 report, the secretary of war discussed the merits of slaves as soldiers but concluded, "My own judgment does not yet . . . perceive the necessity" of doing so, as "we have within the military age as large a proportion of our whole population as will be required." In that same month, Congress debated a resolution stipulating that "no exigency now exists, nor is likely to occur . . . to justify the placing of negro slaves in the army as soldiers." During that debate, H. C. Chambers of Mississippi maintained that the "whole matter hinged upon the simple question, 'Are we approaching exhaustion?'" He believed that the answer was no and that a better enforcement of the current laws would bring more men into the army—which, he added, was already as large as it had ever been.[25]

Not until March 1865 did a majority in Congress decide that the Confederacy was close enough to exhaustion to approve the conscription of slaves. It passed the bill on March 9, with Davis signing it four days later. One Richmond official described it in his diary as "the desperate remedy for the very desperate case." His diagnosis of the direness of both the cure and the condition of the patient was accurate. He optimistically hoped that the measure might bring in 300,000 soldiers, but it raised very few men. The weakness in the Confederate manpower formula caught up to the nation before this new variable could be added to the equation. The case was indeed critical. Within weeks, and before a significant number of slaves could be recruited, the Union army captured Richmond, and on April 9, General Lee surrendered.[26]

The brief experiment in African American soldiers had begun just as the Bureau of Conscription's life ended. On March 29, Adjutant General Cooper sent out General Order 17, section 9 of which declared that "the Bureau of Conscription and the camps of instruction are hereby abolished." In theory, conscription continued. It had preceded the bureau's creation and supposedly would go on under the direction of the general of reserves in each state. As late as April 12, President Davis, fleeing through North Carolina, still expressed the naive hope that new conscripts could save the Confederacy. Of course, conscription policy under any authority needed men to conscript, and many Confederates contended there were few to be found. In July 1864, David Comfort III received a letter listing only three exempts left in a Georgia neighborhood. Now, in April 1865, the situation had become grimmer, as a different correspondent informed Comfort simply that "we have no people left."[27]

Discussions of Confederate math and the idea that no conscripts remained in the Confederacy raises the question of conscription's numerical impact. How many men entered the army? How many were exempt? How many provided substitutes? Regrettably, Confederate conscription numbers are incomplete, contradictory, and untrustworthy. In November 1864, during a debate on the exemption of state officers, Representative William N. H. Smith of North Carolina made this point. He fumed over the "false and unreliable" numbers supplied by the Bureau of Conscription, which impugned his state's patriotism. He found it implausible that North Carolina had 28,055 men exempted for physical disability while Georgia only had 2,053, or that his state had three times as many doctors exempted. Sensitive to slights against North Carolina, Smith complained, "The inconsistency of the table was so glaring and its fallacy so apparent that any one would see it who would merely glance at its figures."[28]

Four months after this diatribe, Josiah Turner, a fellow North Carolina representative, reviewing a new set of numbers, returned to Smith's theme. He offered a series of resolutions, including one asserting that General Preston, as head of the Bureau of Conscription, "shows laxity and neglect" in his execution of the laws, and another maintaining that Preston "is in errour [*sic*] as to the number of conscripts furnished by the State of North Carolina." In defending his resolutions, he complained of the "gross injustice" shown to his state, as Preston's incorrect figures "did violence to all rules of conjecture and good guessing." In response, South Carolina representative William Porcher Miles accused Turner, who "seemed dissatisfied with everybody and anything," of trying to sow discord in Congress when unity was required. In his defense of General Preston, Miles admitted that "mistakes might have occurred in the complicated figures statisticks . . . It was unavoidable."[29]

All three congressmen were correct. Even a cursory examination of Confederate conscription figures supports Smith's and Turner's contentions that they are flawed. In this case, a table that showed North Carolina with more men exempted for physical disability than the combined totals for Alabama, east Louisiana, east Tennessee, Florida, Georgia, Mississippi, South Carolina, and Virginia was undoubtedly mistaken. The bureau admitted as much. On November 28, 1864, it issued circular no. 34, which scolded commandants of conscription for recent reports that "exhibited frequent inaccuracies." Three days later, General Preston specifically admonished Colonel Mallett, the head of conscription in North Carolina, for "utterly false and unreliable" figures. Mallett's subordinates had mistakenly counted the same officials multiple times. In monthly reports, a local officer might list forty state exempts. Each month thereafter, he listed those same forty men. Mallett's staff mistakenly added these numbers together, so after two months these forty men became eighty, and after three months the error compounded, with the forty state officers now transforming into 120. Although Mallett now confessed the errors, the damage had been done, as Preston had submitted his own reports based on the faulty data, and thus the colonel's gaffes had "falsif[ied] the solemn returns of this bureau."[30]

Miles, however, was also correct that mistakes were unavoidable. The overworked and understaffed bureau had to get accurate information from conscription officials in several states. Some of these states faced federal occupation, and enrolling officers in the field were already overburdened. Often coming from the pool of medically exempt or light-duty men, these soldiers lacked the stamina to do their unrelenting jobs. On top of all these difficulties, they sometimes misunderstood what the Richmond government required. A seemingly simple request for the number of state officials exempt resulted in some enrollment officers returning the total possible number of positions which could be exempted while others returned just the number of men they tried to enroll who claimed such exemptions. In describing his own figures on the number of exempted state officials, Preston admitted, "I do not regard them as accurate." Representative Turner even seemed to concede some of these problems when he accused the general of violating the rules of "good guessing." If the numbers were truly complete, guessing—good or bad—would not have been required.[31]

Like these Confederates, historians are also left to speculate based on incomplete evidence. Turner's anger had stemmed from Preston's February 1865 report on the results of almost three years of conscription in the Confederacy. This report is possibly the best source for the measure's numerical impact, but before presenting its tables, Preston acknowledged some of its flaws. In trying to ascertain the number of volunteers since April 1862, he admitted, "There is no record of them at the camps and no means of making an estimate." Yet, on the very next page, the report proceeds to make an estimate for each state east of the Mississippi River. Additionally, he concludes his page-long introduction of the tables with a disclaimer. Preston had delayed its submission to the secretary of war "in order to render the report as accurate as the imperfect agencies allowed to the enrolling service will admit." In other words, the tabulation—based on incomplete and inaccurate state reports—was the best he could do, given the difficult circumstances existing in the Confederacy in 1865.[32]

The report provides a wealth of information on conscription's cumulative impact. Its eleven charts (plus explanations) take up twelve pages in the *Official Records of the War of the Rebellion.* The data in each table is generally divided out by each of the nine Confederate states east of the Mississippi River. In the cases of Louisiana and Tennessee, it stipulates that it only includes information from the eastern regions. West Louisiana, on the opposite side of the river, was part of the separate Trans-Mississippi Department, and west Tennessee was occupied before the onset of conscription. The tables contain a variety of lists: total conscripts enrolled, volunteers since conscription started, men working in various military departments, exemptions by occupations, and details by categories. It concludes with the number of deserters returned to the army and a recapitulation of the first ten tables. Many of the charts are further subdivided into age ranges (17–18, 18–45, and 45–50) to provide a sense of how many of the exemptions and details were going to the youngest and oldest portions of the manpower pool.

At first glance, table A of the report, listing the numbers of conscripts assigned through camps of instruction, is surprising. Given the time spent on conscription, and the animosity over it, one might anticipate a report of hundreds of thousands of soldiers. Yet according to the bureau's calculations, only 81,993 conscripts had joined the army through this method. This figure clearly represents the minimum possible total. State-level reports indicate that the bureau undercounted conscripts in Louisiana and Virginia, calling into question the totals for the other states. Also, the table does not include the men brought in directly by military conscription (through the efforts of Pillow in 1863 and generals of reserves in 1864) or those from west of the Mississippi River. With these additional troops, historians estimate a figure closer to 120,000. North Carolinians, such as representatives Smith and Turner, who had repeatedly complained that their state never got the recognition it deserved, undoubtedly noticed that report credited the Tar Heel state with the most conscripts, at 21,348, a figure that represented 26 percent of all men assigned to the army through this system.[33]

In the next table, General Preston provides some context for the low total of conscripts: an estimate of the number of men who had volunteered since April 1862. Preston believed that these 72,292 men should be credited to the Bureau of Conscription. In his clarifying note, he explains that these men volunteered because they "regarded it as disgraceful to be conscribed." Consequently, they might technically be volunteers but "their service was compulsory, and should be accredited to the energy exhibited in the enforcement of conscription." In 1863, the secretary of war suggested that Preston vastly underestimated the number of volunteers to credit to the bureau as he maintained that for every man conscripted, three men volunteered.[34]

In providing county totals for conscription in North Carolina, a newspaper offered backing for these conclusions. It explained that some counties contributed few conscripts because men there "volunteered to escape enrollment." A Virginian's rant offers further support. He complained that "compelling men to volunteer" was an oxymoron. He found it "absurd," for the soldier could "not say with truth, 'I am a volunteer.'" As if to highlight this distinction, the table's title refers not to volunteers but to "men who have joined the army . . . without passing through camps of instruction." Here, Georgians stood tall—perhaps because of their governor's disdain for the conscription process. The Peach State represented 26,400 (36.5 percent) of the estimated volunteer totals.[35]

The inclusion of any volunteers in Preston's tables highlights the difficulty in using numbers to evaluate conscription. First, as the general notes, the bureau did not keep track of volunteers, so the totals in his tables (and in the secretary of war's report) are educated guesses. Second, volunteering continued long after it lost any official sanction. Even as late as 1865, southerners requested permission to volunteer, and it was unlikely that understrength units turned them away. Third, even if one could discover the precise number of post–April 1862 volunteers, it would be impossible to determine how many of them joined primarily because they feared being conscripted. In *Reluctant Rebels,* Kenneth Noe offers an excellent analysis of these reputed volunteers. According to his figures, 180,000 men enlisted after 1861. His numbers on later enlistees exceed those in the chart, both because he both considers the entire Confederacy and because he includes all of 1862, not just the months after the passage of the conscription law in April.[36]

Thus, on the positive side of the ledger, conscription potentially contributed more than 250,000 men to the army. This sum includes the 81,993 men listed as conscripts and the 72,292 volunteers. Conscripts from west of the Mississippi River, plus those brought in through military conscription, boosted this figure. Then, the addition of perhaps more than 30,000 substitutes—with estimates ranging as high as 150,000—further increased this total. Coming a year after substitution ended, the February report does not offer any sense of the number of substitutes in the army. Additionally, when searching for conscripts, the bureau often found deserters instead. Preston estimated that the bureau had returned 33,056 deserters to the ranks. Thus, these totals might even greatly exceed 250,000 men, but so many of them—even with the supposed detailed record keeping of the bureau—are approximations that coming up with a definitive figure is impossible. Conscription's proponents could add that the original act's transformation of almost 200,000 one-year volunteers into soldiers for the war (with a way station as three-year volunteers) might actually have been the measure's most valuable contribution.[37]

There is an additional problem when trying to ascertain conscription's numerical effect on the Confederate army. Ideally, to determine the percentage of conscripts fighting for the Confederacy, one would simply divide the number of conscripts (or all the men credited to the bureau) by the total number of soldiers. As demonstrated, the numerator of this fraction is flawed by incomplete data and by the question of how to count reluctant rebels, returned deserters, and substitutes. Further complicating matters, there also is no consensus on the denominator of the fraction. In the conclusion of his 1924 book on conscription, Albert Burton Moore, in speculating on the total number of Confederate soldiers, observed, "We seem to be no nearer a common agreement than at the outset" and predicted it will "continue to be a matter of speculation until more complete records are unearthed." His range went from 600,000 to 1.1 million. One hundred years later, most historians accept a slightly narrower range, between 750,000 and 1 million, but have not achieved a consensus. In ascertaining conscription's impact on the army, therefore, it could range from a low of 8.2 percent (the 81,993 conscripts in Preston's report, divided by 1 million) to a high exceeding 33 percent (the 250,000+ men influenced by conscription, divided by 750,000).[38]

Even the latter number might be far too low a percentage. Another way of solving the quandary of conscription's effect is take the army's total enlistment and subtract the number of soldiers *not* affected by the measure. In this approach, the difference between these two figures would be the number of men influenced by conscription. In February 1862, the army possessed 332,750 soldiers, but only 92,275 enrolled for the war (the other 240,475 were enrolled for twelve months).[39] Conscription played a role in extending the terms of the twelve-month men and in almost all subsequent enrollments. Thus, one can only conclusively prove that conscription did not impact these 92,275 volunteers. Viewed from this perspective, the measure might have directly or indirectly impacted 80 percent to 90 percent of the Confederacy's soldiers.

It is, of course, impossible to prove whether each of these men joined the army because conscription nudged them in this direction. Also, even if one accepts the proposition that conscription affected more than 80 percent of the army, this conclusion does not render a verdict on Confederate nationalism. The U.S. Army drafted 10 million soldiers in World War II (slightly more than 60 percent of the men who served), but this does not render a verdict on twentieth-century American patriotism.

While compelling an unknown number and an unknown percentage of men to the join the army, enrolling officers provided others with legal permission to stay home. In December 1864, a war clerk, John B. Jones, for the second time during the war, scribbled in his diary that the agency should rightfully be termed the "Bureau of *Exemption.*" Preston's report provides support for this accusation, as it gives information on the significant number of men who crossed paths with enrollment officers but did not end up in the army. According to his figures, conscription officers exempted 66,586 men and detailed another 20,809, for a total of 87,395. A simple comparison of this total with the 81,993 conscripts leads to the conclusion that the bureau almost precisely balanced the needs of home front and battlefront. As noted, the bureau's contribution to the army greatly exceeded that figure, but a legislator viewing the numbers in Preston's report could easily conclude that Jones's appellation was correct.[40]

The 66,586 exemptions are based solely on the February 1864 law. Thus, there are no principals listed, as well as no millers, blacksmiths, or shoemakers. Records from a year earlier likely would have included even more exempts. Taken together, 26,598 medical exemptions (39.6 percent) and 17,787 state officers (26.5 percent) represented almost two-thirds of the exemptions. Virginia and North Carolina appeared to be the sickliest states. While sending 13,933 conscripts into the army, Virginia had almost half that number (6,745) receive medical exemptions. North Carolina exceeded its northern neighbor in its total medical exemptions, but its 7,885 represented only about one-third of the 21,348 conscripts it sent into the field. Richmond officials were not surprised to see that Georgians led the way in avoiding conscription. Altogether, 15,371 of Joe Brown's citizens received exemptions, in contrast to the 8,993 conscripts sent into the army. More than half of those exemptions (8,229) went to state officials. In other words, Georgia had almost as many exempt state officials as conscripts, and it had nearly as many state officers as the other states combined.[41]

The bureau's report also reflects both the explicit reduction in exempt occupations and the implicit pressure to put all men into the army. The only occupations with more than 1,000 exemptions were overseers and agriculturalists (5,617), railroad employees (4,747), physicians (3,448), ministers (2,714), and teachers (1,353). Eliminating key occupations from the list of exemptions, however, did not suddenly mean that the home front no longer needed millers, blacksmiths, tanners, or shoemakers. Some men who had previously received occupational exemptions now received details. For instance, 5,803 men received details for "public necessity," which included these and other occupations. They, however, represented only 27.9 percent of the 20,809 details. Most details still worked directly for the Confederacy, with bureau employees, contractors, and artisans and mechanics totaling 12,289 (59.1 percent). The 2,717 agricultural details also recognized the common refrain that both the army and the home front needed to be fed. Southerners who feared that pedantic conscription officials only used the rules to benefit the rich at the expense of the poor might have been relieved to see 1,122 detailed for "indigent circumstances" and another 550 detailed for the vague and discretionary category of "equity, justice, and necessity."[42]

The February report is the best extant comprehensive record of conscription across the Confederacy. Its timing, however, reduces some of its value in understanding the measure's effect. Obtaining accurate data at any time during the conflict was difficult, but by 1865, with the Confederacy's borders, army, logistics, and prospects shrinking, the figures in these tables must be viewed with extra caution. For instance, some of the totals unquestionably undercount the measure's true impact. East Louisiana is only credited with eighty-one conscripts, but a report to that state's adjutant general credits that region with almost five times that number of conscripts (401) in just the final eight months of 1862. Similarly, 13,933 conscripts are attributed to Virginia, whereas that state's records enumerate 15,699 conscripts after September 1862 (and imply a few thousand before that date). Moreover, in trying to determine a complete picture of conscription, the timing presents other difficulties. As mentioned, by 1865, substitution and other exemptions had ended, the Twenty Negro Law had been amended to the fifteen–field hand law, and the bureau was fighting for its existence.[43]

A detailed set of state-level Virginia records can supplement this national report. They include both monthly reports on "the progress made in the execution of the conscription law" from September 1862, when a camp of instruction opened at Camp Lee in Richmond, until the end of the war, as well as a separate compilation of exemptions made from the onset of conscription until November 1, 1863. For Camp Lee, Confederate officials recorded the disposition of 23,423 men processed there. Each column starts with the number of soldiers on hand at the start of the month (previously enrolled conscripts who had not yet been assigned to units) and then records the number of new men received. The "men received" figure is compiled after an unspecified number of medical and other exemptions. This amount is then adjusted by subtractions for various causes, including "furnished substitutes," "deserted," "discharged," "Dunkard," "died," "referred to medical board," and "absent with or without leave." The penultimate row lists the number of men "assigned to command," with the final row labeled "to be assigned," which then generally serves as the basis for the number of men on hand for the next month. According to the table, 15,699 conscripts went from Camp Lee to the army, and maybe as many as 5,000 conscripts were assigned prior to the camp's opening.[44]

The rows listing adjustments to "men received" provide further insight into conscription. The 3,034 details represent the largest group not assigned to commands. More than half of these details (1,698) occurred from November 1864 until the end of the war. As Congress decreased the number of exemptions, details increased. Additionally, General Kemper had called for a reexamination of details and exemptions. During these months, then, the bureau brought men into camp who had been detailed for because of age or health complications, and then immediately sent them back home. Also, perhaps the enrolling officers recognized that many of the potential conscripts truly were needed more at home than in the army. In January 1865, the general in charge of reserves in North Carolina recommended to the adjutant general a "liberal allowance" of details for men between forty-five and fifty "to enable them to provide for their families during the winter." Virginia officials followed this advice.[45]

In the monthly totals, just 153 men are listed as having furnished substitutes. This figure, however, only includes men who provided replacement soldiers while training at Camp Lee. More than 90 percent of Virginia principals brought their substitute with them to the camp and thus were released before their training started. As a result, they were listed as exempts and not considered among "men received" at the camp. The charts indicate that 1,468 (6.3 percent of arrivals) deserted, with that number spiking after alterations in the conscription law. The three months that saw more than one hundred desertions included February and March 1864—after the sharp reduction in exemptions and the end of substitution—and December 1864—during Kemper's military conscription and after the end of details. Almost as many potential soldiers (1,299) were listed as "discharged," with no explanation, and another 320 were listed as "improperly enrolled."[46]

In a separate record, there is a cumulative (up to November 1, 1863) exemption report that divides the state's 12,045 exempts into fifty categories (in contrast, the 1865 national report only has twenty categories). This table does not include medical exemptions, which totaled approximately 5,000 at that point in the war. Some tentative conclusions can be drawn. First, once again, the appellation "Bureau of Exemption" might be considered appropriate. While the data is difficult to interpret precisely, it appears that the number of healthy exempts nearly equals the number of men received at Camp Lee during that period. Prior to September 1, 1862, Virginia's enrolling officers processed 4,849 men, and the sum of the months through November 1863 adds another 7,836, for a total of 12,685. With the subtractions listed previously, the camp might have ended up sending only 9,000 conscripts to the army through November 1863, or 3,000 fewer than they exempted.[47]

Second, by far the largest percentage of all exempts—27.1 percent—were principals. When conscripted, 3,270 Virginians paid men to serve in their places. With 153 principals providing substitutes while training at Camp Lee, the total rises to 3,423, perhaps lending some credence to the joke which said it was "easier for a camel to go through the eye of a needle than for a rich man to enter Camp Lee." These 3,423 replacement soldiers, assuming that they did not immediately desert, should be considered part of the state's contribution to the army. So perhaps Camp Lee was more effective at providing soldiers than it first appears. Oddly, as in Preston's 1865 report, the substitutes seemingly disappear from any calculations, unintentionally supporting the anecdotal evidence that many of these mercenaries received their payment, enrolled in the army, and then quickly disappeared from camp. In other words, the records strangely treat substitutions as a subtraction from the army, when the process, if it followed the law, should not have affected the total number of soldiers.[48]

No other category represented more than 1,000 exemptions. The occupations representing more than 5 percent of the exemptions were primarily tradesmen: shoemakers (909, 7.5 percent), railroad employees (797, 6.6 percent), millers (753, 6.3 percent), and blacksmiths (680, 5.6 percent.) Agriculture seemingly had fewer exemptions, with 725 farmers exempt and an additional two hundred planters paying the $500 fee for an overseer exemption. More than likely, other farmers received details that are not included in the chart. Also, many of the sixty-nine men who received executive clemency exemptions might have farmed. Religious Virginians benefited from exemptions, with 184 ministers joined by 418 members of pacifist denominations, the latter paying a $500 fee in lieu of military service. The combination of the eight separate categories of state employees accounted for 417 exemptions. As the home of the Confederate capital, Virginia possessed more exemptions for men working in the national government's various departments (more than seven hundred) than for state employees.[49]

The plurality of substitutes on the exemption list, ironically, supports a lower-than-expected number of substitutes in the Confederacy. National records do not provide a precise account of either how many men paid for replacements or how many substitutes deserted. At the end of 1863, the House of Representatives requested this data from the secretary of war. The War Department could not provide a conclusive answer. The adjutant general explained that his office had neither the time nor the staff to compile a total, and he feared even if they had, the result would be inaccurate. President Davis fumed that this answer "cannot be regarded as a response." Without exact records, Confederates relied on educated guesses. Both the secretary of war and South Carolina's head of conscription estimated that 50,000 conscripts had provided substitutes. Earlier in the year, an assistant secretary of war calculated more than 50,000, two-thirds of whom had deserted. Some officers believed that these Richmond officials severely underestimated the practice. They maintained that the army had enrolled 150,000 substitutes, but very few remained in the army.[50]

If Virginia's total of 3,270 (or 3,423) was accurate, however, and if the percentage of substitutes was consistent across the Confederacy, conjecture and good guessing support a much smaller number, perhaps only 20,000 principals in the nation. North Carolina data provides further support for this hypothesis. According to a detailed, county-by-county breakdown of exemptions, North Carolina had only 2,040 substitutes as of November 1863, which also extrapolates into approximately 20,000 principals in the Confederacy. Nevertheless, other numbers contradict these low figures. In January 1864, a conscription officer attempting to obtain the number of potential soldiers in the Confederacy assumed that North Carolina had 2,040 principals, South Carolina 791, Virginia 15,000, and Georgia 7,050. The first two numbers, which appear more precise, point toward approximately 20,000 substitutes in the Confederacy, while the latter two indicate a total closer to 70,000. The significant discrepancy in his total for Virginia (15,000) compared to the state reports (3,270 or 3,423) illustrates the difficulty in searching for reliable conscription numbers. That being said, based on the detail of the state figures and their correlation to the numbers from the Carolinas, my best estimate is 20,000 to 30,000 principals.[51]

Overall, an examination of the numbers associated with conscription—whether at the state or federal level—is just as discouraging today as it was for President Davis or Confederate congressmen. Reports are maddeningly incomplete and inconsistent. Substitution numbers remain a mystery. The motives of men who volunteered after April 1862 are impossible to quantify, and conscription outside the scope of the bureau (whether in the Trans-Mississippi Department or done by the army) is difficult to assess. An 1864 report, for example, complained that under General Pillow's military conscription, much of the work was "carried on without any record having been kept." Regardless of these qualifiers, one conclusion can be drawn: conscription did not produce a home front completely denuded of white men. Enrolling officers left a significant minority (and some evidence indicates that it was possibly a majority) of southerners they encountered at home, as medically unfit, in exempt occupations, detailed, or as principals.[52]

Confederate officials came to the same conclusion. In October 1862, the secretary of war, in seeking to discover how many men the Confederacy could put into the field, assumed that three-sevenths (42.9 percent) of prospective conscripts received exemptions. Almost a year later, a math professor at Georgia Military Institute, in trying to figure out how many healthy men remained in the state, arrived at a similar inference. His analysis contended that the state had sent 80,000 men into the field, but approximately 60,000 remained home through occupational or medical exemptions. Three months after that, a Confederate officer analyzing conscription in four states found an even higher percentage of exemptions. He came up with the following approximation: out of every six men the bureau examined, two entered the army, one was detailed, and three were exempted. In April 1864, Preston, in arguing that his bureau had thoroughly harvested the conscription crop with only "scanty gleanings" left, released a report on the prior four months, which contrasted 9,835 conscripts with 26,472 exempts.[53]

Given the considerable percentage of men enrolling officers left at home, why did Confederate officials receive so many claims that communities retained very few, if any, military-age men? Were these claims simply exaggerations designed to gain sympathy and secure unnecessary exemptions? No. First and foremost, the calculations greatly overestimate the percentage of men who remained at home. They are based on the men whom the enrolling officers encountered, which, by definition, did not include those who volunteered in 1861. For instance, a separate set of numbers for Virginia claimed that conscription had put 31,725 men into the army, detailed 11,251, and exempted 25,000. Although these figures—like the previous ones—make it appear that one-half of eligible Virginians stayed home, such a conclusion fails to take into account a separate total in the report: the 110,900 Virginians who had volunteered prior to conscription. When the volunteers are considered, 80 percent of state's adult white male population fought for the Confederacy, thereby severely depleting the home front. In his comprehensive study of Virginians' military service, Aaron Sheehan-Dean posits an even greater figure, asserting, "Nearly 90 percent of military-age men in those part of Virginia controlled by the Confederacy served in the army."[54]

Also, in totaling exemptions, enrolling officers most likely counted some men more than once. For example, if a prospective conscript lost his exemption as a state legislator when his term ended, but then received a medical exemption, he probably was counted in both categories. Similarly, when a substitute reached eighteen, the principal was now eligible again. If that principal now received an exemption as an overseer, overworked enrolling officers almost certainly did not resubmit adjusted figures for the month he provided a substitute. In sum, as in trying to figure out conscription's overall numerical effect on the army, trying to ascertain what percentage of men enrolling officers left at home represents another fraction with both a flawed numerator and a flawed denominator.

Additional factors explain the sense of a home front devoid of white men. Exemptions generally favored skilled occupations, but aside from the Twenty Negro Law, they rarely helped agriculturalists directly. Thus, farm families might have suffered disproportionately. Similarly, in balancing home and country, men who had a greater number of dependents might have chosen to wait for conscription to bring them into the army. Historian Joseph Glatthaar finds that conscripts were more likely to be married farmers who had children but only modest means. Consequently, the removal of a conscript might have caused more suffering than the absence of a volunteer. Also, physical disabilities made up the plurality of exemptions. If truly disabled, these men just added dependents to the home front. They consumed but did not produce, or at least did not produce as much as a healthy man. Finally, conscription did not proceed evenly across the South. Enrolling officers had easier access to areas near camps of instruction that were completely under Confederate control. These regions were more likely to be barren of white men than areas that conscription officers had trouble reaching.[55]

Ordinary Confederates, of course, did not have access to these conscription figures, and even if they did, the statistics probably would not have greatly changed their view of conscription. In trying to balance the needs of their homes and communities with the army's requirements, the aggregate data and the percentage of potential conscripts sent home were less important than how it affected their own lives. If a family needed a doctor, the fact that enrolling officers in Virginia exempted 369 physicians was less important than whether they had exempted *their* doctor. Similarly, families were primarily concerned with the farmer who headed their household, not with the knowledge that the state had exempted at least 725 farmers and provided details for numerous others. Overall, while some requesters may have exaggerated their plight and the cupboard was not completely bare, clearly many on the home front suffered from the absence of vital producers.[56]

Throughout the war, Confederates struggled to find a way to protect both home and country. In his opening message to the Second Congress, President Davis had stressed these combined goals: "The defense of home, family, and country is universally recognized as the paramount political duty of every member of society." Since the onset of conscription, Confederates had not disputed this assessment. Instead, they disagreed on how each member of society best defended their home, family, and country; the priority ranking of home, family, and country; and by late 1864, whether the Confederacy possessed enough men to defend both home and country. For those, like Davis, who placed country first, conscription pushed to its limits made sense. A week later, however, a senator expressed the opposite concern. He worried that "the tendency of our legislation was to put every man into the army." He reminded his colleagues, "This must not be carried so far as to destroy the country." In his opinion, Confederate destruction would not result from the military defeat of an outnumbered army with too few conscripts but instead from an internal collapse if too few men remained at home.[57]

That same month, Virginia congressman John Baldwin received a letter that reiterated this home front–first perspective. Calling for a suspension of conscription in Rockingham County, the plea reminded Baldwin of the importance of family and community. If the government called the last producers in Rockingham into the army, it would have devasting effects on both the county and the army. When a soldier's family suffers from want, he "will become uneasy in his place, and will weigh the duty he owes his country and then weigh the duty he owes his family." The letter writers contended that the Confederacy needed to consider both duties in their conscription policies, and the best way to do that would be to continue to allow men to remain at home on agricultural details. Detailed men would take care of both their families and soldiers' families, boosting army morale and thereby strengthening the Confederacy.[58]

Conscription's ability to tip the balance of home and battlefront remained consistent throughout the policy's three years. Opponents of an expanded conscription repeatedly stressed that both the army and civilians needed to be fed. In 1865, Alabama congressman William P. Chilton employed this refrain: "Some one must be left at home . . . or we shall fail for want of food." While others might think soldiers resented exempts, Chilton emphasized that the men in the ranks viewed the situation through the lens of community. In his opinion, "soldiers are sensible as well as patriotick [*sic*]." They would not be fooled "by the cry of class legislation, when meat and bread and liberty are at stake." If stay-at-homes fed, clothed, and protected soldiers' families, they, too, provided a service to the Confederacy. In an admonition applicable to anyone who studies conscription, Chilton challenged his colleagues to "take a comprehensive view of our entire situation." The following day, a South Carolinian, after examining conscription broadly, chided his colleagues, declaring that he "thought the present law very good if *properly enforced.*" Unfortunately, that had never been the case. A North Carolina congressman sounded a similar refrain in emphasizing that there would be much less suffering "if all the proper men were in their proper places."[59]

These goals were more easily voiced than accomplished. As the Bureau of Conscription neared the end of its administrative life, General Preston offered an assessment of its "unappreciated" accomplishments. He pointed out that the "the silent, but sure, legal working of the conscription authority" had to overcome "popular prejudice, the opposition of State Executives and judicial authorities, the weakness of its own agencies, the clamor of ignorant and interested officials." It had done so, "filling the ranks as far as the law allowed." The *Richmond Examiner* offered an assessment that rebutted Preston's claims. It maintained that the bureau was "too cumbrous and slow in action . . . Those who are desirous of avoiding service can do so by mere delay and circumlocution; months and even years pass, the enrolled conscript grows old or he has removed to another part of the country." In short, one Confederate's patience and careful scrutiny was another's inefficiency.[60]

The three-year battle over the utility or futility of conscription was resolved not by consensus on the best plan but by military defeat in April 1865. The Confederacy surrendered just as the final alterations of conscription—drafting slaves and eliminating the bureau—went into effect. Conscription had not prevented Confederate defeat. In the end, as long as the United States remained committed to using its numerical superiority to win the war, the Confederacy did not possess enough men to both fight the Union army and farm. Almost a year before the end of the war, the head of the Bureau of Conscription recognized this dilemma. While General Lee wanted more men, Preston reportedly did not want to see any more agriculturalists forced into the army. A war department official claimed Preston "thinks the limit has been past already at which weakness rather than strength results." The official concurred: "There is no doubt of this."[61]

Ever since its defeat in 1865, the Confederacy's epitaph has been chiseled, erased, and rechiseled on its tombstone. Regardless of what critics contend led to the death of the nation, many of them see the operation of conscription as a symptom of their chosen fatal malady. Conscription was a military policy designed to help the Confederacy win the war. Since it lost, conscription can be judged a component of that defeat. In particular, for those seeking an explanation based on internal explanations, conscription often serves as a useful component of their theses. It can be portrayed as negatively impacting states' rights, social class divisions, and slavery. For some, the mere fact that the Confederacy had to institute conscription demonstrates that southerners lacked commitment to their cause. Viewing the opposite side of the coin, others have argued that such a standard of patriotism is too high. Instead, they point out that the policy saved the nation in 1862 and enabled the army to remain in the field. If the Confederacy lost because of external factors, primarily the strength of the Union army, then conscription should be credited with helping to prevent this defeat for three years.

The debate over whether conscription weakened the Confederacy began almost as soon as the war ended. In its immediate aftermath, Vice President Stephens forcefully contended that conscription had been an unconstitutional usurpation of states' rights, "exceedingly injurious to our cause," and that this example of executive despotism had helped doom the Confederacy. To him, conscription "plainly violated not only the spirit but the letter of the Constitution." He also, surprisingly, but in the true spirit of Georgia politicians, argued that the Confederacy produced enough troops without resorting to the measure. Unfortunately, these potential soldiers, according to Stephens, "were utterly unwilling to be placed in a position, where it seemed they were required to do so by compulsion," adding that "no people are worthy of liberty who have to be compelled to fight."[62]

On conscription—and on numerous other issues—Stephens and Jefferson Davis did not see eye to eye. During the conflict, Davis and his allies had repeatedly vouched for the constitutionality and necessity of conscription, and they continued to do so afterwards. Unlike Stephens, Davis did not believe that the Confederacy foundered on the shoals of states' rights ideals. In *The Rise and Fall of the Confederate Government* (1881), he praises the measure, for its "good effects were seen in the increased strength and efficiency of our armies." He does acknowledge that conscription received some misplaced states' rights criticism. To prove that conscription did not violate states' rights, Davis includes the full text of one of his 1862 letters to Joseph Brown, in which he lectures the Georgia governor on the measure's constitutionality and instructs him that the law was not only necessary but "absolutely indispensable." Davis believed his explanation convinced the Confederate people, as he optimistically contends that opposition "soon became limited."[63]

With regard to states' rights and conscription, most, but certainly not all, historians have come to agree with Davis. The president's argument is more persuasive. Confederates did not generally oppose conscription itself but only how it was (or was not) enforced. Even critics who harped upon the measure's threats to Confederate ideology did very little to hinder the measure. Governor Brown might have shielded more state employees than he should have, but even he did not prevent the enrollment of Georgians in the Confederate army. His criticisms were aimed more at ensuring his popularity among Georgians (and his 1863 reelection) than at truly undermining the Davis administration. Ultimately, whether Davis or Stephens and Brown were correct about the measure is less important than the fact that they all argued as Confederates. Conscription inspired multiple dialogues on what the Confederacy stood for, but these dialogues generally involved two sides dedicated to achieving the same end: Confederate independence.

This conflict between Confederates who viewed conscription differently played out across the nation. In Mississippi, W. L. Brandon, the general in charge of recruiting reserves, tangled with Governor Charles Clark over who controlled exemptions. Despite considering Clark's actions a threat to the success of conscription, Brandon acknowledged that the governor acted from "patriotic motives"—the defense of his state—rather than "a factious spirit of opposition." In April 1863, Florida governor John Milton forwarded President Davis a troubling circular. The anonymous document advocated the formation of an opposition party, something that both Milton and Davis opposed. Much of the circular addressed the unconstitutionality of conscription. It justified those who disagreed with the measure, reminding its readers that "there are men opposed to the Administration whose purposes are as high as that of the loftiest patriots on the side of the Administration." Likewise, in his memoirs, Texas senator William Oldham trumpeted the loyalty of dissenters like himself. A states' rights opponent of conscription, Oldham recounted that most southerners who challenged conscription were "actuated by patriotic motives."[64]

In pointing out the patriotism of conscription's opponents, these Confederates recognize more nuance than many historians who have used the measure to support their theses of internal fissures destroying the Confederacy. These scholars argue that conscription epitomized the centralizing tendencies of the national government, which destroyed Confederate nationalism. Conscription policy neatly corresponds to the argument that the Confederacy collapsed from within, as Davis failed in his attempt to build a nation because he neglected the needs of the common people. In this scenario, conscription policy proved to yeomen that all men did not share the burdens of the war equally. Wealthy planters and their relatives avoided service in the army by purchasing substitutes, by owning twenty or more slaves, or by taking advantage of loopholes in exemption laws. Remaining home, they further weakened the cause by exploiting soldiers' families. In short, conscription is easily portrayed as unfair class legislation undermining the Confederacy. It forced yeomen farmers to the conclusion that they were to be cannon fodder in a conflict that provided them no benefit. Consequently, they quickly abandoned the Confederacy.[65]

Historians who contend that conscription undermined the Confederacy often make two key errors. First, they portray conscription as a monolithic policy, failing to take into account its evolution. Passed in April 1862, the policy changed significantly in October 1862 and again in January and February 1864, and it was receiving further alterations as the war ended. Far from a rigid policy imposed from above, conscription policy represented a give-and-take among various stakeholders, including the executive branch, the legislative branch, the army, governors, state judges, prospective conscripts, and ordinary Confederates.

In July 1863, Senator James Phelan feared for the future of the Confederacy. Writing to President Davis, he saw only a single solution: "Let the *one idea* of the country be 'the conscription,—the conscription,'" but not the conscription currently in place. Phelan wanted the army in charge of the policy, and he urged the end of substitution, the reduction of exemptions, and the closure of camps of instruction. Davis did not immediately put the senator's suggestions into practice, but over the next two years, Congress and the president debated and implemented each of these alterations.[66]

Second, these historians conflate anger over or criticism of Confederate policies with opposition to the Confederacy. Conscription critics from Joseph Brown to Alexander Stephens to Williamson Oldham to Richmond Pearson to James Phelan considered themselves defenders of Confederate ideals. Similarly, ordinary citizens who attacked the measure generally advocated for equity and shared sacrifice, not for the defeat of the nation. They disliked the policy because it forced some to endure more suffering than others. They detested speculators, disliked special privileges, and wanted the government to take care of its people, but they made these arguments as loyal Confederates. In fact, Phelan's proposals to the president had looked simultaneously to helping the army and to satisfying these home front critics. In advocating the end of substitution, the senator believed in this idea of shared sacrifice as "nothing would do more to quiet discontent and infuse new life into the army." To improve civilian morale, all men, regardless of wealth or connections, needed to face conscription.[67]

In 1862, southerners greeted conscription with emotions ranging from relief to anger, but regardless of where their opinion fell on the spectrum of reactions, they accepted it. Like Senator Phelan, other Confederates, in the subsequent three years, condemned its flaws: the abuse of substitution, the haughtiness of conscription officers, the preferential treatment given to exempt classes, and the threats to states' rights. The measure served as a convenient scapegoat for the difficulties faced by common Confederates. This anger, however, did not lead to Confederate collapse, partly because leaders listened to their constituents. They altered conscription to address these complaints, and they tried to ensure that everyone served the cause. Officials also tried to balance the competing needs of home front and battlefront, trying to come up with a perfect yet elusive formula for allocating men to satisfy these competing demands. The operation of Confederate conscription supports the arguments that civilians were willing to accept hardships if everyone had to sacrifice equally, that officials responded to their constituents, and that the Confederacy succumbed because of the enemy's superior numbers rather than because of internal dissent.[68]

In sum, conscription tried to solve an unsolvable problem—finding enough men to both fight and farm without allowing for special privileges—or even the perception of special privileges. A letter Robert E. Lee wrote to Braxton Bragg in September 1864, which is rife with contradictions, exemplifies the difficulties faced by the Bureau of Conscription. Lee complained of the excessive number of Virginians with exemptions or details. He had heard from General Kemper that the total number of these men, combined with those on furlough while awaiting the decision on their appeals for exemptions or details, exceeded 40,000. Given that embarrassing situation, he declared conscription to be "a very imperfect system of recruiting our armies." Rather than suggesting a different system, however, he then does an about-face and admits, "It is possible that nothing better can be done." Similarly, he decried the men who should be on the front lines but instead hid in the bureau. He preferred that "none but reserves and disabled should be employed to collect conscripts." Then he abruptly declares that in "no department of the service are energy, intelligence and practical ability more vitally important to our success."[69]

Most Confederates probably agreed with Lee's oxymoronic description of conscription. They considered the system imperfect, but they rarely offered alternative methods of filling the army. Other than the occasional cries from Georgia officials that they preferred state quotas, no one seriously believed the Confederacy could survive without conscription. Similarly, Confederates wanted enrolling officers to make sure that all southerners did their duty. They had to diligently search all the local hiding places, carefully investigate all claims of medical exemptions, and thoroughly research all occupational exemptions. Yet southerners expected this superhuman effort to come from disabled and elderly soldiers and to make sure that, in addition to filling the army, enough producers remained at home. Simply put, Confederates demanded that all southerners share the sacrifices of the Civil War, and conscription policy needed to enforce that scenario. For three years, Confederates both debated how the policy could best achieve this lofty goal and repeatedly altered its formula in an effort to achieve success. Reality could never meet their expectations.

# Notes

## ABBREVIATIONS

| | |
|---|---|
| DU | David M. Rubenstein Rare Book & Manuscript Library, Duke University |
| EU | Archives and Special Collections, Emory University |
| GA | Georgia Archives, University System of Georgia |
| LC | Library of Congress, Manuscript Division, Washington, D.C. |
| LLMVC | Louisiana and Lower Mississippi Valley Collections, Louisiana State University |
| LV | Library of Virginia, Archives and Manuscripts Department |
| *OR* | *Official Records of the War of Rebellion* |
| *PoJD* | *Papers of Jefferson Davis* |
| SHC | University of North Carolina, Chapel Hill, Southern Historical Collection |
| *SHSP* | *Southern Historical Society Papers* |
| VHS | Virginia Historical Society, Richmond, Va. |

## INTRODUCTION

1. Sam Watkins, *Company Aytch: Or, a Side Show of the Big Show* (1882; repr., New York: Plume, 1999), 31–32.

2. Robert P. Brooks, "Conscription in the Confederate States of America, 1862–1865," *The Military Historian and Economist* 1 (October 1916), 441; Albert Burton Moore, *Conscription and Conflict in the Confederacy* (1924; Columbia: University of South Carolina Press, 1996), 17, 354; Walter C. Hilderman III, *They Went into the Fight Cheering!: Confederate Conscription in North Carolina* (Boone, N.C.: Parkway Publishers, 2005), 21, vii.

3. Paul D. Escott, *After Secession: Jefferson Davis and the Failure of Confederate Nationalism* (Baton Rouge: Louisiana State University Press, 1978); Stephen E. Ambrose, "Yeoman Discontent in the Confederacy," *Civil War History* (September 1962), 268; David Williams, *Rich Man's War: Class, Caste, and Confederate Defeat in the Lower Chattahoochee Valley* (Athens: University of Georgia Press, 1998), 4; David Williams, *A People's History of the Civil War: Struggles for the Meaning of Freedom* (New York: New Press, 2005); James M. McPherson, *Battle Cry of Freedom: The Civil War Era* (New York: Oxford University Press, 1988), 432. In most of his works, Williams inaccurately contends that the wealthy could pay a commutation fee to avoid the draft. This option existed in the Union but not the Confederacy. The literature emphasizing the role of internal dissent in the Confederacy's defeat is vast. In addition to the Escott and Williams titles, it includes Armstead Robinson, *Bitter Fruits of Bondage: The Demise of Slavery and the Collapse of the Confederacy, 1861–1865* (Charlottesville: University of Virginia Press, 2005); David Williams, *Bitterly Divided: The South's Inner Civil War* (New York: New

Press, 2008); Richard Beringer et al., *Why the South Lost the Civil War* (Athens: University of Georgia Press, 1986); Charles W. Ramsdell, *Behind the Lines in the Southern Confederacy* (Baton Rouge: Louisiana State University Press, 1944); and Georgia Lee Tatum, *Disloyalty in the Confederacy* (Chapel Hill: University of North Carolina Press, 1934).

4. Abraham Lincoln to Horatio Seymour, August 7, 1863, in Roy P. Basler, ed., *The Collected Works of Abraham Lincoln*, vol. 6, *1862–1863* (New Brunswick, N.J.: Rutgers University Press, 1953), 371. *Draft* and *conscription* are often viewed as synonyms, but they are not precisely the same. In a draft, men are not automatically enrolled in the army. They are called into service if their name or number is drawn. In a true conscription, all men of a particular age range are assumed to be in the army unless assigned elsewhere or exempted. Thus, conscription allows the government greater control of the nation's manpower.

5. Norman D. Brown, ed., *One of Cleburne's Command: The Civil War Reminiscences and Diary of Capt. Samuel T. Foster, Granbury's Texas Brigade, CSA* (Austin: University of Texas Press, 1980), 49; *Richmond Enquirer*, February 10, 1865; E. Merton Coulter, *The Confederate States of America, 1861–1865* (Baton Rouge: Louisiana State University Press, 1950), 440; Susan B. Carter, ed., *Historical Statistics of the United States, Earliest Times to the Present* (Cambridge: Cambridge University Press, 2006), 5:351; William L. Shaw, "The Confederate Conscription and Exemption Acts," *American Journal of Legal History* 6 (1962), 377–379; Michael Clodfelter, *Warfare and Armed Conflicts: A Statistical Encyclopedia of Casualty and Other Figures, 1494–2007* (Jefferson, N.C.: McFarland, 2007), 292; Thomas L. Livermore, *Numbers and Losses in the Civil War in America, 1861–65* (New York: Houghton, Mifflin, 1900), 21–22. Despite these difficulties, I will guardedly use numbers when possible. For a fuller discussion of the numbers associated with conscription, see chapter 7 in the present volume.

6. John Williams to Sister, February 19, 1864, John Williams Papers, VHS; *Charleston Mercury*, September 18, 1862.

7. Circular 1, February 13, 1865, in Theophilus Holmes Papers, DU. Exemptions allowed entire classes to stay home, whether millers, overseers, or ministers, while details provided a more precise control of manpower. In details, the Confederacy enrolled men and then decided on an individual (rather than an occupational) basis whether to assign them to the army or the home front.

8. Circular, December 1, 1864; John Preston to James Seddon, September 9, 1864, *OR*, ser. 4, vol. 3, 887, 630–633.

9. Anne Sarah Rubin, *A Shattered Nation: The Rise and Fall of the Confederacy, 1861–1868* (Chapel Hill: University of North Carolina Press, 2005), 6; Petition for Joseph Schappers, August 20, 1863, John A. Coke Papers, New York Historical Society.

10. Jefferson Davis, October 3, 1864, in William J. Cooper Jr., ed., *Jefferson Davis: The Essential Writings* (New York: Modern Library, 2003), 348; George C. Rable, *Civil Wars: Women and the Crisis of Southern Nationalism* (Urbana: University of Illinois Press, 1989), 73–90; Stephanie McCurry, *Confederate Reckoning: Power and Politics in the Civil War South* (Cambridge, Mass.: Harvard University Press, 2010), 133–177.

11. Augusta (Ga.) *Daily Constitutionalist*, September 21, 1862.

12. Harris Flanagin to Jefferson Davis, January 5, 1863, *POJD*, 9:10. For an excellent discussion of the harmony of defending home and nation in Virginia, see Aaron Sheehan-Dean, *Why Confederates Fought: Family and Nation in Civil War Virginia* (Chapel Hill: University of North Carolina Press, 2009).

13. William Alan Blair, *Virginia's Private War: Feeding Body and Soul in the Confederacy, 1861–1865*

(New York: Oxford University Press, 2000); Gary Gallagher, *The Confederate War: How Popular Will, Nationalism, and Military Strategy Could Not Stave Off Defeat* (Cambridge, Mass.: Harvard University Press, 1997).

14. Jefferson Davis to Zebulon B. Vance, November 1, 1862, in Frontis W. Johnston, ed., *The Papers of Zebulon Baird Vance,* vol. 1, *1843–1862* (Raleigh, N.C.: State Department of Archives and History, 1963), 296.

## CHAPTER ONE

1. Jefferson Davis to the Senate and House, March 28, 1862; Jefferson Davis to Gentlemen of the Congress, April 29, 1861, both in James D. Richardson, ed., *A Compilation of the Messages and Papers of the Confederacy* (Nashville: United States Publishing Company, 1906), 1:205–206, 82.

2. David S. Heidler and Jeanne T. Heidler, eds., *Encyclopedia of the American Civil War: A Political, Social, and Military History* (Santa Barbara, Calif.: ABC-CLIO, 2000), 1:110. Some historians offer different totals, but regardless of the precise ratio and the exact number of men, the larger point remains: the Confederacy needed to put as great a percentage of men as possible in the army.

3. Davis to the Senate and House, March 28, 1862, in Richardson, *Messages and Papers,* 205–206.

4. James M. Matthews, *Public Laws of the Confederate States of America, Passed at the Second Session of the First Congress* (Richmond, Va.: R. M. Smith, 1862), 77–79. By the end of 1862, the War Department would create a Bureau of Conscription to enforce the policy.

5. Wilmington (N.C.) *Daily Journal,* April 17, 1862.

6. Jefferson Davis Speech, June 1, 1861, *PoJD,* 7:184; diary entry, May 15, 1861, in John Q. Anderson, ed., *Brokenburn: The Journal of Kate Stone, 1861–1868* (Baton Rouge: Louisiana State University Press, 1995), 13; T. B. Deaver to Thomas Hendricks, October 8, 1861, in Josie Armstrong McLaughlin, ed., *Cherished Letters of Thomas Wayman Hendricks* (Birmingham, Ala., 1947), 25; *OR,* ser. 4, vol. 1, 380 (June report), 497 (July report). On *rage militaire,* see James McPherson, *For Cause and Comrades: Why Men Fought in the Civil War* (New York: Oxford University Press, 1997), 16–17.

7. George Huntley to Dear Friends, February 25, 1862, in Michael W. Taylor, ed., *The Cry Is War, War, War: The Civil War Correspondence of Lts. Burwell Thomas Cotton and George Job Huntley, 34th Regiment North Carolina Troops* (Dayton, Ohio: Morningside House, 1994), 63–64. Thanks to Robert Brown for pointing me to this soldier's account. Frederick R. Taber to Mother, December 13, 1861, Frederick R. Taber Papers, LLMVC; Joseph D. Shields Jr. to Joseph D. Shields, July 1, 1861, Joseph D. Shields Papers, LLMVC.

8. Robert G. Tanner, *Stonewall in the Valley: Thomas J. "Stonewall" Jackson's Shenandoah Valley Campaign, Spring 1862* (Mechanicsburg, Pa., Stackpole, 2002), 91 (first and third soldiers); John Garibaldi to Sarah A. W. Poor, January 30, 1862 (second soldier), "John Garibaldi Correspondence, 1862–1864. Transcriptions," VMI Archives Digital Collections, Virginia Military Institute, http://digitalcollections.vmi.edu/digital/collection/p15821coll11/id/2011/rec/1; Larry Logue, *To Appomattox and Beyond: The Civil War Soldier in War and Peace* (Chicago: I. R. Dee, 1996), 22.

9. *OR,* ser. 4, vol. 1, 763.

10. Robert E. Lee, in *OR,* ser. 1, vol. 6, 350; Thomas J. Goree to My Dearest Mother, January 18, 1862, in Thomas W. Cutrer, ed., *Longstreet's Aide: The Civil War Letters of Major Thomas J. Goree* (Charlottesville: University of Virginia Press, 1995), 68; John Kinyoun to Wife, April 4, 1862, Kinyoun Papers, DU.

11. Shreveport (La.) *South-Western,* December 11, 1861; *Richmond Examiner,* November 19, 1861, quoted in John M. Daniel, *The Richmond Examiner During the War* (1868; repr., Arno Press, 1970), 31–32.

12. *OR,* ser. 4, vol. 2, 44; Emory Upton, *The Military Policy of the United States* (Washington, D.C.: Government Printing Office, 1912), 460; Douglas Southall Freeman, *Robert E. Lee: A Biography* (New York: Scribner, 1934), 2:26.

13. *OR,* ser. 4, vol. 1, part 1, 869 (act), 962–963 (Benjamin's numbers); Jefferson Davis, Message to Congress, February 25, 1862, in Richardson, *Messages and Papers,* 190–191; *Report of the Chief of the Department of the Military of South Carolina* (Columbia, S.C.: Charles P. Pelham, State Printer, 1862), 37.

14. Charles Edward Cauthen, *South Carolina Goes to War, 1860–1865* (1950; Columbia: University of South Carolina Press, 2005), 144–146; James B. Griffin to Leila Griffin, January 5, 1862, in Judith N. McArthur and Orville Burton, eds., *A Gentleman and an Officer: A Military and Social History of James B. Griffin's Civil War* (New York: Oxford University Press, 1996), 134; *Report of the Chief of the Department of the Military of South Carolina,* 7; diary entry, March 19, 1862, in C. Vann Woodward, ed., *Mary Chesnut's Civil War* (New Haven, Conn.: Yale University Press, 1981), 314.

15. Thomas Goree to Dr. Pleasant W. Kittrell, February 15, 1862, in Cutrer, *Longstreet's Aide,* 74; Gideon Lincecum to John H. Lewis, March 15, 1862, in Jerry Bryan Lincecum, Edward Hake Phillips, and Peggy Redshaw, eds., *Gideon Lincecum's Sword: Civil War Letters from the Texas Home Front* (Denton: University or North Texas Press, 2001), 181, 183; Appleton H. Justice to William M. Moxley, January 11, 1862, in Thomas. W. Cutrer, ed., *Oh, What a Loansome Time I Had: The Civil War Letters of Major William Morel Moxley, Eighteenth Alabama Infantry, and Emily Beck Moxley* (Tuscaloosa, University of Alabama Press, 2002), 104; *Shreveport* (La.) *Semi-Weekly News,* February 18, 1862.

16. "To Arms! To Arms! $50 Bounty. Do Not Wait To Be Drafted, but Volunteer!!," Virginia recruiting poster, Documenting the American South, Academic Affairs Library, University of North Carolina at Chapel Hill, http://docsouth.unc.edu/imls/toarms/image.html; "Recruits Wanted for the Bartow Invincibles," *Southern Confederacy* (Atlanta), April 9, 1862.

17. McPherson, *For Cause and Comrades,* esp. 19–22; Zebulon Vance, April 29, 1862, in Johnston, *Papers of Zebulon Baird Vance,* 135; John Ellis to E. P. Ellis, November 4, 1862, in E. P. Ellis and Family Papers, LLMVC. For the political connection between liberty and slavery, see William J. Cooper Jr., *Liberty and Slavery: Southern Politics to 1860* (New York: McGraw Hill, 1983).

18. John Achilles Harris to Becky Harris, no date, and December 7, 1861, John Achilles Harris Letters, LLMVC; Reuben A. Pierson to James F. Pierson, February 2, 1862, in Thomas W. Cutrer and T. Michael Parrish, eds., *Brothers in Gray: The Civil War Letters of the Pierson Family* (Baton Rouge: Louisiana State University Press, 1997), 78; Lt. Charles C. Jones Jr. to Rev. C. C. Jones, February 21, 1862, in Robert M. Myers, ed., *The Children of Pride: A True Story of Georgia and the Civil War* (New Haven, Conn.: Yale University Press, 1972), 850; Augustus P. Adamson to Father and Mother, February 17, 1862, in Richard B. Abell and Fay A. Gecik, eds., *Sojourns of a Patriot: The Field and Prison Papers of an Unreconstructed Confederate* (Murfreesboro, Tenn.: Southern Heritage Press, 1998), 37.

19. *Charleston Mercury,* February 8, 1862; *Baton Rouge Gazette and Comet,* March 29, 1862; John H. Chamberlayne to Sally Grattan, March 1, 1862, in Ham Chamberlayne, ed., *Letters and Papers of an Artillery Officer in the War for Southern Independence* (Richmond, Va.: Press of the Dietz Printing Co., 1932), 72; *Georgia Weekly Telegraph,* March 28, 1862, quoting speech from Rockbridge, Va., from March 3, 1862; Reuben A. Pierson to James F. Pierson, January 24, 1862, in Cutrer and Parrish, *Brothers in Gray,* 73.

20. George Washington to Patrick Henry, May 17, 1777, quoted in Michael A. McDonnell, *The*

*Politics of War: Race, Class, and Conflict in Revolutionary Virginia* (Chapel Hill: University of North Carolina Press, 2007), 275–276. For an excellent discussion of the draft in Revolutionary War–era Virginia, see chapters 8, 9, and 12 of that volume.

21. For a the best discussion of Monroe's conscription proposal, see Jack Franklin Leach, *Conscription in the United States: Historical Background* (Rutland, Vt.: Charles E. Tuttle Publishing Co., 1952), 30–126 (quotes, pages 46 and 77); Joseph Davis to Jefferson Davis, April 20, 1862, *PoJD,* 8:148.

22. *Georgia Weekly Telegraph,* April 4, 1862; *Baton Rouge Gazette and Comet,* April 19, 1862; *Memphis Daily Appeal,* April 6, 1862. Throughout this work, all emphasis, whether underlines or italics, is from the original text.

23. Augusta (Ga.) *Daily Constitutionalist,* April 10, 1862; *Charleston Mercury,* March 8, 1862.

24. Jefferson Davis, March 28, 1862, in Richardson, *Messages and Papers,* 205–206; William J. Cooper Jr., *Jefferson Davis: American* (New York: Knopf, 2000), 384.

25. Joseph Brown to Alexander Stephens, May 7, 1862, Alexander Hamilton Stephens Collection, EU.

26. *SHSP,* 45:26–29 (Wigfall, 27–28).

27. *SHSP,* 45:28–29; Clayton E. Jewett, ed., *Rise and Fall of the Confederacy: The Memoir of Senator Williamson S. Oldham, CSA* (Columbia: University of Missouri Press, 2006), 108. For an excellent discussion of the ideological tension created by conscription, see George Rable, *Confederate Republic: A Revolution Against Politics* (Chapel Hill: University of North Carolina Press, 1994), 138–143.

28. *SHSP,* 26–27 (Sparrow and Clark); Thomas S. Ashe to William H. Battle, April 1, 1862, Battle Family Papers, SHC; Mary S. Estill, ed., "Diary of a Confederate Congressman, 1862–1863," *Southwestern Historical Quarterly* 38 (April 1935), 277–278 (Sexton). See also Thomas B. Alexander and Richard E. Beringer, *The Anatomy of the Confederate Congress* (Nashville: Vanderbilt University Press, 1972), 137–138. Their analysis examines conscription throughout the war. In doing so, they also assert that whether a member's district was under Union control played an important role. This was not a significant issue in 1862. Vote totals in *Journal of the Congress of the Confederate States of America,* 2:154 (Senate) and 5:228 (House).

29. *OR,* ser. 4, vol. 1, 1095.

30. Frederick Maurice, ed., *Lee's Aide de Camp: Charles Marshall* (Lincoln, Neb.: Bison Books, 2000), 30–43; Rembert W. Patrick, *Jefferson Davis and His Cabinet* (Baton Rouge: Louisiana State University Press, 1944), 123–124; Archer Jones, "Some Aspects of George W. Randolph's Service as Confederate Secretary of War," *Journal of Southern History* 26, no. 3 (1960), 303–305; Davis to Congress, April 17, 1862, *OR,* ser. 4, vol. 1, 1069–1070.

31. Robert M. Magill, *Magill Family Record* (Richmond: R. E. Magill, 1907), 175; Malcolm Stuart to J. Stuart, July 26, 1862, Auman Family Papers, SHC.

32. Rable, *Confederate Republic,* 140.

33. W. A. Hauser to Sister, August 8, 1861, Jones Family Papers, SHC.

34. Richmond (Va.) *Daily Dispatch,* April 4, 1862. Five days after conscription's passage, the Confederate Congress would pass its first list of occupational exemptions. See chapter 2 in the present volume for the debate over exemptions.

35. George Huntley to Dear Friends, December 3, 1861, and February 25, March 19, April 3, 1862; Huntley to Dear Father, March 6, 1862. All in Taylor, *The Cry Is War, War, War,* 40, 63–71.

36. J. C. Nunn to His Family, May 12, 1862, in Mills Lane, ed., *"Dear Mother: Don't Grieve About Me.*

*If I Get Killed, I'll Only Be Dead": Letters from Georgia Soldiers in the Civil War* (Savannah, Ga.: Beehive Press, 1977), 118; E. Jefferson Lee to Jordan G. Taylor, May 20, 1862, in Frank Vandiver, ed., "A Collection of Louisiana Confederate Letters," *Louisiana Historical Quarterly* 26, no. 4 (October 1943), 966; John Offield to Joseph Offield, April 17, 1862, in Leona Taylor Aiken, ed., "Letters from the Offield Brothers, Confederate Soldiers from Upper East Tennessee," *East Tennessee Historical Society's Publications* 46 (1974), 119; Thomas J. Goree to Mother, February 21, 1862, in Cutrer, *Longstreet's Aide,* 77; diary entry, August 19, 1862, in Anderson, *Brokenburn,* 138.

37. *Charleston Mercury,* July 30, 1862; James B. Griffin to Leila Griffin, March 20, 1862, in *A Gentleman and an Officer: A Military and Social History of Major James B. Griffin's Civil War,* 175; Atlanta *Southern Confederacy,* March 6, 1862; W. D. Rutherford to Sallie F. Rutherford, April 19, 1862, William Drayton Rutherford Papers, University of South Carolina Library (digital collections).

38. Joseph Brown to Alexander Stephens, May 7, 1862 (first and third quote), Stephens Collection, EU; Brown to Thomas W. Thomas, April 12, 1862, Executive Letterbook, GA; Letcher Message, May 5, 1862, in Accompanying Documents, p. iii, of *Journal of the House of Delegates of the State of Virginia for the Session of 1861–1862;* Gov. Henry T. Clark to Peter Mallett, June 24, 1862, quoted in W. Buck Yearns and John G. Barrett, eds., *North Carolina Civil War Documentary* (Chapel Hill: University of North Carolina Press, 1980), 131; Shorter quote in John B. Robbins, "Confederate Nationalism: Politics and Government in the Confederate South, 1861–1865" (PhD diss., Rice University, 1964), 96.

39. Letcher Message, May 5, 1862; Clark quote in R. Matthew Poteat, "'A Modest Estimate of His Own Abilities': Governor Henry Toole Clark's and the Early Civil War Leadership of North Carolina," *North Carolina Historical Review* 84, no. 2 (April 2007), 138–139; Joseph Brown to Officers and Soldiers of the State Troops, April 16, 1862, Executive Letterbook, GA. W. Buck Yearns, ed., *The Confederate Governors* (Athens: University of Georgia Press, 1985) argues this same point—that most governors voiced displeasure but rarely acted upon it.

40. Mississippi Private Wilborn Smith, in Dick Stanley, "The Conscription Act," *13th Mississippi Infantry Regiment,* December 11, 2010, http://13thmississippi.com/2010/12/11/the-conscription-act; Charles Liebermann to Lenora Liebermann, April 25, 1862, Liebermann Family Papers, VHS; William L. Sullivan to A. S. Caddell, April 26, 1862, Artemus S. Caddell Papers, DU; Eglantine Agours to Cousin, April 21, 1862, Eglantine Agours Papers, DU; R. C. Puryear to Henry T. Clark, April 23, 1862, quoted in Rable, *Confederate Republic,* 141; Charles Hutson to Father, May 13 and 16, 1862, Charles Hutson Papers, SHC.

41. Augusta (Ga.) *Daily Constitutionalist,* April 10, 1862.

42. Samuel D. Sanders to Mary Sanders, November 27, 1861, March 22, 1862, in Walter Rundell Jr., ed., "'If Fortune Should Fail': Civil War Letters of Dr. Samuel D. Sanders," *South Carolina Historical Magazine* 65 (July 1964), 133, 135; Lewis Warlick to Cornelia McGimsey, June 3, 1862, Cornelia McGimsey Papers, SHC; diary entry, August 2, 1862, in J. V. Frederick, ed., "War Diary of W. C. Porter," *Arkansas Historical Quarterly* 11, no. 4 (Winter 1952), 299; John Achilles Harris to Becky, December 7, 1861, November 1861, Harris Letters, LLMVC.

43. Edwin Fay to Sarah Fay, June 23, 1862, in Bell I. Wiley, ed., *"This Infernal War": The Confederate Letters of Sgt. Edwin H. Fay* (Austin: University of Texas Press, 1958), 96; Isaac Walker to Holley Walker, April 30, July 30, 1862, in Allan C. Richard and Mary M. Richard, *The Defense of Vicksburg: A Louisiana Chronicle* (College Station: Texas A&M University Press, 2004), 60–61, 63; Thomas Settle to John Gilmer, May 1862, Thomas Settle Papers, SHC.

44. *OR,* ser. 4, vol. 1, 1095.

45. William L. Sullivan to Mr. A. S. Caddell, April 26, 1862, Caddell Papers, DU; J. M. Tate to Dear Sister, April 23, 1862, in Robert E. Bonner, *The Soldier's Pen: Firsthand Impressions of the Civil War* (New York: Hill and Wang, 2007), 155; John Wilkinson to Micajah Wilkinson, April 16, 1862, in Micajah Wilkinson Papers, LLMVC; William H. Hill, diary entry of April 21, 1862, in Stanley, "Conscription Act"; James B. Griffin to Leila Griffin, April 6, 1862, in *A Gentleman and an Officer,* 191.

46. *OR,* ser. 1, vol. 10, part 1, 780–781.

47. James B. Griffin to Leila Griffin, April 25, 1862, in McArthur and Burton, *Gentleman and Officer,* 200; Augustus P. Adamson to Dear Father, April 27, 1862, in Abell and Gecik, *Sojourns of a Patriot,* 49; John Kinyoun to Wife, April 4, 1862, Kinyoun Papers, DU; Charles Hutson to Mother, April 28, 1862, Hutson Papers, SHC.

48. Charles Hutson to Mother, April 26, 1862, Hutson Papers, SHC; Ham Chamberlayne to Sally Grattan, March 1, 1862, and Chamberlayne to My Dear Mother, February 23, 1862, in Chamberlayne, *Letters and Papers,* 66–69, 70–72; Charles Liebermann to Lenora Liebermann, March 11 and 23, and April 25, 1862, Liebermann Family Papers, VHS; J. W. Reid, February 7, 1862, in J. W. Reid, *History of the Fourth Regiment of S.C. Volunteers from the Commencement of the War Until Lee's Surrender* (Greenville, S.C.: Shannon & Co., 1892), 68; Raleigh *Semi-Weekly Standard,* January 25, 1862.

49. Charles W. Truehart to My Dear Sisters, April 22, 1862, in Edward B. Williams, ed., *Rebel Brothers: The Civil War Letters of the Truehearts* (College Station: Texas A&M University Press, 1995), 53–54; Dr. Harvey Black to My Dear Wife, April 4, 1862, in Glenn L. McMullen, ed., *The Civil War Letters of Dr. Harvey Black: A Surgeon with Stonewall Jackson* (Baltimore, Md.: Butternut and Blue, 1995); James B. Gordon to Frank, April 19, 1862, in Christopher M. Watford, ed., *The Civil War in North Carolina: Soldiers' and Civilians' Letters and Diaries, 1861–1865,* vol. 2, *The Mountains* (Jefferson, N.C.: McFarland, 2003), 40; James B. Griffin to Leila Griffin, March 20, 1862, in McArthur and Burton, *Gentleman and an Officer,* 176.

50. James M. Holloway to Wife, December 18, 1861, and January 28, 1862, John Williams Holloway Papers, VHS; Samuel A. Burney to Dearest Wife, April 27, 1862, in Nat S. Turner, ed., *A Southern Soldier's Letters Home: The Civil War Letters of Samuel A. Burney, Cobb's Georgia Legion* (Macon, Ga.: Mercer, 2003), 158; J. S. Hubard to Uncle, February 21, 1862, Hubard Family Letters, and Henry H. Dedrick to M. E. A. Dedrick, January 22, 1862, Henry H. Dedrick Papers, both in "Valley of the Shadow," University of Virginia Library, https://valley.lib.virginia.edu/VoS/personalpapers/documents/augusta/p2dedrickletters.html; diary entries of February 1 and May 9, 1862, in Anderson, *Brokenburn,* 87, 103.

51. *Baton Rouge Gazette and Comet,* April 19, 1862 (military despotism); Eglantine Agours to Cousin, April 21, 1862, Agours Papers, DU; J. W. Reid to Family, April 18, 1862, in Reid, *History of the Fourth Regiment,* 75; William L. Sullivan to A. S. Caddell, April 26, 1862, Caddell Papers, DU; Charles Liebermann to Lenora Liebermann, April 25, 1862, Liebermann Papers, VHS; Sgt. W. D. Bishop to Susan Bishop, April 4, 1862, quoted in Poteat, "Henry Toole Clark's Civil War Leadership," 136.

52. *Richmond Enquirer,* April 18, 1862; E. D. Tracy to C. C. Clay, February 22, 1862, C. C. Clay Papers, DU. For a description of the Shiloh battle, see James M. McPherson, *Battle Cry of Freedom: The Civil War Era* (New York: Oxford University Press, 1988), 405–414.

53. Richmond *Daily Dispatch,* April 1, 1862; *Raleigh Standard,* April 5, 1862.

54. *OR,* ser. 4, vol. 2, 43 (August 1862 report); George W. Bolton to Dad, April 1862, in Sue Lyles

Eakin and Morgan Peoples, eds., *In Defense of My Country . . .": The Letters of a Shiloh Confederate Soldier* (Bernice, La., 1983), 19; William Hill, diary, April 21, 1862; Gov. Clark to Peter Mallett, June 24, 1862, in Yearns and Barrett, *North Carolina Civil War Documentary,* 131.

55. *Charleston Mercury,* March 31 (age range), April 3, 1862 (sooner); *Richmond Examiner,* April 4, 1862, quoted in Daniel, *Richmond Examiner During the War,* 47–48; Samuel A. Burney to Dearest wife, April 27, 1862, in Turner, *Southern Soldier's Letters Home,* 158; Tally Simpson to Caroline Virginia Taliaferro Miller, April 30, 1862, in Guy R. Everson and Edward H. Simpson Jr., eds., *"Far, Far from Home": The Wartime Letters of Dick and Tally Simpson, 3rd South Carolina Volunteers* (New York: Oxford University Press, 1994), 119.

56. *Wilmington Daily Journal,* April 17, 1862; *Raleigh Semi-Weekly Standard,* January 25, April 16, 1862; Joseph Brown to Alexander Stephens, May 7, 1862, Stephens Collection, EU (quote); Brown to Thomas W. Thomas, April 12, 1862, Executive Letterbook, GA; Brown to Davis, April 22, 1862 (quotes); Brown to Davis, May 9, 1862, in *Correspondence Between Governor Brown and President Davis on the Constitutionality of the Conscription Act* (Atlanta: Atlanta Intelligencer, 1862).

57. James Chesnut to Jefferson Davis, April 20, 1862, and council declaration in Cauthen, *South Carolina Goes to War,* 145.

58. Cauthen, *South Carolina Goes to War,* 145.

59. Diary entry, April 22, 1862, in Robert S. Durham, *The Blues in Gray: The Civil War Journal of William Daniel Dixon* (New York: Arno Press, 1970), 79; Shreveport *South-Western,* April 16, 1862, in Perry A. Snyder, "Shreveport, Louisiana During the Civil War and Reconstruction" (PhD diss., Florida State University, 1979), 83.

## CHAPTER TWO

1. John Conrad to Sally Conrad, April 17, 1862, John Thomas Conrad Papers, State Archives of North Carolina.

2. Jonathan Worth to A. G. Foster, May 1, 1862, in Joseph G. de Roulhac Hamilton, ed., *The Correspondence of Jonathan Worth* (Raleigh: North Carolina Historical Commission, 1909), 1:168; William Beavans to Dear Sister, April 20, 1862, William Beavans Diary and Letters, SHC.

3. *Military Laws of the Confederate States* (Richmond, Va.: J. W. Randolph, 1863), 58–61 (substitution), 67–68 (exemption); *OR,* ser. 4, vol. 1, 1099. The act simply stated "Persons not liable for duty may be received as substitutes," allowing the secretary of war to provide regulations for how the process would work.

4. Moore, *Conscription and Conflict in the Confederacy,* 354; Coulter, *Confederate States of America,* 327; Escott, *After Secession,* 116; Mark Weitz, *More Damning Than Slaughter: Desertion in the Confederate Army* (Lincoln: University of Nebraska Press, 2005), 157; McPherson, *Battle Cry of Freedom,* 432.

5. Moore, *Conscription and Conflict in the Confederacy,* 51; Escott, *After Secession,* 117; Bell Irvin Wiley, *The Life of Johnny Reb: The Common Soldier of the Confederacy* (1943; Baton Rouge: Louisiana State University Press, 2005), 125; Mary L. Wilson, "Profiles in Evasion: Civil War Substitutes and the Men Who Hired them in Walker's Texas Division," *East Texas Historical Journal* 43 (2005), 25–38; Armstead Robinson, *Bitter Fruits of Bondage,* 150–156, at 153; Lowell H. Harrison, "Conscription in the Confederacy," *Civil War Times Illustrated* 9 (July 1970), 10–18, at 12, 13.

6. Patrick J. Doyle, "Replacement Rebels: Confederate Substitution, and the Issue of Citizenship,"

*Journal of the Civil War Era* (March 2018), 3–31, at 5, 11. Aaron Sheehan-Dean makes a similar point in his study of Virginia soldiers. Sheehan-Dean, *Why Confederates Fought*, 96–97.

7. Upton, *Military Policy of the United States*, 35, 77–79, 122–123; John K. Mahon, *History of the Militia and the National Guard* (New York: Macmillan, 1983), 53. This work specifies that all fifteen states in the 1790s allowed substitutes. Sally Hadden, *Slave Patrols: Law and Violence in Virginia and the Carolinas* (Cambridge, Mass.: Harvard University Press, 2001), 75, 103.

8. *OR*, ser. 4, vol. 1, 694–695, 975; Richmond *Daily Dispatch*, March 1862; *Charleston Mercury*, March 10, 1862. On March 5, in a one-sentence order, the Confederate army revoked the October substitute regulations, but it is unclear what that meant. The order did not say that it ended the practice of substitution, just the October regulations on substitution. Units continued to accept them after this revocation. *OR*, ser. 4., vol. 1, 971.

9. William Larue to Eliza Grantham, May 26, 1861[2], in Larue Family Papers, VHS (first quote); John A. Williams to "Dear Sister," February 10, 1863, in John A. Williams Letters, VHS (second quote); *OR*, ser. 4, vol. 1, 1093 (one per month). According to the secretary of war's February report, there were 240,475 twelve-month men in the army. An undetermined number of these were younger than eighteen or older than thirty-five.

10. For reminders that conscription was "prospective," see Peter Mallett to J. H. Haughton, December 1, 1862, Mallett to Secretary of War, December 1, 1862, and Mallett to Hon. B. Gaither, December 12, 1862, Peter Mallett Papers, SHC.

11. Charles Friend to Mary Friend, July 1, 1862, Blanton Family Papers, VHS. For a soldier over thirty-five years of age complaining about being kept past July 16, see J. W. Carter to H. C. Wayne, July 18, 1862, Adjutant General's Letters, GA.

12. *Petition of Certain Non-Conscripts Respectfully Presented to the Confederate States Congress*, August 8, 1862; Petition from Privates of the 17th La. Regiment to his Excellency Governor Moore, September 30, 1862, Thomas Overton Moore Papers, LLMVC; John Ellis to Sister, October 29, 1862, John Ellis to E. P. Ellis, November 4, 1862, in E. P. Ellis and Family Papers, LLMVC.

13. Weitz, *More Damning than Slaughter*, 52–116.

14. Kenneth W. Noe, *Reluctant Rebels: The Confederates Who Joined the Army After 1861* (Chapel Hill: University of North Carolina Press, 2010), 103–121, esp. 116–118. For Edwin Fay's background, see Wiley, *"This Infernal War,"* 4–7. Though he considered his wife's views, only his letters are extant. Noe offers an excellent quantitative discussion of 1862 enlistees (reluctant rebels), conscription, and substitution. His group includes both Fay and Grant Taylor.

15. Edwin Fay to Sarah Fay, May 20 and 25, June 15, 18, and 23, August 2, 1862, all in Wiley, *"This Infernal War,"* 56–57, 84, 90 (first two quotes), 96 (third quote).

16. Edwin Fay to Sarah Fay, May 25 and 27, June 15, 18, and 23, 1862, in Wiley, *"This Infernal War,"* 84, 90, 96, 64.

17. Grant Taylor to Malinda Taylor, June 27, July 7, 13, and 19, 1862, in Ann K. Blomquist and Robert A. Taylor, eds. *This Cruel War: The Civil War Letters of Grant and Malinda Taylor* (Macon, Ga.: Mercer University Press, 2000), 55, 57, 62. For Grant's background, see viii–ix. "Old Rily" was in his forties, making him less than a decade older than Grant.

18. Malinda to Grant Taylor, July 19, August 1, 1862, Grant to Malinda Taylor, August 6 and 8, 1862, in Blomquist and Taylor, *This Cruel War*, 62, 74, and 76. If Grant disliked the offer because the numbers added up to $770 rather than $800, he did not say so.

19. Grant to Malinda Taylor, August 8 and 14, 1862, Malinda to Grant Taylor, August 14 and 24, 1862, in Blomquist and Taylor, *This Cruel War,* 77, 83, and 86.

20. Abner Ford to Mollie Ford, January 4 (first quote), 7, 17, 23 (second quote), and 26 (third quote), 1863, Abner Dawson Ford Papers, VHS.

21. Abner Ford to Mollie Ford, February 1, March 26, April 14, May 20 and 23, July 17, August 29, September 19, 1863, Abner Dawson Ford Papers, VHS.

22. Edwin Fay to Sarah Fay, June 23 and 27, July 10 and 13, October 2, 1863, in Wiley, *"This Infernal War,"* 101, 292, 338; Grant Taylor to Malinda Taylor July 22, 1862, in Blomquist and Taylor, *This Cruel War,* 64. Fay and Ford died in the 1890s and Taylor died in 1908.

23. All wealth and slaveholding data from the 1860 census and slave schedules on Ancestry.com.

24. Abner Ford to Mollie Ford, January 23, 1863, Ford Papers, VHS; Edwin Fay to Sarah Fay, May 20, 1862, Wiley, *"This Infernal War,"* 56.

25. Lewis Warlick to Laura McGimsey, June 3, 1862, McGimsey Papers, SHC; John Williams to My Dear Sister, May 13, 1862, and Williams to Mary Williams, June 21, 1862, in John A. Williams Letters, VHS.

26. A. J. Gilkeson to Brother [probably Hugh], October 6, 1862, Hugh Gilkeson Collection, "Valley of the Shadow," https://valley.lib.virginia.edu/papers/A1102; John M. Harris to Henry St. George Harris, March 24, 1863, Henry St. George Harris Papers, DU; J. B. Gaither to Father, March 20, 1863, October 18, 1863, and undated, Gaither Family Papers, SHC.

27. Diary entries, June 8, 1862 (secessionists), July 16, 1862 (Cavett), in Gary D. Joiner, ed., *No Pardons to Ask, Nor Apologies to Make: The Journal of William Henry King, Gray's 28th Louisiana Infantry Regiment* (Knoxville: University of Tennessee Press, 2006), 30, 54. A month later, King would record that the substitute died, having sold his life for a slave woman and $500 (63). James Calvin Marcom Diary, May 30, 1863, DU; Edgar Richardson to Sister, June 21, July 13, 1862, Richards to Dear Mother, October 10, 1862, in Richardson Family Letters, GA.

28. Edwin Fay to Sarah Fay, June 27, 1862, in Wiley, *"This Infernal War,"* 102; William Larue to Nellie Grantham, May 8, 1861[3], Larue Family Papers, VHS.

29. Samuel A. Burney to My Dearest Wife, June 22 and 25, July 14, 1862, in Turner, *A Southern Soldier's Letters Home,* 185, 187, 195.

30. Charles Liebermann to Lenora Liebermann, April 25, 1862, Liebermann Family Papers, VHS. For further discussion of substitution's connection to the "rich man's war, poor man's fight" theme, see chapter 3 of the present volume. Liebermann most likely underestimated the cost of a substitute.

31. *Richmond Daily Dispatch,* March 7, 1862; February 13 and 17, 1863, entries in Bureau of Conscription, Conscript Journal, LV.

32. Tolivar Davis to Governor Vance, September 11, 1862, in Watford, *Civil War in North Carolina,* 2:58; John Thompson to Governor Vance, September 27, 1862, in Christopher M. Watford, ed., *The Civil War in North Carolina: Soldiers' and Civilians' Letters and Diaries, 1861–1865,* vol. 1, *The Piedmont* (Jefferson, N.C.: McFarland, 2003), 73.

33. Malinda Taylor to Grant Tayor, June 11, 1862, in Blomquist and Taylor, *This Cruel War,* 37; Ham Chamberlayne to Lucy Parke Chamberlayne, May 6, 1862, in Chamberlayne, *Letters and Papers,* 79–80.

34. George W. Randolph to James Chesnut, May 13, 1862, *OR,* ser. 4, vol. 1, 1121.

35. Jonathan Worth to A. G. Foster, May 1, 1862, in Hamilton, *Correspondence of Jonathan Worth,*

168; W. H. Lineberry to Jonathan Worth, December 11, 1862, in Jonathan Worth Papers, SHC; J. P. M. Brown and Samuel Hope to Secretary of War Randolph, May 6, 1862 (dental goods), in Letters Received by the Secretary of War, National Archives.

36. All petitions in Charlotte County (Va.) records, 1763–1896, VHS. Only the blacksmith petition has a date (March 17, 1862), but it appears that all of the petitions are from March 1862. Carroll County Petition, May 1, 1862, in Letters Received by the Secretary of War, National Archives; McCurry, *Confederate Reckoning*, 138–161; Amy E. Murrell, "'Of Necessity and Public Benefit': Southern Families and Their Appeals for Protection," in Catherine Clinton, ed., *Southern Families at War: Loyalty and Conflict in the Civil War South* (New York: Oxford University Press, 2000).

37. *OR*, ser. 1, vol. 6, 850–851; E. S. to John Perkins, September 12, 1862 (first quote), and William M. Pew to John Perkins, August 5, 1862, John Perkins Papers, SHC; Ladies of Halifax quoted in Poteat, "Henry Toole Clark's Civil War Leadership of North Carolina," 142; Daniel Ruggles to General S. Cooper, Adj. Gen'l CSA, October 3, 1862, *OR*, ser. 1, vol. 15, 821; W. B. Overstreet to Joseph Brown, April 26, 1862, in Mills Lane, ed., *Times That Prove People's Principles: Civil War in Georgia* (Savannah, Ga.: Beehive Press, 1993), 124. For the Mississippi slave conspiracy, see Winthrop D. Jordan, *Tumult and Silence at Second Creek: An Inquiry into a Civil War Slave Conspiracy* (Baton Rouge: Louisiana State University Press, 1993).

38. James Chesnut to G. W. Randolph, *OR*, ser. 4, vol. 1, 1106; Joseph Brown to Jefferson Davis, April 22, 1862, in *Correspondence Between Governor Brown and Jefferson Davis on the Constitutionality of the Conscription Act* (1862), 5–6.

39. Jefferson Davis to Governor Pettus, May 30, 1862, in *OR*, ser. 4, vol. 1, 1138 (with enclosure from Secretary of War Randolph).

40. David W. Siler to Zebulon Vance, November 3, 1862, in Watford, *Civil War North Carolina*, 2:70–71.

41. Peter Brock, ed., *Liberty and Conscience: A Documentary History of the Experiences of Conscientious Objectors in America through the Civil War* (New York: Oxford University Press, 2002), 163.

42. Church data taken from *Eighth Census of the United States*, 497–498; *OR*, ser. 1, vol. 12, part 3, 835 (Stonewall Jackson quote); Christ Good quote in Christian B. Keller, "Pennsylvania and Virginia Germans During the Civil War: A Brief History and Comparative Analysis," *Virginia Magazine of History and Biography* 109, no. 1 (2001): 73. Dunkers, who practiced three-time immersion baptism, were also referred to as Tunkers, Dunkards, and Brethren.

43. James O. Lehman and Steven M. Nolt, *Mennonites, Amish, and the American Civil War* (Baltimore, Md.: Johns Hopkins University Press, 2007), esp. 56–75; Samuel Horst, *Mennonites in the Confederacy: A Study in Civil War Pacifism* (Scottsdale, Pa.: Herald Press, 1967), 26–29, 39–43, 70–80; secretary of war quoted in Richmond *Daily Dispatch*, July 29, 1862; Peter S. Hartman, *Reminiscences of the Civil War* (Lancaster, Pa.: Eastern Mennonite Associated Libraries and Archives, 1964), 8–13; Delphina Mendenhall to John B. Crenshaw, September 29, 1862, John B. Crenshaw Papers, Guilford College.

44. Samuel Horst, *Mennonites in the Confederacy*, 112. For more on Rockingham County, see John M. Sacher, "The Loyal Draft Dodger? A Reexamination of Confederate Substitution," *Civil War History* (June 2011), 153–178.

45. *OR*, ser. 4, vol. 1, 1106 (S.C. overseers), 1140 (state list); *Charleston Mercury*, May 16, 1862 (creative reading). Virginia's March 1862 draft also exempted overseers.

46. Brown to Davis, June 21, 1862, *OR*, ser. 4, vol. 1, 1169. Privately, he acknowledged that he would "reserve the question of the constitutionality of the act . . . [until] the earliest day when it can be done without serious embarrassment to the Confederacy in the prosecution of the war." Joseph Brown to Alexander Stephens, May 7, 1862, in Stephens Collection, EU.

47. Joseph Brown to Davis, April 22, 1862 (quotes); Brown to Davis, May 9, 1862, in *Correspondence Between Governor Brown and President Davis*, 7, 9; Brown to Secretary of War Randolph, May 26, 1862, *OR*, ser. 4, vol. 1, 1128.

48. Davis to Brown, July 10, 1862 (first and last quote), 47; May 29, 1862 (second quote) in *Correspondence Between Governor Brown and President Davis*, 29.

49. For Watts's opinion, see Rembert W. Patrick, ed., *The Opinions of the Confederate Attorneys General 1861–1865* (Buffalo, N.Y.: Dennis & Co., 1950), 94–98.

50. Davis to Brown, May 29 (first quote), July 10 (second quote), 1862, *Correspondence Between Governor Brown and President Davis*, 17, 48; Atlanta *Southern Confederacy*, May 28, 1862.

51. Clay Alexander to Joseph Brown, September 15, 1862 (typescript), Governor's Correspondence, GA; Augustus P. Adamson to Sister, June 22, 1862, in Bender, *Sojourns of a Patriot*, 74; For an example of Stephens's views, see Alexander H. Stephens, *A Constitutional View of the Late War Between the States* (Philadelphia: National Publishing Co., 1868), 2:572. Paul Escott portrays this battle over conscription as the beginning of the break between the Richmond government and the planter class. Escott, *After Secession*, 81–90.

52. "An Act to Organize Bands of Partizan Rangers," April 21, 1862, in *Military Laws of the Confederate States*, 65; Miller Francis to James Francis, May 12, 1862, in James P. Pate, ed., *When This Evil War Is Over: The Correspondence of the Francis Family, 1860–65* (Tuscaloosa: University of Alabama Press, 2006), 77–78; John T. Ault to Gov. Brown, June 6, 1862, Governor's Correspondence, GA; *OR*, ser. 4., vol. 2, 31 (Governor Clark discusses popularity of Ranger service).

53. Peter Mallett to Samuel Cooper, July 24, 1862 (first quote), Mallett to General French, August 29, 1862, Mallett to Cooper, August 9, 1862, Mallett to Cooper, September 2, 1862 (second quote), Mallett to General Martin, September 16, 1862, all in Peter Mallett Papers, SHC.

54. *OR*, ser. 4, vol. 2, 5 (Clark and Randolph), 26 (General Order 53); Assistant Secretary of War Bledsoe quoted in Daniel E. Sutherland, *A Savage Conflict: The Decisive Role of Guerrillas in the American Civil War* (Chapel Hill: University of North Carolina Press, 2013), 101; *OR*, ser. 1, vol. 51, part 2, 526 (Heth).

55. Thomas Overton Moore to Secretary of War George Randolph, June 13, 1862 (quote), Moore to President Davis, June 12, 1862, Randolph to Moore, July 3, 1862, all in Records of the Louisiana State Government in the War Department Collection of Confederate Records, 1850–1888, National Archives (microfilm M359, reel 4).

56. Jordan S. Council to Mary A. Council, April 27, 1862, in Watford, *Civil War in North Carolina*, 2:43; Charles C. Jones to Rev. and Mrs. C. C. Jones, July 14, 1862, in Myers, *The Children of Pride*, 931. For a greater discussion of the motivations of men who enlisted in the Confederate army in 1862, see Noe, *Reluctant Rebels*. For a discussion of the problems of trying to count conscripts, see chapter 7 in the present volume.

57. Troop figures from *OR*, ser. 4, vol. 1, 962–963, vol. 2, 278; casualty estimate from McPherson, *Battle Cry of Freedom*, 432; *Charleston Mercury*, August 29, 1862; Vance inaugural (typescript), Septem-

ber 8, 1862, in James O. Carr Papers, SHC. While the 449,439 soldiers is the most commonly cited figure, a separate report indicates 473,004 men. *OR*, ser. 4, vol. 2, 380.

58. Diary entry, July 28, 1862, Thomas Bragg Diary, SHC; Randolph Report, August 12, 1862, in *OR*, ser. 4, vol. 2, 42–49.

## CHAPTER THREE

1. Peter Mallett to Samuel Cooper, September 16, 1862, Letterbook, Peter Mallett Papers, SHC; *OR* ser. 4, vol. 2, 53–56 (Davis address, 54); 42–49 (secretary of war's report).

2. For a succinct discussion of the eastern theater in 1862, see James M. McPherson, *Antietam: The Battle That Changed the Course of the Civil War* (New York: Oxford University Press, 2002).

3. *SHSP*, 46:89 ("extended debate"); *SHSP*, 45:206 (Barksdale), 208 (Singleton), 209 (Dargan).

4. Samuel Burney to Wife, September 6, 1862, in Turner, *Southern Soldier's Letters Home*, 203; James C. Bates to Mom, n.d. (August/September 1862), in Richard Lowe, ed., *A Texas Cavalry Officer's Civil War: The Diary of James C. Bates* (Baton Rouge: Louisiana State University Press, 1999), 163.

5. Richmond *Daily Dispatch*, August 29, September 26, 1862; *Charleston Mercury*, August 29, 1862.

6. Rable, *Confederate Republic*, 155; "Speech of W. S. Oldham of Texas, Upon the Bill to Amend the Conscript Law, Made in the Senate, September 4, 1862."

7. Alexander and Beringer, *Anatomy of the Confederate Congress*, 109; Jewett, *Rise and Fall of the Confederacy*, 109.

8. Foote in *SHSP*, 45:182, 203–204; Ben Wynne, *The Man Who Punched Jefferson Davis: The Political Life of Henry S. Foote, Southern Unionist* (Baton Rouge: Louisiana State University Press, 2018), 223–230, at 223.

9. *SHSP*, 46:74–75 (Semmes); 45:213–214 (Herbert). For more on the Texas frontier conflict, see David P. Smith, "Conscription and Conflict on the Texas Frontier, 1863–1865," *Civil War History* (September 1990), 250–261.

10. *Speeches of William L. Yancey, Esq., Senator from the State of Alabama* (Montgomery, Ala., 1862), 19, 23, 30; *SHSP*, 46:90. See also Eric H. Walther, *William Lowndes Yancey and the Coming of the Civil War* (Chapel Hill: University of North Carolina Press, 2006), 339, 348–352.

11. Diary entries, August 23 (first quote), August 25, September 25 (second quote), 1862, in Thomas Bragg Papers, SHC; diary entries, August 19 and 22, 1862, in Estill, ed,. "Diary of a Confederate Congressman, 1862–3," 208.

12. Milledgeville *Southern Recorder*, July 1, 1862; *SHSP*, 46:108–109 (Barksdale); *SHSP*, 45:208 (Miles); *SHSP*, 46:69–70 (Gentry).

13. General John Forney to John Milton, September 8, 1862, Milton to Secretary of War Seddon, December 6, 1862, in M. Edward Hughes, ed., *Civil War Correspondence of Florida's Governor John Milton* (Victoria, B.C.: FriesenPress, 2015), 314, 418.

14. *OR*, ser. 4, vol. 2, 45 (secretary of war); *SHSP*, 45:222, 252 (Wigfall).

15. *SHSP*, 45:250–252. Even though Missouri did not secede from the Union, it had representatives in the Confederate Congress.

16. *SHSP*, 45:271–274, at 271, 272; *SHSP*, 46:6.

17. *SHSP*, 45:201 (Military Committee), 272 (Barnwell).

18. Robert E. Lee to Jefferson Davis, September 23, 1862, Robert E. Lee to Gustavus W. Smith, September 24, 1862, *OR*, ser. 1, vol. 19, 622–625.

19. *OR*, ser. 4, vol. 2, 53–56, 132; John A. Williams to Dear Sister, September 9, October 8, 1862, John A. Williams Letters, VHS; William R. Stilwell to Dear Molly, August 22, 1862, in Ronald H. Moseley, ed., *The Stilwell Letters: A Georgian in Longstreet's Corps, Army of Northern Virginia* (Macon, Ga.: Mercer University Press, 2002), 33; *Charleston Mercury*, July 20 (quote), September 10, 1862; diary entry dated September 29, 1862, in Joiner, *No Pardons to Ask*, 53. The secretary of war maintained there were 145,000 men between thirty-five and forty and 101,500 between forty and forty-five in the Confederacy. He estimated that three-sevenths of these men would receive exemptions.

20. Tolivar Davis to Governor Vance, September 11, 1862, in Watford, *Civil War in North Carolina*, 2:58; John Pool to Governor Vance, September 18, 1862, in Johnston, *Papers of Zebulon B. Vance*, 198–201; Governor Brown to Jefferson Davis, October 18, 1862, in Allen D. Candler, *Confederate Records of Georgia* (Atlanta: C. P. Byrd, 1910), 3:294–302, at 296.

21. *SHSP*, 47:805, 809, 810; diary entry, October 11, 1862, in Beth Crabtree, ed., *Journal of a Secesh Lady: The Diary of Catherine Ann Devereux Edmondston* (Raleigh: North Carolina Division of Archives, 1979), 272; Chandra Manning, *What This Cruel War Was Over: Soldiers, Slavery, and the Civil War* (New York: Knopf, 2007), 106–110, at 106. For reactions to the Emancipation Proclamation, see James L. Roark, *Masters Without Slaves: Southern Planters in the Civil War and Reconstruction* (New York: Norton, 1977), 75.

22. *SHSP*, 44:182, 190.

23. *Daily Constitutionalist*, September 10, 1862 (army of consumers); *Military Laws of the Confederate States*, 84–87; "Bureau of Exemption" in diary entry, February 16, 1863, in John B. Jones, *Rebel War Clerk's Diary at the Confederate States Capital* (Philadelphia: J. B. Lippincott & Co., 1866), 1:260.

24. *Military Laws of the Confederate States*, 84–87.

25. Mary Wilkinson to Micajah Wilkinson, October 29, 1862, Micajah Wilkinson Papers, LLMVC; *Military Laws of the Confederate States*, 70–71 (expansion of the age range, September 27, 1862), 78 (allows enrollment outside of state of residence, October 8, 1862).

26. *Richmond Enquirer*, November 7, 1862 (East Tennessee); *OR*, ser. 4, vol. 1, 1152–1153 (lists of camps), vol. 2, 286 (January 1863 report), ser. 1, vol. 15, 872 (suspension); Louis Bush to senators Sparrow and Semmes, August 30, 1862, in Letters Received by the Secretary of War; Lucius J. Dupre to Jefferson Davis, *PoJD*, 8:440–441.

27. *Opelousas Courier*, October 25, 1862; Petition from the Citizens of Stanly's Precinct, Rapides Parish, December 1, 1862, Moore Papers, LLMVC; David Siler to Governor Vance, November 3, 1862, in Watford, *Civil War in North Carolina*, 2:70–71.

28. For a discussion of the misunderstandings surrounding the measure, see John M. Sacher, "Reconsidering the 'Twenty-Negro' Law as the Overseer Exemption," *Journal of the Civil War Era* (June 2017), 269–292. Much of the material from the next several pages comes from this article. For examples of condemnations of the act, see Roark, *Masters Without Slaves*, 47; Escott, *After Secession*, 121; Williams, *People's History of the Civil War*; Robinson, *Bitter Fruits of Bondage*, 188.

29. O. F. M. Holladay to Alexander Stephens, November 30, 1862, Stephens Collection, EU; Bell I. Wiley, *Plain People of the Confederacy* (Baton Rouge: Louisiana State University Press, 1943), 65 (Mississippi and North Carolina); Manning, *What This Cruel War Was Over*, 103 (Georgia soldier); J. W. Courtney to mother and sister, February 7, 1864, Joel A. Stokes Family Papers, LLMVC; Augusta

Evans, quoted in Sarah E. Gardner, *Blood and Irony: Southern White Women's Narratives of the Civil War, 1861–1937* (Chapel Hill: University of North Carolina Press, 2004), 23.

30. *Public Laws of the State of North Carolina Passed by the General Assembly, 1862–63* (Raleigh, N.C., W. W. Holden State Printer, 1863), 49–50; McCurry, *Confederate Reckoning*, 138–177, at 164; Rable, *Civil Wars*, 73–86; *OR*, ser. 1, vol. 17, part 2, 790.

31. Watkins, *Company Aytch*, 32; Marshall, *Lee's Aide de Camp*, 40, 42.

32. Bennett quote, October 1862, and Colin Woodward's own quote, in Woodward, *Marching Masters: Slavery, Race, and the Confederate Army in the Civil War* (Charlottesville: University of Virginia Press, 2014), 48.

33. J. A. Campbell to Herschel V. Johnson, December 17, 1862, *OR*, ser. 4, vol. 2, 244.

34. Peter Mallett to Dr. A. Patterson, November 1, 1862 (first quote), Mallett to R. P. Howell, November 27, 1862 (second quote), Mallett Papers, SHC; James M. Mathews, ed., *The Statutes at Large of the Confederate States of America, Passed at the Third Session of the First Congress* (Richmond, Va.: R. M. Smith, 1863), 158–159; Escott, *After Secession*, 120; Roark, *Masters Without Slaves*, 47.

35. Peter Mallett to Hon. B. Gaither, December 12, 1862, Mallett Papers, SHC; Endorsement of Jesse G. Shepherd to Zebulon B. Vance, April 3, 1863, in Joe A. Mobley, ed., *The Papers of Zebulon Baird Vance*, vol. 2, *1863* (Raleigh: North Carolina Division of Archives and History, 1995), 107; *OR* ser. 4, vol. 2, 287. Attorney General Thomas Watts offered an opinion that out of all exemptions, the overseer was the only one that could possibly be considered retroactive. He equivocated that he was "by no means certain that even this can be so considered." T. H. Watts to George Randolph, October 18, 1862, *Opinions of the Confederate Attorneys General*, 165. I have encountered no evidence that the army ever considered it retroactive. The secretary of war's declaration that it was not a discharge came three months after Watts offered his opinion.

36. Jonathan Worth to D. G. Worth, November 1, 1862, D. G. Worth to Jonathan Worth, January 24, 1863, in Hamilton, ed., *Correspondence of Jonathan Worth*, 1:191, 226–227. By the next year, David had been appointed North Carolina salt commissioner—a position which carried an exemption. Worth might have urged his son to be reputable, but he employed more questionable—though still legal—means to get his own overseer exempted. Lacking twenty slaves, Worth persuaded slaveholders from the eastern part of the state to send their slaves to him so he could meet the twenty-slave threshold and secure his overseer's exemption. See Richard L. Zuber, *Jonathan Worth: A Biography of a Southern Unionist* (Chapel Hill: University of North Carolina Press, 1965), 133–135.

37. Williams, *People's History of the Civil War*, 77 (quote); Moore, *Conscription and Conflict*, 108.

38. Record of Exemptions in Virginia, Record Group 109, chap. 1, vol. 251, National Archives, Washington, D.C.; Rockingham (Va.) Enrolling Books, 1862–1864, VHS; J. S. Preston Report, Confederate Imprint 1285, VHS. Preston's report includes Virginia, but since the previous sentences covered this, I removed that state from these calculations. Enrollment Statistics, March 1865, Louisiana State Archives; *OR*, ser. 1, vol. 15, 919–920 (quote).

39. Jefferson Davis to Zebulon B. Vance, November 1, 1862, in Johnston, *Papers of Zebulon B. Vance*, 296; Davis to Benjamin H. Hill, October 23, 1862, *PoJD*, 8:460 (prediction).

40. Clay Alexander to Joseph Brown, September 15, 1862, Governor's Subject Files, GA (Brown's response in postscript); Brown to Jefferson Davis, October 18, 1862, in Candler, *Confederate Records of Georgia*, 300.

41. Wigfall in *SHSP*, 46:45; J. Henly Smith to A. Stephens, June 21, 1862, Alexander Stephens

Papers, LC (digital); *Savannah Republican,* in T. Conn Bryan, *Confederate Georgia* (Athens: University of Georgia Press, 1953), 87.

42. Smith to Stephens, June 21, 1862, Stephens Papers, LC; "Georgia" letter in Augusta *Daily Constitutionalist,* September 17, 1862; Thomas E. Schott, *Alexander H. Stephens of Georgia: A Biography* (Baton Rouge: Louisiana State University Press, 1988), 361; diary entry, July 28, 1862, Bragg Papers, SHC.

43. Superior court decision in *Daily Constitutionalist,* September 28, 1862; *Jeffers v. Fair, 1862,* GA; Robert David Carlson, "Breach of Faith: Conscription in Confederate Georgia" (PhD diss., Emory University, 2009), 78–84; Jefferson Davis to William M. Browne, November 28, 1862, *OR,* ser. 4, vol. 2, 216; Jefferson Davis to Augustus H. Kenan, November 11, 1862, *PoJD,* 8:487.

44. *Ex Parte Hill* (1863) in *Opinions of the Judges of the Supreme Court of Alabama in 'Conscript Cases'* (Montgomery, 1863); *Davis Simmons v. J. H. Miller* (1864). For a discussion of the state supreme courts and conscription, see Donald J. Stelluto, "'A Light Which Reveals Its True Meaning': State Supreme Courts and the Confederate Constitution" (PhD diss., University of Maryland, 2004), esp. 118–166; for Alabama, see John P. Norman, "'Self-Preservation Is the Supreme Law': State Rights vs. Military Necessity in Alabama Civil War Conscription Cases," *Alabama Law Review* 60, no. 3 (January 2009): 727–749.

45. *Ex Parte Coupland* (1862); William P. Ballinger, diary, January 17, 1863, quoted in Robbins, "Confederate Nationalism," 125.

46. Atlanta *Southern Confederacy,* November 19, 1862 (Brown quote), November 26, 1862 (Stephens quote); Linton Stephens to Alexander Stephens, December 29, 1862, Stephens Collection, EU.

47. *Daily Constitutionalist,* November 13, 1862; Joseph H. Parks, *Joseph E. Brown of Georgia* (Baton Rouge: Louisiana State University Press, 1977), 206; Henry C. Wayne to Capt. William A. Hadden, November 11, 1862 (quote), Wayne to Paudling Tatnall, September 19, 1862, B. B. deGraffenried to Lt. West Harris, November 28, 1862, Adjutant General's Letter Book, GA; James Walker to Henry C. Wayne, December 22, 1862, Civil War Miscellany, GA.

48. *Atlanta Southern Confederacy,* November 19, 1862; Joseph Brown to General Assembly, November 6 and 13, 1862, in Candler, *Confederate Records of Georgia,* 2:283–305, 317–321 (quotes at 285, 305, 321).

49. *Journal of the Senate of the State of Georgia, at the Annual Session of the General Assembly,* (Milledgeville, Ga., 1862), 119–121; Carlson, "Breach of Faith," 183–195. George Rable offers a similar conclusion, portraying Georgia's legislature as searching for an "elusive middle ground" between Brown and Davis. Rable, *Confederate Republic,* 161.

50. "Speech of Hon. George A. Gordon, of Chatham, on the Constitutionality of the Conscription Laws, Passed by the Congress of the Confederate States, Delivered in the Senate of Georgia, on Tuesday, 9th of December, 1862," Documenting the American South, https://docsouth.unc.edu/imls/gordong/gordon.html.

51. Moore, *Conscription and Conflict,* 354; Frank L. Owsley, *State Rights in the Confederacy* (Chicago: University of Chicago Press, 1925), 279, 75; Coulter, *Confederate States of America,* 327.

52. Curtis Arthur Amlund, *Federalism in the Southern Confederacy* (Washington, D.C.: Public Affairs Press, 1966), 94–114; Yearns, *Confederate Governors;* Beringer et al., *Why the South Lost the Civil War,* 234; Michael A. Powell, "Confederate Federalism: A View from the Governors" (PhD diss., University of Maryland, 2004), 117–172; David J. Eicher, *Dixie Betrayed: How the South Really Lost the Civil War* (New York: Brown, 2006), 134–140. While the authors of *Why the South Lost the Civil War* contend that states' rights did not negatively affect conscription, they do argue that conscription (especially later in the war) sapped Confederate morale (306–307).

53. Joseph Brown to Alexander Stephens, September 1, 1862, in U. B. Phillips, ed., *The Correspondence of Robert Toombs, Alexander H. Stephens, and Howell Cobb* (1913; New York: DaCapo Press, 1970), 605; John Gill Shorter, *An Appeal to the People of Alabama* (1862); Ben H. Severance, *A War State All Over: Alabama Politics and the Confederate Cause* (Tuscaloosa: University of Alabama Press, 2020), 75–78; Lubbock, in Francelle Pruitt, "'We've Got to Fight or Die': Early Texas Reaction to the Confederate Draft, 1862," *East Texas Historical Journal* (1998), 36:1, 14.

54. Davis to Vance, November 1, 1862, in Johnston, *Papers of Zebulon B. Vance,* 296; David D. Scarboro, "North Carolina and the Confederacy: The Weakness of States' Rights During the Civil War," *North Carolina Historical Review* 56 (April 1979), 133–149.

55. William Browne to Jefferson Davis, December 23, 1862, Jefferson Davis Papers, DU; "slippery gentleman" in Parks, *Joseph E. Brown,* 228; Browne to Howell Cobb, January 21, 1863, Howell Cobb Papers, University of Georgia (digital).

56. "Speech at Jackson," in Crist, *PoJD,* 8:568–560, at 568.

57. "Speech at Jackson," in Crist, *PoJD,* vol. 8:569. In his study of the president's rhetoric, R. Jarrod Atchison contends that Davis, in his Mississippi speech, employed civic republican tradition in highlighting the virtuous intent of the overseer exemption. For Davis, this intent trumped any unintended consequences. Atchinson, *A War of Words: The Rhetorical Leadership of Jefferson Davis* (Tuscaloosa: University of Alabama Press, 2017), 57.

58. Yancey speech, *Southern Recorder,* February 3, 1863; John Witherspoon DuBose, *The Life and Times of William Lowndes Yancey* (New York: Peter Smith, 1942), 2:674; *Daily Constitutionalist,* January 23, 1863.

59. Seddon Report, January 3, 1863, *OR,* ser. 4, vol. 2, 279–294, at 287. Seddon's report is almost entirely devoid of numerical assessments. While maintaining that the army is larger than ever before, he acknowledges it still is not sufficient. He then states, "It is not deemed requisite to state its precise aggregate" (280). Either he did not know the number or he wanted to keep the figures from the public.

60. Joseph Brown to Alexander Stephens, September 1, 1862, in Phillips, *Correspondence,* 605.

## CHAPTER FOUR

1. Leonidas L. Polk to wife, April 19, 1863, in Reid Mitchell, *Civil War Soldiers* (New York: Penguin, 1997), 157; John David Workman to Mary Workman, October 15, 1863 (first quote), September 17, 1863 (second quote) Wright-Boyd Family Papers, LLMVC; Charles C. Jones Jr. to Rev. and Mrs. C. C. Jones, July 14, 1862, in Myers, *Children of Pride,* 930. The officers were called both enrolling officers and conscript officers. I will use the terms interchangeably.

2. J. M. Little to Col. Mallett, January 1864, Confederate States of America, Bureau of Conscription, Seventh North Carolina Congressional District, SHC (hereafter, N.C. Conscript Bureau); Peter Mallett to Major Duffield, May 31, 1864, Mallett Papers, SHC.

3. John S. Preston to James Seddon, March 18, 1864, *OR,* ser. 4, vol. 3, 222–225, at 225. North Carolina was one of the few states where conscription began in a timely manner and continued throughout the war, so it possessed more conscription records than any other Confederate state. While this chapter describes a cumbersome process in North Carolina, my assumption is that other states had even less efficient systems. The flawed North Carolina bureau—with less Union invasion and a consistent leadership—might have represented the best system in the Confederacy. Official conscription records (though incomplete) credit North Carolina with more conscripts than any other state.

4. Several important books look at resistance to the Confederacy. While resisters undoubtedly opposed conscription and/or deserted from the Confederate army, their fights generally stemmed from much larger factors—such as Unionism or neighborhood feuds—that predated conscription. Because their stories are already eloquently told, I have chosen not to highlight them here. Works on these areas include Victoria Bynum, *The Free State of Jones: Mississippi's Longest Civil War* (Chapel Hill: University of North Carolina Press, 2001); Richard B. McCaslin, *Tainted Breeze: The Great Hanging at Gainesville, Texas, 1862* (Baton Rouge: Louisiana State University Press, 1994); Barton Myers, *Rebels Against the Confederacy: North Carolina Unionists* (Cambridge, Mass.: Harvard University Press, 2014), esp. 54–78; Daniel E. Sutherland, ed., *Guerrillas, Unionists, and Violence on the Confederate Home Front* (Fayetteville: University of Arkansas Press, 1999). As Myers notes, much of the time it is impossible to distinguish Unionists, deserters, and recusant conscripts.

5. For examples of this behavior, see Gustave A. Breaux, diary entries of February 21 and July 10, 1864, MS 489, TU; John David Workman to Mary Workman, October 15, 1863, Wright-Boyd Family Papers, LLMVC; B. Jenkins to Prudhomme, October 5, 1864, Prudhomme Papers, Louisiana State Archives (quote); Hyatt, diary, August 30, 1863 (bribery), and Hugh Montgomery to A. W. Hyatt, October 14, 1864, Arthur W. Hyatt Papers, LLMVC.

6. "Circular Instructions for Enrolling Officers," Bureau of Conscription, May 14, 1863, 8; George and John Lucas Petition, undated, N.C. Conscript Bureau, SHC.

7. John King Petition, March 8, 1864, N.C. Conscript Bureau, SHC; H. Bicknalls to S. A. Sharpe, October 6, 1863, John McKee Sharpe Papers, SHC; Elisa Fortner Petition, January 20, 1864, John Logan Papers, SHC.

8. Horace Sinbury Petition, John Wood Petition, October 19, 1863, John Hancock Petition, October 17, 1863, N.C. Conscript Bureau, SHC; Poindexter report, June 25, 1864, John A. Coke Papers, New York Historical Society.

9. Gary B. Mills, "Alexandria, Louisiana: A 'Confederate' City at War with Itself," 179 (first quote); Mills, "Alien Neutrality and the Red River Campaign," in Arthur Bergeron, ed., *The Civil War in Louisiana: Part B, The Home Front* (Lafayette, La: Center for Louisiana Studies, 2002), 166–167; W. C. Corsan, *Two Months in the Confederate States: An Englishman's Travels Through the South* (1863; repr., Baton Rouge: Louisiana State University Press, 1998), 41; Mobile consul quoted in David T. Gleeson, *The Green and the Gray: The Irish in the Confederate States of America* (Chapel Hill: University of North Carolina Press, 2013), 62.

10. Jeremiah Dansby Petition, March 19, 1864, David Hentshel Petition, March 23, 1864, Coke Papers, New York Historical Society; Special Orders and Circulars Relating to Conscription, October 15, 1863, Trans-Mississippi Department General Orders (quote), LSA; John David Workman to Mary, September 17, 1863, Wright-Boyd Family Papers, LLMVC; A. G. Magrath, *Liability of Alien Residents to Conscription: Opinion of Judge Magrath in the Confederate Court, South Carolina District* (n.d.), 19.

11. Charles Hardee to A. Fullarton, January 22, 1863, Great Britain Consulate Records, DU; Peter Mallett to Vice Consul Pinckney Walker, October 4, 1862, in Letterbook, Mallett Papers, SHC; Langley Petition, May 22, 1864, Letterbook, N.C. Conscript Bureau, SHC.

12. Peter Mallett to John Harrison, September 2, 1862, G. W. Lay (comment) on Henry Gross Petition, January 26, 1863 (handle with caution); Mallett to Walker, October 4, 1862, in Letterbook, Mallett Papers, SHC.

13. George Symms to Molyneaux, October 13, 1862, J. J. Kelly to Fullarton, November 11, 1862, J. A. Knott to Fullarton, January 25, 1863, in Great Britain Consulate Records, DU.

14. John Weems to Hon. A. Fullarton, October 30, 1862, George W. Randolph to Fullarton (telegraph, n.d.), Weems to Fullarton, November 7, 1862, and Randolph to Fullarton, November 11, 1862, all in Great Britain Consulate Papers, EU.

15. *Correspondence of the Department of State in Relation to the British Consuls Resident in the Confederate States* (Richmond, 1863), especially Judah P. Benjamin to James Mason, June 6, 1863 (quote), Jefferson Davis Revoking Exequatur of Consul Moore, June 5, 1863, Benjamin to John Slidell, October 8, 1863, and Benjamin to Fullarton, October 8, 1863; Ella Lonn, *Foreigners in the Confederacy* (Chapel Hill: University of North Carolina Press, 1940), 386–416; Eugene Berwanger, *The British Foreign Service and the American Civil War* (Lexington: University Press of Kentucky, 1994), 92–124. Viewing the measure from the consuls' perspective, Berwanger, in his insightful work, emphasizes Confederate officials overstepping their bounds. In contrast, looking at the measure from the perspective of enrolling officers, I stress consuls abetting prospective conscripts' duplicity.

16. Mallett to Capt. Duffield, June 27, 1864, Mallet Papers, SHC; *OR*, ser. 4, vol. 3, 507.

17. Charles C. Jones Jr. to Rev. and Mrs. C. C. Jones, July 15, 1862, in Myers, *Children of Pride*, 932; April 1, 1864 petition (newspaper), July 1864 petitions (poorhouse), Coke Papers, New York Historical Society; W. G. Meachem to Pearson, July 4, 1864 (hiding out and nitre), N.C. Conscript Bureau, SHC; John Gorder for C. M. Gordon, January 10, 1863, Bureau of Conscription, Conscript Journal, LV.

18. John Curry substitute paperwork, May 12, 1862, John Coke to Colonel Shields, February 5, 1863, Binford notation on bottom of this request, Coke Papers, New York Historical Society.

19. Capt. Haughton to Pearson, July 23, 1864, Spaugh Petition, February 20, 1864, Letterbook, N.C. Conscript Bureau, SHC; William Harnie (Commissary Agent) to Mrs. Elliott, July 26, 1864, Elliott and Gonzales Family Papers, SHC; Alex Bourman to James Coke, April 28, 1863, Coke Papers, New York Historical Society.

20. Raleigh *Semi-Weekly Standard*, January 2, 1863; Frank Johnson, February 2 and March 14, 1864, DeButts Family Papers, VHS.

21. "A Lover of Public Justice" to John Coke, March 14, 1864, Coke Papers, New York Historical Society; Peter Mallett to Haynes Lenoir, July 24, 1862, Mallett to Sec. of War George W. Randolph, September 24, 1862, in Letterbook, Mallett Papers, SHC.

22. Lt. Josiah Jones to Capt. J. M. Little, June 9, 1864, Mallett Papers, SHC.

23. B. C. Burgess Petition, June 13, 1864, Cicreo Holmes Petition, March 1864, Letterbook, N.C. Conscript Bureau, SHC.

24. Henry and Jefferson Keneth Petition, March 27, 1863, Nathan York Petition, June 14, 1864, S. W. Swain Petition, July 1, 1864, Hinshaw Petition, December 12, 1864 (superior's response on back, dated December 30, 1864), N.C. Conscript Bureau, SHC.

25. Delphina Mendenhall to John B. Crenshaw, January 10, 1863, Elihu Mendenhall to Crenshaw, April 10, 1863, Thomas W. Johnson to Crenshaw, April 23, 1863, Crenshaw Papers, Guilford College.

26. John C. Smith, Petition, February 4, 1863, John Welborn to Maj. McClaine, October 28, 1864, N.C. Conscript Bureau, SHC; William Elliott Jr. to Emmie Elliott, April 28, 1864, Elliott to Dear Mother, April 1, Elliott and Gonzales Family Papers, SHC.

27. D. C. Pearson to Col. Mallett, March 21, 1864, Pearson Report, March 3, 1864, Josiah James (for

Mallett) to Pearson, March 29, 1864, Sgt. Brown Investigation, June 3, 1864, Pearson to Little, June 5, 1864, Mallett Papers, SHC (all but the March 21, 1864, letter in Letterbook).

28. Cooper Report, *OR,* ser. 4, vol. 3, 859–863.

29. Smith Petition, March 8, 1864, Ambrose Beck Petition, undated, James Holt Petition, undated, Col. Bradshaw for Tobias Beaver, March 26, 1864, John Carnes Petition, May 7, 1864, Jared Harny Petition, July 1, 1864, N.C. Conscript Bureau, SHC.

30. Unnamed Petition, June 8, 1864, Susannah McDaniel for George McDaniel, June 16, 1864, John Cassady, June 14, 1864, N.C. Conscript Bureau, SHC.

31. A. H. Merriot et al, for Dawson April 11, 1863, Benjamin Harris for Elias H. Brooks, E. J. Bell Petition, May 13, 1864, B. F. Lambeth Petition, May 13, 1864, Augustus Alston Petition, May 18, 1864, Letterbook, N.C. Conscript Bureau, July 21, SHC. Dawson's exemption was refused, but it is unclear whether Brooks's was accepted or denied. For more on overseer exemptions, see chapter 3 in the present volume.

32. Thomas Clark Petition, June 3, 1863, William Long Petition, July 15, 1864, William N. Moore Petition, April 23, 1863, N.C. Conscript Bureau, SHC.

33. Jonathan Cox Petition, May 15, 1863, Henry London to James Seddon, July 20, 1863, Richard Smith on behalf of James Smith, July 10, 1863, N.C. Conscript Bureau, SHC.

34. Jesse Richardson Petition, March 10, 1864, N.C. Conscript Bureau, SHC; Campbell endorsement on William K. Cooper Petition, March 9, 1863, Bureau of Conscription, Conscript Journal, LV.

35. Unnamed Petition, June 8, 1864, Susannah McDaniel for George McDaniel, June 16, 1864, Duncan Niven Petition, December 12, 1863, Reucher to Capt. Little, January 21, 1864, William Bell Petition, June 13, 1864, Willis Dameron Petition (addressed to "His Excellency President Davis"), November 4, 1862, N.C. Conscript Bureau, SHC.

36. Isaac Pragg, March 12, 1864, Abner Lasitens Petition, May 13, 1864, N.C. Conscript Bureau, SHC; Woods Petition, February 18, 1863 (Seddon on back), Bureau of Conscription, Conscript Journal, LV.

37. W. S. McIntosh to John Logan, October 30, 1863, John Logan Papers, SHC; John Graffenedt Petition, May 26, 1863, Capt. Albright to Peter Mallett, May 9, 1863, N.C. Conscript Bureau, SHC.

38. F. Darby to Col. Little, November 28, 1863, Harner and Stuts Petition, July 17, 1863, James M. Covington Petition, July 1864, Alvis Snipes Petition, March 10, 1864, William Hill Petition, May 21, 1864, N.C. Conscript Bureau, SHC. A note on the back of Covington's petition indicates that a superior officer overturned this initial rejection, not because he considered Covington loyal but because there were "many poor and many families of soldiers . . . dependent upon [him] for the necessaries of life."

39. George W. Randolph to Jefferson Davis, August 12, 1862, *OR,* ser. 4, vol. 2, 44; Zebulon Vance to Peter Mallett, May 18, 1863, Unknown to Capt. Little, January 12, 1864, General Order 7 (election day), July 29, 1864, N.C. Conscript Bureau, SHC. On state judges and conscription, see chapters 5 and 6 of the present volume.

40. *OR,* ser. 4, vol. 3, 1102 (number of state officials).

41. Capt. Little to Col. Mallett, February 5, 1864, Charles Barney (CSA Nitre Bureau) to Capt. Wood, August 31, 1864, General Order 32, N.C. Conscript Bureau, SHC; Josiah Gorgas to James Seddon, October 13, 1864, *OR,* ser. 4, vol. 3, 733–734, at 734.

42. Capt. Pearson report, undated (May or June 1864), Letterbook, N.C. Conscript Bureau, SHC; S. M. Parish to Thomas Webb, Pres. of NC RR Co. Shops, June 17, 1864, Mallett Papers, SHC.

43. Capt. Little to Mallett, January 14, 1864, N.C. Conscript Bureau, SHC; C. C. Davenport to George Logan, December 1, 1863, John Logan Papers, SHC; Zebulon Vance to James Seddon, April 22, 1863, in Mobley, *Papers of Zebulon Baird Vance*, 127 (on fears that General D. H. Hill was enlisting men outside conscription, without any regard for the exemption process). In 1863, the army tried to take over conscription. For discussion of that conflict, see chapter 5 of the present volume.

44. Virginia governor in *OR*, ser. 4, vol. 2, 1021–1022; H. C. Walter to J. W. C. Watson, December 29, 1864, *OR*, ser. 4, vol. 3, 976; George Logan to Major E. Surget, April 15, 1863, John Logan Papers, SHC.

45. For examples of Mallett informing men that they needed to come to camp as soon as their health permitted, see Mallett to O. H. Blocker, September 12, 1862, in Letterbook, Mallett Papers, SHC; G. W. Lay, *Circular to Commandants of Conscription*, June 23, 1863.

46. Walter T. Davenport to Governor Brown, April 24, 1862, Governor's Subject Files, GA; J. A. Little to Peter Mallett, January 5 and 8, 1864, N.C. Conscript Bureau, SHC.

47. Harvey Black to My Dear Wife, April 23, 1862, McMullen, *Civil War Letters of Dr. Harvey Black*; Eli Sinberry, July 7, 1864, Willis Crawford Petition, undated [May 1864], Zebulon Pearce Petition, April 14, 1863, John Cassady Petition, June 14, 1864, Reilly Johnson Petition, June 18, 1864, Letterbook, N.C. Conscript Bureau, SHC; Frederick Nims to Medical Board for Examining Conscripts, March 11, 1864, Nims, Rankin, and Spratt Family Papers, SHC; Malinda Taylor to Grant Taylor, May 8, 1862, Blomquist and Taylor, *This Cruel War*, 14–15 (shooting off fingers).

48. Andrew R. Barber to Mary Anna Sibert, August 30, 1864, Evans-Sibert Family Papers, "Valley of the Shadow," https://valley.lib.virginia.edu/papers/A7509; Gustave A. Breaux, diary, February 21, July 10 (quote), 1864, MS 489, TU; Nellie Sheffey to John Sheffey, February 11, 1863, in James I. Robertson, ed., *Soldier of Southwestern Virginia: The Civil War Letters of Captain John Preston Sheffey* (Baton Rouge: Louisiana State University Press, 2004), 142; Lt. Charles C. Jones Jr. to Rev. and Mrs. C. C. Jones, in Myers, *Children of Pride*, 930.

49. J. Julian Chisolm, *A Manual of Military Surgery for the Use of Surgeons in the Confederate States Army*, 3rd ed. (Columbia, S.C.: Evans and Cogwell, 1864), 15, 441–448, at 441, 448.

50. Diary entry, August 22, 1862, in Joiner, *No Pardons to Ask*, 45; Kate Cumming, *A Journal of Hospital Life in the Confederate Army of Tennessee from the Battle of Shiloh to the End of the War* (Louisville, Ky., J. P. Morgan, 1866), 167.

51. "Record of Conscripts Examined by Surgeons Composing the Examining Board in the 7th Congressional District of North Carolina for the month of August 1864," N.C. Conscript Bureau, SHC.

52. Peter Mallett to Colonel Cowles, August 27, 1862, Mallett to Col. Martin, September 19, 1862, in Letterbook, Mallett Papers, SHC.

53. Peter Mallett to Thomas Robards, November 1 and 3, 1862, Letterbook, Peter Mallett Papers, SHC.

54. Capt. Haughton to Pearson, June 29 and July 9, 1864, N.C. Conscript Bureau, SHC.

55. Capt. Haughton to Pearson, July 4, 1864, N.C. Conscript Bureau, SHC; Wilse Dial Letter, July 29, 1863, SHC; George Lay to John Preston, September 2, 1863, *OR*, ser. 4, vol. 2, 783–785, at 784. For an excellent discussion of opposition to conscription in North Carolina, see William T. Auman, *Civil War in the North Carolina Quaker Belt: The Confederate Campaign Against Peace Agitators, Deserters, and Draft Dodgers* (Jefferson, N.C.: McFarland, 2014), esp. chapter 3. For a discussion of a violent incident on the western edge of North Carolina in January 1863, see Phillip Shaw Paludan, *Victims: A True Story of the Civil War* (Knoxville: University of Tennessee Press, 1981).

56. Capt. Haughton to Pearson, July 11 and July 14, 1864, N.C. Conscript Bureau, SHC.

57. John C. Whitner to Howell Cobb, August 12, 1862, in Phillips, *Correspondence*, 603; John Smith, quoted in Margaret Storey, *Loyalty and Loss: Alabama's Unionists in the Civil War and Reconstruction* (Baton Rouge: Louisiana State University Press, 2004), 69; diary entry, November 20, 1863, in Joiner, *No Pardons to Ask*, 121; H. C. Walter to J. W. C. Watson, December 29, 1864.

58. *OR*, ser. 4, vol. 3, 354; July 1864 Reports for Randolph, Davidson, Chatham, Stanly, Moore, and Anson Counties, N.C. Conscription Bureau, SHC.

59. *OR*, ser. 4, vol. 3, 976; Johnson to Raines, January 9, 1863, Letterbook, Mallett Papers, SHC; Hilderman, *They Went into the Fight Cheering*, 63–83. Captain Johnson served under Colonel Thomas August, but when Johnson wrote this letter, August had yet to arrive at the camp. Mallett would return to duty in March 1863.

60. James Phelan to Jefferson Davis, December 9, 1862, *OR*, ser. 1, vol. 17, 790, and ser. 4, vol. 3, 356–357. On those unfit for field duty, see March 13, 1863, A. J. Beal Detail, February 5, 1864, J. A. Thompson, April 6, 1864, Stanley County, Men Engaged in Enrolling Service, August 1864, N.C. Conscript Bureau, SHC; Mallett to Duffield, June 21, 1864, Mallett Papers, SHC.

61. Peter Mallett to Dr. Richard Anderson, October 22, 1862, Mallett to Samuel Cooper, October 31, 1862, in Letterbook, Mallett Papers, SHC.

62. Zebulon Vance to James Seddon, May 18, 1863, in Mobley, *Papers of Zebulon Baird Vance*, 157–158 (accusation of extortion); Circular 5, February 3, 1864, Circular 3, April 5, 1864, N.C. Conscript Bureau, SHC; William Elliott Jr. to Dear Mother, March 5, 1864, Elliott and Gonzales Family Papers, SHC. For Georgia, see David Carlson, "The 'Loanly Runagee': Draft Evaders in Confederate South Georgia," *Georgia Historical Quarterly* 84, no. 4 (Winter 2000), 607–608.

63. J. A. Shinfer to Capt. Pearson, June 13, 1864, Miles Hobson Petition, April 1864, Letterbook (rebuke of Pearson on back), N.C. Conscript Bureau, SHC; Lt. Josiah Jones to Pearson, July 2, 1864, Mallett Papers, SHC.

64. Trans-Mississippi Department General Orders, Special Orders and Circulars relating to Conscription, October 15, 1863, LSA.

65. Bureau of Conscription, "Circular No. 6," April 1, 1864, Documenting the American South, https://docsouth.unc.edu/imls/circular6/circular.html.

66. Lt. Jones to Capt. J. M. Little, June 9, 1864, Mallett Papers, SHC; *Salem Press*, quoted in *Raleigh Register*, July 26, 1862, in Memory F. Mitchell, *Legal Aspects of Conscription and Exemption in North Carolina 1861–1865* (Chapel Hill: University of North Carolina Press, 1965); General Order No. 1, January 3, 1862[3], Adjutant and Inspector General's Office, in *Circular Instructions for Enrolling Officers*, 2–3.

## CHAPTER FIVE

1. Jefferson Davis to Senate and House of Representatives, January 12, 1863, in Richardson, *Messages and Papers*, 294–295.

2. *SHSP*, 49:80.

3. *The Statutes at Large of the Confederate States of America Passed at the Third Session of the First Congress* (Richmond, Va.: R. M. Smith, 1863), 158–159. The only other change involved a clarification of which state officials were exempt. The secretary of war had suggested exempting one man in areas with eight to ten "helpless whites," but Congress did not act on this proposal. *OR*, ser. 4, vol. 2, 288.

4. General Order 112, December 30, 1862, Special Order 1, January 2, 1863, *OR*, ser. 4, vol. 2, 266, 279; diary entries, January 7 and 8, 1863, Jones, *Rebel War Clerk's Diary*, 1:233–234.

5. Gallagher, *Confederate War; OR*, ser. 4, vol. 2, 530.

6. John S. Lewis to Mrs. Nancy Lewis, January 12, 1863, in Robert Evans, ed., *The 16th Mississippi Infantry: Civil War Letters and Reminiscences* (Jackson: University Press of Mississippi, 2002), 135; John D. Hyman to Zebulon Vance, April 30, 1863, James O. Carr Papers, SHC; *Macon Daily Telegraph*, December 31, 1863; J. F. Morton to Governor Brown, December 24, 1863, in Lane, *Times That Prove People's Principles*, 135.

7. George A. Mercer, diary, November 4, 1862, in Lane, *Times That Prove People's Principles*, 69; *Military Laws of the Confederate States*, 84–87; Wiley, *Johnny Reb*, 136. Soldiers' pay remained at the 1861 level until June 1864, when it increased to $18 per month.

8. Atlanta *Southern Confederacy*, October 30, 1862; *Montgomery Weekly Advertiser*, August 5, 1863; *Southern Literary Messenger*, August 1862.

9. Robert Hudson to Jefferson Davis, October 5, 1863, *OR*, ser. 4, vol. 2, 857; George Richards to Zebulon Vance, December 19, 1862, in Watford, *Civil War in North Carolina*, 1:88; John Ellis to Sister, December 12, 1862, Ellis Family Papers, LLMVC; Enrolling Officer Report, August 7, 1863, *OR*, ser. 4, vol. 2, 772.

10. John A. Harris to Becky Harris, February 14, 1863, John Achilles Harris Letters, LLMVC; congressman in *SHSP*, 49:82; diary entry, January 21, 1863, in Jones, *Rebel War Clerk's Diary*, 1:243.

11. John Thompson to Governor Vance, September 27, 1862, in Watford, *Civil War in North Carolina*, 1:73; Gideon Lincecum to R. B. Hannay, October 22, 1863, in Lincecum, Phillips, and Redshaw, *Gideon Lincecum's Sword;* General Order 8, April 26, 1863, *OR*, ser. 1, vol. 51, pt. 2, 694; Officers of the Army of Tennessee to Samuel Cooper, July 25, 1863, *OR*, ser. 4, vol. 2, 670; F. Manson to W. A. Burwell, July 26, 1863, Burwell Family Papers, SHC.

12. D. W. Hood to Dear Father, March 23, 1863, John C. Hood Papers, DU; G. W. Poindexter to Aunt, April 27, 1863, John F. Poindexter Collection, DU; George to Ma and Pa, January 4, 1863, anonymous Civil War letter, LLMVC; Edgard Richardson to Dear Dugan, December 21, 1863, Richardson Family Letters, GA; Hugh S. Gookin Letter, December 3, 1863, LV; George (unknown) to David F. Kagey, January 30, 1864, Henry Kagey Papers, DU.

13. George Guess to S. H. Cockrell, September 9, 1863, Monroe F. Cockrell Papers, SHC; Diary entry, November 20, 1863, in Joiner, *No Pardons to Ask*, 121; William Speer to Father, August 15, 1863, in Allen Paul Speer, ed., *Voices from Cemetery Hill, Civil War Diary, Reports and Letters of Colonel William Henry Asbury Speer (1861–1864)* (Johnson City, Tenn.: Overmountain Press, 1997), 113; Theophilus Holmes to Harriet Holmes, July 17, 1863, in M. Jane Johansson, ed., *Widows by the Thousand: The Civil War Letters of Theophilus and Harriet Perry, 1862–1864*, ed. M. Jane Johansson (Fayetteville: University of Arkansas Press, 2000), 150.

14. Theophilus Holmes to Harriet Holmes, July 12, 1863, in Johansson, *Widows by the Thousand*, 147–148; Gideon Lincecum to Maj. Green Wood, February 15, 1863, in Lincecum, Phillips, and Redshaw, *Gideon Lincecum's Sword*, 215; D. H. Hill to Governor Vance, April 26, 1863, James O. Carr Papers, SHC.

15. Edwin Fay to Wife, February 27 (patriots), April 23, and October 23 (cowards), 1863, in Wiley, *"This Infernal War,"* 350; Samuel Pickens, diary, February 7, 1864, in G. Ward Hubbs, ed., *Voices from Company D: Diaries by the Greensboro Guards, Fifth Alabama Infantry Regiment, Army of North-*

*ern Virginia* (Athens: University of Georgia Press, 2003), 216; August 28 and September 7, 1863, in William B. Stype, ed., *Writing & Fighting the Confederate War: The Letters of Peter Wellington Alexander* (Kearny, N.J.: Belle Grove Publishing, 2002), 186, 190.

16. Peter Wellington Alexander, August 28, 1863, in Stype, *Writing & Fighting the Confederate War,* 186; John S. Lewis to Nancy Lewis, July 21, 1863, in Evans, *16th Mississippi Infantry,* 183.

17. Jeremiah Gage to Mary Sanders, April 24, 1863, Mollie Wendel to Jeremiah Gage, May 8, 1863, Gage Family Collection, University of Mississippi Digital Archive; Mary P. Davis to Cousin Ben, August 9 (first quote) and July 28 (second quote), 1863, Mary P. Davis Papers, DU. Two months later, Jeremiah died of wounds received at Gettysburg. It is unclear if he took their advice or just never located a substitute.

18. For background on the Neblett family, see Erika L. Murr, ed., *A Rebel Wife in Texas: The Diary and Letters of Elizabeth Scott Neblett, 1852–1864* (Baton Rouge: Louisiana State University Press, 2001), 1–20.

19. Lizzie Neblett to Will Neblett, April 26, August 11, August 18, 1863, Will to Lizzie, August 25, 1863, in Murr, *Rebel Wife in Texas,* 94, 132, 142, 145.

20. Lizzie Neblett to Will Neblett, August 18, 1863, Will to Lizzie, August 25, 1863, in Murr, *Rebel Wife in Texas,* 141, 145–146.

21. William Neblett to Lizzie, August 3, 1863, Lizzie to William, August 11, 13, 18/19, and November 13, 1863, in Murr, *Rebel Wife in Texas,* 126, 130–131, 135–137, 142, 203. For restrictions on substitution, see *OR,* ser. 4, vol. 2, 611.

22. Diary, December 20, 1862, July 25, 1863, November 1, 1863, in Jones, *Rebel War Clerk's Diary,* 1:219, 387, 2:85; Samuel Davis, January 2, 1863, Joseph Vidal and Family Papers, LLMVC; diary, March 25, 1863, Favrot Family Papers, TU; Richards diary, July 18, 1863, in Wendy Hamand Venet, ed., *Sam Richards's Civil War Diary: A Chronicle of the Atlanta Home Front* (Athens: University of Georgia Press, 2009), 189; Sarah Lois Wadley, diary, November 16, 1863, Sarah Lois Wadley Papers, SHC.

23. Lizzie to William Neblett, November 13, December 13, 1863, January 21, 1864, in Murr, *Rebel Wife in Texas,* 203, 241–243, 311. Fortunately for Jim, he discovered his substitute was supposedly fifty-two years old. Lizzie to Will, January 9, 1864, 283.

24. D. H. Hill, General Order 8, April 24, 1863, *OR,* ser. 1, vol. 51, part 2, 694; John A. Harris to Becky Harris, January 20, 1863, John Achilles Harris Letters, LLMVC; Wadley diary, October 15, November 16, December 10, 1863, in Sarah Lois Wadley Papers, SHC.

25. *OR,* ser. 4, vol. 2, 171; Abram G. Jones to Ellick, January 10, 1863, Jones Family Papers, SHC; *Rockingham Register,* June 27, 1862 (soldier quote), January 2, 1863 (suicide).

26. *Richmond Daily Dispatch,* December 31, 1863; George Lay to James Seddon, June 9, 1863, *OR,* ser. 4, vol. 2, 582–583.

27. Order from May 28, 1863; Order from J. C. Shields, December 12, 1862, Jas. H. Binford to Capt. J. S. Byers, September 12, 1863, Shields and Binford to J. D. H. Ross, February 23, 1863, Shields to Byers, September 16, 1863; circular, October 13, 1863; Byers to County Enrolling Officers, October 24, 1863, all in Rockingham, Virginia, Enrolling Books, VHS; *OR,* ser. 4, vol. 2, 808, 820, 827, 1070–1072.

28. Robert Hudson to Jefferson Davis, October 5, 1863, *OR,* ser. 4, vol 2, 857; Sacher, "Loyal Draft Dodger?," 153–178; Records of the U.S. House of Representatives, Southern Claims Commission, 1871–1880, National Archives & Records Administration Microfilm P2257, Claims no. 2550.

29. Fields Fox Petition, April 16, 1864, J. B. Bynum, June 11, 1864, N.C. Conscript Bureau, SHC.

30. Davis Proclamation, *OR,* ser. 4, vol. 2, 635; diary, July 14, 1863, in Edward Younger, ed., *Inside the Confederate Government: The Diary of Robert Garlick Hill Kean* (1957; Baton Rouge, Louisiana State University Press, 1985), 81.

31. Jefferson Davis to Reuben Davis, July 20, 1863, *PoJD,* 9:290; 75,000 prediction in *The American Annual Cyclopaedia and Register of Important Events of the Year 1863* (New York: Appleton, 1870), 17; Harriet to Theophilus Holmes, September 15, 1862, in Johansson, *Widows by the Thousand,* 30. In April, the House defeated a bill to repeal the substitution laws, by a vote of 39 to 48; see *SHSP,* 49:83.

32. *Daily Constitutionalist,* February 8, 1863; D. Y. Milling to Brother, January 10, 1863, D. Y. Milling Correspondence, LLMVC.

33. Conscription Circulars, February 27, July 21, 1863, *OR,* ser. 4, vol. 2, 412, 654; diary, December 24, 1862, January 8, 1863, in Joiner, *No Pardons to Ask,* 73–74.

34. For discussions of Pearson and conscription, see M. Mitchell, *Legal Aspects of Conscription,* 38–60; Jennifer Van Zant, "Confederate Conscription and the North Carolina Supreme Court," *North Carolina Historical Review* 72 (1995): 54–75; J. G. de Roulhac Hamilton, "The North Carolina Courts and the Confederacy," *North Carolina Historical Review* 4 (1927), 366–403; Mark E. Neely Jr., *Southern Rights: Political Prisoners and the Myth of Confederate Constitutionalism* (Charlottesville: University of Virginia Press, 1999), 64.

35. H. C. Jones, ed., *Cases of Habeas Corpus, Decided by the Supreme Court of North Carolina at the June term, 1863* (Salisbury, N.C.: J. J. Bruner, 1863). Available at Documenting the American South, https://docsouth.unc.edu/imls/nccourt/nccourt.html.

36. *In re Huie,* in H. C. Jones and P. H. Winston, eds., *Cases Argued and Determined in the Supreme Court of North Carolina from June Term, 1863, to December Term, 1864, Inclusive* (Raleigh, N.C.: News Publishing Co., 1878), 166. Numerous applications for habeas corpus demonstrate Pearson's pro-individual, anticonscription view. See, for example, Angel v. Orrill, February 6, 1863, P. D. Jones, October 15, 1863, George Wilkins Application, October 8, October 17, 1863, John G. Foster Application, October 8, 1863, James Brown, October 19, 1863, all in Richmond Mumford Pearson Papers, SHC.

37. Campbell to Peter Mallett, May 11, 1863, James Seddon to Zebulon Vance, June 15, 1863, in Mobley, *Papers of Zebulon Baird Vance,* 156, 193; Campbell to Barksdale, July 21, 1863, *OR,* ser. 4, vol. 2, 656; David Carlson, "'The Distemper of the Times': Conscription, the Courts, and Planter Privilege in Civil War South Georgia," *Journal of Southwest Georgia History* 14 (1999), 1–24; *In re Meroney,* in *Cases of Habeas Corpus, Decided by the Supreme Court of North Carolina at the June term, 1863* (quote).

38. John W. Graham to William A. Graham, January 13, 1863[4], in Max R. Williams and J. G. de Roulhac Hamilton, eds., *Papers of William A. Graham* (Raleigh: North Carolina Office of Archives and History), 5:441–442; Sam Richards, March 4, 1863, in Venet, *Sam Richards's Civil War Diary,* 166.

39. *Cases of Habeas Corpus, Decided by the Supreme Court of North Carolina at the June term, 1863,* 59; R. F. Armfield to Gov. Vance, February 19, 1863, *OR,* ser. 1, vol. 18, 886–887; Daniel G. Fowle to Richmond Pearson, May 22, 1863, quoted in Mitchell, *Legal Aspects of Conscription,* 43. Without providing much evidence, Mitchell asserts, "The constant battle between the civil courts and the military authorities proved to be a major factor . . . to surrender" (91). On the disruption caused by Pearson, see May 3 and 20, 1863, in Kean, *Inside the Confederate Government,* 55, 64. On North Carolina soldiers' deserting because they believed that Pearson had declared conscription unconstitutional, see W. D. Pender to Maj. W. H. Taylor, April 23, 1863, *OR,* ser. 1, vol. 25, part 2, 746–747; Vance to Davis, May 13, 1863, quoted in Joe A. Mobley, *"War Governor of the South": North Carolina's Zeb Vance in the Confed-*

*eracy* (Gainesville: University Press of Florida, 2005), 47. Mark Neely asserts that the judge "made rather a show of avoiding any ruling on [conscription's constitutionality]." Neely, *Southern Rights,* 69.

40. For Pearson and Vance's disagreement, and the text of many of their letters, see Hamilton, "North Carolina Courts and the Confederacy," 378–388. For more on North Carolina conservatives, see Marc W. Kruman, *Parties and Politics in North Carolina, 1836–1865* (Baton Rouge: Louisiana State University Press, 1983), 241–270.

41. Zebulon Vance to Col. T. P. August, March 20, 1863, Vance to James Seddon, May 22, 1863, Vance to Jefferson Davis, March 31, 1863, Davis to Vance, July 14, 1863, Gabriel Rains to Vance, March 25, 1863, Vance to Rains, March 31, 1863, all in Mobley, *Papers of Zebulon Baird Vance,* 90–91, 97, 102, 214, 104.

42. Vance to Rains, March 31, 1863, Joseph Brown to Vance, April 11, 1863, John G. Shorter to Vance, April 7, 1863, Vance to Peter Mallet, April 20, 1863, S. F. Phillips to Vance, April 11, 1863, all in Mobley, *Papers of Zebulon Baird Vance,* 104, 114–115, 111, 121–125. Tennessee had a similar provision regarding invasions and insurrections. The Confederate attorney general said that conscription applied only to "service as is ordinarily required of the militia." T. H. Watts to President Davis, December 4, 1862, in Patrick, *Opinions of the Confederate Attorneys General,* 185–187.

43. Edmund Kirby Smith to Jefferson Davis, June 16, 1863, *PoJD,* 9:222; Richmond *Daily Dispatch,* February 17, 1863.

44. Circular, *OR,* ser. 4, vol. 2, 305.

45. *OR,* ser. 1, vol. 20, part 2, 498, and ser. 4, vol. 2, 362, 387–388; Thomas L. Connelly, *Autumn of Glory: The Army of Tennessee* (Baton Rouge: Louisiana State University Press, 2001), 109; Douglas C. Purcell, "Military Conscription in Alabama During the Civil War," *Alabama Review* 34, no. 2 (1981), 94–106.

46. Braxton Bragg to President Davis, February 23, 1863, *OR,* ser. 1, vol. 52, part 2, 426; Gideon Pillow to Capt. Falconer, March 19, 1863, Pillow to James A. Seddon, February 17, 1863, Pillow to Col. Brent, March 22, 1863, *OR,* ser. 4, vol. 2, 442–445, 403–404, 449–450.

47. Zebulon Vance to James A. Seddon, April 7, 1863, in Mobley, *Papers of Zebulon Baird Vance,* 108–109; S. F. Darwin, March 21, 1863, Virginia Conscript Journal, LV; Gideon Pillow to James A. Seddon, February 17, 1863, G. J. Rains to James A. Seddon, March 10, 1863, *OR,* ser. 4, vol. 2, 403, 430–440.

48. G. J. Rains to James A. Seddon, March 10, 1863; circular, March 30, 1863, Rains to Seddon, April 7, 1863, *OR,* ser. 4, vol. 2, 430–440, 463, 473–475.

49. James A. Seddon to Joseph E. Johnston, March 2, 1863, James Campbell to Braxton Bragg, April 13, 1863, Gideon Pillow to Benjamin Ewell, July 15, 1863, General Order 1, *OR,* ser. 4, vol. 2, 415–416, 482, 636–637, 675–676.

50. Gideon Pillow to James Seddon, August 23, 1863, Isham Harris to Seddon, August 8, 1863, Pillow to Seddon, August 26, 1863, Pillow to Gholson, August 26, 1863, Pillow to Cooper, August 28, 1863, *OR,* ser. 4, vol. 2, 741–743, 752, 758–759, 775; *Richmond Daily Dispatch,* September 21, 1863; James Phelan to Jefferson Davis, July 29, 1863 (quote), Jefferson Davis Collection, Clements Library; Phelan to Davis, September 5, 1863, Leonidas Polk to Davis, August 9, 1863, *PoJD,* 9:370–371 (quote), 335.

51. Gideon Pillow to Benjamin Ewell, July 15, 1863, John Preston to James Seddon, August 25, 1863, Joseph Brown to Seddon, August 10, 1863, *OR,* ser. 4, vol. 2, 680–681, 749–751, 753.

52. John Preston to William Porcher Miles, January 8, 1863, Preston to James Seddon, August 17, 1863, Walthall to Lay, August 6, 1863, Isham Harris to Seddon, August 8, 1863, Shorter to Seddon, August 13, 1863, *OR,* ser. 4, vol. 2, 307, 723–726, 726–727, 752, 754.

53. James Seddon to Joseph E. Johnston, August 25, 1863, Samuel Cooper to Gideon Pillow, October 7, 1863, Johnston to Cooper, October 10 and 11, 1863, Report of the Secretary of War, November 26, 1863, *OR,* ser. 4, vol. 2, 748, 859, 867–869, 996; John Preston to William Porcher Miles, n.d., *OR,* ser. 4, vol. 3, 883–886.

54. Report of the Secretary of War, November 26, 1863, Gideon Pillow to James Seddon, August 23, 1863, Pillow to Cooper, November 27, 1863, *OR,* ser. 4, vol. 2, 996, 741–743, 1019–1020; Special Order 298, *OR,* ser. 1, vol. 31, part 3, 836; Pillow to Brent, March 22, 1863, Confederate Military Records, National Archives ("moral obligation" and "fallacy" underlined). Also, without underlines, in *OR,* ser. 4, vol. 2, 449–450.

55. While the election occurred prior to the December congressional meeting, the victors in the election did not take their seats until later, in 1864. Nevertheless, the elections provide a chance to gauge the nation's attitude toward conscription in 1863.

56. Rable, *Confederate Republic,* 215; Robbins, "Confederate Nationalism," 206; Rob Andrew, "The Essential Nationalism of the People: Georgia's Confederate Congressional Election of 1863," in Lesley J. Gordon and John C. Inscoe, eds., *Inside the Confederate Nation: Essays in Honor of Emory M. Thomas* (Baton Rouge: Louisiana State University Press, 2007), 205.

57. Shreveport *Semi-Weekly News,* October 13, 1863; Robinson, *Bitter Fruits of Bondage,* 248.

58. Kruman, *Parties and Politics in North Carolina,* 249–255; *Daily Carolina Watchman,* August 31 (Lander), October 16 (Ramsay), 1863, quoted in Yearns, *North Carolina Civil War Documentary,* 316.

59. James T. Leach Election Circular, September 17, 1863, James Thomas Leach Papers, SHC; "To the Voters of the 5th Congressional District," September 1, 1863, A. H. Arrington Papers, SHC.

60. Andrew, "Essential Nationalism of the People," 128–143, at 130, 137, 132; Munnerlyn letter in Milledgeville *Southern Recorder,* August 4, 1863. In a study of Georgia's first district, William Alexander Percy finds that "conscription did not emerge as an issue," but a more accurate assessment might be that it did not emerge as a *divisive* issue. William Alexander Percy, "Localizing the Context of Confederate Politics: The Congressional Election of 1863 in Georgia's First District," *Georgia Historical Quarterly* (Spring 1995): 192–209, at 200.

61. *Macon Daily Telegraph,* September 12 (Trawick) and 28 (soldier), 1863; Milledgeville *Southern Recorder,* August 11 and 25, September 8, 1863; Athens *Southern Banner,* August 26, 1863; *Macon Daily Telegraph,* October 1, 1863.

62. Milledgeville *Southern Recorder,* September 1 (quote), 15 (Furlow letter), 22, and 29, and October 6, 1863.

63. *Daily Intelligencer,* September and October 1863.

64. *Daily Intelligencer,* September 15 and 27, 1863; *Southern Watchman,* November 18, 1863 (quote); Milledgeville *Southern Recorder,* September 22, October 6, 1863.

65. W. Buck Yearns, *The Confederate Congress* (Athens: University of Georgia Press), 50. In his recent study of Alabama politics in 1863, Ben Severance concludes that prior interpretations of that state's congressional elections, which stressed that Peace Democrats defeated prowar Democrats, is mistaken. Instead, he describes a situation somewhat akin to what I have found in North Carolina and Georgia, with no candidates seeking to overturn conscription. The results, even when incumbents lost, demonstrated "a stoic affirmation of the cause." Severance, *War State All Over,* 12.

66. Reuben Davis to Jefferson Davis, August 2, 1863, Civil War Collection, American Antiquarian Society. Reuben Davis and Jefferson Davis were not related.

67. Reuben Davis to Jefferson Davis, August 2, 1863.

## CHAPTER SIX

1. For the military situation at the beginning of 1864, see McPherson, *Battle Cry of Freedom,* 718–722.

2. Robert E. Lee to Jefferson Davis, November 29, 1863, *OR,* ser. 1, vol. 29, part 2, 853; *Confederate Speller* quoted in Rubin, *Shattered Nation,* 30–31.

3. Secretary of War Report, November 26, 1863, Army totals, December 21, 1863, *OR,* ser. 4, vol. 2, 995, 1073; Robert E. Lee to Jefferson Davis, November 29, 1863, *OR,* ser. 1, vol. 29, part 2, 853; Lee to James Seddon, September 10, 1864, *OR,* ser. 4, vol. 3, 661. Additional information on troop totals in E. B. Long and Barbara Long, *The Civil War Day by Day: An Almanac, 1861–1865* (Garden City, N.Y.: Doubleday, 1971), 706.

4. Wigfall in *SHSP,* vol. 50:153.

5. *SHSP,* 50:51; "Augusta County: Diary of Joseph Addison Waddell (1855–1865)," December 25, 1863, in "Valley of the Shadow," http://valley.lib.virginia.edu/papers/AD1500.

6. John Milton to Jefferson Davis, May 23, 1863, in Hughes, *Civil War Correspondence of Florida's Governor John Milton,* 451; Governor's Message, in *Journal of the Senate of South Carolina, Being the Session of 1863* (Columbia, S.C.: P. Pelham, 1863), 45; *Journal of the House of Representatives of the State of Mississippi, December Session of 1862, and November Session of 1863* (Jackson, Miss., 1864), 153, 175; Brown, in *Richmond Daily Dispatch,* November 19, 1863; *SHSP,* vol. 50:40.

7. John Sink to Michael Sink, December 27, 1863, in Watford, *Civil War in North Carolina,* 1:141; James Barr to Rebecca Barr, December 18, 1863, in Thomas D. Mays, ed., *Let Us Meet in Heaven: The Civil War Letters of James Michael Barr, 5th South Carolina Cavalry* (Abilene, Tex.: McWhiney Foundation Press, 2001), 168–169; Richmond *Daily Dispatch,* December 9, 1863, *SHSP,* 50:51, 106; Theophilus Holmes to Harriet Holmes, January 18, 1864, in Johansson, *Widows by the Thousand,* 197. For a discussion of the number of substitutes in the Confederate army, see chapter 7 of the present volume.

8. Theophilus Holmes to Harriet Holmes, January 18, 1864, in Johansson, *Widows by the Thousand,* 197; "Augusta County: Diary of John R. Hildebrand (1864–1865)," January 29, 1864, "Valley of the Shadow," http://valley.lib.virginia.edu/papers/AD6088; Brown, in *Richmond Daily Dispatch,* November 19, 1863; *Staunton Spectator,* December 15, 1863; *SHSP,* 50:106 (Clark of Georgia calls it a "breach of faith"), 122, 129–130 (Orr).

9. Jefferson Davis to Congress, December 7, 1863, Davis to Congress, February 13, 1864, in Richardson, *Messages and Papers,* 370–371, 404–405.

10. "State of the Country: Speech of Hon. A. G. Brown of Mississippi, in the Confederate Senate, December 24, 1863," Documenting the American South, https://docsouth.unc.edu/imls/browna/browna.html.

11. "State of the Country."

12. *SHSP,* 50:120; James M. Matthews, *The Statutes at Large of the Confederate States of America, Passed at the Fourth Session of the First Congress; 1863–4* (Richmond, Va.: R. M. Smith, 1864), 172; William Henry Asbury Speer to James Speer, January 26, 1864, in Speer, *Voices from Cemetery Hill,* 116; Charles Truehart to Minnie, January 3, 1864, in *Rebel Brothers,* 87; J. J. Wilson to James E. Wilson, January 24, 1864, in *16th Mississippi Infantry,* 236; Thomas C. Hindman to Jefferson Davis, January 16, 1864, *PoJD,* 10:180–181; Abner Ford to Mollie Ford, January 31, 1864, Abner Dawson Ford Papers, VHS. The vote in favor of ending substitution was 52 to 13 in the House and 17 to 2 in the Senate.

13. Samuel Melton to James Seddon, November 11, 1863, Seddon Report, November 26, 1863, *OR*, ser. 4, vol. 2, 946, 997; W. L. Cunningham to Jefferson Davis, January 16, 1864, *PoJD*, 10:177; Richmond *Daily Dispatch*, December 9, 1863.

14. Jefferson Davis to Congress, December 7, 1863, Davis to Congress, November 7, 1864, in Richardson, *Messages and Papers*, 370–371, 491.

15. *Staunton Spectator*, January 12, 1864; "The Great Speech of Hon. A. H. Stephens, Delivered Before the Georgia Legislature, on Wednesday Night, March 16th, 1864, to Which Is Added Extracts prom [*sic*] Gov. Brown's Message to the Georgia Legislature," Documenting the American South, https://docsouth.unc.edu/imls/stephens/stephens.html; *SHSP*, vol. 50:144, 204–206.

16. Matthews, *Statutes at Large . . . Fourth Session*, 211–215; Jefferson Davis Veto, June 6, 1864, *OR*, ser. 4, vol. 3, 472–473.

17. Matthews, *Statutes at Large . . . Fourth Session*, 211–215; Blair, *Virginia's Private War*, 104; Richard F. Bensel, *Yankee Leviathan: The Origins of Central State Authority in America, 1859–1877* (New York: Cambridge University Press, 1990), 183–186.

18. Conscription Record for Robert Edmond, 1864, John A. Coke Papers, New York Historical Society.

19. Circular 23, June 24, 1864, *OR*, ser. 4, vol. 3, 507. The Confederacy did not plan to send enrolling officers to Maryland. This provision mainly affected men already in the ranks whose terms expired in 1864 and prevented men within the Confederacy's borders from trying to escape conscription by falsely claiming to be Marylanders.

20. William R. King, diary, December 24, 1863, January 1, 1864, in Joiner, *No Pardons to Ask*, 133, 136; Edwin Fay to Wife, January 1, 1864, in Wiley, *"This Infernal War,"* 383–384; Waddell diary, December 25, 1863.

21. Waddell diary, December 31, 1863; Richmond *Daily Dispatch*, January 12, 1864; *SHSP*, 50:176, 343; Thomas Webb to Peter Mallett, June 28, 1864, Josiah Gorgas to James Seddon, October 13, 1864, *OR*, ser. 4, vol. 3, 599–600, 734.

22. Burr Powell Noland to James K. Kemper, September 30, 1864, Bailey Family Papers, VHS; *SHSP*, 50:107; Joseph Brown to James Seddon, January 29, 1864, in Governor's Correspondence, GA; David L. Swain to William Alexander Graham, May 3, 1864, in Williams, *Papers of William Alexander Graham*, 6:84; Orlando Cox Petition, November 28, 1864, N.C. Conscript Bureau, SHC; Kean diary, September 25, 1864, Kean, *Inside Confederate Government*, 174; Bureau of Conscription, "Circular No. 6," April 1, 1864.

23. A. W. Montgomery to N. D. Tomlin, September 4, 1863, Samuel Hilton Steelman Papers, SHC; James Barr to Rebecca Barr, January 10, 1864, in Mays, *Let Us Meet in Heaven*, 177–178; Richmond *Daily Dispatch*, January 5, 1864; diary entry, February 1, 1864, Jones, *Rebel War Clerk's Diary*, 2: 140; Circular 1, January 13, 1864, Report of the Bureau of Conscription, April 30, 1864, *OR*, ser. 4, vol. 3, 24–25, 355; John A. Williams to Dear Sister, January 25, 1864, John A. Williams Letters, VHS; Lazerus H. Davis to Jefferson Davis, January 27, 1864, *PoJD*, 10:206–207; diary entry, January 15, 1864, Woodward, *Mary Chesnut's Civil War*, 540.

24. December 25 and 31, 1863, January 30, February 13 and 20, 1864, in Venet, *Sam Richards's Civil War Diary*, 207–208, 206–219.

25. Report of the Bureau of Conscription, April 30, 1864, Howell Cobb to James Seddon, January 26, 1864, *OR*, ser. 4, vol. 3, 355, 48–49; Francis H. Board to Milton, February 11, 1864, Francis H. Board

Letter, LV; Thomas Nicholson to Governor Vance, January 23, 1864, in Yearns, *North Carolina Civil War Documentary,* 149–150.

26. *SHSP,* 50:140, 152, 243, 347–348.

27. "Enrollment of Principals of Substitutes in 7th Congressional District, N.C., for the Month of _____ 1864," N.C. Conscript Bureau, SHC. One man was listed in each of the following categories: "By Sec. of war," "Doctor extends for 30 days," "Wagon maker," "shoemaker," "millwright," "Rec. for provost duty," "physician," "tanner," and "militia officer." Regardless of occupation, it is impossible to conclude definitively whether some of these men had been eligible for conscription when they provided substitutes. Their status would potentially depend on whether they were practicing the occupation at the time and which conscription laws were in effect when they provided their substitute.

28. "Enrollment of Principals." Sixteen had no dates of enlistment, three were listed in 1863, and the other sixty-six had been enrolled in 1862 (including twenty-seven substitutes enrolled in February or March 1862, before national conscription had begun).

29. William Daniel Dixon, diary, December 1863, January 6, 1864, in Durham, *Blues in Gray,* 192; *SHSP,* 50:133.

30. For some examples of men discharged by Pearson, see the following petitions: George Wilkins, October 18, 1863, F. W. Kirk, October 19, 1863, Robert Mathews, November 9, 1863, John G. Foster, October 14, 1863, Henry Snow, October 20, 1863, and James Hutchins, October 17, 1863, all in Pearson Papers, SHC; Kean, *Inside the Confederate Government,* February 26, 1864, 137–138; W. H. C. Whiting to Jefferson Davis, February 25, 1864, *OR,* ser. 1, vol. 33, 1198. For a detailed discussion of the 1864 judicial battles over conscription in North Carolina, see Mitchell, *Legal Aspects of Conscription,* 61–91; and Neely, *Southern Rights,* 64–79. For all state courts, see Moore, *Conscription and Conflict,* 177–190.

31. Jefferson Davis to House of Representatives, February 3, 1864, *OR,* ser. 4, vol. 3, 67–70; Matthews, *Statutes at Large of the First Congress of the Confederate States,* 4th session, 187–189; John B. Robbins, "The Confederacy and the Writ of Habeas Corpus," *Georgia Historical Quarterly* (Spring 1971), 83–101; *Savannah Republican,* quoted in Yearns, *Confederate Congress,* 157. The suspension would last until ninety days after the start of the next session of Congress.

32. Alexander Stephens to Georgia Legislature, March 16, 1864, Lawrence Keith to Stephens, April 13, 1864, Stephens Papers, LC; General Assembly of Georgia, March 19, 1864, Joseph Brown to George T. Anderson, in *OR,* ser. 4, vol. 3, 234–235, 372–374; Brown to Alexander Stephens, February 20, 1864, Robert Toombs to Stephens, April 1, 1864, in Phillips, *Correspondence,* 633, 639; *Salisbury Carolina Watchman,* February 15, 1864, quoted in Mitchell, *Legal Aspects of Conscription,* 65; *Early County News,* February 24, 1864, quoted in David Williams, Teresa Crisp Williams, and David Carlson, *Plain Folk in a Rich Man's War: Class and Dissent in Confederate Georgia* (Gainesville: University Press of Florida, 2002), 116; Kean, *Inside the Confederate Government,* January 9, 1864, 132; Jones, *Rebel War Clerk's Diary,* January 30, February 19, 1864, 2:153.

33. *Ex Parte Walton,* in Jones and Winston, *Cases Argued and Determined,* 222; Kemp Battle to Sam Watkins, March 15, 1864, Battle Family Papers, SHC.

34. *Wilmington Journal,* quoted in *Carolina Watchman* (Salisbury, N.C.), March 14, 1864; James Seddon to Thomas Bragg, March 19, April 2, 1864, Zebulon Vance to Seddon, February 29, 1864, Seddon to Vance, March 5, 1864, *OR,* ser. 4, vol. 3, 238, 267, 176, 197–198; Jones, *Rebel War Clerk's Diary,* March 1 and 2, 1864, 343–344; Pearson, quoted in Hamilton, "North Carolina Courts," 397. The *Caro-*

*lina Watchman* article states that Pearson rejected seven of the first thirty-five habeas corpus cases he heard, and Hamilton says he rejected nine of twenty-seven in 1863 (369).

35. James Seddon to Zebulon Vance, March 5, 1864, Jefferson Davis to Thomas Bragg, March 7, 1864, Bragg to Seddon, March 15 and 29, 1864, *OR*, ser. 4, vol. 3, 197–198; 200–291, 213, 256; "act of madness" in Neely, *Southern Rights*, 69.

36. Peter Mallett to Thomas Bragg, June 14, 1864, Mallett Papers, SHC; Mitchell, *Legal Aspects of Conscription*, 66–77; *Gatlin v. Walton*, in Jones and Winston, *Cases Argued and Determined*, 325.

37. *Burroughs v. Peyton*, in *Opinion of the Supreme Court of Appeals of Virginia in Regard to Liability to Military Service of the Principals of Substitutes* (Richmond: James E. Goode, 1864); *Fitzgerald v. Harris*, Executive Letterbook, GA; Stelluto, "A Light Which Reveals Its True Meaning," 65–79, at 75 (Georgia Supreme Court).

38. Archer Anderson to Braxton Bragg, June 22, 1864, July 18, 1864, James Kemper to Samuel Cooper, July 26, 1864, *OR*, ser. 4, vol. 3, 504–506, 539–542, 558; James Chesnut to John Preston, October 1, 1864, Preston-Davie Papers, VHS.

39. Petition for James Johnson, June 13, 1864, Randolph County Board of Investigation, June 8, 1864, N.C. Conscript Papers, SHC; James Saunders to James Seddon, January 29, 1864, Saunders Family Papers, VHS.

40. Daniel N. Moxley to William M. Moxley, May 3, 1864, in Cutrer, *Oh, What a Loansome Time I Had*, 154; Joseph G. Penn to Sarah R. Hay, June 11, 1864, Joseph Goodman Penn Letter, LV.

41. James M. Holloway to Annie Holloway, July 23, 25, and 27, 1864, in John W. Holloway Papers, VHS.

42. King diary, June 28, 1864, in Joiner, *No Pardons to Ask*, 179; William H. A. Speer to James Speer, January 26, 1864, in Speer, *Voices from Cemetery Hill*, 116–117; Mary Helm Tompkins to Jefferson Davis, January 8, 1864, *PoJD*, 10:164; *Communication from the Secretary of War, Relative to the Number of Men Liable to Conscription Removed from the Commissary and Quartermasters Departments, to Give to Disabled Soldiers*, January 1864; *SHSP*, 50:36, 105, 115–116, 243; diary entry, June 9, 1864, Jones, *Rebel War Clerk's Diary*, 2:228. "Fat, sleek, able-bodied" became an epithet similar to "speculator." It appeared repeatedly in congressional discussions. See *SHSP*, 50:36 (Foote), 106 (Clark), 116 (Gaither).

43. David Cumming to Joseph Brown, July 4, November 1, 1864, Governor's Correspondence, GA.

44. Joseph Brown to James Seddon, January 29, 1864, circular, July 1, 1864, *OR*, ser. 4, vol. 3, 61–63, 524; John Milton to Seddon, January 11, 1864; Milton to L. B. Northop, January 13, 1864, Milton to Seddon, January 26, 1864, Seddon to Milton, February 11, 1864, in Hughes, *Civil War Correspondence*, 546, 549–551, 574–575, 583–584.

45. C. C. Henkel to David Kagey, January 25, 1864, Henry Kagey Papers, DU; Samuel D. Knight to Governor Brown, February 22, 1864, in Mills, *Times That Prove People's Principles*, 137; H. W. Walter to J. W. C. Watson, December 29, 1864, *OR*, ser. 4, vol. 3, 976–979; H. W. Walter Report, March 30, 1864, Braxton Bragg Papers, DU; Unknown to Jefferson Davis, August 15, 1864, *PoJD*, 10:612; John Milton to Jefferson Davis, October 5, 1863, in Hughes, *Civil War Correspondence*, 517–519.

46. Report of the Bureau of Conscription, April 30, 1864, General Order 73, September 22, 1864, *OR*, ser. 4, vol. 3, 354–364, 675.

47. Circular 5, January 29, 1864, John Preston to James Seddon, March 18, 1864, Report of the Bureau of Conscription, April 30, 1864, *OR*, ser. 4, vol. 3, 57, 224–225, 354–364.

48. *OR*, ser. 4, vol. 3, 354–364; Blair, *Virginia's Private War*, 125.

49. James Seddon to Jefferson Davis, April 28, 1864, *OR*, ser. 4, vol. 3, 334–335.

50. Braxton Bragg to Jefferson Davis, September 5 and 7, 1864, *OR*, ser. 4, vol. 3, 609–610, 624. For Goldthwaite's age, see *OR*, ser. 4, vol. 3, 631. Judith Lee Hallock, *Braxton Bragg and Confederate Defeat* (Tuscaloosa: University of Alabama Press, 1991), 2:150–187, esp. 176–179.

51. John Preston to James Seddon, September 9, 1864, Medical Examining Board Report, *OR*, ser. 4, vol. 3, 630–633.

52. John Preston to James Seddon, September 9, 1864, Seddon to Jefferson Davis, September 14, 1864, Preston to Seddon, November 5, 1864, *OR*, ser. 4, vol. 3, 633–634, 640–641, 785–789.

53. Diary entry, September 20, 1864, Jones, *Rebel War Clerk's Diary*, 2:287; Frank L. Owsley, "Local Defense and the Overthrow of the Confederacy," *Mississippi Valley Historical Review* 11 (March 1924), 514, 525; "Resolutions Concerning Certain Acts of the Late Congress of the Confederate States," May 28, 1864, in Yearns and Barrett, *North Carolina Civil War Documentary*, 279.

54. Diary, May 20, 1863, in Joseph G. de Roulhac Hamilton, ed., *The Papers of Randolph A. Shotwell* (Raleigh: North Carolina Historical Commission, 1929), 1:471; J. C. Mather to Jefferson Davis, March 31, 1864, James A. Seddon to Howell Cobb, December 30, 1864, *OR*, ser. 4, vol. 3, 259, 981; A. C. Walker to Governor Brown, January 18, February 24, 1864, in Governor's Correspondence, GA. In *Johnson v. Mallett*, a case involving the conscription of a police officer, the North Carolina court declared that the state had unlimited power to determine which state officers to keep at home. Van Zant, "Confederate Conscription," 72–73.

55. List of the Number of State Officers, November 23, 1864, John Preston to James Seddon, November 29, 1864, Preston to Peter Mallett, December 1, 1864, H. W. Walter to J. W. C. Watson, December 29, 1864, February 1865 Report, *OR*, ser. 4, vol. 3, 851, 866–874, 894, 976, 1102, 976; Henry Wayne to Charles Harris, December 18 and 26, 1863, Attorney General's Letterbook, GA.

56. Joseph Brown Proclamation, March 1, 1864, Alexander Stephens to Herschel V. Johnson, April 8, 1864, *OR*, ser. 4, vol. 3, 197, 279; Herschel V. Johnson to Jefferson Davis, 1864, Jefferson Davis Papers, DU; Kean, *Inside the Confederate Government*, March 13, 1864, 140.

57. Howell Cobb to Joseph Brown, April 21, 1864, *OR*, ser. 4, vol. 3, 347–349; Cobb to Jefferson Davis, July 7, 1864, *PoJD*, 10:506.

58. Joseph Brown Proclamation, March 1, 1864, Brown to Cobb, May 5, 1864, *OR*, ser. 4, vol. 3, 197, 381–384; Brown to Alexander Stephens, April 5, 1864, in Phillips, *Correspondence*, 640; Brown to Cobb, May 3, 1864, Governor's Letterbook, GA.

59. Howell Cobb to Joseph Brown, May 12 and 23, 1864, Brown to Cobb, May 20 and 30, 1864, Cobb to Samuel Cooper, June 7, 1864, *OR*, ser. 4, vol. 3, 417–422, 431–439, 442–444, 455–457, 476.

60. James Seddon to William Browne, July 5, 1864, *OR*, ser. 4, vol. 3, 530–531; Seddon to Howell Cobb, July 21, 1864, *OR*, ser. 1, vol. 52, 710.

61. P. G. T. Beauregard to President Davis, James Seddon endorsement to Mr. Shepherd, October 10, 1864, *OR*, ser. 1, vol. 39, part 3, 800; William Browne to Howell Cobb, January 28, 1865, ser. 4, vol. 3, 1049.

62. William H. A. Speer to Father & Mother, April 4, 1864, in Speer, *Voices from Cemetery Hill*, 124; Governor Vance, Message to General Assembly, May 17, 1864, Documenting the American South, https://docsouth.unc.edu/imls/govern64/govern64.html; S. E. Watney to Kemp Battle, March 3,

1864, Battle Family Papers, SHC. For the 1864 governor's race, see Kruman, *Parties and Politics in North Carolina*, 259–267, at 263.

63. Zebulon Vance to Governor M. L. Bonham, September 23, 1864, Governors' Resolutions, October 17, 1864, *OR*, ser. 4, vol. 3, 684–685, 735–736. The governors represented Alabama, Georgia, Mississippi, North Carolina, South Carolina, and Virginia.

64. Governors' Resolutions, October 17, 1864, Zebulon Vance to General Holmes, October 25, 1864, *OR*, ser. 4, vol. 3, 735–736, 746.

65. Message of the Governor of Virginia to the General Assembly, December 7, 1864, *OR*, ser. 4, vol. 3, 906; Statement Exempting Thomas E. Bienvenu from Military Service, n.d., St. Martin Parish Papers, LLMVC. Bienvenu was conscripted in 1864, with the decision coming in 1865.

66. *Ex Parte Tate*, in *Report of Cases Argued and Determined in the Supreme Court of Alabama 1864*, 39:257.

67. Upton, *Military Policy of the United States*, 490; Fred A. Shannon, *The Organization and Administration of the Union Army, 1861–1865* (Cleveland, Ohio: Arthur H. Clark Company, 1928), 1:269; Emory M. Thomas, *The Confederate Nation, 1861–1865* (New York: Harper Torchbooks, 1979); and Thomas, *The Confederacy as a Revolutionary Experience* (Englewood Cliffs, N.J.: Prentice-Hall, 1971), 59, 70; Bensel, *Yankee Leviathan*; Michael Brem Bonner, *Confederate Political Economy: Creating and Managing a Southern Corporatist Nation* (Baton Rouge: Louisiana State University Press, 2016), esp., 128–141.

68. "Great Speech of Hon. A. H. Stephens," March 16, 1864, Documenting the American South. For troop totals, see Long and Long, *Civil War Day by Day*, 706. These totals include men absent from the ranks. When they are removed, the discrepancy is even greater: 630,924 to 196,016.

## CHAPTER SEVEN

1. Conrad, *SHSP*, 50:345–346; December 25, 1864, diary entry, in Kean, *Inside the Confederate Government*, 181.

2. Augusta Speech, in Cooper, *Jefferson Davis: The Essential Writings*, 347; President's Message, November 7, 1864, *OR*, ser. 4, vol. 3, 796; diary entry of November 7, 1864, Jones, *Rebel War Clerk's Diary*, 2:325 (detail on the weather).

3. Secretary of War Report, November 3, 1864, President's Message, November 7, 1864, James A. Seddon to Howell Cobb, December 30, 1864, *OR*, 759–760, 796, 981.

4. *SHSP*, 51:143, 306.

5. *SHSP*, 51:305–308, 186, 180, 494.

6. John Preston to James Seddon, October 22, 1864, *OR*, ser. 4, vol. 3, 744.

7. Kemper to Cooper, July 26, 1864, *OR*, ser. 4, vol. 3, 557; Kean, *Inside the Confederate Government*, September 25, October 18, 1864, 174–177.

8. General Order 73, John Preston to James Seddon, October 22, 1864, *OR*, ser. 4, vol. 3, 675, 744–745.

9. General Order 76, October 5, 1864, General Order 77, October 8, 1864, General Order 81, October 14, 1864, *OR*, ser. 4, vol. 3, 712–713, 715, 734, 751; Robert E. Lee to Samuel Cooper, October 10, 1864, *OR*, ser. 1, vol. 42, 1144; diary entry, October 18, 1864, in Jones, *Rebel War Clerk's Diary*, 2:310. General Order 77 merely clarified some language in General Order 76.

10. John Preston to President Davis, October 18, 1864, Preston to James Seddon, October 18 and 22, November 5, 1864, *OR*, ser. 4, vol. 3, 739, 742, 744–745, 785–789.

11. John Preston to Jefferson Davis, November 28, 1864, James Kemper to Davis, December 7, 1864, *OR*, ser. 4, vol. 3, 854–856, 858.

12. General Orders 83, November 1, 1864, J. L. Kemper to John Preston, November 22, 1864, Preston to Secretary of War, November 29, 1864, *OR*, ser. 4, vol. 3, 749–751.

13. Cooper Report, *OR*, ser. 4, vol. 3, 859–863.

14. John Preston to President Davis, Preston to James Seddon, December 18, 1864, *OR*, ser. 4, vol. 3, 946–947; Preston to William Porcher Miles, undated, *OR*, ser. 4, vol. 3, 880–882. Preston knew how to play the political game. He had maneuvered to get promoted from colonel to brigadier general in the summer of 1864. Kean, *Inside the Confederate Government*, 161–162.

15. H. W. Walter to J. W. C. Watson, December 29, 1864, *OR*, ser. 4, vol. 3, 976; *SHSP*, 52:302, 344, 343, 368, 374. House vote was 50 to 13.

16. Veto Message, March 13, 1865, *OR*, ser. 4, vol. 3, 1129; *SHSP*, 52:480 (Davis veto); diary entries, February 15, March 22, 1865, in Jones, *Rebel War Clerk's Diary*, 2:423, 456.

17. Circular 1, February 13, 1865, Theophilus Hunter Holmes Papers, DU.

18. Wigfall in *SHSP*, 52:181; circular in *Southern Banner* (Athens, Ga.), November 16, 1864; John Campbell to John C. Breckinridge, March 5, 1865, Campbell Family Papers, SHC; Anonymous Writer to Howell Cobb, January 3, 1865, in Phillips, *Correspondence*, 656.

19. Howell Cobb to James Seddon, January 8, 1865, Seddon Report, November 3, 1864, *OR*, ser. 4, vol. 3, 1009–1010, 756; Bruce Levine, *Confederate Emancipation: Southern Plans to Free and Arm Slaves During the Civil War* (New York: Oxford University Press, 2006), 26–28.

20. Levine, *Confederate Emancipation; Macon Telegraph*, quoted in Phillip D. Dillard, *Jefferson Davis's Final Campaign: Confederate Nationalism and the Fight to Arm the Slaves* (Macon: Mercer University Press, 2017), 127; *SHSP*, 52:292. See also Robert F. Durden, *The Gray and the Black: The Confederate Debate on Emancipation* (Baton Rouge: Louisiana State University Press, 1972). Levine's, Dillard's, and Durden's books led me to many of the sources in the following pages.

21. Cleburne Proposal *OR*, ser. 1, vol. 52, part 2, 586–592, at 588.

22. September 29, 1864, in Sarah W. Wiggins, *The Journals of Josiah Gorgas, 1857–1878* (Tuscaloosa: University of Alabama Press, 1995), 134; Henry W. Allen to James Seddon, September 26, 1864, *OR*, ser. 1, vol. 41, 774; *Message of the Governor of Virginia, to the General Assembly* (Richmond, Va.: James E. Goode, Senate Printer, 1864); Robert E. Lee to Andrew Hunter, January 11, 1865, *OR*, ser. 4, vol. 3, 1012.

23. Warren Akin to Nathan Land, October 31, 1864, in Bell Irvin Wiley, ed., "The Letters of Warren Akin, Confederate Congressman, Part II," *Georgia Historical Quarterly* 42, no. 2 (1958): 200; other two Georgians quoted in Levine, *Confederate Emancipation*, 37, 117.

24. Levine, *Confederate Emancipation*, 37–38. *Message of the Governor of Virginia, to the General Assembly.*

25. Secretary of War Report, November 3, 1864, *OR*, ser. 4, vol., 3, 762; *SHSP*, 51:292–294.

26. Levine, *Confederate Emancipation*, 118; diary entry, March 17, 1865, in Jones, *Rebel War Clerk's Diary*, 2:451; Cooper, *Jefferson Davis*, 526.

27. M. J. Cave to David Comfort III, July 21, 1864, A. W. Clisby to David Comfort III, April 20, 1865, in Comfort Family Papers, VHS; General Orders No. 17, *OR*, ser. 4, vol. 3, 1176.

28. *SHSP*, 51:333–334.

29. *SHSP,* 52:428–429 (Turner), 431 (Miles).

30. List of the Number of State Officers, November 23, 1864, Circular No. 34, John Preston to Peter Mallett, December 1, 1864, *OR,* ser. 4, vol. 3, 851, 853, 894.

31. John Preston to James Seddon, November 29, 1864, *OR,* ser. 4, vol. 3, 866–867; chart in *SHSP,* 51:333.

32. Preston's report, February 1865 *OR,* ser. 4, vol. 4, 1099–1110. Further evidence pointing to the incompleteness of this report is that, just three months earlier, Preston had claimed the bureau had evaluated 360,000 men in two years, yet this report adds up to only 275,000. Preston to James Seddon, November 5, 1864, *OR,* ser. 4, vol. 3, 789.

33. *OR,* ser. 4, vol. 3, 1100–1101. The 120,000 figure appears in James M. McPherson, *Ordeal by Fire: The Civil War And Reconstruction* (New York: Knopf, 1982), 182.

34. McPherson, *Ordeal by Fire;* Secretary of War Report, *OR,* ser. 4, vol. 3, 995, 1101.

35. Raleigh *Semi-Weekly Standard,* November 20, 1863; C. A. James to Cousin, date unknown, Bidgood Family Papers, VHS; *OR,* ser. 4, vol. 3, 1101. The summation of table B is listed as 76,206, but the totals add up to 72,292

36. Noe, *Reluctant Rebels,* 2 (estimate of volunteers).

37. *OR,* ser. 4, vol. 3, 1110.

38. Moore, *Conscription and Conflict,* 357. The 8.2 percent figure represents the lowest possible numerator divided by the highest denominator, whereas the 33 percent represents the reverse—the highest numerator and lowest denominator. It is possible that the numerator could be even higher.

39. *OR,* ser. 4, vol. 1, 962–963.

40. *OR,* ser. 4, vol. 3, 1100–1101. December 27, 1864, in Jones, *Rebel War Clerk's Diary,* 2:114. He had made the same joke on February 16, 1863; see 1:260.

41. *OR,* ser. 4, vol. 3, 1100–1101. By percentage, Floridians were perhaps more successful in dodging conscription (362 conscripts compared to 748 exempts) than Georgians, but their small (and certainly inaccurate) numbers made their evasion less remarkable.

42. *OR,* ser. 4, vol. 3, 1100–1101.

43. Louisiana figures in Napier Bartlett, *Military Record of Louisiana: Including Biographical and Historical Papers Relating to the Military Organizations of the State* (1875; Baton Rouge: Louisiana State University Press, 1996), 254; "Report of Progress Made in the Execution of the Conscription Law in Virginia," chapter 1, vol. 250, RG 109, National Archives.

44. "Report of Progress Made."

45. T. H. Holmes to Samuel Cooper, January 8, 1865, Theophilus H. Holmes Correspondence, SHC.

46. "Report of Progress Made."

47. "Record of Exemptions in Virginia." The 12,685 figure is a slight underestimate, as the figures for January 1863 are missing. The numbers in this paragraph differ from those in previous paragraphs because, in order to correspond with the period covered in the exemption records, these numbers only consider until November 1, 1863, rather than the entire duration of the war. The different dates on exemptions, medical exemptions, and camp data further complicate any analysis of conscription. The exemption report lists a total of 12,641 exempts. However, it omits a column with forty-four militia officers that is barely visible, smashed in the gutter of the book. Medical exemptions are listed at 5,512 as of September 1864.

48. Edward A. Pollard, *The Lost Cause: A New Southern History of the War of the Confederates* (New York: E. B. Treat & Co., 1868), 646 (quote). For the opinion that less than 1 percent of substitutes remained in the army, see Officers of the Army of Tennessee to Cooper, July 25, 1863, *OR*, ser. 4, vol. 2, 670–671.

49. "Record of Exemptions in Virginia." State employees included militia officers, magistrates, commissioners of revenue, sheriffs, commonwealth attorneys, clerks of court, members of the legislature, and other state officers. Confederate employees included government contractors, mail contractors, members of the treasury, and the quartermaster, ordnance, subsistence, navy, and medical departments. In addition to the 418 religious men exempt, another thirty-six men were released from camp as Dunkards. All thirty-six were released in October and November 1862. Most likely, these men were conscripted before enrolling officers were aware how to apply the October 1862 revision, which allowed for this exemption, or before or before the Dunkards could cobble the money together.

50. Report of the Secretary of War, Samuel Cooper to James A. Seddon, December 16, 1863, Melton to Seddon, November 11, 1863, James Campbell to Senator Barksdale, July 21, 1863, officers of the Army of Tennessee to Cooper, July 25, 1863, *OR*, ser. 4, vol. 2, 996, 1058–1059, 946, 655–656, 670–671.

51. "Report of Progress Made"; *OR*, ser. 4, vol. 3, 95–103. According to the 1860 census, Virginia represented 18% of the Confederacy's total population, 19.2% of its white population, and 19.8% of its free population (including free African Americans). Much like all conscription extrapolations, this one is flawed—Virginia's numbers in 1860 include the counties that formed West Virginia. Also, this list does not include Virginia soldiers already in the army who provided substitutes. Regardless, if the total of 3,270 (or 3,423) principals in Virginia is even close to accurate, it is hard to envision 50,000 (let alone 150,000) substitutes in the Confederacy. For North Carolina figures, see Raleigh *Semi-Weekly Standard*, November 20, 1863. For an estimate of 20,000 substitutes (plus 10,000 fraudulent substitute papers), see *The American Annual Cyclopaedia and Register of Important Events of the Year 1863* (New York: Appleton, 1870), 17. While not trying to ascertain a total figure on substitutes, Joseph Glatthaar's contention that they composed less than one percent of Lee's army would also support a very low total of substitutes across the Confederacy. Joseph T. Glatthaar, *General Lee's Army from Victory to Collapse* (New York: Free Press, 2008), 399. Notably, in almost every case, precise figures indicate a low number of principals, whereas broad estimates or quotes from substitution's critics support a high number.

52. *OR*, ser. 4, vol. 3, 95.

53. *OR*, ser. 4, vol. 2, 132, 739–741, 939, vol. 3, 363. While the math professor's report makes the dubious assumption that each of Georgia's 132 counties would have the same number of men practicing each occupation, providing substitutes, and occupying the youngest and oldest age ranges, its broader point still applies.

54. *OR*, ser. 4, vol. 3, 95–103; Sheehan-Dean, *Why Confederates Fought*, 3, and Sheehan-Dean, "Everyman's War: Confederate Enlistment in Civil War Virginia," *Civil War History* (March 2004), 5–26. The discrepancy between the 80 percent and 90 percent figures most likely stems from the fact that the lower figure includes all of Virginia (including modern-day West Virginia), whereas the higher figure just includes modern-day Virginia. William Blair maintains that 93 percent of military-age males in Virginia were either in the army or in "war-related work." Blair, *Virginia's Private War*, 125.

55. Joseph T. Glatthaar, *Soldiering in the Army of Northern Virginia: A Statistical Portrait of the Troops Who Served Under Robert E. Lee* (Chapel Hill: University of North Carolina Press, 2011), 10–11.

56. Virginia figures from "Report of Progress Made."

57. Jefferson Davis to Congress, November 7, 1864, *OR,* ser. 4, vol. 3, 796; *SHSP,* 40:307.

58. Wm. McWartmann and John T. Harris to John B. Baldwin, November 23, 1864, *OR,* ser. 4, vol. 3, 845–846.

59. *SHSP,* vol. 52:142–144, 149, 194.

60. John Preston to James Seddon, October 22, 1864, *OR,* ser. 4, vol. 3, 744–745; *Richmond Examiner,* quoted in Moore, *Conscription and Conflict,* 338–339.

61. Diary entry, April 3, 1864, in Kean, *Inside the Confederate Government,* 144.

62. Stephens, *Constitutional View,* 570, 572–573.

63. Jefferson Davis, *The Rise and Fall of the Confederate Government* (1881; New York: Da Capo, 1990), 1:434–435.

64. Circular in John Milton to Jefferson Davis, *OR,* ser. 4, vol. 2, 490–491; W. L. Brandon to Jefferson Davis, November 15, 1864, Brandon to James Seddon, December 5, 1864, *OR,* ser. 4, vol. 3, 823–824, 902–903; Oldham, *Memoirs,* 108.

65. For some examples of this argument, see Escott, *After Secession;* and David Williams, *People's History of the Civil War.*

66. James Phelan to Jefferson Davis, July 29, 1863, Jefferson Davis Collection, Clements Library.

67. James Phelan to Jefferson Davis, July 29, 1863.

68. For a similar argument, see Blair, *Virginia's Private War.*

69. Robert E. Lee to Braxton Bragg, September 10, 1864, in Douglas Southall Freeman, *Lee's Dispatches* (New York: G. P. Putnam's Sons, 1915), 297–298. The previous day, Lee had suggested to President Davis the consolidation of the bureau with the general of reserves and the moving of all able-bodied men out of the bureau. Lee to Jefferson Davis, September 9, 1864 (294).

# Bibliography


## MANUSCRIPT COLLECTIONS

### *American Antiquarian Society*

Civil War Collection

### *Documenting the American South (all digital)*

Bureau of Conscription Circulars

Governor Vance, Message to General Assembly, May 17, 1864.

The Great Speech of Hon. A. H. Stephens, Delivered Before the Georgia Legislature, March 16th, 1864.

Opinion of the Supreme Court of Appeals of Virginia in Regard to Liability to Military Service of the Principals of Substitutes. Richmond: James E. Goode, 1864.

Speech of Hon. George A. Gordon, of Chatham, on the Constitutionality of the Conscription Laws, Passed by the Congress of the Confederate States, Delivered in the Senate of Georgia, on Tuesday, 9th of December, 1862.

State of the Country: Speech of Hon. A. G. Brown of Mississippi, December 24, 1863.

Virginia Recruiting Poster

### *Duke University*

Artemus S. Caddell Papers

Braxton Bragg Papers

C. C. Clay Papers

Eglantine Agours Papers

Great Britain Consulate Records

Henry Kagey Papers

Henry St. George Harris Papers

James Calvin Marcom Diary

Jefferson Davis Papers

John C. Hood Papers

John F. Poindexter Collection

John H. Kinyoun Papers
Mary P. Davis Papers
Theophilus Hunter Holmes Papers

### *Emory University*

Alexander Hamilton Stephens Collection
Great Britain Consulate Papers

### *Georgia Archives*

Adjutant General's Letter Book
Attorney General's Letter Book
Civil War Miscellany
Executive Letterbook
Governor's Subject Files (Joseph Brown)
Richardson Family Letters

### *Library of Congress*

Alexander Stephens Papers

### *Library of Virginia*

Bureau of Conscription, Conscript Journal
Francis H. Board Letters
High S. Gookin Letter
Joseph Goodman Penn Letter

### *Louisiana and Lower Mississippi Valley Collections, LSU*

Anonymous Civil War Letter
Arthur W. Hyatt Papers
D. Y. Milling Correspondence
E. P. Ellis and Family Papers
Frederick R. Taber Papers
Joel A. Stokes Family Papers
John Achilles Harris Letters
Joseph D. Shields Papers

Joseph Vidal and Family Papers
Micajah Wilkinson Papers
St. Martin Parish Papers
Thomas Overton Moore Papers
Wright-Boyd Family Papers

### *Louisiana State Archives*

Enrollment Statistics
Prudhomme Papers
Trans-Mississippi Department Papers

### *National Archives*

Letters Received by the Secretary of War
Record of Exemptions in Virginia
Records of the US House of Representatives, Southern Claims Commission, 1871–1880
Report of Progress Made in the Execution of the Conscription Law in Virginia
War Department Collection of Confederate Records

### *New York Historical Society*

John A. Coke Papers

### *State Archives of North Carolina*

John Thomas Conrad Papers (digital)

### *Southern Historical Collection, UNC*

A.H. Arrington Papers
Auman Family Papers
Bailey Family Papers
Battle Family Papers
Burwell Family Papers
Campbell Family Papers
Charles Woodward Hutson Papers
Confederate States of America, Bureau of Conscription, 7th North Carolina Congressional District Records, 1862–1865

Cornelia McGimsey Papers
Elliott and Gonzales Family Papers
Gaither Family Papers
James O. Carr Papers
Jason Thomas Leach Papers
John Logan Papers
John McKee Sharpe Papers
John Perkins Papers
Jonathan Worth Papers
Jones Family Papers
Monroe F. Cockrell Papers
Nims, Rankin, and Spratt Family Papers
Peter Mallett Papers
Richmond Mumford Pearson Papers
Samuel Hilton Steelman Papers
Sarah Lois Wadley Papers
Theophilus H. Holmes Correspondence
Thomas Bragg Papers
Thomas Settle Papers
William Beavans Diary and Letters
Wilse-Dial Letter

### *Tulane Archives*

Gustave A. Breaux Diary
Favrot Family Papers

### *University of Georgia*

Howell Cobb Papers (digital)

### *University of Michigan, Clements Library*

James S. Schoff Civil War Collection
Jefferson Davis Collection,

### *University of Mississippi Digital Archive*

Gage Family Collection (digital)

*University of South Carolina Library*

William Drayton Rutherford Papers (digital)

*Valley of the Shadow Project*

Evans-Sibert Family Papers
Henry H. and Mary E.A. Dedrick Papers
Hubard Family Letters
Hugh Gilkeson Collection
John R. Hildebrand Diary
Joseph Addison Waddell Diary
William Hill Diary

*Virginia Historical Society*

Abner Dawson Ford Papers
Bidgood Family Papers
Blanton Family Papers
Charlotte County (Va.) Records
Comfort Family Papers
DeButts Family Papers
J. S. Preston Report
John A. Williams Letters
John W. Holloway Papers
Larue Family Papers
Liebermann Family Papers
Preston-Davie Papers
Rockingham, Virginia, Enrolling Books
Saunders Family Papers

*Virginia Military Institute*

John Garibaldi Correspondence (digital)

WEBSITE

13th Mississippi Infantry Regiment—History, Rosters, Diaries, Letters

## GOVERNMENT DOCUMENTS

*Circular Instructions for Enrolling Officers.* 1863.

*Communication from the Secretary of War, Relative to the Number of Men Liable to Conscription Removed from the Commissary and Quartermasters Departments, to Give to Disabled Soldiers.* Richmond, Va., 1864.

*Correspondence Between Governor Brown and President Davis on the Constitutionality of the Conscription Act.* Atlanta: Atlanta Intelligencer, 1862.

*Correspondence of the Department of State in Relation to the British Consuls Resident in the Confederate States.* Richmond, Va., 1863.

*Eighth Census of the United States,* 1860.

Jones, H. C., ed. *Cases of Habeas Corpus, Decided by the Supreme Court of North Carolina at the June Term, 1863.* Salisbury, N.C.: J. J. Bruner, 1863.

Jones, H. C., and P. H. Winston, eds. *Cases Argued and Determined in the Supreme Court of North Carolina from June Term, 1863, to December Term, 1864, Inclusive.* Raleigh, N.C.: News Publishing Co., 1878.

*Journal of the Congress of the Confederate States of America, 1861–1865.* Washington, D.C., 1904–1905.

*Journal of the House of Delegates of the State of Virginia for the Session of 1861–1862.* Richmond, Va., 1861.

*Journal of the House of Representatives of the State of Mississippi, December Session of 1862, and November Session of 1863.* Jackson, Miss., 1864.

*Journal of the Senate of South Carolina, Being the Session of 1863.* Columbia, S.C.: P. Pelham, 1863.

*Journal of the Senate of the State of Georgia, at the Annual Session of the General Assembly.* Milledgeville, Ga., 1862.

Magrath, A. G. *Liability of Alien Residents to Conscription: Opinion of Judge Magrath in the Confederate Court, South Carolina District* (n.d.).

Matthews, James M. *Public Laws of the Confederate States of America, Passed at the Second Session of the First Congress.* Richmond, Va.: R. M. Smith, 1862.

———. *The Statutes at Large of the Confederate States of America Passed at the Third Session of the First Congress.* Richmond, Va.: R. M. Smith, 1863.

———. *The Statutes at Large of the Confederate States of America, Passed at the Fourth Session of the First Congress; 1863–1864.* Richmond, Va.: R.M. Smith, 1864.

*Message of the Governor of Virginia, to the General Assembly.* Richmond, Va.: James E. Goode, Senate Printer, 1864.

*Military Laws of the Confederate States.* Richmond, Va.: J. W. Randolph, 1863.

*Opinions of the Judges of the Supreme Court of Alabama in 'Conscript Cases.'* Montgomery, Ala., 1863.

*Petition of Certain Non-Conscripts Respectfully Presented to the Confederate States Congress.* Richmond, Va., 1862.

*Public Laws of the State of North Carolina Passed by the General Assembly, 1862–63.* Raleigh, N.C.: W. W. Holden State Printer, 1863.

*Report of Cases Argued and Determined in the Supreme Court of Alabama, 1864.*

*Report of the Chief of the Department of the Military of South Carolina.* Columbia, S.C.: Charles P. Pelham, State Printer, 1862.

Richardson, James D., ed. *A Compilation of the Messages and Papers of the Confederacy.* Vol. 1. Nashville, Tenn.: United States Publishing Company, 1906.

Shorter, John Gill. *An Appeal to the People of Alabama.* 1862.

*Southern Historical Society Papers.* 52 vols. Richmond: Virginia Historical Society, 1876–1959.

Speech of W. S. Oldham of Texas, Upon the Bill to Amend the Conscript Law, September 4, 1862.

*Speeches of William L. Yancey, Esq., Senator from the State of Alabama.* Montgomery, Ala., 1862.

*The Statutes at Large of the Confederate States of America Passed at the Third Session of the First Congress.* Richmond, Va.: R. M. Smith, 1863.

*The War of the Rebellion: A Compilation of the Official Records of the Union and Confederate Armies,* 128 vols. (Washington, D.C.: Government Printing Office, 1880–1901.

## COURT CASES

*Davis Simmons v. J. H. Miller* (1862)

*Ex Parte Coupland* (1862)

*Jeffers v. Fair,* (1862)

## NEWSPAPERS

### *Alabama*

*Montgomery Weekly Advertiser*

### *Louisiana*

*Baton Rouge Gazette and Comet*

*Opelousas Courier*

*Shreveport Semi-Weekly News*

Shreveport *South-Western*

### *Georgia*

Athens *Southern Banner*
Athens *Southern Watchman*
Atlanta *Daily Intelligencer*
Atlanta *Southern Confederacy*
Augusta *Daily Constitutionalist*
*Georgia Weekly Telegraph*
*Macon Daily Telegraph*
Milledgeville *Southern Recorder*

### *North Carolina*

*Daily Carolina Watchman*
Raleigh *Semi-Weekly Standard*
*Raleigh Standard*
Wilmington *Daily Journal*

### *South Carolina*

*Charleston Mercury*

### *Tennessee*

*Memphis Daily Appeal*

### *Virginia*

*Richmond Daily Dispatch*
*Richmond Enquirer*
*Richmond Examiner*
*Rockingham Register*
*Southern Literary Messenger*
*Staunton Spectator*

## PUBLISHED PRIMARY SOURCES

Abell, Richard Bender, and Fay A. Gecik, eds. *Sojourns of a Patriot: The Field and Prison Papers of an Unreconstructed Confederate.* Murfreesboro, Tenn.: Southern Heritage Press, 1998.

Aiken, Leona Taylor, ed. "Letters from the Offield Brothers, Confederate Soldiers from Upper East Tennessee." *East Tennessee Historical Society's Publications* 46 (1974): 116–125.

*The American Annual Cyclopaedia and Register of Important Events of the Year 1863*. New York: Appleton, 1870.

Anderson, John Q., ed. *Brokenburn: The Journal of Kate Stone, 1861–1868*. Baton Rouge: Louisiana State University Press, 1995.

Bartlett, Napier. *Military Record of Louisiana: Including Biographical and Historical Papers Relating to the Military Organizations of the State*. 1875. Baton Rouge: Louisiana State University Press, 1996.

Basler, Roy P., ed., *The Collected Works of Abraham Lincoln*. Vol. 6, *1862–1863*. New Brunswick, N.J.: Rutgers University Press, 1953.

Blomquist, Anna K., and Robert A. Taylor, eds. *This Cruel War: The Civil War Letters of Grant and Malinda Taylor*. Macon, Ga.: Mercer University Press, 2000.

Bonner, Robert E. *The Soldier's Pen: Firsthand Impressions of the Civil War*. New York: Hill and Wang, 2007.

Brock, Peter, ed. *Liberty and Conscience: A Documentary History of the Experiences of Conscientious Objectors in America through the Civil War*. New York: Oxford University Press, 2002.

Brown, Norman D., ed., *One of Cleburne's Command: The Civil War Reminiscences and Diary of Capt. Samuel T. Foster, Granbury's Texas Brigade, CSA*. Austin: University of Texas Press, 1980.

Candler, Allen D. *Confederate Records of Georgia*. Atlanta: C. P. Byrd, 1910.

Carter, Susan B., ed., *Historical Statistics of the United States, Earliest Times to the Present*. Cambridge: Cambridge University Press, 2006.

Chamberlayne, Ham, ed. *Letters and Papers of an Artillery Officer in the War for Southern Independence*. Richmond, Va.: Press of the Dietz Printing Co., 1932.

Chisolm, Julian. *A Manual of Military Surgery for the Use of Surgeons in the Confederate States Army*. 3rd ed. Columbia, S.C.: Evans and Cogwell, 1864.

Cooper, William J., Jr., ed. *Jefferson Davis: The Essential Writings*. New York: Modern Library. 2004.

Corsan, W. C. *Two Months in the Confederate States: An Englishman's Travels Through the South*. 1863. Reprint, Baton Rouge: Louisiana State University Press, 1998.

Crabtree, Beth, ed. *Journal of a Secesh Lady: The Diary of Catherine Ann Devereux Edmondston*. Raleigh: North Carolina Division of Archives, 1979.

Crist, Linda, et al., eds. *Papers of Jefferson Davis*. 14 vols. Baton Rouge: Louisiana State University Press, 1971–2015.

Cumming, Kate. *A Journal of Hospital Life in the Confederate Army of Tennessee from the Battle of Shiloh to the End of the War*. Louisville, Ky.: J. P. Morgan, 1866.

Cutrer, Thomas W., ed. *Longstreet's Aide: The Civil War Letters of Major Thomas J. Goree.* Charlottesville: University of Virginia Press, 1995.

———. *Oh, What a Loansome Time I Had: The Civil War Letters of Major William Morel Moxley, Eighteenth Alabama Infantry, and Emily Beck Moxley.* Tuscaloosa: University of Alabama Press, 2002.

Cutrer, Thomas, and T. Michael Parrish, eds. *Brothers in Gray: The Civil War Letters of the Pierson Family.* Baton Rouge: Louisiana State University Press, 1997.

Daniel, John M. *The Richmond Examiner During the War.* 1868. Reprint, New York: Arno Press, 1970.

Davis, Jefferson. *The Rise and Fall of the Confederate Government.* 1881. New York: Da Capo, 1990.

Durham, Robert S., ed. *The Blues in Gray: The Civil War Journal of William Daniel Dixon.* Knoxville: University of Tennessee Press, 2000.

Eakin, Sue Lyles, and Morgan Peoples, eds. *"In Defense of My Country . . .": The Letters of a Shiloh Confederate Soldier.* Bernice, La., 1983.

Estill, Mary S., ed. "Diary of a Confederate Congressman, 1862–1863." *Southwestern Historical Quarterly* 38, no. 4 (April 1935): 270–301.

Evans, Robert, ed. *The 16th Mississippi Infantry: Civil War Letters and Reminiscences.* Jackson: University Press of Mississippi, 2002.

Everson, Guy R., and Edward H. Simpson Jr, eds. *"Far, Far from Home": The Wartime Letters of Dick and Tally Simpson, 3rd South Carolina Volunteers.* New York: Oxford University Press, 1994.

Frederick, J. V., ed. "War Diary of W. C. Porter." *The Arkansas Historical Quarterly* 11, no. 4 (Winter 1952): 286–314.

Freeman, Douglas Southall, ed. *Lee's Dispatches.* New York: G. P. Putnam's Sons, 1915.

Hamilton, Joseph G. de Roulhac, ed. *The Correspondence of Jonathan Worth.* Raleigh: North Carolina Historical Commission, 1909.

———. *The Papers of Randolph A. Shotwell.* Vol. 1. Raleigh: North Carolina Historical Commission, 1929.

Hartman, Peter S. *Reminiscences of the Civil War.* Lancaster, Pa. Eastern Mennonite Associated Libraries and Archives, 1964.

Hubbs, G. Ward, ed. *Voices from Company D: Diaries by the Greensboro Guards, Fifth Alabama Infantry Regiment, Army of Northern Virginia.* Athens: University of Georgia Press, 2003.

Hughes, M. Edward, ed. *Civil War Correspondence of Florida's Governor John Milton: Florida in the Civil War 1861–1865.* Victoria, B.C.: FriesenPress, 2015.

Jewett, Clayton E., ed. *Rise and Fall of the Confederacy: The Memoir of Senator Williamson S. Oldham, CSA.* Columbia: University of Missouri Press, 2006.

Johansson, M. Jane, ed. *Widows by the Thousand: The Civil War Letters of Theophilus and Harriet Perry, 1862–1864.* Fayetteville: University of Arkansas Press, 2000.

Johnston, Frontis W., ed. *The Papers of Zebulon Baird Vance,* Vol. 1, *1843–1862.* Raleigh, N.C.: State Department of Archives and History, 1963.

Joiner, Gary D., ed. *No Pardons to Ask, Nor Apologies to Make: The Journal of William Henry King, Gray's 28th Louisiana Infantry Regiment.* Knoxville: University of Tennessee Press, 2006.

Jones, John B. *A Rebel War Clerk's Diary at the Confederate States Capital.* 2 Vols. Philadelphia: J. B. Lippincott & Co., 1866.

Lane, Mills, ed. *"Dear Mother: Don't Grieve About Me. If I Get Killed, I'll Only Be Dead": Letters from Georgia Soldiers in the Civil War.* Savannah, Ga.: Beehive Press, 1977.

———. *Times That Prove People's Principles: Civil War in Georgia.* Savannah, Ga.: Beehive Press, 1993.

Lincecum, Jerry Bryan, Edward Hake Phillips, and Peggy Redshaw, eds. *Gideon Lincecum's Sword: Civil War Letters From the Texas Home Front.* Denton: University of North Texas Press, 2001.

Lowe, Richard, ed. *A Texas Cavalry Officer's Civil War: The Diary of James C. Bates.* Baton Rouge: Louisiana State University Press, 1999.

Magill, Robert M. *Magill Family Record.* Richmond, Va.: R. E. Magill, 1907.

Mays, Thomas D., ed. *Let Us Meet in Heaven: The Civil War Letters of James Michael Barr, 5th South Carolina Cavalry.* Abilene, Tex.: McWhiney Foundation Press, 2001.

McLaughlin, Josie Armstrong. *Cherished Letters of Thomas Wayman Hendricks.* Birmingham, Ala., 1947.

McMullen, Glenn L., ed. *The Civil War Letters of Dr. Harvey Black: A Surgeon with Stonewall Jackson.* Baltimore: Butternut and Blue, 1995.

Mobley, Joe A., ed. *The Papers of Zebulon Baird Vance.* Vol. 2, *1863.* Raleigh: North Carolina Division of Archives and History, 1995.

Moseley, Ronald H., ed. *The Stilwell Letters: A Georgian in Longstreet's Corps, Army of Northern Virginia.* Macon, Ga.: Mercer University Press, 2002.

Murr, Erika L., ed. *A Rebel Wife in Texas: The Diary and Letters of Elizabeth Scott Neblett, 1852–1864.* Baton Rouge: Louisiana State University Press, 2001.

Myers, Robert M., ed. *The Children of Pride: A True Story of the Civil War.* New Haven, Conn.: Yale University Press, 1972.

Pate, James P., ed. *When This Evil War Is Over: The Correspondence of the Francis Family, 1860–65.* Tuscaloosa: University of Alabama Press, 2006.

Patrick, Rembert W., ed. *The Opinions of the Confederate Attorneys General 1861–1865.* Buffalo, N.Y.: Dennis & Co., Inc., 1950.

Phillips, Ulrich B., ed. *The Correspondence of Robert Toombs, Alexander H. Stephens, and Howell Cobb.* 1913. Reprint, New York: DaCapo Press, 1970.

Pollard, Edward A. *The Lost Cause: A New Southern History of the War of the Confederates.* New York: E. B. Treat & Co., 1868.

Reid, J. W. *History of the Fourth Regiment of S.C. Volunteers from the Commencement of the War Until Lee's Surrender.* Greenville, S.C.: Shannon & Co., 1892.

Robertson, James I., ed. *Soldier of Southwestern Virginia: The Civil War Letters of Captain John Preston Sheffey.* Baton Rouge: Louisiana State University Press, 2004.

Rundell, Walter Jr., ed. "'If Fortune Should Fail': Civil War Letters of Dr. Samuel D. Sanders." *The South Carolina Historical Magazine* 65 (July 1964): 129–144.

Speer, Allen Paul, ed. *Voices from Cemetery Hill, Civil War Diary, Reports and Letters of Colonel William Henry Asbury Speer (1861–1864).* Johnson City, Tenn.: Overmountain Press, 1997.

Stephens, Alexander H. *A Constitutional View of the Late War Between the States: Its Causes, Character, Conduct and Results Presented in a Series of Colloquies at Liberty Hall.* Philadelphia: National Publishing Co., 1868.

Stype, William B., ed. *Writing & Fighting the Confederate War: The Letters of Peter Wellington Alexander.* Kearny, N.J.: Belle Grove, 2002.

Taylor, Michael W., ed. *The Cry Is War, War, War: The Civil War Correspondence of Lts. Burwell Thomas Cotton and George Job Huntley, 34th Regiment North Carolina Troops.* Dayton, Ohio: Morningside House, 1994.

Turner, Nat S., ed. *A Southern Soldier's Letters Home: The Civil War Letters of Samuel A. Burney, Cobb's Georgia Legion.* Macon: Mercer, 2003.

Vandiver, Frank E, ed. "A Collection of Louisiana Confederate Letters," *Louisiana Historical Quarterly* 26, no. 4 (October 1943): 937–974.

Venet, Wendy Hamand, ed. *Sam Richards's Civil War Diary: A Chronicle of the Atlanta Home Front.* Athens: University of Georgia Press, 2009.

Watford, Christopher M., ed. *The Civil War in North Carolina: Soldiers' and Civilians' Letters and Diaries, 1861–1865.* 2 vols. Jefferson, N.C.: McFarland, 2003.

Watkins, Sam. *Company Aytch: Or, a Side Show of the Big Show.* 1882. Reprint, New York: Plume, 1999.

Wiggins, Sarah W. *The Journals of Josiah Gorgas, 1857–1878.* Tuscaloosa: University of Alabama Press, 1995.

Wiley, Bell I., ed. "The Letters of Warren Akin, Confederate Congressman, Part II," *Georgia Historical Quarterly* 42, no. 2 (1958): 193–214.

———. *"This Infernal War": The Confederate Letters of Sgt. Edwin H. Fay.* Austin: University of Texas Press, 1958.

Williams, Edward B., ed. *Rebel Brothers: The Civil War Letters of the Truehearts.* College Station: Texas A&M University Press, 1995.

Williams, Max R., and J. G. de Roulhac Hamilton, eds. *Papers of William Graham.* Vols. 5–6. Raleigh: North Carolina Office of Archives and History, 1973.

Woodward, C. Vann, ed. *Mary Chesnut's Civil War.* New Haven, Conn.: Yale University Press, 1981.

Yearns, W. Buck, and John G. Barrett, eds. *North Carolina Civil War Documentary.* Chapel Hill: University of North Carolina Press, 1980.

Younger, Edward, ed. *Inside the Confederate Government: The Diary of Robert Garlick Hill Kean.* 1957. Reprint, Baton Rouge: Louisiana State University Press, 1985.

## BOOKS

Alexander, Thomas B., and Richard E. Beringer. *The Anatomy of the Confederate Congress.* Nashville, Tenn.: Vanderbilt University Press, 1972.

Amlund, Curtis Arthur. *Federalism in the Southern Confederacy.* Washington, D.C.: Public Affairs Press, 1966.

Atchinson, R. Jarrod. *A War of Words: The Rhetorical Leadership of Jefferson Davis.* Tuscaloosa: University of Alabama Press, 2017.

Auman, William T. *Civil War in the North Carolina Quaker Belt: The Confederate Campaign Against Peace Agitators, Deserters, and Draft Dodgers.* Jefferson, N.C.: McFarland, 2014.

Bensel, Richard F. *Yankee Leviathan: The Origins of Central State Authority in America, 1859–1877.* New York: Cambridge University Press, 1990.

Bergeron, Arthur, ed. *The Civil War in Louisiana: Part B, the Home Front.* Lafayette, La.: Center for Louisiana Studies, 2002.

Beringer, Richard, Harman Hattaway, Archer Jones, and William N. Still Jr. *Why the South Lost the Civil War.* Athens: University of Georgia Press, 1986.

Berwanger, Eugene. *The British Foreign Service and the American Civil War.* Lexington: University Press of Kentucky, 1994.

Blair, William Alan. *Virginia's Private War: Feeding Body and Soul in the Confederacy, 1861–1865.* New York: Oxford University Press, 2000.

Bonner, Michael Brem. *Confederate Political Economy: Creating and Managing a Southern Corporatist Nation.* Baton Rouge: Louisiana State University Press, 2016.

Bryan, T. Conn. *Confederate Georgia.* Athens, Ga.: University of Georgia Press, 1953.

Bynum, Victoria. *The Free State of Jones: Mississippi's Longest Civil War.* Chapel Hill: University of North Carolina Press, 2001.

Cauthen, Charles Edward. *South Carolina Goes to War, 1860–1865.* 1950. Reprint, Columbia: University of South Carolina Press, 2005.

Clinton, Catherine, ed. *Southern Families at War: Loyalty and Conflict in the Civil War South.* New York: Oxford University Press, 2000.

Clodfelter, Michael. *Warfare and Armed Conflicts: A Statistical Encyclopedia of Casualty and Other Figures, 1494–2007.* Jefferson, N.C.: McFarland, 2007.

Connelly, Thomas L. *Autumn of Glory: The Army of Tennessee.* Baton Rouge: Louisiana State University Press, 2001.

Cooper, William J., Jr. *Jefferson Davis: American.* New York: Knopf, 2000.
———. *Liberty and Slavery: Southern Politics to 1860.* New York: McGraw Hill, 1983.
Coulter, E. Merton. *The Confederate States of America, 1861–1865.* Baton Rouge: Louisiana State University Press, 1950.
Dillard, Phillip D. *Jefferson Davis's Final Campaign: Confederate Nationalism and the Fight to Arm the Slaves.* Macon, Ga.: Mercer University Press, 2017.
Dubose, John Witherspoon. *The Life and Times of William Lowndes Yancey.* 2 vols. New York: Peter Smith, 1942.
Durden, Robert F. *The Gray and the Black: The Confederate Debate on Emancipation.* Baton Rouge: Louisiana State University Press, 1972.
Eicher, David J. *Dixie Betrayed: How the South Really Lost the Civil War.* New York: Brown, 2006.
Escott, Paul D. *After Secession: Jefferson Davis and the Failure of Confederate Nationalism.* Baton Rouge: Louisiana State University Press, 1978.
Freeman, Douglas Southall. *Robert E. Lee: A Biography.* Vol. 2. New York: Scribner, 1934.
Gallagher, Gary. *The Confederate War: How Popular Will, Nationalism, and Military Strategy Could Not Stave Off Defeat.* Cambridge, Mass.: Harvard University Press, 1997.
Gardner, Sarah E. *Blood and Irony: Southern White Women's Narratives of the Civil War, 1861–1937.* Chapel Hill: University of North Carolina Press, 2004.
Glatthaar, Joseph T. *General Lee's Army from Victory to Collapse.* New York: Free Press, 2008.
———. *Soldiering in the Army of Northern Virginia: A Statistical Portrait of the Troops Who Served Under Robert E. Lee.* Chapel Hill: University of North Carolina Press, 2011.
Gleeson, David T. *The Green and the Gray: The Irish in the Confederate States of America.* Chapel Hill: University of North Carolina Press, 2013.
Gordon, Lesley J., and John C. Inscoe, eds. *Inside the Confederate Nation: Essays in Honor of Emory M. Thomas.* Baton Rouge: Louisiana State University Press, 2007.
Hadden, Sally. *Slave Patrols: Law and Violence in Virginia and the Carolinas.* Cambridge, Mass.: Harvard University Press, 2001.
Hallock, Judith Lee. *Braxton Bragg and Confederate Defeat.* Vol. 2. Tuscaloosa: University of Alabama Press, 1991.
Heidler, David S., and Jeanne T. Heidler, eds. *Encyclopedia of the American Civil War: A Political, Social, and Military History.* Santa Barbara, Calif.: ABC-CLIO, 2000.
Hilderman, Walter C. III. *They Went into the Fight Cheering!: Confederate Conscription in North Carolina.* Boone, N.C.: Parkway Publishers, 2005.
Horst, Samuel. *Mennonites in the Confederacy: A Study in Civil War Pacifism.* Scottsdale, Penn.: Herald Press, 1967.
Jordan, Winthrop D. *Tumult and Silence at Second Creek: An Inquiry into a Civil War Slave Conspiracy.* Baton Rouge: Louisiana State University Press, 1993.

Kruman, Marc W. *Parties and Politics in North Carolina, 1836–1865*. Baton Rouge: Louisiana State University Press, 1983.

Leach, Jack Franklin. *Conscription in the United States: Historical Background*. Rutland, Vt.: Charles E. Tuttle Publishing Co., 1952.

Lehman, James O., and Steven M. Nolt. *Mennonites, Amish, and the American Civil War*. Baltimore, Md.: Johns Hopkins University Press, 2007.

Levine, Bruce. *Confederate Emancipation: Southern Plans to Free and Arm Slaves During the Civil War*. New York: Oxford University Press, 2006.

Livermore, Thomas L. *Numbers and Losses in the Civil War in America, 1861–65*. New York: Houghton, Mifflin and Company, 1900.

Logue, Larry. *To Appomattox and Beyond: The Civil War Soldier in War and Peace*. Chicago: I. R. Dee, 1996.

Long, E. B., and Barbara Long. *The Civil War Day by Day: An Almanac, 1861–1865*. Garden City, N.Y.: Doubleday, 1971.

Lonn, Ella. *Foreigners in the Confederacy*. Chapel Hill: University of North Carolina Press, 1940.

Mahon, John K. *History of the Militia and the National Guard*. New York: Macmillan, 1983.

Manning, Chandra. *What This Cruel War Was Over: Soldiers, Slavery, and the Civil War*. New York: Knopf, 2007.

Maurice, Frederick, ed. *Lee's Aide de Camp: Charles Marshall*. Lincoln, Neb.: Bison Books, 2000.

McArthur, Judith N., and Orville Burton, eds. *A Gentleman and an Officer: A Military and Social History of James B. Griffin's Civil War*. New York: Oxford University Press, 1996.

McCaslin, Richard B. *Tainted Breeze: The Great Hanging at Gainesville, Texas, 1862*. Baton Rouge: Louisiana State University Press, 1994.

McCurry, Stephanie. *Confederate Reckoning: Power and Politics in the Civil War South*. Cambridge, Mass.: Harvard University Press, 2010.

McDonnell, Michael A. *The Politics of War: Race, Class, and Conflict in Revolutionary Virginia*. Chapel Hill: University of North Carolina Press, 2007.

McPherson, James M. *Antietam: The Battle That Changed the Course of the Civil War*. New York: Oxford University Press, 2002.

———. *Battle Cry of Freedom: The Civil War Era*. New York: Oxford University Press, 1988.

———. *For Cause and Comrades: Why Men Fought in the Civil War*. New York: Oxford University Press, 1997.

———. *Ordeal by Fire: The Civil War And Reconstruction*. New York: Knopf, 1982.

Mitchell, Memory F. *Legal Aspects of Conscription and Exemption in North Carolina 1861–1865*. Chapel Hill: University of North Carolina Press, 1965.

Mitchell, Reid. *Civil War Soldiers.* New York: Penguin, 1997.

Mobley, Joe A. *"War Governor of the South": North Carolina's Zeb Vance in the Confederacy.* Gainesville: University Press of Florida, 2005.

Moore, Albert Burton. *Conscription and Conflict in the Confederacy.* 1924. Columbia, SC: University of South Carolina Press, 1996.

Myers, Barton. *Rebels Against the Confederacy: North Carolina Unionists.* Cambridge, Mass.: Harvard University Press, 2014.

Neely, Mark E., Jr. *Southern Rights: Political Prisoners and the Myth of Confederate Constitutionalism.* Charlottesville: University Press of Virginia, 1999.

Noe, Kenneth W. *Reluctant Rebels: The Confederates Who Joined the Army After 1861.* Chapel Hill: University of North Carolina Press, 2010.

Owsley, Frank L. *State Rights in the Confederacy.* Chicago: University of Chicago Press, 1925.

Paludan, Phillip Shaw. *Victims: A True Story of the Civil War.* Knoxville: University of Tennessee Press, 1981.

Parks, Joseph H. *Joseph E. Brown of Georgia.* Baton Rouge: University of Louisiana Press, 1977.

Patrick, Rembert W. *Jefferson Davis and His Cabinet.* Baton Rouge: Louisiana State University Press, 1944.

Rable, George. *Civil Wars: Women and the Crisis of Southern Nationalism.* Urbana: University of Illinois Press, 1989.

———. *Confederate Republic: A Revolution Against Politics.* Chapel Hill: University of North Carolina Press, 1994.

Ramsdell, Charles W. *Behind the Lines in the Southern Confederacy.* Baton Rouge: Louisiana State University Press, 1944.

Roark, James L. *Masters Without Slaves: Southern Planters in the Civil War and Reconstruction.* New York: W. W. Norton and Co., 1977.

Robinson, Armstead. *Bitter Fruits of Bondage: The Demise of Slavery and the Collapse of the Confederacy, 1861–1865.* Charlottesville: University of Virginia Press, 2005.

Richard, Allan C., and Mary M. Richard. *The Defense of Vicksburg: A Louisiana Chronicle.* College Station: Texas A&M University Press, 2004.

Rubin, Anne Sarah. *A Shattered Nation, The Rise and Fall of the Confederacy, 1861–1868.* Chapel Hill: University of North Carolina Press, 2005.

Schott, Thomas E. *Alexander H. Stephens of Georgia: A Biography.* Baton Rouge: Louisiana State University Press, 1988.

Severance, Ben H. *A War State All Over: Alabama Politics and the Confederate Cause.* Tuscaloosa, Ala.: University of Alabama Press, 2020.

Shannon, Fred A. *The Organization and Administration of the Union Army, 1861–1865.* Vol. 1. Cleveland, Ohio: Arthur H. Clark Company, 1928.

Sheehan-Dean, Aaron. *Why Confederates Fought: Family and Nation in Civil War Virginia.* Chapel Hill: University of North Carolina Press, 2009.

Storey, Margaret. *Loyalty and Loss: Alabama's Unionists in the Civil War and Reconstruction.* Baton Rouge: Louisiana State University Press, 2004.

Sutherland, Daniel E. *A Savage Conflict: The Decisive Role of Guerrillas in the American Civil War.* Chapel Hill: University of North Carolina Press, 2013.

———, ed. *Guerrillas, Unionists, and Violence on the Confederate Home Front.* Fayetteville: University of Arkansas Press, 1999.

Tanner, Robert G. *Stonewall in the Valley: Thomas J. "Stonewall" Jackson's Shenandoah Valley Campaign, Spring 1862.* Mechanicsburg, Penn.: Stackpole, 2002.

Tatum, Georgia Lee. *Disloyalty in the Confederacy.* Chapel Hill: University of North Carolina Press, 1934.

Thomas, Emory M. *The Confederacy as a Revolutionary Experience.* Englewood Cliffs, N.J.: Prentice-Hall, 1971.

———. *The Confederate Nation, 1861–1865.* New York: Harper Torchbooks, 1979.

Upton, Emory. *The Military Policy of the United States.* Washington, D.C.: Government Printing Office, 1912.

Walther, Eric H. *William Lowndes Yancey and the Coming of the Civil War.* Chapel Hill: University of North Carolina Press, 2006.

Weitz, Mark. *More Damning than Slaughter: Desertion in the Confederate Army.* Lincoln: University of Nebraska Press, 2005.

Wiley, Bell Irvin. *The Life of Johnny Reb: The Common Soldier of the Confederacy.* 1901. Reprint, Baton Rouge: Louisiana State University Press, 2005.

———. *Plain People of the Confederacy.* Baton Rouge: Louisiana State University Press, 1943.

Williams, David. *Bitterly Divided: The South's Inner Civil War.* New York: New Press, 2008.

———. *A People's History of the Civil War: Struggles for the Meaning of Freedom.* New York: New Press, 2005.

———. *Rich Man's War: Class, Caste, and Confederate Defeat in the Lower Chattahoochee Valley.* Athens: University of Georgia Press, 1998.

Williams, David, Teresa Crisp Williams, and David Carlson. *Plain Folk in a Rich Man's War: Class and Dissent in Confederate Georgia.* Gainesville: University Press of Florida, 2002.

Woodward, Colin. *Marching Masters: Slavery, Race, and the Confederate Army in the Civil War.* Charlottesville: University of Virginia Press, 2014.

Wynne, Ben. *The Man Who Punched Jefferson Davis: The Political Life of Henry S. Foote, Southern Unionist.* Baton Rouge: Louisiana State University Press, 2018.

Yearns, W. Buck, ed. *The Confederate Congress.* Athens: University of Georgia Press, 1960.

———. *The Confederate Governors.* Athens: University of Georgia Press, 1985.

Zuber, Richard L. *Jonathan Worth: A Biography of a Southern Unionist.* Chapel Hill: University of North Carolina Press, 1965.

## ARTICLES

Ambrose, Stephen E. "Yeoman Discontent in the Confederacy." *Civil War History* (September 1962): 259–268.

Brooks, Robert P. "Conscription in the Confederate States of America, 1862–1865." *Military Historian and Economist* 1 (October 1916): 419–442.

Carlson, David. "'The Distemper of the Times': Conscription, the Courts, and Planter Privilege in Civil War South Georgia." *Journal of Southwest Georgia History* 14 (1999): 1–24.

———. "The 'Loanly Runagee': Draft Evaders in Confederate South Georgia." *Georgia Historical Quarterly* 84, no. 4 (Winter 2000): 589–615.

Doyle, Patrick J. "Replacement Rebels: Confederate Substitution and the Issue of Citizenship." *Journal of the Civil War Era* (March 2018): 3–31.

Hamilton, J. G. de Roulhac. "The North Carolina Courts and the Confederacy." *North Carolina Historical Review* 4 (1927): 366–403.

Harrison, Lowell H. "Conscription in the Confederacy." *Civil War Times Illustrated* 9 (July 1970): 10–18.

Jones, Archer. "Some Aspects of George W. Randolph's Service as Confederate Secretary of War." *Journal of Southern History* 26, no. 3 (1960): 299–314.

Keller, Christian B. "Pennsylvania and Virginia Germans During the Civil War: A Brief History and Comparative Analysis." *Virginia Magazine of History and Biography* 109, no. 1 (2001): 37–86.

Norman, John P. "'Self-Preservation is the Supreme Law': State Rights vs. Military Necessity in Alabama Civil War Conscription Cases." *Alabama Law Review* 60, no. 3 (January 2009): 727–749.

Owsley, Frank L. "Local Defense and the Overthrow of the Confederacy." *Mississippi Valley Historical Review* 11 (March 1924): 490–525.

Percy, William Alexander. "Localizing the Context of Confederate Politics: The Congressional Election of 1863 in Georgia's First District." *Georgia Historical Quarterly* (Spring 1995): 192–209.

Poteat, R. Matthew. "'A Modest Estimate of His Own Abilities': Governor Henry Toole Clark and the Early Civil War Leadership of North Carolina." *North Carolina Historical Review* 84, no. 2 (April 2007): 127–155.

Pruitt, Francelle. "'We've Got to Fight or Die': Early Texas Reaction to the Confederate Draft, 1862." *East Texas Historical Journal* 36, no. 1 (1998): 3–17.

Purcell, Douglas C. "Military Conscription in Alabama during the Civil War." *Alabama Review* 34, no. 2 (1981): 94–106.

Robbins. John B. "The Confederacy and the Writ of Habeas Corpus." *Georgia Historical Quarterly* (Spring 1971): 83–101.

Sacher, John M. "The Loyal Draft Dodger? A Reexamination of Confederate Substitution." *Civil War History* (June 2011): 153–178.

———. "Reconsidering the 'Twenty-Negro' Law as the Overseer Exemption." *Journal of the Civil War Era* (June 2017): 269–292.

Scarboro, David D. "North Carolina and the Confederacy: The Weakness of States' Rights During the Civil War." *North Carolina Historical Review* 56 (April 1979): 133–149.

Shaw, William L. "The Confederate Conscription and Exemption Acts." *American Journal of Legal History* 6 (1962): 368–405.

Sheehan-Dean, Aaron. "Everyman's War: Confederate Enlistment in Civil War Virginia." *Civil War History* (March 2004): 5–26.

Smith, David P. "Conscription and Conflict on the Texas Frontier, 1863–1865." *Civil War History* (September 1990): 250–261.

Van Zant, Jennifer. "Confederate Conscription and the North Carolina Supreme Court." *North Carolina Historical Review* 72 (1995): 54–75.

Wilson, Mary L. "Profiles in Evasion: Civil War Substitutes and the Men Who Hired Them in Walker's Texas Division." *East Texas Historical Journal* 43 (2005): 25–38.

## THESES AND DISSERTATIONS

Carlson, Robert David. "Breach of Faith: Conscription in Confederate Georgia." PhD diss., Emory University, 2009.

Powell, Michael A. "Confederate Federalism: A View from the Governors." PhD diss., University of Maryland, 2004.

Robbins, John B. "Confederate Nationalism: Politics and Government in the Confederate South, 1861–1865." PhD diss., Rice University, 1964.

Snyder, Perry A. "Shreveport, Louisiana during the Civil War and Reconstruction." PhD diss., Florida State University, 1979.

Stelluto, Donald J. "'A Light Which Reveals Its True Meaning': State Supreme Courts and the Confederate Constitution." PhD diss., University of Maryland, 2004.

# Index